# Maybe It'll Be Good:
## My Life As Marc With A C

## By Marc Sirdoreus

*This book is dedicated to the memory of Domenico Marini.*

# INTRODUCTION

"Most people will not like what you write."

That sticks in my head often. There's around 7 billion people accounted for on Earth, and I can't remember the last time I've heard of anything even moving 6 billion units. You can't be universal. It's simply not possible. You might as well write what you'd like because writing to please others will nearly always turn out to be a fool's errand.

When I first started scribbling lyrics and poems in elementary school, I wasn't concerned about who'd like them. In fact, I didn't bother to show them to hardly anyone. I wanted to make something, so I did.

As I write this introduction, I know that these words will be seen. Even if the eyes that receive my thoughts are small in numbers, they're still being seen.

If I'm not going to reach 6 billion people, why write at all? For the same reasons I made up songs and poems when I was 7 years old.

Something in me wants to write and communicate. I'm able, and unless I find myself turning out to be immortal, I won't always have the opportunity. There is only now and the decay of the memory of now.

At the moment, I'm best known for making records for a small-but-loyal cult of dedicated listeners as well as hosting a podcast about records. I like it, and it certainly beats digging ditches. At best, I break even on whatever I make. Sometimes I even make a small profit.

To do this, though? It's a morning, noon, and night job. There are no days off. There will also never be enough hours in any given day. I live, eat, breathe, and vomit being an entity named Marc With a C all day, every day. Most good things that have happened to that act? They happened right as I planned a break, to sleep in, to shut off for a day.

And to do it above board with any semblance of quality, ethics, and professionalism? I can get lost in admin and production work until I realize I haven't even touched an instrument for two weeks straight.

Yet I continue. Because it's what I do.

But still, why bother to write when most people probably won't like what I will write?

- "The right people will get it."

- "Maybe it'll be good."

Those are the motivators to show off whatever I've concocted. You might not hate it. You might giggle. You might get bored. Or?

Maybe it'll be good.


Love on ya,
Marc With a C, 2019

# Part I: Memoir

BEFORE HUMAN SLUSHY:

At various times in my life, I've sort of written off the first proper Marc With a C album and the preceding years. Truth be told, it has more to do with me growing out of the person I was at the time. That person hadn't had an easy life, but in comparison to others, I hadn't ever experienced what could be considered "true hardship." I was born into a life and family that had the ability to appear middle-class but ultimately didn't have much of anything. Most of what I felt by the onset of my early adult years was entitlement, really. I felt – as many people do in their 20s – that the world owed me something.

They say you have your whole life to come up with your first album but only six months to write your second one. I would normally agree, but it doesn't feel that way for me. I guess it's sort of anachronistic, but in a way, yes, *Human Slushy* – what became my first album – does sum up *some* of who I was in the first 23 or so years of my life. And then I heard it, lived with it, and decided I didn't want to be anything like that person anymore. In that regard, it's "important." At least, as important as any set of songs can be.

Really, it's just the prequel to becoming the "Marc With a C" that is writing this strange and possibly/probably/very likely unnecessary memoir/diary.

To bring you up to speed, here's the general overview of my life prior to that album: I was born. I had a lot of health problems. I moved around a lot. My family isn't quite as important to the story as you might think, not to my record-making life. I'll touch on them here and there, but it's not really the aim – hope we're on the same page about that. The matriarchal person in my life felt more like a fair-weather friend and roommate, and the patriarchal role was a different person every day and happened to just live in the same body. Sadly, that "different person" was almost always an individual that wasn't very nice. This all made it next to impossible to figure out how to be a "good kid."

I wasn't well-liked by my peers, and I lived the rather predictable lifestyle of any child that doesn't have many pals but is constantly told by those in a position of authority that they are special due to scoring high on tests that mattered to adults. This was right at the dawn of the supposed "everybody gets a trophy just for showing up" years, so it did a bit of a number on my head. A weird mix of ego and feeling worthless before puberty. I escaped into music at an early age and only felt right when I disappeared into song worlds.

My parents separated when the state of Florida got involved due to me saying the wrong thing to the right educator, and I was forcibly removed from the situation. There was guilt on my part, though I now know that I unwittingly did the right thing. I spent some time in San Diego with more family. I lived in a neighborhood where nearly every single door had the same pattern. San Diego is a beautiful city, both culturally and geographically. I had a friend from school that invited me over one day, and it turned out that he lived just a few doors down from me. I had no idea that there was a house in that spot. From the street, the dwelling was completely obscured by foliage that wasn't native to California, which my new pal's father obsessively cultivated. Never met that guy, but I respected his efforts at defying science while having his house swallowed up by his own man-made ecosystem.

I ended up in a religious school for a while because it was the best option available at the time. It was the first time that I really and truly felt that someone was "out to get me" – because they actually were. I'm sure if I dug hard enough, I could come up with the police records to prove it, but I don't think that it's really necessary.

They'd break into my house to rid me of sinful possessions. The meanest people I'd ever met, and I don't say that lightly, because I'd once upon a time literally lived in a loop dedicated to the procurement and distribution of illegal drugs – just so a family member could have easy access to them. Those folks were at least kind some of the time, excluding the aforementioned family member that moved us into the decrepit shack to begin with.

After a few more moves, I ended up living in a very small town in Florida named Mascotte. The same types of folks that I'd met in the religious school populated the place for the most part. I had very long hair and dressed in dark clothes and didn't look "right," so I always felt singled out. Probably had to do with people whipping bottles at me out of cars just for walking down the street, yelling "f*ggot," "devil worshiper," and also ... wolf-whistling?

They were just as confused as I was.

I didn't do very well in those small-town schools because, for one, the curriculum was so relatively dumbed down compared to the West Coast that I was bored. I was also distracted by the authority figures' constant indictment for looking different than their preferred brand of "god-fearing" teenagers who will one day grow up to sell tractors or something. One day early on in the new school, a classmate who probably meant well asked, "Did everybody look like you where you come from?" This cemented the fact that I seemed positively alien to these folks but was really just an awkward teenager by any other standards.

I'd gone from existing in very large cities with wonderful radio stations and always having another record store just a few blocks away to living in a rural town with no traffic lights, few peers that understood my points of view, and absolutely no way to consume popular media besides spotty cable service. My relationship to "the outside world" came in the forms of occasional gateway drugs that I would sometimes imbibe just to feel like I fit in. That's the funny part about small towns. A lot of the inhabitants of the one I lived in didn't actually seem to like each other; there just wasn't any hope to leave it. You clung to the few people that you could stand like a life preserver, but, ultimately, you'd leave them behind in an instant for something more interesting or challenging. I've proved that to the people I knew there, and they proved it right back to me.

One of my biggest teenage salvations was a junk store that had an aisle of LPs for a dollar apiece. Literally somewhere in the neighborhood of 20,000 records piled on top of each other. It was actually dangerous to be in that aisle because they were stacked so haphazardly that you could be crushed to death by albums, and no one would know for a while. I'm not sure how these records ended up there because there was really, really cool stuff for such a one-horse town. Tons of new wave, no wave, and psych rock were just hiding away in a store in the town least likely to ever sell them. I'd save my lunch money and buy a few each day. The owner would allow me to bring back the ones I didn't like and trade them in on a two for one basis. It was like the ultimate library-cum-training ground for a budding music nerd. Each day I'd sink into a new album, and sometimes you'd even find a stash of an intoxicating substance hidden in a gatefold to make it easier to drown out the deafening silence of a small town.

Of course, the town wasn't always quiet. You'd hear shotguns going off at night and, interestingly, teenagers doing doughnuts in crappy cars while blaring hair metal out of their car radios – never mind that hair metal was dead and gone to the world at large by this time. Word didn't reach this place overnight, and I'll admit, it was a contagious tone for a lonely kid that didn't have anywhere to go, let alone a way to get there. My metal phase will be very entertaining in another book, one day.

I lived for Saturday afternoons because, on a clear day, I could pick up *The Banana Split Show* on Tampa's WMNF on my horrific little boombox. The host Lana's voice and record collection would be the soundtrack to cleaning my room, and it's here that I discovered groups like Sloan, The Soft Boys and The Rubinoos. Groups that no one else was playing on the radio at all at the time. Groups that would teach me that melody was not an enemy but rather a boon to what might be otherwise "difficult music" for some.

NON-ACCIDENTAL DRUG USE:

The junk store in Lake County was a pretty pivotal place for me. I don't know the real name of a particular employee who worked there, but we all referred to him as "Chong." You couldn't miss him, not only because looked like a Very Famous Stoner, but because he ingratiated himself onto any conversation being held in the vicinity of this shop.

One day, I was picking up a Blue Oyster Cult album. I liked "Don't Fear The Reaper," and I was interested in hearing more. On my way out, Chong cut me off at the pass and, apparently being a massive fan of BOC, he was very excited that a young teenager would be picking up something as obscure as the *Club Ninja* album. He quizzed me on my knowledge of the group – which really only extended to a short live album called *Some Enchanted Evening* – and asked if I'd ever listened to the band properly. I couldn't come up with an incorrect way to hear the song "Godzilla," so I responded in the positive.

"No, no. Have you ever listened to BOC *on shrooms*?"

I knew a bit about drugs, but they didn't really cover mushrooms in the D.A.R.E. program. I was just completely ignorant on them, but I wanted to sound cool, so I pretended like I was an old veteran of imbibing psychedelics that grew in cow manure.

"Of course, I have!"

Before I could say "Cities on Flame With Rock And Roll," Chong had made plans to come to my house the very next day when I got home from school. He'd be bringing his homebrewed mushroom tea with him, and we were to listen to BOC "properly." He gave me a few guidelines: make sure that no one is home, don't eat anything greasy, and don't make any plans for about 10 hours.

I know, I know. The man in his 40s asking the young teenager if he could come over with some drugs while no one was home should have raised a lot of red flags. I have a nasty habit of ignoring those.

He showed up at the agreed-upon time and saw me eating some turkey. This displeased him – apparently that was too greasy. Regardless, he pulled two heroic-sized mason jars full of a purplish liquid from his backpack and put them on the dresser in my bedroom. Was telling me how "primo" this stuff was until a car pulled up in the driveway. A family member had come home.

Chong was unhappy about this and frankly shockingly nervous. He literally climbed out of my bedroom window to leave, and when I asked him what to do with the jars? He yelled for me to just keep them. I quickly went and hid them in the back of the crisper drawer of the refrigerator. No one would be reaching for vegetables tonight, hopefully.

It only took 20 minutes for my curiosity to get the best of me. I didn't know how to do this stuff or how much I was even supposed to ingest, but it made sense that since there were two of us and two jars? One of them was meant for me. I smuggled one receptacle back into my room and chugged the nauseating liquid down. The whole hipster-sized mason jar.

After 45 minutes, I'd come to two conclusions: this drug didn't work, and the *Club Ninja* album wasn't my thing. And that's when someone knocked on my bedroom door.

It was the aforementioned family member. They were holding the other mason jar and demanded to know what it contained. I didn't see any reason to lie because this crud wasn't doing anything for me. I told them the truth: it was mushroom tea, and I had no intentions of ingesting it. This was technically true, as I'd already drank a big jar of it, so I wouldn't need to drink the one they were holding.

This family member sat me down and started telling me all of the horrible things that would assuredly happen to me if I were to take mushrooms, and that's when everything seemed very funny and terrifying at the same time. They were telling me about how I'd go blind and eat my own tongue, and I tried my best to concentrate despite how fascinating looking at my hand had just become. I mean, have you ever really looked at your hand? There's some amazing stuff going on in there, especially when you've got BOC on in the background and ... oh, crap.

When they'd finished their terrifying speech, I only knew for certain that I was assuredly going to die that day, so I'd better work very hard to enjoy my final day on earth. They had me pour the purple liquid down the sink – which looked amazing at that moment, by the way. And simultaneously, when I first learned what "peaking" was? Another member of our household that was also unaware that I'd drank the death serum came inside to say, "Hey, I fixed the lawnmower. You should go and take care of the yard." I figured that I might as well do something nice for the household before they had to plan for my funeral.

As I walked outside, I was struck by two things. Firstly, I'd forgotten just how big the earth was. And secondly, I didn't know that some substances would make you hear sort of a "buzzing" sound, which I (honestly) mistook as being the sound of the lawnmower being left on. I walked to it and pushed, assuming that the hallucinogenic properties of the drug were kicking in. It only looked like the grass was growing back, right?

A neighbor kid that I was friends with walked up to the fence and stared for a bit. I wasn't talking to him because I had to get this lawn manicured before I found out if there was life after death, and since the grass kept growing back, I didn't have time for idle conversation.

"Do you notice a problem?" he asked.

I said, "Yes. But can you see it, too?"

He sighed and asked if I'd considered turning on the mower. He was also holding a cup in the shape of a woman's breast, but from where I was standing, he was holding a severed body part, so I shrieked, ran inside, and barricaded myself in my room. I rode out the nightmarish storm through a sleepless night. I was still tripping when I had to go to school the next day, so I hid in the bathroom, making sure I didn't speak to anyone.

At the beginning of first period, my science teacher turned on the overhead projector and squirted the laminate with a spray bottle of water to clear the previous text, which had been written in many colors, creating a bright liquid swirl, much like a Fillmore East light show.

From my seat and vantage point? She'd just opened a portal to hell on the wall. I promptly stood up and said, "Nope." Got up and walked 5 fucking miles home without alerting anyone.

I've never touched mushrooms since. Don't even ask.

BEFORE HUMAN SLUSHY PART TWO:

By the time I got to high school – which was no mean feat, as the last few schools didn't even want me there, let alone to allow me to succeed – I met some other folks that weren't "normal," and I surrounded myself with them. Probably adhered myself to them like a leech, now that I think about it. I was surprised when ladies wanted to date me because it honestly hadn't ever crossed my mind that someone might see me in a romantic way.

All the women that I dated in high school went on to be interesting people. Some are dead now, some travel the world, some redefined their gender identity completely, and some just ended up strung out. All of them had one thing in common: they broke up with me. I didn't know what was wrong with me. However, while I was certainly self-absorbed at the time, I was not very self-aware. Looking back, I can completely see why I needed to improve myself, but rejection was all I felt. I didn't search for internal reasons. I just blamed it on them for "what they did to me."

That's pretty much what defined the early songs I'd make up. My maternal grandmother had given me a cheap Spanish guitar, and I threw myself into trying to figure that thing out with aplomb. I didn't do it to impress the objects of my affection because, again, I was very surprised when people saw me in a romantic light. But when they no longer saw me that way, I'd fill notebooks with crappy teenage prose. Really nonsensical stuff. To even call it stream of consciousness would be giving the words too much praise.

Eventually, I'd just start rambling the lyrics while I played some chords that sounded okay together, and I found that if you did that enough times, you'd remember it. If you mostly stopped and started it the same ways, you could even convince people that these were "songs," and the insides could stay malleable enough that you could change it up on a whim or even consider the piece to be in a perpetual state of flux.

When I found myself nursing teenage heartbreak, I'd hole myself up in my room, stringing things together this way. I'd play each song a few times and then record it on a 90-minute cassette tape using one of those cheap-o karaoke machines for primitive overdubs. Each time I'd fill a tape up, I'd give it a name, call it an album, make dubs for some friends, and move on to doing it all over again.

The material was whiny, simplistic, and overly derivative. My performances were not even good enough to be called amateurish, but, hey, these were "songs," so I started fancying myself a "songwriter."

I'd found myself in an on-again/off-again relationship with a deeply flawed/

very pretty lady that was roughly my age. I won't be talking about her much because I think it'd be highly disrespectful to do so considering how things panned out, but I'm willing to say that she had the capacity to be a very nice, funny, and generous person. The other 50 percent of the time she was highly intoxicated or just not very nice to me. I wasn't always nice either. We both came from broken homes and dysfunctional families, so there wasn't a template for either of us to even pretend to trace. Something just kept drawing us back into each other's lives and beds, and it was far from healthy.

Not long after entering high school, I'd had enough of ritualized schooling. I wasn't doing well with my grades, many of my teachers refused to give me a chance due to my hair and manner of dress, and I'd been pulled into the principal's office for actual sermons.

Seriously. Rehearsed sermons with sticky notes marking pages in a worn Bible and everything.

That particular authority figure would just call me out of class if, say, there had been some unexplained vandalism in the school. Now, I wasn't the culprit – graffiti isn't my bag. If I'm being a jerk on purpose, I tend to prefer more subtle things. No matter, though. If something bad happened, and he couldn't explain it, he'd call me out of class, pull said Bible out of his desk, and start reading to me from it.

This would happen several times a week. He'd often punish me for these things that I had not done – and in some cases hadn't even seen proof of. If I dared protest, he'd tell me, "You reap what you sow." If I'd call him out about the sermonizing, he'd flat out ask me if I thought that anyone would believe me with "the way I looked."

After one too many of these situations, I opted instead to go to the school where they sent the pregnant ladies and "troublemakers." I didn't have the organs necessary to be the former, but I had a track record that made a good case that I was the latter. And around this time, I started a band to play my silly songs. The name of the group isn't terribly important because none of the members were ever happy with it, and someone always insisted that I'd change it every couple of shows. We went through a bunch of nomenclatures that were all terrible, and the band had a fluctuating lineup usually consisting of people that openly didn't even like my songs very much in the first place:

- There was a drummer that couldn't play but got the job because he owned a dusty kit.

- There was another drummer that was full of raw talent but was struggling with mononucleosis, so his stamina was questionable at best.

- And then there was the drummer who wouldn't finish any songs because he'd declare them all to be "butt rock" but wouldn't offer alternative ideas. He mostly just complained. I made a mental note during one of those impossible practices: "Don't whine if you have no ideas on how things can improve."

- Once, we had a rhythm guitarist that really wanted us to be a heavier band. He'd later go on to be very successful with making merchandise related to horror films.

- There was a bassist that mostly stayed throughout the lineups that sometimes seemed to want to be there but mostly complained about every single song I'd written. On the rare occasions he'd actually bring material to the table, they'd be missing all of the elements that would complete them: melodies, chords, tempos, etc. I'd write those things around his lyrics, and then he'd claim that they belonged to him. His exact words were, "That's what I would have written anyways." He'd also brought in another guitarist once at a rehearsal that I wasn't invited to. I didn't think much of it until multiple sources that liked drama claimed that the bass player bragged that he was replacing me. On the rare occasions I'd try to break out of this situation and play shows by myself — keeping in mind that this bassist would always insist that I was better as a solo act — he'd allegedly send his roommates (according to them at the time) to the shows to spy on me to make sure I didn't play any of "our" songs.

That band was around for a few years with hints of local college radio love, but after a few years of false starts, I just didn't want to deal with the drama that came with having a group. I don't remember who quit first, but I do remember that out of the two people that were in the band most often, I was interested in writing new songs, and the bass player would rather play poker.

Despite all this, the bass player and I were close friends. It was only in "working circumstances" that we'd quibble. He'd charitably take me to see Smashing Pumpkins and The Lemonheads when I wanted to go but was far too poor to afford tickets. And together, we got to see what ended up being David Bowie's longest ever concert appearance in a club in Fort Lauderdale. We had a huge effect on each other without question, but when we picked up instruments, we simply couldn't get along.

Since there weren't many musicians to choose from in the redneck wasteland, I decided to just stick to doing things by myself. Not that I really had much of a choice, but it was ultimately the easier option.

For work, I'd done a lot of odd things ranging from fast food to cleaning pools to graveyard shifts at convenience stores. But most of the time? I worked in record stores. During one particularly formative period, I'd found myself working at the sadly defunct Borders Books & Music chain. Oddly, I was put in charge of their sorely neglected classical music section, but any reason to work around records was better than any other task that a company could give me money for. Working for Borders was good for me in a number of ways:

- The on-again/off-again lady that I'd been dating? She was pregnant, and I needed money. The pregnancy itself had actually made our relationship rockier than ever, which I'll get to later, and while I wasn't getting rich from working at Borders, the money was manna. Every two weeks. Before I handed it off to someone else.

- I got lots of promotional compact discs that turned me on to music I'd have otherwise not have heard.

- When the aforementioned relationship was "off," it was a great place to meet potential mates. Because, well, you knew that they read books. It was nice to know that every person I struck up a conversation with in that building liked to think. I know – I was in my 20s, and intelligence levels probably shouldn't have mattered, right? I'd almost always been a "brains before beauty" sort of guy when it comes to potential romantic/sexual partners, and it's as if the Borders front door was a great filtration system to know if someone would be worth talking to. Most memorably, I met an intriguing young lady that introduced herself to me as a human slushy. I asked her what that meant and wrote a song based on the self-imposed nickname, though not inspired by her description.

- I had a fellow employee that we'll refer to as "Ska Steve." When it came down to it, we actually had very, very little in common, but we had a strangely immediate and tight connection that would last for a number of years.

- Most importantly, this Borders wanted to run an open mic night, and they handed me the task of organizing and hosting it. This was a challenge because all of my musical connections were about an hour away in Lake County, and if you were to put a microphone in front of me, I'd end up swearing like a sailor without fail, which wouldn't really do well in a family-friendly bookstore.

So, there it was. Every Wednesday night, I'd host an open mic where kids from local high schools would come and show off songs, stand-up comedy, and monologues to their friends. As the host, I started to cultivate a personality to glue the show together. It was sort of a cross between someone that was entirely too confident but alternately had no idea how they'd gotten the hosting job. Really, it was just an exaggerated extension of myself, but it was a good way to practice being in front of people. I had no idea at the time what I was actually building.

You see, each week, I'd need to come up with a reason for people to show up. Open mic nights aren't really a big draw on their own. Nobody looks in the entertainment listings of the newspaper and says to themselves, "Boy, I'd sure like to go out for an evening of entertainment, but I want it to be mostly amateurs, and I want to have no idea what I'm going to see." Rarely happens.

I'd have to be entertaining on my own and have material ready for those nights when only a few performers show up, even if there's no audience, because as I learned, if I didn't stretch the night and fill the two hours, I didn't get paid. This meant that I started writing down every single idea I had. The type of silly thing you'd sing to yourself while washing the dishes? That's what I'd call a "song." If it failed to entertain people, I could still fall back on the "I don't know how I got this job" part of the act. If people cheered? Well, the overconfidence came into play. And I got to practice every week, and somehow, a few people started coming just to see ... me?

I needed new material constantly. And I found that I was better able to convey a song if it was more direct, rather than obscuring the meanings through poetry or typical lyrics. I stood apart when I was singing conversational lyrics. There was something to that whole "three chords and the truth" motif I'd read about after all.

Of course, I also had actual menial tasks from the job to tangle with. I often spent late nights there, working on getting their very neglected but highly perused classical music section up to snuff. One particular night, I was leaving at around 4 a.m. and I needed to be back by 11 a.m. It was an hour drive to get home. At best, I had a nap to look forward to, but I really, really needed that nap.

I'd absent-mindedly locked my keys in my aging Chevrolet Celebrity, so I grabbed a chair from a nearby diner and smashed in the back window so I could enter the car and go home. Not one of my brighter moments, but I didn't have the money for a locksmith, and even if I were to suck it up and sleep in the parking lot, I'd still need shelter because it was raining. It felt like the right thing to do at the time, and, ultimately, the car was my possession, so why not? Sometimes it was fun to be an adult, even if it meant that I'd be sitting in gross, mildew-covered car seats for a few months until I could afford a new window.

HUMAN SLUSHY:

I'd been especially taken with an Orlando group named Heronymus. Their sound was a cross between prog rock and jam band leanings, all punctuated by a horn section and a very theatrically minded lead vocalist named Tim Williams. For a short while, I lived and died for their shows. I hadn't seen a band on a local level that could bring a completely different show for every booking and still pack the dance floor with a bevy of enthusiastic fans. They had something really special, and I made it a point to go to every single show they'd do. When possible, I'd record the performances on a dilapidated Walkman. I felt like there was something here that really needed to be captured for posterity, which would come in handy years later when the band got back together as a one-off and couldn't remember some of their songs.

Heronymus shows were always good fun, but on one particular evening at a club that was once named Barbarella's, they'd booked an intensely bizarre opening act that I didn't know anything about named Precious. Most opening acts will go on about an hour before the headliner, keeping the show on track, getting the crowd warmed up. It's not a foreign concept that needs much explanation. And that sort of tradition was paramount to a Heronymus show, as they usually tended to play until closing time. Time was of the essence.

After numerous delays due to the lead vocalist of the mysterious Precious band not having the correct microphone stand, they finally went onstage close to midnight. And not everyone got it. Distorted fuzz bass; an eccentric front man that sang like a cross between Hank Williams, Billy Corgan, and Thom Yorke; and a balding drummer with the stage presence of a true-blue Motely Crue fanatic playing the most impressive off-kilter times and polyrhythms, seeming to be the only glue in a show that consisted of berating the audience, broken guitars that would be danced upon – it was almost as if this band that had kept us all waiting was in the middle of deconstructing themselves right before our eyes.

I was hooked. I'd never seen anything like them, and I quietly swore allegiance to them, thinking "just because they're local doesn't mean they aren't one of the greatest bands on earth." I came away with a different understanding of how to present yourself to an audience. You could wear your heart on your sleeve if things weren't going your way, and that could enhance the show. It didn't matter that some people wouldn't like you. Half the Heronymus crowd disliked Precious, but I walked away with newfound purpose and inspiration. All that mattered in art was just that the RIGHT people got it.

Very soon afterward, I ingratiated myself into the band's circle by sort of showing up everywhere they went. It wasn't in a stalker-type of way – just going to all of their gigs. Eventually, the band noticed me and started striking up conversations with me, particularly the bassist Joe Panton, and the guitarist and vocalist Steve Garron. They thought enough of me to offer me money if I'd help them load in their gear and sell their merchandise during their shows. I was into that because I liked the extra cash, and it meant that I could go to every single Precious show without paying to get in – and I got to consider it "going to work."

In the meantime, I'd been continuing to exist in the small town. Sometimes working at Borders, sometimes whiling away nights working the graveyard shift at a convenience store, sometimes jumping from record store to record store, and sometimes going without work completely. It was hard to find steady work where I lived because you had to drive for an hour to get to anywhere you'd actually want to spend your days. This meant I often literally only came home to sleep. Between the Precious shows, day jobs, night jobs, and the disintegrating relationship with the mother of my newly born daughter, I sometimes didn't even see my own bed for days at a stretch.

I suppose I should talk about my daughter here. It seems like the kind of thing that one would record in a memoir, doesn't it? But, no. She's her own person, and if she wants her story told, she's free to tell it. I'm merely here to navigate you to the parts of my life that intersected with you knowing about Marc With a C in the first place. And the same goes for her mother, out of respect.

I can say the following: as I've previously mentioned, my daughter's maternal half had a massive problem with substance abuse. I would like to tell you the extents of the addiction, and I'd also like to share the situation that led her to become so immersed while enabling her to come after me legally for daring to leave her once and for all after seeing too much damage in one place, but I really, really should not do that.

Of course, I'm perfectly *capable* of telling you, but that type of thing shouldn't be mapped out in excruciating detail. I'm hoping that despite this disclosure, you'll trust that the legal aspects placed me in completely unwinnable situations that I continue to feel the ramifications of every day. Also, things that take place inside of court rooms often trigger panic attacks for me, so each new hurdle created a world of mild PTSD that you'll simply have to accept and believe.

Now, where were we before I broke chronological narrative?

Working at the Precious shows had its benefits. On one particularly fateful night in December 1999, the band was slated to play at a benefit show in the now-defunct Kit Kat Club. (Thankfully, that club wasn't much into alliteration.) I don't remember much about the evening except for the fact that as the time for Precious to perform grew nigh, Steve Garron was nowhere to be found.

This wasn't unusual. Despite his known penchant for substances that would alter his consciousness, he was also a rather ill man with kidney problems that had plagued him as long as he was able to recall. Also, he wasn't much for sitting idly. As such, he'd show up to play right at (or shortly after) stage time and often take off into the night the very second he was done. Going on early simply wasn't in the cards.

This package show had either run just a little bit short, or a band had canceled. I don't recall. I just remember the lady that was putting on the show frantically looking for some way to fill time. I mentioned to her that I wrote some silly songs, and I'd be happy to play a couple of things to tide everyone over. I mean, I'd already set up Steve's gear, so there was a guitar waiting on the stage, right? I was fully expecting to be shot down, but her eyes lit up, and she escorted me to the stage.

She asked my name. I told her. She jotted down "MARK" on her notecard and started up the steps to the stage to introduce me, and – look, I don't know why it mattered to me, but I said, "No, no. It's Marc. M-A-R-C. With a C," as if the spelling would matter to the impatient people in the audience that absolutely had not come to see me. But, she scratched it out, walked onstage, and, with all the bravado of a deflated balloon, spoke into the microphone: "Ladies and gentlemen? This is Marc" – pausing for an eyeroll so epic that I was shocked at her corneal capabilities before continuing in a huff – "with a 'C'."

She left, and, dammit, I had to entertain an audience. I had no idea how long I was supposed to play, or what these people would like, so I launched into a shaky version of the theme song to *Laverne & Shirley*. When I was done, the venue erupted into cheers, much to my surprise. I did things that were only half-written: embryonic versions of "Victoria's Girls," "Why Don't Girls Like Me," and "Left For Her." And somehow, the stars aligned for me while a very packed venue listened to everything with rapt attention.

Out of the corner of my eye, I spotted Steve Garron walking into the club, looking a bit surprised that I was onstage, playing his guitar. And then in classic Steve style? He made a face that looked as if to say, "Well, he's got it covered," and walked right back out the door. I kept playing.

Afterward, I was asked over and over for my "card," my "CD," and other things that I did not have. Ladies who felt very, very out of my league wanted to buy alcoholic beverages for me. Men wanted to intimidate me because ladies were paying attention to me. But most importantly, people wanted to book me. Almost every person I gave my phone number to that night called the next day, asking about my availability.

That off-the-cuff performance? It was now a persona, and I had to keep delivering it. It was miles from the Very Serious Artist that I saw myself as in my head, but it was also the road to getting paid to play music, so I decided to keep doing it. I figured I could gradually shift gears, and nobody would notice.

I'm still in that gear shift today.

On precisely one occasion, I met and slept with a lady simply due to the fact that I made up songs, and she happened to like them. It didn't feel natural, but it felt like what I was supposed to want as a musician. In her case, she had driven a very long distance to see my show and had not made plans for lodging. I offered to put her up for the night. We had a fine time, but as the night wore on, I started feeling not so great about the situation. Despite enjoying her general company, I didn't know much of anything about her, and she only seemed to like what I did for a living.

But importantly, hours after she'd left, I started getting phone calls from her very concerned friends. Yes, dear reader, she'd told a bunch of her pals that she'd be driving to Orlando to see my show and sleep with me. When she hadn't reappeared, people started digging for personal details about me and assumed I'd done something awful to her. Scared me half to death, and I vowed to never repeat that behavior. I mostly stuck to that vow, which was impressive because I was stubborn about everything but resolutions about vices.

But after the dissolution of my longtime on-again/off-again relationship, I did my share of playing the field. I entered into long-distance relationships with people I'd met via the internet, which would last for a week or so until we got bored with the lack of physical intimacy. I dated people that I met through odd circumstances like the old personal lines you used to see advertisements for on late-night television. I slept with friends I'd known since high school because there simply wasn't a more attractive option available to either of us at the time, which would temporarily convince you that you liked someone more than you actually did. But mostly, I stayed up late, watched videotaped reruns of *That '70s Show,* and smoked far too many cigarettes. The rituals of serial dating were exhausting, and I'd tell myself that I wasn't interested, but loneliness would always win. It led me to feel a sort of an entitlement – not to casual sex but to a lasting, loving, and healthy relationship. And that's what dominated my songwriting at the time. And misdirection.

Well, attempts at misdirection, anyways.

Joe Panton of Precious had noticed that I had a knack for knocking out a catchy tune or two, and we made plans to record some songs. He wanted to get his feet wet with producing other artists, and I wanted to have music to sell at shows so people could take home souvenirs. I'd heard and been obsessed with enough albums that I figured I could knock out a good one pretty easily. Joe played me a production he'd been working on, a silly ditty called "Pigtails." It was just irreverent enough to convince me that Joe and I could make a pretty good team. I should note that the production was forward-thinking enough that I had to ask where he'd recorded the material. Once he told me that it was recorded in the very living room we were sitting in, I was even more interested. And when I asked how much it might cost to have him produce an album, I couldn't refuse the princely sum of "nothing, just credit me as a producer."

We knocked out "Why Don't Girls Like Me?," the first version of "Laura, I Need Medicine," and a regrettable slice of TMI called "Well Fucked Sailor" in precisely one evening. Mixed, mastered, out the door with a master CD. This was early 2001, and I thought we'd have an album ready to go in just a few short weeks.

We settled on the schedule of reserving every Sunday for recording. I didn't know Joe was battling some personal demons that were both debilitating and alienating to those closest to him, so when he'd cancel for the week, I would try to be understanding but ultimately be crushed. Sometimes I'd drive for one hour to his house on nothing more than gas fumes, hoping I could borrow a few dollars from him to get home, only to find out that he'd already called to cancel, and I wasn't home to receive the news. This stretched the process out beyond my comfort level because I like to work quickly. But I couldn't complain – it was free.

In these off weeks, I'd write new material to bring into the sessions and show him embryonic versions of them, but he wouldn't like them very much. He preferred to make things that were in line with the loud pop bands we shared a common love for, notably Canadians like Sloan and Blinker The Star. I'd argue that since I'd often be performing these songs solo, we should do the tracks as stripped down as possible. He argued that a record was very different from a live show, and we should include every single instrument available to us at the time to create an impenetrable wall of sound. I countered with the notion that the songs simply didn't call for that type of production, and he'd respond by telling me to go home and write some. So I'd hastily write a throwaway track like "Groupie Sex" in 20 minutes to try and appeal to both of our sensibilities. He liked that one, while I had reservations about the compromises. But I couldn't complain – it was free.

There was an extra problem introduced due to Joe's aversion to recording things stripped down and quickly: I couldn't really play much of anything besides some passable rhythm guitar at that time. I could offer the personality of my voice. That was it. This meant any idea that Joe had, Joe would have to play on the album. At the end of each session, I'd take home a rough mix, listen to it in the car, and notice that my voice and acoustic guitar was completely drowned out by loud rock guitars, pummeling bass lines, Moog synthesizers, and Joe's drumming. But I couldn't complain – it was free.

Now, I wasn't a pleasure to work with, either. I'd go out for interminable cigarette breaks, make demands that were likely unrealistic and force Joe into time crunches due to self-imposed due dates. Mostly, I just wanted an album out, and the longer the process took, the more I didn't really care what was on it. I needed something to sell at shows because people were asking for them. I became increasingly demanding of Joe's free time and probably wasn't terribly kind when things didn't go my way. During the recording of what would become my first proper album, I became convinced that I actively disliked the record-making process. But really? I just didn't play well with others – despite the fact that it was free.

I got very impatient for the album to be finished, especially when "Why Don't Girls Like Me?" and "Laura, I Need Medicine" began getting airplay on the local Clear Channel affiliate and then spread to surrounding regions. That was no mean feat, and it had happened without much prodding from me. I became increasingly obsessed that an album needed to be available post-haste to go along with these tracks, and I put my foot down on the proverbial gas pedal, speeding past Joe's own comfort zone, and demanded that we release it immediately. The momentum of a single is very, very fleeting, and I didn't want to miss my window of opportunity.

I had showed up one day, and a backing track for the initially acoustic "A Very Special Episode" was just magically ready for me to sing on. I may be mixing this up with the never-released outtake called "Mall Sluts With Cell Phones," but it's probably similar: Joe had produced this sort of Spanish disco-sounding song with Rentals-esque synth parts. I wasn't thrilled by that but decided to trust his instincts. The problem was that he'd recorded these backing tracks in E, which was not the key of the song. I really strained my voice doing multiple painful takes, and overall, we should have scrapped it and started fresh in a less-demanding key.

A similar situation sprouted up for the title track. It was written in A minor, but Joe felt it would have more punch if we'd bring it up to B minor, insisting that I'd only have to sing it correctly once. Trouble was, when these things happened, the strain in my voice was very evident on the album, so not only was the acoustic guitar very, very swallowed up in the mix, but my voice sounded weary, thin, and less than capable.

I should note that what Joe produced was actually quite a good pop record. What was "wrong" with it was my guitar and voice in the mix of all this. That's something I had a problem with and would take me a long time to come to grips with. Joe had made a good record. It just wasn't the right record for ME, and I own that. In truth, the record would have made more sense if it had been equally co-billed to Joe Panton and Marc With a C.

When the record was done – and by "done" I mean that I got tired of the endless tinkering and decided we were going to release it by August of 2002, no matter what the producer felt about how much more really could have been tweaked – there were tons of things that could have/should have been changed. But, there was airplay and demand, so we kept the release date, and I didn't really think about the future implications. As the date for the record release party grew nearer, I realized I'd somehow have to integrate the very dense *Human Slushy* songs into a solo performance that was known for being offensive, antagonistic, and straddling a line between performance art and self-aware "bleeding heart on the sleeve" confessionals. You could love or hate my shows, but you couldn't ignore them once you were in the building.

I wouldn't have to be concerned about it for too long because Joe had insisted on playing drums at the release party. And, unbeknownst to me, he'd also hired a bass player named Aaron Zacktan to play in the band. I just hoped that we'd get along. Thankfully, during our first rehearsal, Aaron had really nailed being able to play the whole *Human Slushy* album from front to back, and there was no need to worry. A band just up and appeared, and I wasn't about to fight that.

Reactions to the album were mixed from fans. It didn't represent the shows, and most were less than impressed with it. Alternately, if a fan heard the album first, liked it, and would come and see me playing a solo gig? They'd be disappointed that it didn't sound anything like the record. People got mad that I'd sometimes throw the setlist out the window, hardly represent the album at all, and just stand on stage, whiling away my set time by smoking, drinking, and telling stories. Not that I'd planned it that way; I was just willing to do anything necessary to make a room remember me. Unfortunately, the album wasn't as malleable and fizzled without distribution, despite leading me to being nominated for (and eventually winning) local awards, which felt very odd but strangely gratifying because I wasn't getting many accolades in other facets of my life.

"I'll get it right next time," I quietly promised myself.

HEY RAPE GIRL, VOLUME ONE:

On one fateful evening in 2002, I was playing a show at a coffeehouse in Orlando. I was on a double bill with the bass player from my first band, and any time that happened, I felt as if he was in some weird competition with me. That notion probably stemmed from the times he reportedly tried to replace me in my own band, or it could have all been in my imagination, but it was palpable to those around me, who would mention it first without fail before I could ever bring it up. I didn't ever personally enter those types of mental spaces with him. I just showed up and put on the best show I could. After the show, a young man named Chris Zabriskie introduced himself to me, offering his services to increase and improve my internet presence. I was on dial-up and had barely mastered using AOL, so this idea seemed especially attractive to me. I gave him my number so we could talk about it further, and we quickly became the best of friends.

It was an odd pairing to look back on. I was in my mid-20s. I drank like a fish during performances, smoked my own body weight in cheap cigarettes, and played in nightclubs and strip joints. He had just entered his 20s and was a devout, lifelong Mormon. Our lifestyles were so foreign to each other that I believe we ended up with a mutual fascination. We'd talk on the phone for hours, and he soon became my confidant and creative partner. I couldn't offer the same to him, as he was – among many things – a budding yet naturally gifted musician that didn't know what he wanted to do with his output, and I couldn't really see things from his very innocent perspective.

I'd mentioned quite often to him that I just wanted to record in more immediate ways. Have the idea, commit it to tape, and get it out into the public sphere as quickly as possible. I wanted people to be excited about new music at the same time that I was. I'd tell him of some of the more grandiose things I wanted to produce, and no matter how strange the idea would sound leaving my lips, Chris would always say it was a worthwhile idea to try, which I wasn't used to hearing.

For a little while, I had a roommate to try and help make ends meet. I didn't check into any of his credentials because he was once a touring member of Meat Puppets, and I was too blinded by fanboy-isms to really think the situation through. He mostly depended on me for rides to work, smoked all my cigarettes, ate all my food, took every consumable pill in the cabinets – even the antibiotics – and had a nasty habit of sleepwalking. Sometimes you wouldn't hear from him for days, and sometimes he would drain your attention.

But mostly I lived for the times we'd sit in the living room with our acoustic guitars, jamming on old Meat Puppets songs. I'd occasionally show him something I'd cooked up, and he'd interrupt and say, "You're just so obviously ripping off Jonathan Richman." I actually hadn't really explored much of Jonathan's work at the time, so I took great offense to such a suggestion but brought home a Modern Lovers album from work for research purposes. I was hooked from the first note. Best thing that came out of that roommate situation. One day he just stopped coming home, and I never really heard from him again.

As I met people that actually did seem to like me, I still felt a red and pulsating hole within myself where a solid relationship could have been. I took to fascinations and incurable crushes. Some examples:

- A lady named Jessica had caught my eye as we happened to inhabit the same buildings more often than not but seemingly accidentally. I wrote a theme song for her radio show on WPRK, a community radio station in Winter Park, Florida that operated out of a bomb shelter that had been converted into a basement. She had me on as a guest, and I would do everything in my power to make her notice me. Eventually I got up the courage to ask her about getting together outside of work circumstances to have a meeting where we could possibly talk about the in's and out's of the theoretical probability of maybe-considering-one-day going on a date; while making it clear that I had very little money, and our shared time together would be about all I could ever truly offer her. She accepted and suggested a fast food joint for said meeting before a show we were going to do together. In one of my least classy moves, I opened the dinner conversation with the explanation that I wasn't sure that I actually had any romantic feelings for her but rather that I was so desperate to have her in my life as a close friend that my brain was tricking me into trying to date her, though I merely wanted very close friendship. And of course, I meant all of this in a very sweet and sincere way (and was somewhat lying about my feelings in some misguided attempt to be "noble"). Later that night, she performed roughly four songs before just walking off of the stage and out of the building completely. I don't know that the two things were related because we never talked about the incident in-depth again, but either way, I thought I'd cemented a friendship and just ended up feeling like a jackass.

- I'd met a very nice lady at some shows I'd played, sharing a bill with some of her friends. Her name was Amy, and we got along very well. Our activities together mostly included eating food, listening to records, drinking wine, and watching bad television. Eventually, it was mutually decided that we were really just friends, and all of the physical stuff complicated that. Although quiet to the point of unresponsiveness at times, Amy would eventually have an immeasurable impact on my life.

By the tail-end of 2002, I was already tired of promoting *Human Slushy* as a solo act and only pushed it during the rare full-band shows that Joe could make time for. We eventually ran into a brick wall with Aaron Zacktan in that he had a lot of trouble writing bass lines. So, if I handed him a demo, he couldn't make anything up to go along with it. This impeded the band playing pretty much anything but the 12-song album that no one seemed all that impressed by. We'd have to come up with something else and fast. Of course, we didn't succeed at that, and with all of the love and respect in the world, we waved goodbye to Aaron with absolutely no idea what to do next.

I had all but given up on trying to include songs from *Human Slushy* in my solo shows besides the radio singles. And while those singles seemed to be getting a few people in the door, said people seemed to be returning for the antics, almost all of which were fueled by alcohol and drugs.

So here's the pithy and predictable part where I tell you that I didn't really want to be yelling at the audience, telling jokes, and getting hammered onstage. I felt that I was at least a pretty good songwriter, but how would the audience know unless I got them to listen? But of course, if you got the room's attention with something outlandish, that's what they'd remember, not the song. This is where I had my first bit of inner contention: am I an entertainer or an artist?

The bookings were steady enough at this time that I didn't have time to decide. I'd try to start off each show rather calmly, but then I'd have to revert to showboating by the end to keep them there. People were coming just to see what I'd do next. I can't blame them. I was a train wreck. Meeting the expectations of my own reputation was not an easy task while sober, and that wasn't a problem because most clubs I worked preferred to pay you in libations and other substances rather than actual money that you could buy food with – though I did like playing at the places that served food because you could talk them out of day-old bread that they were about to throw out, and you could eat something the next day.

But the antics, they were out of control. I'm sure that other people have clearer memories of them than I do, though based on what I've heard retold, I think that they are also exaggerating. But there were two shows that I remember most vividly:

- One took place at the Midtown Tavern, which was a hole-in-the-wall bar where I had a monthly residency. Since I had the safety of that residency, and they hardly paid me anything, I began to show up to these gigs completely unprepared, expecting the night to dictate what I'd do. On this particular evening, I was playing with a weird outsider group that I liked very much called Shaking Babies. During an extended call-and-response chant of "rock and rock and rock and rock and rock and rock and rock and roll" – which I found quite inspiring – they'd managed to chase most of the patrons out of the room. My set was performed to a few nice folks at the bar, my friends, and the entourage of Shaking Babies. The folks at the bar liked my opening tune enough to send some shots of hard liquor up to the stage. I'd never performed under that particular influence. I smelled popcorn (possibly my biggest weakness) and asked if I could have some. The next thing I remember was forcing an audience member onto all fours, riding him like a horse, asking him if he liked "Have a Drink On Me" by AC/DC and pouring the shots onto his head. I also chewed up some popcorn, spat it out and had him suck it up like a human vacuum cleaner. I don't remember playing at Midtown Tavern again afterward.

- The other was an ill-conceived show called the Orlando Punk Awards. There was precisely one of these events, and I was asked to host it. I was far more vulgar than usual, and the audience was there to see the short performances by the local punk cognoscenti. Interminable delays led to a restless and drunk audience that threw bottles at me. In turn, I drank even more heavily than usual. I brought one of the bottles on the stage and spat a mouthful of beer at the crowd members. They responded by slapping me in the ear, causing a giant hole in my ear drum. My balance was already questionable due to the combination of beer and pills I'd slammed down my gullet, but now I had no equilibrium to speak of at all. I quit the show then and there and simply waited for it all to end so I could collect my pay and go home. Plus, I was never given a schedule with which to write my own script, and I should have known to say no to it. Just a terrible combination all the way around. When I think back on the show, though, it probably would have been pretty fun to attend if I hadn't been hired.

After the fiasco at the punk awards, Amy and I made our way to Orlando's Heritage Park, which was really just a courtyard of grass and some cement alligators. We sat together as I ruminated about where this all went so incredibly wrong. She spoke up to say only one thing, which was "I don't like THAT you," motioning toward the club we'd just left. She then pointed at me and said, "I like this you."

At that very moment, I made the decision to not drink until I could handle it better and to transition my act to a more sustainable and honest one. Two things the people who paid money on a regular basis to see my performances probably weren't going to be too pleased by.

Of course, I didn't go completely sober overnight. I was taking painkillers to quell the pain from what turned out to be a more serious ear injury than originally thought. A kind soul had given me some hash brownies for my 25th birthday, and I hadn't yet reached the age were these things would make me paranoid and anxious.

I had a lot of ideas percolating, and I wanted to record them all. One particular idea was to write from the perspective of an amalgamation of a few women that I'd known who were absolutely endeared to the concept of consensual non-consent. It wasn't a mindset that I thought I could relate to, nor could I understand why a number of the women I'd dated wanted to dabble in it with me. I hadn't really seen myself as an "alpha male" unless it came to a musical vision that I wanted to get across. The ensuing collection of songs that would appear were heavily influenced by a dear friend of mine that we'll call Lea. Somewhat based on her experiences, somewhat based in fiction, and sometimes based in the realities of other friends of mine.

Under the influence of the aforementioned special brownies, I completed the harrowing and defiantly lo-fi *Hey, Rape Girl* EP on a four-track borrowed from Jessica. I had the cassette machine so I could complete basic tracks for an EP by our occasional country side project called Not Like Other Girls but found myself more inspired to work on the six songs with "rape" in the title. Even family members took umbrage at me throwing the word around – but I wasn't educated in any proper terminology at the time. And I couldn't shake everyone by the shoulders and explain the very true reality that, yes, some people sought out fantasy rape because they got off on it, and that's what this was based on. In no way did I intend to glorify the horrific realities of actual nonconsensual rape. No matter how much it angered them, **these very real people would continue craving those situations**, so it might help to try and understand it from their perspective rather than just assuming they were sick and twisted, as so many had done to them when coming clean about what they were as sexual beings.

At least one song was based on an article I'd read on "bug chasing." This was a phenomenon specific to mostly gay males: they could not go through the motions of pregnancy and instead would hope to be "impregnated" with the HIV virus in hopes that they could raise it and nurture it. It didn't make any sense to me, but I figured I could try to come to terms with it via song.

This project also marked the first official appearance of "Long Distance Dedication." The song dated back to a zygote of the track that I'd brought in for one of my earlier rockin' teenage combos, but we never found the correct groove for it. Or rather, when we did, the bassist wasn't there yet, and when he finally showed up, he didn't have anything kind to say about the song. Regardless, the song meant a lot to me, as Jessica really liked it and kept telling me that I needed to follow my heart to produce more of this type of material. She could tell that it came from someplace real.

"Long Distance Dedication" itself was much like the other songs earmarked for this project: yet another amalgamation of various times, situations, people and places, with a refrain lifted from one of the subject's old AOL profiles, which I'd learn much later was a lyric that she'd lifted from another song altogether. Either way, it was a dynamic tune, and one of the first where I really felt as if I was getting the hang of this whole songwriting thing.

The resulting EP was a hard thing to truly complete. I had been reading about the ability to induce nausea through specific stereo frequencies, and despite my best attempts to fill the *Hey Rape Girl* EP with those sounds, it ultimately fell flat. My left ear was still suffering damages, and I couldn't tell if I was doing it right. Instead, I mixed the tracks to mostly mono in one sweaty afternoon at a very supportive friend's house. We released it digitally through Chris Zabriskie's burgeoning digital label, Celestial Bison, and I moved on to other projects.

Or rather, I tried to. I alternately got hate mail about the EP and electronic letters that thanked me for putting into words and sounds what the sender had been unable to express. At least the reaction wasn't indifference. Still felt weird playing the songs in public, though. The one time that I performed the EP to completion, I left the stage during the middle of the closing song, "Long Distance Dedication," finding myself entirely too emotional and vulnerable to continue the short opening set, or even the song. Chris Zabriskie had told me that it was the finest performance he'd seen from me. This transition to a different kind of stage show might work after all.

But there were other things to be completed. One was the Not Like Other Girls EP, which I felt a bit of resentment toward. I liked playing songs with Jessica, but she seemed more excited to accept show offers than to rehearse, or at least that's how I felt at the time. We had roughly six original songs and a few covers we could draw from. We hardly had enough for a half-hour set, and our rehearsals at a nearby park would usually either simply become a friendly hang-out session or an argument – if they occurred at all. I resented not only doing the lion's share of the work to meet imposed deadlines but also our inability to consistently play a show worth seeing – but that's completely due to my penchant for assuming that if we didn't work ourselves blind, it couldn't be any good. I'm sure that there were other underlying issues, especially that of not being happy with the results of the EP sessions, and a brand new deadline of having to complete said recording before she up and left the state. It wouldn't be the last time I found myself in the position of rushing to complete something that couldn't be promoted due to abandonment of a locale, and I never grew a taste for it.

Another project was one that had sprouted wings in 1999. When the mood struck me, I'd use a different and barely held together four-track cassette recorder with melted capstans (You'd have to put it in the freezer for a little while before use, and then you had about two takes before it got too warm.) to record slow and mournful versions of songs from the *Rocky Horror Picture Show* sequel, *Shock Treatment*. People hadn't been kind to the film, but I found it fascinating and ahead of its time. I spent many a lonely night in Lake County trying to will myself into sleep watching a worn-out VHS of the movie and started noticing hints of actual desperation in the songs.

I may have been a privileged white guy, but I still lived in a town that gave me a hard time for being who I was and looking strange to them. If I played guitar too loudly in the house, cops would be alerted to calm down the satanic sounds I was conjuring up. I was trying to kick every illicit substance I'd been putting into my body cold turkey. My daughter didn't live with me, and her mother had dragged me through some legal troubles that would warrant their own book to properly discuss. Having sex wasn't a problem, but the possibility of any lasting connection with someone seemed too remote to even imagine. I'd meet people online that seemed to want to date me, but they were all too far away, too dishonest, or terrifyingly clingy to really pursue a future with. Once my ancient computer fried itself, my only way to reach out for gigs was the phone. I didn't have much money to make any long-distance calls because Lake County didn't share an area code with almost anyone that I felt a real connection to anymore, and, as a starving artist, I didn't have the money for phone bills.

Not to mention that the house I was living in was falling into disrepair. The water heater was broken, and eventually the main heater followed suit, so I spent an interesting winter where I wasn't homeless, but the shelter over my head simply could not be warmed. People make a lot of jokes about Florida's weather, but if you're poor and lonely? Those winters are simply intolerable if you're accustomed to overwhelming heat and humidity. So why wouldn't I connect to the inherent loneliness of the *Shock Treatment* film?

Occasionally, in just the right mindset, I'd go through the process of freezing the four-track and trying out a take or two of a song from the movie. If I blew it, no work was done that day, and the embattled deck would make its way back into the freezer until I could try again. You could eat up an entire day in this fashion and not get a single usable basic track. I felt lost and practically dead inside, and I couldn't tell if it was circumstantial or the reappearance of an emotional disorder. I just tried to stay alive.

BUBBLEGUM ROMANCE, PART ONE:

Joe Panton called one day to remind me that I'd apparently once told him that I would happily be his roommate. He also told me that I'd be moving in by the end of the week. I tried to protest, but he'd been banking on me doing this thing that I had no recollection of agreeing to. Joe had that way about him. I felt that I should probably do it because I'd live with the guy that was recording me, and it'd be just like The Monkees. We'd have wacky adventures, lean on each other when we were low, and make great music, right?

I loaded up what turned out to be rather meager possessions into a moving van that was far too big for the job and made my way to Orlando without any actual employment to speak of. And it soon became apparent that while I'd been doing okay with putting my addictions behind me, besides the cigarettes, Joe had a whole set of problems that he wasn't ready to face, let alone conquer.

We'd slowly begun working on what was intended to be my second full-length album, though it didn't have a title. I made it overtly clear that I wanted this new record to only have the bare minimum of sound necessary to get each song across. Each song would be its own sovereign nation, built from the ground up. And it'd be done quickly, too. I was overflowing with tunes, and I wanted to completely bury *Human Slushy*. The first song we worked on was "Music Can Heal," a sincere track that was met with much derision at my shows as I'd try to strike a balance between the silliness and honesty. Once we'd hit on the third hour of trying to make ringing cordless phones harmonize with each other, I could feel in my bones that things weren't quite right between us. But hey, Joe had the equipment, and maybe he knew best, so I went along with it.

The sessions dragged on and on. Every few weeks, I'd twist Joe's arm into doing some work when he seemed coherent enough for it, wasn't working with Precious, and wasn't in the throes of a massive depression from losing his job at a mom-and-pop music store that was being swallowed up by one of the big impersonal chain shops.

And sometimes, I'd even get him to rehearse for shows. There was nothing more he seemed to dislike than rehearsing. We'd drafted Chris Zabriskie to play bass in place of Aaron Zacktan, but this became problematic for a number of reasons:

- Joe was a bassist by trade and disliked that Chris favored riding the root notes.

- To the best of my recollections, Chris did not own a bass guitar and could not rehearse unless he came over.

- Joe might've hated to rehearse, but Chris hated it more.

- I would spend hours on the phone, ringing it off of the hook in hopes that they'd be over to learn the songs at the same time.

- This scared them both off from working with me because I seemed completely obsessive and insane.

We dubbed ourselves Marc With a C & The Malk, and that tension actually ended up making us into a live force to be reckoned with, though it wasn't exactly a boon to our interpersonal relationships.

Orlando wasn't bad to live in, though. There were always nearby coffee shops where I could play for a few bucks, and I dated a number of interesting people. One memorable young lady we'll call Emily had tried to predict our future via rune stones, and that's when I headed for the door with a loud "NOPE." She then tried to flush the rocks down the toilet, and I didn't have the heart to explain why I was leaving for good as the pipes burst. I didn't know how badly I'd upset her until she called frantically at the end of a long first date I'd had with someone else, giving me the impression that she'd been nearby watching the entire time. This made sense, as Emily had a habit of showing up at places I'd be despite telling me she wouldn't be attending. It felt like she wanted to catch me in the act of wronging her, and I suppose that I ultimately didn't disappoint.

But that first date that she'd interrupted with her frantic phone call? It was memorable in its own right: a lady we'll call Ellen who I'd been trying to pitch woo to for a little while had taken me up on the offer to see each other. She'd been pretty shattered from the remains of her most recent relationship and wasn't too sure about my intentions. And I only had positive ones. We did a lot of very childlike things together, but that shared arrested development would lead to misunderstandings and long, stubborn arguments for approximately one year.

In-between the beginning and end of that relationship, though? The inspiration was astounding. I don't know if it was specifically who I was dating, or just that I had found freedom in Orlando. I was lucky to live in a pretty neat neighborhood that had a thriving art scene. There was always a cool open mic on, or some people would be huddled outside of houses with instruments, or some just mixed the two with open jams in DIY spaces. I'd find myself composing songs clearly in my head, able to walk to all of the places one would need to go, humming lines like "I'm In Love With Everyone I Know" to myself and jotting them down when I'd get home. Fun song ideas would introduce themselves from simply watching Ellen and my daughter coloring pictures together, and next thing I knew? I'd be scribbling something down about colonies full of brine shrimp.

As the *Bubblegum Romance* sessions wore on endlessly, I would sometimes find Joe nodding out at the controls. We'd blown a ton of release dates, and this was problematic because the new songs I'd been introducing at shows were surpassing the popularity of even my meager radio tunes. People were especially clamoring for "Bounce Bounce Bounce," which was a song written while watching my daughter jump on the bed tirelessly. And a little ditty called "Nerdy Girls," which would go on to be one of my most enduring tunes. But it wasn't designed that way.

Well, kinda.

You see, "Nerdy Girls" was a fairly calculated move on my part. Here's the components of what went into that particular song, in case you've ever wondered just how much I think about each and every aspect of songs that I make up:

- I wanted to write an "anthem." And in all of my obsessive reading about pop music history, it seemed that most worthy anthems said something about the audience that was absorbing it. And I'd noticed that quite often, the audience looking back at me was socially awkward, and when the lights would hit the sea of glasses? It'd look like a crowd full of Stormtroopers.

- This was the early 2000s. As a society, we were still kind of okay with The Baha Men. Being socially awkward not only wasn't in vogue; some of the very, very attractive ladies that came to my shows saw their nerdiness as something to hide. In some cases, they would rue their glasses, feeling the opposite of pretty when they'd wear them.

- There weren't exactly a million songs celebrating the virtues of ladies in glasses at the time that I knew of, let alone songs that championed intelligent women that liked what they liked unapologetically, so I thought I'd fill that gap until someone else could do it more effectively.

- I'd gotten tired of hearing people say that they like "everything but rap and country" because we're all basically using the same 12 notes (give or take a few semitones), so I thought that it'd be an interesting twist to write so specifically about my audience that they couldn't help but relate to it – and they'd be too busy enjoying the lyrical content to notice that it was actually a style of music that they claimed to dislike.

I had an inkling that the song would be popular within my modest-at-best fan base, but I had no idea just how beloved it would become. To many, it remains my signature song. There are worse things to be remembered for, I suppose.

On one fateful day in 2003, I was contacted by an A&R representative for a Very Large Record Label. They were requesting a sampling of my latest material based on the airplay that I'd garnered on Clear Channel stations – a nearly impossible feat unless a mandate had come down from up on high. Chris was in the room when I received the correspondence, and he did some digging to make sure the person was legit. They were. I talked Joe into finishing at least a few mixes from the sessions we'd been slaving over, and we sent them off on a disc with some of the already-known radio singles.

We waited. And the wait was interminable. They'd received songs like "Freezing In Florida" and "Liana," the latter of which didn't see an official release for a number of years. I believed that I was becoming a "real" songwriter, and, at the time? I had an increasing disdain for the more punchline-oriented material.

On one of the days while we waited to hear something back about our musical fates, I'd shown Chris two songs I'd written in the same session: "Just a Few Words" and "RetroLowFi." We'd spent the bulk of the day digging for records at that shockingly well-stocked junk store in Groveland, Florida, and the latter was inspired by that visit. I knew it was catchy, and it was really a statement of purpose for me. It'd definitely stick around. But the former, "Just A Few Words"? I thought it was too heartfelt, and that Marc With a C audiences would never go for it. He bluntly asked why I couldn't just be known for both, as they were two sides of the same psyche. He was right, and I started changing my tune.

That was easier said than done, though. I'd begun retiring the sort of trashy "Well Fucked Sailor" as the set closer at shows and started replacing it with that 6-minute dirge written on a sleepless and sad night called "Music Can Heal." It was rough going. People wanted me to make dick jokes. They wanted me to be abrasive. On more than a few occasions, patrons would actually throw objects at me when I'd leave out "Why Don't Girls Like Me" and play "Music Can Heal" in its place. I tried hard to make room for both, but some audiences just simply weren't having it. And while I've always changed my setlist greatly from show to show, I started becoming picky about the types of material I'd play because it's no fun to have a bottle whiz past your head for telling the truth. There was a balancing act between being an entertainer and being an artist, and I had yet to master it.

And let's face it: having that type of identity crisis wasn't the best thing to go through while making an album with a controlling soul like Joe. He wanted to make a loud rock record, and when the label interest had shown up, he'd gone into overdrive about making the album as accessible and radio-ready as possible. He mostly wanted to wow people with not just his production abilities but his own playing. At one point, his exact statement to me was, "Let's show everyone who the real rock god in this town is," referring to himself. It wasn't just a dig at me, but he lived in Steve Garron's larger-than-life shadow in Precious. When he'd suggested that the album art should literally be me buried in his musical equipment, he probably didn't realize just how appropriate that would have been.

The *Human Slushy* trend had continued: we'd record the basic tracks with me playing guitar and him playing drums. And then he'd layer a bunch of things on top, sometimes replacing the parts I'd played altogether. He seemed determined to use every single instrument he owned at some point during the record, despite my protests. I'd remind him that I wanted the album to be simple and stripped-down, and he'd just continue making his own album out of my songs. It seemed that he was intentionally letting each promised release date go by unchecked because he wanted the album out on a big label.

I didn't have those lofty goals. I just wanted what was best for the songs, and I wasn't really keen on trying to become the biggest thing since sliced bread - I valued my privacy and artistic freedom but agreed it'd be nice for the album to have wider distribution. Joe and I were at an impasse, one that does show a healthy dollop of faith in the quality of the material I was writing on Joe's part, all cards shown.

That impasse wasn't an "agree to disagree" situation. We'd spent the better part of two years on an album that I had barely played on, and while he wasn't in a good way with his addictions and overall outlook, I needed an album out, and it had to happen soon. Joe's attention was divided because Precious had been signed by an upstart label that would eventually become the home of acts like Whole Wheat Bread, Astronautilus, and Grand Buffet. And said label had made the decision to give a trio featuring two members with insatiable addictions a rather large signing advance. I got it in my head that Joe was really just holding out with my record for another advance, and it increasingly felt like he wanted to run the damn show. He'd tell me to "shut up" if my banter was taking too long at shows for his tastes, or just flat out talk over me and make the gig all about him. I couldn't put out this album without him, as he was my key to recording, but I also couldn't play shows with him. Chris was just sort of caught in the crossfire.

We did have a good time together now and again. One memorable night was my birthday in early 2004 at a long-defunct venue called Guinevere's. We'd played as a band, but I'd played an acoustic guitar instead of an electric one, and we actually did a very nice gig to a full room. Or rather, it was easy to fill the room, as Guinevere's was really just a tiny art gallery.

Of course, no good time is without its consequence. After the show, Ellen continued to refer to me by her ex-boyfriend's name, and I was in a foul mood as a result. I just wanted to get out of there. Joe really wanted me to drive him to his dealer's house, which I refused to do. I made it home refusing to speak to either of them. The next morning, I'd driven back to that general area to return some library books while still wearing my pajamas and a Precious T-shirt. I was pulled over by a police officer who'd made it his business to take me to jail due to what can only be referred to as one of the most massive clerical errors in the history of massive clerical errors: my driver's license had been suspended. Trust me when I tell you that you don't want to go to the county jail in the garb that I was wearing. As a matter of fact, the guards were so busy making fun of my clothes, kitty cat slippers, and plastic Krusty The Clown watch that someone had literally escaped right before my eyes.

They set my bail at $500, which miraculously happened to be the exact amount of money I had on my person at the time. I paid my own bail and expected to be sent on my way. In actuality, the jail went into full-scale lockdown due to the aforementioned escape artist, and I was held for over 24 hours. My phone calls to try to get Joe to come to the jail fell on deaf ears, literally.

When I got home, I'd found that Joe had simply turned the volume of the answering machine down as far as possible, presumably because he was tired of me calling and was still mad at me from the night before.

The first Very Large Record Label had decided that I wasn't ready for prime time as it were unless I was willing to drop all of the serious stuff and hand over a bunch of comedic material for further consideration. There was a "thanks but no thanks," and that was the end of that. Joe wasn't pleased, but it was especially surprising as he almost always immediately dismissed any material that could possibly elicit a chuckle from someone. And the more I thought about it, he didn't seem to like the other songs unless he could give them all a complete and total makeover.

I'd passed on the label that had signed Precious with a disc full of lo-fi demo songs that might end up on a second record if I had my druthers about the way it'd turn out. They had the same philosophy as Joe: do comedic material, and they'd market me to the college crowds.

But me? I needed to get a record out. It wasn't so much about self-expression but that this was something I was put here to do, and every second that I wasn't working on it, I was squandering my time on Earth. It needed to be done my way because I was the only person that could make records from my perspective.

That may not seem important to someone that hasn't heard me yet, but I had art to create that poured out of me, and it needed the canvas that I deemed appropriate. And Joe was making his own version of my art. *Bubblegum Romance* started feeling more like a remix album than my own creation.

To accentuate to all involved parties that we needed to get this album out as soon as possible, not just for my career but for my mental health, I set an arbitrary release date for August of 2004. I also found myself booked on a popular local radio show on a Clear Channel affiliate where I was to premiere the intended single from the album, "No London In Brazil." And that's when I ended up with the first full rough mix of the album, which I listened to on the way to the station. When I arrived, after hearing the whole she-bang? I knew that I couldn't release it.

The album wasn't anywhere near ready, and I simply could not get Joe to do the album in the manner that these songs called for. I gamely did the interview, and over the air, we played the song while the DJs feigned excitement over it, but it was clear that this album versus what I actually did live were two opposing things. And not in a good way. This was an album that tried its best to be slick but just didn't need to be. If it would come out in this fashion, my heart wouldn't be in it, and I'd still be tied to Joe's schedule for creating art.

I called Chris while taking a break at the dehumanizing call center job I'd found myself stuck in, which was the type of thing I only reserved for having arguments with Ellen, usually over something I'd done wrong. I was especially bad about oversharing at the time, not yet fully understanding the reach of journal sites and social media, and those arguments were rightful and founded for her to start.

I told him that despite all of the work, the album just wasn't right, and neither were things with Joe. I confided that in a perfect world, I'd fire Joe and do a totally different album, but my pesky natural sense of loyalty wouldn't allow it. Chris reassured me that I was right, adding in that basically, if Joe had done the album as quick and lo-fi as we'd initially agreed on, it would have been out already, everyone would have been happy, and we could all just move on. However, the process had taken so long that I'd basically become a different artist altogether in the interim: one that liked using the minimal amount of sound-producing items to get the loudest point across, as well as someone who could now record themselves in a primitive way, and the results never sounded a thing like how Joe thought it should sound. Chris made it clear that we could record the album in roughly one day, in his living room, and still meet the arbitrary release date. We bandied emails back and forth about the tracklist, because at this point, I'd literally written more songs than either of us could count, and we wanted to distill it into around 40 minutes that would define what Marc With a C was from that point on.

There was only one problem: I couldn't fire Joe right then because The Malk had already been booked at the Fringe Festival as a band. To make things more complicated, we still couldn't get into the same room to rehearse. But somehow, we took to the stage, playing a squeaky clean set right before sunset full of songs from an album that two of us knew wasn't going to come out. I hadn't been feeling well – a newly discovered blood disorder had called for an immediate change to my diet, which the hiatal hernia in my chest wasn't taking to very well, and my immune system was letting every imaginable illness through. I tried to take a "show must go on" mentality that might have been less than important at the time.

There were scattered audience members in a field that could hold quite a few people, and while I was trying to jump up and down and give them a good show, Joe would continuously tell me to calm down or make it clear in some way that my actions were not enjoyable for him, usually via the PA system that was loud enough to coat most of downtown Orlando in our voices. We weren't playing well, and everyone on the stage had an issue with someone else up there, and all of those issues that could have been worked out in the rehearsals we didn't have? They came boiling to the surface during that gig. We tried to end the show with one of the few older tunes that had stuck around in the setlist, the title track to *Human Slushy*. Joe counted it in, but it was a little sloppy, so he stopped us, placing Chris and myself squarely in the hot seat. After he sternly said, "Let's give the people a PROPER ending," Chris and I knew precisely what had to happen:

Joe counted to four to kick off "Human Slushy," and Chris and I launched directly into "If You're Happy And You Know It." This led into the longest, slowest version of "Hungry Like The Wolf" that one can imagine, and that morphed into a bastardized version of Pink Floyd's "Interstellar Overdrive." The show literally ended with Joe yelling at us both to stop.

Later that night, I told him I'd be finishing the album elsewhere, and he shrugged it off. I also told him that I was planning on sticking to solo shows. I had sworn off trying to keep a band together, and I was determined to do things my own way. But I'd still need a little help to get it right.

NO LONDON IN BRAZIL:

Often, people ask me what a particular song is about, and I sometimes won't answer with the whole truth. That's not because I'm being evasive, but if I'm often writing so directly that if the listener hasn't picked up on what I'm trying to communicate? I don't really want to destroy what's going on in their heads. This would also explain my natural aversion to music videos. But you, dear reader? There's a better than average chance that you're here because I made up a song that you like at some point. So, let's break away from that point of view for just a moment, and I'll tell you about the situation that inspired one of my most enduring tunes, "No London In Brazil." The *Orlando Weekly* once put it in a list of Best Orlando Songs Ever Of All Time or something of that nature, so it seems like a good candidate for this sort of thing.

I was living in Lake County when these actions took place, and I was a single man. There weren't many places near the town of Mascotte where one could quickly and easily procure food, but one day, I noticed a lady – we'll call her Tina – that worked at one of those precious few fast food joints. She didn't hand me my order or anything, but I saw her through the window, and I thought that she was absolutely beautiful. I thought to myself, it's a small town. I'll eventually run into her at some point, and I drove home.

As luck would have it, I was leaving a convenience store a few blocks from my house at around 8 p.m. one evening, and lo and behold? There she was, sitting on the sidewalk of the shop, reading a fashion magazine. I brazenly decided to go up and talk to her. I introduced myself and gave her some compliments about her level of attractiveness, but I immediately regretted it, figuring that she must have gotten that kind of thing all of the time. But instead?

"OH MY GOD, YOU ARE JUST THE SWEETEST THING," she shrieked in the most Southern and shrill voice that one can imagine. The voice didn't match up with her demeanor or poise in any way, and I was taken aback. But hey, unexpected voice or not? Conversation had been initiated, and I was going to press my luck by inviting her to dinner. I gave her my phone number, she accepted, and I drove home feeling as good as anybody else that had basically just made a date with the current object of their affection.

Now, when I'd given her the number, I'd made mention that it was the number to my office. Of course, I knew what I meant by that: "the office" was a semi-soundproofed room for making music so that the local police would stop coming to the house. If someone called the other line while I was in said office, there was no chance I'd hear the phone ring. But I hadn't really made that distinction to Tina. And as soon as I walked in the door? Office phone was ringing, so I dashed to answer it. It was Tina, who immediately inquired as to why I worked so late. I explained the situation, and she countered with "SO WHEN ARE YOU MAKING ME DINNER ANYWAYS?" I explained that I had plans of ingesting food that evening, and she was welcome to come over and eat some of it with me. She took down my address and biked over.

I barely had time to give myself a once-over in the mirror and check for boogers before she knocked on the door. She'd come directly from the convenience store I'd just seen her at. Barged right into the house while still knocking and asked if she could use the restroom. I didn't see any reason to deny that reasonable request, and as the bathroom door slammed shut behind her, the sound of the faucet being turned on full blast wasn't easy to ignore.

I waited for about 15 minutes, but she didn't reappear. Wanted to go and knock on the door to check on her but didn't want to be rude, so I just got to work making dinner: a simple plate of grilled chicken and a baked potato. She remained in the restroom until I was plating the food, and I was relieved when she reappeared that I wasn't going to have to call the authorities due to Tina gaining squatter's rights from occupying that room for so long.

We dug right into the food, and she would ask me off-the-wall questions like, "DO YOU LIKE NEW AGE MUSIC? YOU KNOW, LIKE 8-BALL AND MJG?," "WHY YOU GOTS SO MANY GUITARS?," and, after only a few bites of food, "CAN I BRAID YOUR HAIR?"

It's important for you to know that at this point, I had hair that was nearly down to my waist.

She was peculiar, but I did in fact want her to play with my hair, despite sensing that something was a little bit off. I mean, we all have our eccentricities, right? I hastily scarfed down the remaining food on my plate while she stood behind me, doing some things to my hair with her lanky fingers. She abruptly stopped and walked in front of me, kneeled keeping eye contact, and with all of the gravity possible, she muttered in an only slightly less shrill voice, "THIS GUY CAME ALL INSIDE OF ME ONCE."

She then waltzed right over to the kitchen, took a cup from the dish rack, grabbed the antibacterial dish soap, squirted some into the glass, added some water, grabbed a spoon, and stirred and drank the entire thing right before my eyes. Threw in a loud "THIS STUFF CLEANS OUT MY INSIDES" for good measure.

I reached behind me to check out the progress on her braiding and realized that not only had she been simply tying my hair into bow-tied knots, but she didn't seem to be intoxicated, so that left one possible scenario: Tina was not in her right mind, and while I was now slightly scared to have her there, I was also morbidly curious as to what my new friend would do next. She didn't seem to pose any sort of threat, and now that I'd mentally taken any possibility of romance off of the table, it was fair game to just let the night play out.

While her dinner sat untouched, she'd mentioned that she really wanted to watch a movie. It just so happened that during this time, I was working part time in a video store – yes, I burnt through a lot of jobs – and had brought home a copy of the Brendan Fraser remake of *Bedazzled* to see just how bad it really was, and she was welcome to watch it with me.

I settled on the couch, ready to watch what was sure to be a less-than-enjoyable 90-minute flick, and Tina? Well, she removed the thick blanket from the loveseat, put it over her head, and said "OKAY, START THE MOVIE."

You have to understand that she had completely wrapped the blanket around her head numerous times, and there was simply no way that she could have seen the screen, and I'm not quite sure that she was able to get enough oxygen really, but she cackled maniacally throughout the film. And I don't just mean the she laughed loudly at the jokes. One continuous fit of laughter lasted for about 40 minutes.

Why only 40 minutes? Because after that show of unprompted laughter, I had decided I was scared to have her in my house all by myself for much longer. So I suggested that we walk up to the convenience store we'd met at just a bit earlier. I don't remember what I pretended to need, but ultimately my hopes were that she'd either notice how late it was getting and excuse herself, or at the very least, I'd be seen with her, and this way people would know who had murdered me that evening.

When I've suggested that Mascotte was a small town, it's something that can't be overstressed. There were a hand full of police officers at best, and if you worked in food service, you knew them all by name, because you'd be expected to give them free drinks and such. But this truck stop/convenience store that we were walking toward? People would set up drug deals between the giant big rigs that were always parked behind the place, and some of these dealers that had driven in to distribute their wares weren't familiar with the local officers. I point this out to you because Tina had recognized one of them who was pretty clearly in the middle of a covert sting and yelled "HEY! I KNOW YOU! YOU'RE THAT POLICE! YOU WANT A SLURPEE OR SOMETHING FROM THE STORE?"

I was severely regretting having her over for dinner, but not as much as when she started confiding things in me on the walk back to my house:

- "I ASK EVERY GUY I MEET HOW LONG HE CAN LAST. AT SEX."

- "I WAS MARRIED BUT I LEFT HIM BECAUSE I DON'T LIKE DOING THE DISHES, BUT I KEPT HIS CREDIT CARDS. MY DADDY WAS HAPPY THAT ME AND MY COUSIN COULD GO BACK TO JUST BEING A FAMILY AGAIN."

- "I THINK I COULD FALL FOR YOU. YOU HAVE YOUR OWN OFFICE."

Understandably, I made hasty excuses for why she couldn't come inside. She was disappointed, but she rode her bike off into the night, and I went inside to call my buddy Ska Steve, because he simply wasn't going to believe the night I'd had. At around 4 a.m., I drifted off to sleep with the help of some type of chemical and was excited to enjoy my upcoming day off.

Until 7 a.m., when the office phone started ringing like crazy. The answering machine would pick up, they'd hang up on it, call back, and repeat the process over and over. Sleep was now out of the question, so I groggily answered, "Hello?"

"HEY, HAVE YOU EVER HEARD THIS SONG?"

She put the phone to the radio speaker as a very distorted version of "Jessie's Girl" by Rick Springfield played through. In its entirety.

"Yes, I have heard that song."

"I'M GONNA COME OVER SO I CAN PLAY IT FOR YOU AND YOU CAN HEAR IT BETTER."

"No. Please don't do that. I know that song, and I want to go back to bed."

"HOW LATE DO YOU SLEEP?"

"I'm an insomniac, and—"

"WELL, YOU ARE UP NOW SO I AM COMING OVER."

"No. Don't. Please, just, give me until noon?"

"OKAY, BUT I'LL BE SICK OF THE SONG BY THEN."

I really didn't want her to come over at all, but I didn't know how to firmly say "no" without upsetting her. And after realizing that she wasn't living on the same plane of existence as most folks, I frantically called Ska Steve, waking him up and begging him to come over so that I wouldn't have to be alone with her. Thankfully, he was an early riser. When I explained the situation to him over a sleepy conversation, it ended something like this:

"So look, will you please come over? I just can't do this by myself, and I'm kind of freaked out."

"Well, she's hot, right?" Ska Steve asked.

"Please try to understand, she's pretty, but she's obviously unstable, and you shouldn't really factor her looks in. You're basically coming over because I can't be around her alone."

"But, she's hot?"

Sighing, I said, "Fine, yes, she's 'hot.' Will you just get over here by noon?"

"I'm on my way."

My warnings fell on deaf ears. He lived 40 minutes away but arrived in 30 minutes flat. This was around 8:30 a.m., and we killed a sleepy morning watching videotapes of Bill Hicks.

Tina arrived shortly before noon armed with a very, very full backpack and what seemed to be a thick coat of liquid gloss covering every inch of her body, soaking through her clothes which were stuck to her skin. I asked her what she'd gotten herself into, and she loudly explained that she'd found a moisturizing lotion, and since she'd never used one before, she thought it'd be a good idea to make up for lost time and use a few bottles worth and really let it soak in. I showed her to the bathroom and gave her every towel in the house while patiently explaining that this wasn't really how those things worked, suggesting that she should definitely clean herself up before sitting on any of my furniture. I closed the door and braced myself.

Seconds later, she peeked her head out to ask in a quiet and childlike voice that I didn't know she was capable of, "Will you show me how to turn on the shower?" She covered herself with a towel and asked me to make the water as cold as possible. This wasn't an issue due to the dead water heater. I felt really bad for her, but I didn't know what to do. I had initially approached her with romantic hopes, learned that she wasn't in a mental position where that type of thing should even be considered, found myself a bit scared of her presence, and also wanted to help her out. It wasn't pity but rather an odd paternal sort of patience and protectiveness. But also, I just wanted it to be over because I didn't know how to handle this type of situation. They didn't really write books on what to do in these cases, and if they did, I hadn't read them.

When I sat down, Ska Steve's eyes met mine as he said, "You're right. She IS hot." If he felt mentally superior to someone that he could not have sex with, it usually became open season for him to fuck with them. I wasn't in favor of that, but I was exhausted and pretty scared of doing the wrong thing, so I gave him the reigns to keep the situation at bay. If he thought she was "hot?" Cool, he'd be trying to impress her, but he'd soon figure out what the score was.

Instead, Ska Steve tried to relate to her on her own level. When she reappeared, freshly showered but still in sticky clothes, I placed a towel on the couch for her to sit on, and on her way to her seat, she bent over, grabbed her butt cheeks, and made the motions of spreading them directly in my face as she passed by. She then announced that we were "in love." I could only plead with my eyes for Ska Steve to help. I wanted to run for the proverbial hills, but, it was my house, and I needed to protect my belongings.

Steve motioned toward her backpack and inquired about the contents. She responded by silently opening it and dumping the contents onto the coffee table. Those contents? Literally around one hundred individual coffee creamers of various flavors, a small notepad, and some pens. I asked where she'd gotten all the cream samplers, and she explained calmly that they just gave these things away at gas stations, so she'd been collecting them for a special occasion.

She offered each of us one of the single-serve creamers. I politely declined, and she yelled, "WELL, FIIIIINE. BE A PUSSY. WE'LL DRINK ALL THE SHOTS BY OURSELVES." She thought that these were alcoholic beverages, something akin to Bailey's.

Steve said, "All right, I'm down," and they went to town downing these shots right in front of me, one after the other. She'd take notes in her notepad about each flavor. She announced that the dark chocolate one was "especially meticulous."

I recall the two of them having nonsensical conversation while I watched in disbelief:

"SO WHERE YOU FROM?"

"Brazil," Ska Steve said

"OH, I HEARD THERE'S A LOT OF CRIME UP THERE."

"Well, I'm from the rich part. It's called London."

"I HEARD THAT PLACE IS NICE. THEY EAT CRICKETS."

This sort of petered out after an hour or so. She'd decided that she and Steve were now "in love," and, right on schedule, their stomachs weren't handling all the creamer. They both left separately, and I only saw Tina on the rare occasions when she'd barge into my house without knocking, asking a random question like "HEY. WHAT IS A LAWNMOWER?," allowing me to half-answer and then disappearing again for a few months.

"No London In Brazil" was a set of lyrics strewn together from stream of consciousness writings about the events with Tina, and as I'd later occasionally learn some odd things about her upbringing via small-town hearsay. Those would later creep up in a lesser-known song of mine called "A Woman's Duty."

If you've ever thought that my songs are bizarre, you should try living them.

I hope Tina is okay, wherever she is.

BUBBLEGUM ROMANCE, PART TWO:

In late May 2004, Chris and I holed up for a day and a half in his living room to record what would eventually become the *Bubblegum Romance* album that you're possibly familiar with today. It was a simple setup with Chris at the controls. We'd made a pact that everything would be a first take unless the equipment malfunctioned, keeping a sense of urgency throughout. I'd brought over the Schecter Diamond Series six-string that I usually played onstage, and there were a few classical guitars at our disposal at Chris's pad. The only things that were even overdubbed were the bass guitars heard on three songs, the buried piano parts on "I Need a Hug" and "No London In Brazil," and any harmony for my own voice. Beyond that, whoever was in the room would be the backing vocalist, and they'd usually have very little warning. Chris captured a vibe in those two days, and as a result, I walked out with a finished master of the album at the end of the second day.

It all seemed so much easier to do it this way. Know the songs, believe in the songs, and record them exactly as they sound. I'd been toying with making demos on a slightly better four-track tape recorder than the one I'd begun on, but I couldn't have set the vibe the way that Chris did. The only thing that felt a little off was the ending of the album. It felt slow but cluttered. At various times, the tracklist included extra songs like "Satellite" and "Music Can Heal," and they were removed at the last minute with frantic calls to the pressing plant.

I now highly regret removing "Music Can Heal" from the album, but that was rectified when the album got its first vinyl issue in 2014. The version from that session was likely the definitive version of the song, and for some reason I'd seen fit to exclude it and replace it with "When You're Not Around." The latter is an okay pop song, but including a song inspired by time apart from Ellen instead of "Music Can Heal" was just not a great judgment call on my part. Especially considering the state of our relationship at the time.

Ellen was not accustomed to the things that my daughter's mother was up to, and once she had seen firsthand evidence of it, she put a series of events in motion that would seem as if they obviously needed to be done but ultimately ended up very tragic instead. I could see things unraveling, and I held Ellen personally responsible.

Plus, at her behest, I'd quit my job at the call center to do some work in the field of activism, which didn't really resonate with me. I enjoyed playing the odd benefit show, but having conversations with complete strangers about the political issues of 2004 mostly ended with me being standoffish. I wasn't good at it, I didn't make much money, and again, I held her responsible. And no matter how much pressure she'd put on me to make these choices, I ultimately made the choice to give in and only had myself to blame.

The strain on our relationship was only exacerbated by a rogue hurricane changing direction at the last minute and knocking out the power for nine consecutive days. We found ourselves staying in a broken-down RV camper at a family member's house for the duration and arguing more than usual.

We did find some time to visit some surrounding thrift stores during this "visit." It was during this time that I'd bought a stack of cassettes that I'd planned to record over for mixtape-makin' purposes, until I'd learned that each tape contained roughly 90 minutes' worth of chilling answering machine messages by a man who had truly gone off the deep end when his girlfriend left him. I composed a song called "Amy, It's Kevin" out of some of the most memorable bits, but it was hard to keep my mind on the job, knowing that we'd return home to a bunch of things ruined by water damage, heat, and humidity. I couldn't shake the feeling that something bigger and scarier was waiting just around the corner at any flash of happiness.

Around this time, what had been somewhat dormant emotional disorders were awoken into a tailspin. I'd find myself walking on air, composing at a mile a minute and then my face would be flooded with mucus and tears at a simple "hello" from someone. It was becoming harder and harder to abstain from alcohol with the emotional mess I was in, and with the entire house smelling like Joe's bongwater, I started caving in and having a drink here and there. It'd soothe my insides momentarily, but alcohol would also push me into further self-loathing for being weak enough to give in to those urges. And Ellen didn't let me live down a single slip.

*Bubblegum Romance* was finally issued in late August of 2004. We celebrated with a release party at a small venue called Austin's in Winter Park, Florida. When I arrived, the place was exceptionally packed, and I had a hard time even making my way to the stage. I could not find room in the venue to actually set up a merch table, and I had to sell the discs from the tiny raised platform I had just sung from after the show was over. Chris Zabriskie backed me up on drums for the show, which he'd been doing on and off for a little while. (My recollections are that he just showed up one day with drums, set them on the stage and decided he was my new backbeat, though he recalls it differently. I'll let him tell you about it in his own memoir).

We played pretty well in a show dominated by new material, every song from *Bubblegum Romance* except for "The Prettiest Girl In The Whole Wide World" for some reason. "Terror Song" also made its debut at that show, including a verse from Pink Floyd's "Astronomy Domine," which Chris had suggested just moments before we went on, and it just stuck.

Our opening acts for the night were:

- Joe Panton, because I felt that I owed him one for producing an entire album's worth of material that I canned. Besides, Precious had pretty much broken up at this point, so it seemed like a good time for him to show off all of the (very, very good) songs he'd been hoarding over the years.

- Chris Zabriskie, because he's probably the best songwriter I've ever physically met, but sometimes that was hard to tell people. My audience mostly knew him as my "sideman," and he played shows so sporadically that he was a little hard to "follow" if you liked what you heard.

- Natalie Weiss of Unicornicopia – or at least I think she played. This was long before she moved to New York and started the DJ school for babies that was featured in all of those magazines.

- Bucket Of Nails.

Now, Bucket Of Nails sure was one interesting band. Back in 2002, when I was working the merch stand for Precious at a House Of Blues show, a very young fan of the group came bounding up to me, looking over the wares for sale. And when I say young, I mean it: he actually looked to be around 9 years old, though he was really around 13. Just a bit small for his age, really.

I sold him his merchandise and introduced myself because it was cool to see kids understanding just how powerful Precious really was. Something about my stage name rang a bell for him, and he gave me sort of a stink-eye before saying, "Are you cool? I heard you're cool." I told him to judge for himself and slid him a copy of *Human Slushy*. That was Patrick Scott Bell, and soon he and his brother Michael started coming to bunches of my shows.

They'd tell me that they'd set out to make the worst band possible. Patrick would play the drums in drag, screeching lyrics like "I HATE PEOPLE THAT THINK IT'S COOL TO SHOP AT THRIFT STORES! YOU'RE STEALING FROM THE HOMELESS," while his brother made caterwauling feedback and played the straight foil to Pat's outrageousness. You either got them or hated them, and I was pleased as punch that I'd had some influence on them.

I'd book the band every chance I got, and I'd revel in watching people squirm. Some couldn't handle them, but most times they'd go over very well. Here were two kids that looked like they weren't even old enough to be in the building, and they were louder and more abrasive than bands that actually applied themselves. I'd go on to produce two albums (*I Checked My Calendar... It's Doomsday* and *Bucket Of Nails and Nico*) and one EP (*Anxiety*) for them.

And while I was enjoying recording music for Bucket Of Nails, as well as finally playing shows to promote an album that I really felt that I could stand behind? Ellen and I had broken up, but were going through the awkward phase where we still lived together, so neither of us could really move on. We'd try our best to be civil to each other, but we'd fail time and time again.

Eventually, during one particularly heated argument, she just pushed me in the chest as hard as she could. It wasn't quite a punch, but if I didn't leave the situation immediately, I couldn't be assured that one wasn't going to follow. This was as we were both just about to leave for a Rilo Kiley concert that we had tickets for, which I belatedly made it to, hoping that the gig would cheer me up. Instead, a bit of a twig snapped in my head, specifically while Jenny Lewis sang "A Man/Me/Then Jim." I became a blubbering mess. Could not stop crying. It didn't subside during the more upbeat songs, either. There's a cliche about "the straw that broke the camel's back," but that's what actually happened.

After the gig, I found myself wandering around downtown Orlando, telling strangers untrue things, chain-smoking, crying, laughing in the faces of people I'd never met for no good reason. I wasn't in my right mind, but I was mindful enough to know that I needed help. I'd been diagnosed as bipolar years earlier, but I'd left it untreated for far too long, and while I'm not afflicted with the most overwhelming case of the illness that you'll have ever seen, when it presents in me, there's no mistaking it. There had been signs that a major depressive episode was coming on for months, but that's the day that it decided to overtake me.

## THIS WORLD IS SCARY AS FUCK, PART ONE:

I spent days driving through Orlando, recognizing that I drastically needed help. Pent-up internal disturbances that I'd been previously able to ignore were bubbling up to the surface, but all the circumstances of the fall of 2004 that should have been upsetting me weren't really coming to mind. It wasn't that I was dwelling on the dissolution of my relationship with Ellen. It wasn't the continuing sting of not having full custody of my daughter. I wasn't even all that troubled about living with Joe, though that was particularly difficult.

It was much simpler: I couldn't control or predict if I'd be running at double full speed or bursting into tears for no good reason at all.

I tried driving to every place I could think of to get some help. I was basically attempting to find a way to get some low-/no-cost therapy. I figured that there had to be some sort of system in place for those that suffered from a mental illness but didn't have insurance, but after stopping at nearly every hospital I could think of, filling out endless applications and being denied repeatedly, I had two choices: I could either do my best to "suck it up," or I could get arrested and hope to be placed into some kind of psychiatric ward. The latter seemed like it would only exacerbate the circumstances, so I went with the former.

*Here's where I attempt make something clear: if you are suffering from depression or a mental illness of any kind, I do not recommend that you self-medicate or attempt to go it alone. If there is an option that does not involve incarceration, please try it. I was out of options, did not have much money, and didn't have much of a support system in place. I do not recommend just going home and trying to "snap out of it."*

I went home to try to snap out of it. But instead, I found alcohol making its way back into my life on a more-than-semi-regular basis. And pills, when I could acquire them. No uppers like one would imagine, either. I've always had off-the-wall reactions to any medication I am handed. Whereas an opiate might make someone else sleepy and groggy, they'd fill me with a euphoric sense of purpose and a false sense of clarity, but mostly, I didn't want to die. I could focus when on those substances, though the focus was ultimately stunted by an inebriation that I was sometimes very, very good at hiding from people.

As a result, I made poor life decisions. More than usual. And actually, the bulk of the period directly following the release of *Bubblegum Romance*, and my mini-breakdown is mostly a blur. But three things do stick out amongst the din surrounding those memories, not listed in order of importance:

- I quickly found myself in what can only be described as a rebound relationship with a lady we'll call Eunice. Neither of us was in a good place in our lives, and we may have pooled our collective misery together. There was an age difference between us that didn't look that wide on paper, but we were miles apart in our ambitions, not to mention our definition of "ambition." We drove each other batty.

- The mother of my daughter passed away. The circumstances of her passing still aren't crystal clear to me, but I think that it would be sound to say that she'd really put her body through the ringer with various manners of self-abuse, and it gave out completely on Thanksgiving of 2004. I don't have the words for the shockwaves that this sent through my family, nor will I attempt to write something about it here. Some things are just too heavy.

- Chris Zabriskie and I had a major falling out. We'd done what was to become the first of my yearly "holiday shows" at the record store I was working at, Hullabaloo. It was really a showcase for his fledgling Celestial Bison label, and I'd been relegated to a short 20-minute set.

Meanwhile, Chris's noise group Struggleburger played for roughly two hours. It was loud and long, and I'd picked up some cheap alcoholic beverages from the nearby corner store to pass the time. I imbibed it, and this did not please him as his values were still very much aligned with the Mormon faith. Nor did what he perceived as my lack of respect for his instruments. See, after the show was over, when the building had emptied out, myself, and the other employee of the shop had jammed on the instruments for a few minutes, as Struggleburger had elected to leave their gear in the store overnight. It was admittedly not the classiest move on my part, but Chris and I had used each other's gear before, so I didn't think it was a big deal. That was an incorrect assumption.

The next day, he'd noticed scratches all over his guitar, and wood shavings from the drum sticks littering the floor. He was under the impression that the impromptu jam session had been much more intense than it was. He wrote me a scathing letter about the situation, completely ignoring that he and his Struggleburger bandmate had beaten the living fucking snot out of their gear for two hours straight. He retaliated by taking my website offline completely, and I had no idea how to fix that. He'd also promised that it'd be back "when he felt better," to paraphrase his words.

I retaliated by making the decision to kill Marc With a C. I'd just gotten out of the situation where each artistic move I made had to be approved by Joe, or it wouldn't get recorded. I wasn't about to enter a situation where Chris could just get pissed off at me and decide to erase my internet presence. It may sound silly to you, but I was bordering on being a luddite at the time and knew nothing about how websites were sent out into the world. I wasn't going to be silenced just because Chris wanted to get a point across. So when the website returned? I told him to announce my final show, which would take place in March of 2005 at BackBooth in Orlando, FL.

The only person who would be allowed to silence the musical act known as Marc With a C was me.

Now, it isn't fair to say that the bullshit that Chris pulled was the sole reason or my rather rash decision. I wasn't sick of making music, but I was tired of the large divide between what I created and how it was perceived. In *Bubblegum Romance*, I'd made an honest, earnest, and real statement with those songs, nary a punchline in site (at least in my mind), but people still had this misconception that I was a comedian. And as of this writing, I'm still not quite sure how or why that tag stuck to me. For every silly song I wrote, I'd write three ballads. I'd never strayed from things that might cause an audience to giggle because humor is an aspect of human reactions and feelings. But often, I was angry onstage. Or sad. Or even just flat out meandering at times. But all that most people remembered were the giggles, and it's dogged me for the bulk of my career.

I didn't want to deal with anyone else when it came to my art any longer. I was tired of telling people that I wasn't there to merely tickle their funny bone but rather to entertain in general.

It'd have to be career suicide.

And despite my foggy mental state, I was serious about it. I didn't plan to stop making music, I just decided that I'd reinvent what I already did in a manner that people not only couldn't have a say-so in, but I'd also be doing it semi-anonymously. It'd take a while to fully develop the idea, but I had already come up with a name for it: Bunnythumbs, which was a nickname I'd earned from being a total thumb war champion. (And if you follow the rules properly, I can probably destroy anyone in a thumb war. Y'all just like to bend the rules when you figure it out. More on that in my upcoming instructional vlog.)

Bunnythumbs would be a website. On said website, music would simply appear. No images, fancy graphics or identifying information. I'd be creating it but with a twist: every day I'd give myself around 90 minutes where I simply had to commit some music to tape. It didn't have to be listenable. It didn't even have to be good. It just had to be **something**. I'd go back and refine ideas and possibly reuse some material if I had a better idea for it. Of course, I'd also be free to create more than just one piece, but either way, in 90 minutes or so every day, something had to be completed, no excuses.

So there it'd be. This mysterious website where some entity was producing music. No attribution to Marc With a C. No contact information. Just music. I'd planned to kick things off with a definable 10-song digital "album" as sort of a starting point and then start uploading the random bits. One could cherry pick songs they enjoyed or choose to see it as a perpetual rehearsal. Services like Bandcamp and SoundCloud weren't even on the horizon, so it was a spectacularly bizarre concept at that time. I looked at it as the digital equivalent to Jandek, and I was ready to devote myself to it.

Besides, lots of other things were changing. Precious had unceremoniously broken up onstage, people were using phones less and less in favor of electronic text communications, and I'd tracked my father down and tried to coax some type of apology out of him for the things that he had done to me and my family in my youth. He wasn't willing to even entertain such an idea and instead implored me to simply stop holding a grudge. He'd also taken me to task for making such "bubblegum" music, which tickled me in a way, truth be told. It seemed like a good time to do something else altogether.

I WILL KEEP YOU:

Let's back up just a bit. When Ellen and I were split up but still living together, I'd done a show at an infamous Orlando establishment called Will's Pub. It was the best sort of hole-in-the-wall dive in its original incarnation, and an act named Meka Nism had asked me to play a show with her. As usual, details were scant about the show. Often times, I'd show up for these things incredibly early because:

- No one planned for low-tier shows terribly well.

- There was nothing better to do on Earth than play a concert.

I've been reminded time and time again that I'm the most punctual musician that most folks have ever worked with. I can count the number of times I've been late to a gig on Mickey Mouse's fingers, and despite the fact that each tardy showing was due to an emergency that was beyond my control? I still browbeat myself for that type of behavior. Lack of punctuality would surely be in my list of "top five pet peeves" if I were to ever make such a thing, but that's a story for another time.

On this particular evening, all I knew was that Meka was going to play a set and that she wanted me to perform one as well. At the time, Meka was an acoustic musician that was heavily inspired by the darkest metal she could get her hands on. Anachronistic for sure, and, for this reason, we were often paired on bills together. No one knew what else to do with us separately.

And of course, we're talking about a low-level concert in the backroom of a pub, behind the room with the main attractions: the pool table, the jukebox, and the alcohol. The finer details of a musical performance just weren't terribly high on anyone's list of priorities in such a situation. As show time grew nearer, I'd occasionally glean another detail: someone had been added to the bill, the running order had been changed, etc. The act of "hurry up and wait" is possibly my least favorite part of public performance, second only to making setlists and changing guitar strings. I was getting increasingly antsy as I tried to put myself in the correct headspace to perform, so I eventually directly asked Meka when I'd be going on.

She said, "Oh, you're going on after the next act. Someone is going to read some stories and poetry for about 10 minutes." I thought to myself, "All right, I can follow poetry. Just a few minutes."

A heart-stoppingly beautiful woman named Nicole made her way to the stage and told some stories of college romance gone wrong, and while I enjoyed her work, I found myself distracted by my inability to stop ogling this redhead spouting the unflinchingly honest material. I was mentally slapping myself on the wrist for not being able to stay tuned to her art.

(It'd only been a few months since Ska Steve and I had gone through a falling out that would irreparably destroy our friendship. We were watching a friend of mine perform, and she was doing a great job, and he kept leaning in to mutter things to me like, "I bet she's a tiger in the sack, though." He'd disrespected my female friends in the performing community a few too many times for my tastes, and once I confronted him about it, he ultimately decided to ditch me altogether rather than accept that this type of behavior could use a bit of work. This was after telling me that he equated our relationship to the one he'd have had with his stillborn sibling, so it stung especially hard. And each time I found myself noticing the physical attributes of the opposite sex after this, I was very hard on myself, unsure if I'd lost my best friend due to my own projection.)

I was especially taken by her, but before I knew it, it was time for me to go up and play my set. I rushed off, got into my pajamas for prime comfort during my performance, played what I remember as a pretty decent set, and then waited around to get paid – and say hello to the beautiful redheaded storyteller. I couldn't do much in the way of conversation, though. Her large boyfriend didn't seem very pleased that I was trying to talk to her. I told her that I liked her performance and that we should look each other up on MySpace.

After that initial meeting, we'd run into each other here and there:

- Once at a show where I was opening for the local *Rocky Horror* shadow cast, The Rich Weirdoes. This was an especially notable performance, as my penis had popped out of my pajama pants, though I'm not sure that anybody noticed. I'm pretty sure it was blocked from the audience's view by my guitar.

- Occasionally at an in-store performance at Hullabaloo, the fledgling music store I was working at that was disintegrating more each day.

- A few times during a radio station marathon where one DJ named Dave Plotkin tried to stay awake and on the air for five days straight. I performed two sets during the marathon, and Nicole was dancing Rockettes-style during "RetroLowFi." It was hard to take my eyes off of her, let alone concentrate on the songs.

I was pretty sure that we were noticing each other, but I couldn't say for sure because I'm uniformly terrible at reading romantic signals. And besides, I was in the throes of ending my hopelessly ill-conceived rebound relationship with Eunice, and Nicole had a boyfriend that hardly ever let me get a word in edgewise when I tried to talk to her.

I was feeling especially low in February of 2005. I had all but ended the toxic relationship I was in with Eunice. The key moment came when I'd made myself so sick on pills that I found myself puking outside of a family member's house on my birthday. I wasn't even sure who I was mad at, so I couldn't "blame" my intake on the actions of someone else. I felt lower than dirt, and I couldn't wait to end Marc With a C and become a hermit that worked in the backroom of a thrift store or something.

And then? An unexpected MySpace message from Nicole: "I miss you."

That was it. It was simple. It wasn't even the type of message that demanded a reply since we hardly knew each other. It was just a very kind message, and I wasn't receiving many of those. It sparked a conversation that evolved into her coming over for soup later that evening.

And dear readers? As our conversation turned toward innermost feelings, secrets, feelings on dominance and submission, and what can only be described as the most intense listening session for an album by Low ever conceived? We dolly back and fade to black.

That was it. The first date never ended. I fell asleep naturally by her side, which is something I couldn't do with others. There was no question for either of us: this is what we'd be doing with the rest of our lives. Oh sure, there could be rocky waters occasionally, but this was for real.

Within a few days, I'd given her a symbolic engagement ring – one of the few family heirlooms I possess – and we made the decision out loud. We were a couple and wouldn't let anything change that. And then we high-fived.

Beyond that, I will not tell you much about the dynamics of our relationship. Those belong to us, and unless our relationship is very important to the story of the music I've made, I will not touch on domestic issues much from here on out.

But by the end of February of 2005? I was walking on air because I was partnered with the most beautiful, kind, intelligent, and funny woman I'd ever met. That'll do wonders for your inner darkness. The relationship saved me because I was certainly only half of a person, and nothing was keeping that half together. That's not to say that anyone else should look to be fixed by a relationship, only that it's what happened in my own case.

THIS WORLD IS SCARY AS FUCK, PART TWO:

The "final" Marc With a C show took place in a half-filled club in March of 2005. Chris Zabriskie did not attend, and while it crushed me inside, I also had to respect that there was a massive divide between us. I played one of the best 90-minute sets of my lifetime because I was sure this would be the end.

Knowing what I know now? I feel like I really screwed every attendee out of the $5 entry fee. If you can prove to me that you were there somehow, I'll send you back the money. My bad. I promise that I thought I was finished at the time.

After the show, Nicole and I went to see a laser light adaptation of *The Wall* by Pink Floyd. However, the operator kept skipping songs and playing things out of order. For example, the wall **went back up** after the trial. I drunkenly hurled insults and pretty much ruined any good times that could have been had in the room. I also got into an argument with a friend named Emily (her actual name, not the Emily from earlier. Boy, I really should have thought these pseudonyms through). Again, I don't know what I was so mad at, but looking back, I think I was mad at myself for not letting the storms pass. I felt like Marc With a C had been taken away from me, but I was conveniently forgetting that I'd personally made the decision to kill it. Funny how that works.

Work continued on the Bunnythumbs project. Tons of weird little things were committed to tape, and the first 10 "songs" for the site had been finished, a full album. It was weirder than anything I'd made thus far, and owed a huge debt to the Guided By Voices, Sebadoh, and early Blinker The Star records I was listening to at the time. During a patch where Chris and I were actually speaking, I let him hear it, and his review was "this is much more melodic than I thought it'd be." I enlisted him to help make the Bunnythumbs website a reality, giving him another chance at webmaster-type-things, still recognizing that I had no head for making those types of internet things occur.

Two things happened very, very close together that changed my plans:

- I hadn't actually previously checked, but any website that used the term Bunnythumbs would lead you to pornography. In retrospect, I really should have bothered to see if the sites were available. And I didn't want to try to come up with another name, so I abandoned the idea altogether, but not the habit of the 90-minute production windows.

- Chris had decided to move away to the Northwestern United States. He'd booked a "going away" show and asked me to play it because he said that it would mean a lot to him. I accepted but asked him not to bill me as Marc With a C. Though my set included almost nothing except cover songs and unreleased Bunnythumbs material, Chris's introduction of me to the audience contained something like, "Here he is, doing his first show since he lied about quitting." I was a little mad because I was doing him a favor as a pal, but, he was also right.

And with Nicole behind me, believing in me even when I didn't, I set on a course of forging forward with the Marc With a C nomenclature. I decided that no matter what the public perception of my art was, I would still produce it without apology. If people thought that I was doing comedy, I'd play shows with nary a laugh in sight – but only if I felt that way on that day. (And besides, my attempt at reinventing myself as the world's first lo-fi hair metal solo artist had failed miserably when the single "Makin' Bacon On The Beach" had fizzled, so I was running out of avenues.)

I started going through the Bunnythumbs material and piecing together some of the best bits into an album that would eventually be known as *This World Is Scary As Fuck*. Numerous songs were spliced together to make wholly new creations ("God Save The Queen From Navy Seals"), some were revitalized from the never-ending pile of unused songs from the *Bubblegum Romance* period

("One Hit Wonder"), and one of my favorites was completed by taking an unfinished chorus about my daughter and then writing the sappiest and most obvious love song lyrics for the verses to make the tune mean something else completely ("Stuck With Me"). Before I knew it, I had an album. Oh sure, it was dark, noisy and depressing, but there were hints of light when I would sing things inspired by Nicole.

And just as I was ready to release it? Joe dropped the bomb: we all had to move out by September 1. He wasn't in good shape, and the money we'd given him for bills didn't always make it to the organization that was owed the debt, as Joe had, erm, *other* bills to pay. Trouble was that he'd told many of these debtors that I was the one with the substance abuse problems, and they were basically kicking me out.

It's true that I didn't know when to say when if an illicit substance came my way at the time. I was certainly trying to plug a hole in my heart through any means available, but I didn't do it with money that I needed for rent. It turns out that if you're a musician, people will often just hand you drugs and alcohol most of the time if they are a fan. I hardly ever spent a dime on those things back then.

Under the gun, Nicole found a cozy little duplex that we'd be able to move into on the same day that we were moving out of the large house on Aloma Avenue. I'd seen a lot of car crashes in front of that house, so any sadness I had felt about moving was quelled by the reminder of some newfound safety.

Moving our things was easy. Joe had a habit of spreading his possessions all over the house and overtaking every single room. Nicole and I were living in what amounted to a very large patio where all of our stuff was, and we occasionally used the kitchen and bathrooms. We were out by 4 p.m. on the allotted day, having fully cleaned only the spaces where our possessions once were. Joe asked if we'd be coming back to "help," but he didn't seem to be doing much. He'd packed a lot of boxes but was still just sitting on the couch, watching television. He didn't seem to be ready to move at all. I didn't see the need to deal with that as he'd basically come very close to making me homeless through his accusations, so I closed the door one final time and was ready to move on.

Considering the confusion at home, I was treading lightly with returning to playing shows in public. I'd book a coffee shop gig here or there, but few gigs would make a big splash. I was feeling a little sheepish because I'd had a bunch of press coverage about "quitting," so it felt weird contacting the same publications six months later in hopes of promotion.

We released *This World Is Scary As Fuck* under the radar. No big promo push, no online sales, just a meek little CD-R sold at gigs – gigs where I was all but refusing to play earlier songs. I figured that since I'd "quit," it didn't really matter what I played anymore. Instead, I opted to perform only current material and things that I could heavily relate to at that moment.

This would frustrate attendees. Sometimes in the generic way of "well, I heard "Laura, I Need Medicine" on the radio, so I came to see you, now please play it." Other times, it'd be the couple that got married to the strains of my "Freezing In Florida" that could be possibly frustrated by my preference of performing relatively difficult material with non-linear lyrics like "I Am Going To Fuck Your Life Up" instead.

I wasn't being difficult on purpose, mind you. I was trying to follow the muse and play a really good gig by only performing the things that I best related to at the time. I had a good handle on which songs of mine people liked best en masse, and that's when the yearly holiday shows became "Okay, just the hits tonight." Which was an interesting balancing act: I didn't have actual "hits" to speak of, but most evenings I wasn't performing the songs that I was barely even known for. I was trying to make new favorites, after all.

But I was hitting a new audience. My experience has been that whatever my newest material happens to be doesn't really connect with an audience for nearly two to five years, by which time I've all but retired the songs out of the assumption that folks didn't like it, or that I'm looking ahead toward what's coming next. But around this time, kids – yes, kids – were coming to my shows that had only just heard *Human Slushy*, and they related to the somewhat whiny and entitled lovelorn concepts put forth in the album.

One younger audience member had found my AOL Instant Messenger screenname, and she sent me a sweeping amount of quandaries about if I'd accompany her to the Warped Tour. I'd been to said festival before, once as an attendee, and once working for Precious. I knew that it wasn't my cup of tea, so I politely declined. She went on and on, not taking no for an answer, telling me all the reasons that I should reconsider my decision. I felt too old to be having this conversation, declined again, and signed off of the service completely.

She went on to update her LiveJournal and MySpace blogs with emotional and sad things because now that this musician she liked wasn't going to a festival with her, no one could understand her pain. The lady in question made sure that I saw this. I picked up my guitar and cheekily set the attitude to music, and Nicole and I had a good laugh about it all. I then tucked the song away, thinking that nobody would get it. It was a very, very specific thing, after all. Catchy tune, though.

LIFE'S SO HARD, PART ONE:

I'd been slowly introducing a new drummer into the shows. He went by the name of Ryan Price, and, as Chris Zabriskie wasn't available for the sideman job, Ryan had volunteered himself for the duties. It was slow going, though. Where Chris was an unpredictable and energetic wildcard who knew my songs like the back of his hand, Ryan was a reserved individual who liked to go over each tune with a fine-toothed comb and play them numerous times each day to enhance his muscle memory.

I wasn't used to working this way, and I didn't immediately grow a taste for it. I felt that if you have the general idea of how a song should go, that was good enough. Because when on a stage, it's sometimes best for me to have to come up with how to connect it with the room on the spot. Otherwise you have a script that you can't deviate from. A nice thought, but this wasn't a Pink Floyd show tied to a click-track. It was a personality-driven gig that could go a number of ways, no matter what was written down on the physical setlist.

Ryan had the capacity to retain the drum patterns to roughly 12-20 songs at a time. I liked him, and I liked drinking fine beer with him as we podcasted, and I taught him the tunes, but it didn't feel natural to play with him. Internally, I felt that I was trying to train us into having a natural stage camaraderie, and that was about as realistic to do as it sounds. I couldn't really get where Ryan was coming from, and I was probably much harder on him than I intended to be. And as I was born equipped with a naturally terse tongue, most sessions would end with at least one of us in tears.

*(Often, it was Ryan. I'm sorry about that, Ryan. You're a good person. Thanks for sticking with me as long as you did.)*

Some of the songs we'd play at the shows most often would be "Stuck With Me," a slightly more up-tempo "I Will Keep You," or "Bite Size Help." We'd occasionally do a cover like "God's Away On Business," but mostly, we stuck to new songs like "The Problem Is Me," "Counting Down," and "Every Single Friend."

I'd been performing a monthly residency at an Orlando venue called Stardust Video & Coffee. The title implies exactly what they were: a coffee shop that rented out videotapes. And not just any videotapes. Besides the first-run new releases they had to offer to stay afloat? This place mostly had b-movies and foreign films in stock, almost universally bootlegged copies. The tapes weren't arranged by title, either. You had to look for things alphabetically ... by director. In the backroom, there was a small, uneven stage, and if you brought 60 people to the gig, you'd feel like a motherfucking sorcerer looking out into that now shoulder-to-shoulder room.

We used these shows to workshop the songs that would go on my next album, but it was a troubled collection from the get-go. It wasn't troubled in the manner of, oh, say, a gaffer falling to their death or a bunch of mishaps leaving tapes erased, but rather a problem that I'd never faced alone: I had far too much unreleased material, and I couldn't focus and find the heart of the newer songs for what felt like a complete album.

Of course, the audience didn't often know that they were watching a workshop. The attendees would understandably show up wanting to hear "I'm In Love With Everyone I Know" or "Why Don't Girls Like Me?" Instead, I'd be trying out a new song called "You Can't Kiss An Emoticon." Of course, if someone showed up the following month and asked for a repeat of the new tune, they'd be out of luck because I'd decide that I didn't like the tune and had already decided to shitcan it.

Plus, you'd get all sorts of people who were just there for the libations. On a particularly memorable evening, a Stardust show was sparsely attended, and that was fine with me. I didn't feel well, as some of my lifelong stomach problems had decided to flare up on that particular day. I wasn't going to cancel, but one older gentleman had made it his business to be louder than everyone else.

This wasn't an issue for me because I was good at drowning those things out back then, either by ignoring the distraction or making them rue the day they were born with snappy banter, but when this guy yelled out things like, "PLAY 'DIXIE' TO HONOR DEAD SOLDIERS," I was completely flabbergasted. So I said, "Okay, let's play 'Dixie' to honor dead soldiers" and instead launched into the very childlike "I Really Wanna Be Your Friend."

This made the audience laugh, but this dude didn't see it as a joke. He continued to yell things that were highly inappropriate for a show with such a twee presentation. By the end of the show, he'd won. I was just not into it, the attendees had become a silent mass, and even though someone might request "I'm In Love With Everyone I Know," and I'd acquiesce in hopes of lightening the mood? Everybody stayed pretty quiet. They were patiently waiting for me to finish up so that they could leave the very uncomfortable situation. You just can't plan for those types of nights.

I was becoming comfortable dealing with difficult people, though. I was trying to help make ends meet by working at a mom-and-pop liquor store a block from my house called Big C. Ultimately, once trucks were unloaded and the bottles were on the shelf? You had a bunch of time to kill between customers, and said customers were an endless stream of inspiration. Sure, you'd sell imported beers to the occasional connoisseur or the couple that just wanted a few drinks to unwind after work, but a large percentage of the stores inhabitants were lifers.

There was a gentleman that was drinking to keep his mind off of his odd case of leprosy, and the guy that worked at the car wash across the street who was always very excited to tell me about his band. I'd scribble thoughts and poems about them, and the owners didn't really care. It pained me to sell liquor to those that were in especially bad shape. I felt guilty parsing out what would ultimately be the cause of death for some of these folks, many of them only making it as far as the parking lot before they'd chug their Novocaine and then turn right back around to buy more from me. I worked there for what felt like a good long while, but I ultimately couldn't handle it anymore when the pseudo-leper literally drank himself to death in front of the store.

WHAT THE HELL WERE YOU ON?:

Though Chris Zabriskie wasn't physically around, I trusted his judgment about my music. He always seemed to understand where I was going even when nobody else did. I'd send him tapes and mp3s of demos, asking for his help in narrowing down what would ultimately show up on the next album. As I previously mentioned, in 2006, it was a lot like the *Bubblegum Romance* period. I had far too many songs for the record, and was having a hard time making it a focused and tight statement.

Many of the songs were far less autobiographical than they'd been in the past, instead leaning toward stories of people in odd situations. I didn't know how to make the two co-exist. How do you make a song about Sergeant Hartman from *Full Metal Jacket* being disappointed in his fictitious daughter sit alongside "Counting Down," a song about my very real daughter? Chris was indispensable in his advice, and *Life's So Hard* as an album would have been very different without his direction.

Though I wasn't drinking much then, just occasionally escaping into a bottle when things felt especially tough, working at the liquor store had changed that. They'd send me home with bottles of things to try so I'd know how to recommend things to the customers with especially discriminating tastes. I took this as "I NOW HAVE BEEN GRANTED PERMISSION TO DRINK ALL OF THE TIME," but I mostly consumed late at night when my antics wouldn't bother anybody.

I've always been an insomniac, so most often, I'd truly look at alcohol as a way to knock myself out. Soon after, I'd seen a doctor about my sleeping woes, and upon his understanding of just how serious the issues were? He'd prescribed a powerful alternating cocktail of things that would basically tranquilize an elephant. But I didn't have a handle on how these things would mix with other stuff, nor did I really get that you should take these medications while lying in bed. How could I do that? It'd be 4 a.m., I'd be bouncing off the walls with my creativity at its peak, and you expect me to take a handful of pills and ... just lie down?

Reading that back, it seems like the obvious thing to do, but internally it didn't make sense. The later it would get in the day, the more manic I'd become, and sleep seemed like a cruel joke invented merely to torment me.

As a result, I'd take the pills on top of whatever else I'd consumed that evening, and then I'd go about my business until I could no longer stand upright. This resulted in conversations that I have no recollection of, friendships forged through late-night chats that I wouldn't even be aware of during my waking hours, and most importantly to you, dear reader? Music that I wouldn't discover until a later date.

The first example of this that I can remember discovering was on a night where I was battling a severe cold. I'd had a few beers, I had imbibed far too much cough syrup, and then I also downed my sleepy-time medicine. And that's about the last thing that I remember.

I woke up late in the afternoon on the following day to see that numerous microphones were set up in the living room. There was a pad of paper; my guitar; and a tape in the four-track that still had the play, record, and pause buttons pushed in. Clearly, I'd recorded something the night before. I played it back, and ... it was an angry song with an odd beat. That was definitely my scratchy voice, but I didn't recognize the tune. It had verses dedicated to a mom and a dad, and I recognized the scenarios from the film *SLC Punk*, though the third verse was rooted in the moment where my dad told me that if I turned out to be homosexual, he'd disown me. There were chords and a beat where a chorus should be, but no lyrics.

I quickly came up with some words for it: "What the hell were you on / When you came up with that one?" I overdubbed it, transferred the mix to the computer, and voila. A song was born, apparently. The downside was that it was in a rather bizarre rhythm that was so simple that it was hard to replicate. It took me years to figure out how it could work in a live context, and, even then, it became a more laid-back shuffle.

It would also take years before I'd get the hang of how one should take care of themselves when nocturnal medication is a part of their lives. I'd make some mistakes along the way, but I'd also make up some of my most well-known songs under the circumstances. The drugs made me unpredictable and combustible, but they also seemed to unlock portions of my brain that I otherwise wouldn't have tapped into creatively.

People don't always believe these stories, and I don't recommend that you try and replicate the results, but that's how it went down, for better or worse.

LIFE'S SO HARD, PART TWO:

Again, narrowing down the tracklist to *Life's So Hard* was a task that I couldn't seem to get right. I knew that the first five songs were exactly the album I needed to be making, but there were other tunes that I just couldn't properly shoehorn into the album. As a rule, I usually prefer that my albums are between 30 and 45 minutes long at most. Just because technology allows for more space, attention spans don't. I wanted my albums to be a thing that you could listen to in one shot without fatigue. Unless you don't like my songs or voice, and then I couldn't really help you.

But the important part to note about the creation of *Life's So Hard* as an album was a sea change that affected my life and music overall: as I've mentioned before, this was the first full album where I really started singing through the eyes of other people. Did I have something to hide? Probably. We all have things we don't want anyone to know. But I'd always been good at letting that type of thing fuel the art.

The trouble was that there was really no trouble at all. I was in a healthy, committed relationship, and while there were some growing pains while Nicole and I settled into the realization that the other party wasn't just going to up and leave, those were problems that were, at worst, worked out in a matter of days. Not the kinds of things that you'd immortalize in song, no matter how relatable they might have been if turned into lyrics.

Reactions to the songs were mostly positive from listeners, some hailing them as a "return to form," though obviously darker? Others couldn't be satisfied. Some folks just wanted *Bubblegum Romance* over and over again. And this is where I say the cliché thing like, "I already made that album, and I have to grow as an artist," which is partially true. The actuality of the situation is that I could write *Bubblegum Romance*-type songs all day long, and I don't find it fulfilling. In fact, it was that exact type of song that I would continuously cut from the tracklist of what became the *Life's So Hard* album, and often for the better. A lot of those songs only matter to me in the short term. But pleasing an audience has to factor in as well, and that's where the eternal internal arguments come from: am I an artist, or am I an entertainer?

I still struggle with this conundrum, but here's how I've made peace with it:

- I am an artist when I'm making a song or a record. I might jot down some ideas here and there, but it's really up to the muse what I'll do with it. Now, what do I mean by "the muse?" One could look at the muse as a Tinkerbell-esque fairy that nudges you while you're doing yardwork and says, "Hey, you should totally write a song about ammonia." So you put down your rake, run inside, and start scribbling, but the muse has taken off and gone to inspire other people. You are left with the fragments and decay of what the muse suggested, and now you have to do something with it. This is how the artist finds "their voice." After enough visits from the muse, one day the muse will show up long enough to whisper, "Okay, collect the best pieces and make a portfolio." That's when I go through everything with a fine-toothed comb and make a collection that I call "an album." I usually don't think about you when I do that, either. I'm making something that I think is good. Now, during this process, I do *hope* that you'll like it, but I can't make these things while taking your interests into consideration. I have to like it first and then cross my fingers that the feelings trickle down to you. Any deviation from this process, and I'm making "a product." To me, the art is the record, and the plastic/vinyl it is delivered to you on is the canvas.

- I am an entertainer when I have to do/be Marc With a C in public. As I'm a prolific writer, there is no correct setlist, ever. If the show is over 30 minutes long, I break it down to a third of songs that I want to sing that day, a third that make sense to sing at that venue on that day, and a third that is a cross-section of songs that people have made clear to me that they like very, very much. The latter is important. I went for years thinking that nobody liked "A Very Special Episode" from my first album, so I didn't play it. Once, I did it at a show on a whim. I saw people tugging at their friend's arms going, "Oh my god, he's playing it!" or just outright cheering. The entirety of the audience sang the song right back to me. And me? I was bewildered. It almost seemed like a synchronized prank on the audience's part. So, if you like a song and don't tell me? Expect the section of "favorites" to stay stagnant. And truth be told, I'm often just throwing setlists against the wall and seeing if they stick. I'm not Laurie Anderson. I'm usually not showing up to do performance art. You've taken time out of your lives to watch me sing songs, and I will never, ever, ever take that for granted. I do not want you to leave that room bummed out. For all I know? You've taken the night off of work. You've paid for a babysitter. You might have paid admission or for parking. It's my job to take you on a journey that can be a little bittersweet but ultimately make you happy. And I make that show out of the existing art.

That became a balancing act around 2006, though. The shows were beholden to which songs Ryan knew how to play, and they'd always have to be paced in similar ways. Things didn't feel as malleable, and I had less material to draw from onstage than ever before. But ultimately? Though Ryan and I were friends, we just didn't have a natural stage chemistry.

Ryan came from a mindset of being fascinated by emerging technologies, while I was taking it upon myself to guard the "old school." He really liked doing podcasts, and we even tried to do one together called *The Zanzibar Lounge*. Nicole would come along for the ride, and we'd have unfocused talks over more than a few drinks. But often? I would get angry at Ryan playing drums in a manner that I felt didn't represent the records or how Chris might've played the drums onstage. It's not that he wasn't good, it's that I expected him to do the impossible: ignore his own style while playing my dilapidated drum kit. Rehearsals grew increasingly tense to the point where we ultimately just did not want to do them. And god forbid that Ryan was late: I'm such a stickler for punctuality, and I didn't have patience for the musical timekeeper being unable to keep track of time. I'd kick him off of many shows for being late to load the gear. And looking back, I get the feeling that I should feel bad about these things. While I do feel not-so-good about causing sorrow in his heart, we weren't cut out to work together, and it was drawn out much longer than it should have been.

The writing was on the wall when Chris Zabriskie came back into town for the 2006 holiday show. For fun, he slipped behind the drumkit while we were hanging out, and after we played a few songs, it felt as if we'd never been away. I made time for them both to play at the annual marathon show, and after Ryan later shared some privileged information that he'd been sworn to secrecy about, I eventually fired him over many tears. We'd occasionally get together for one-off shows, but each time we did it, it was a reminder that we were having to adapt to each other's styles, and those two styles were so disparate that the "mean average" could never make us both happy.

NORMAL BIAS, PART ONE:

The next batch of songs wasn't coming to me as easily. Things in my own life were still relatively settled, and occasionally, the muse would tap me on the shoulder while walking to a diner with my wife ("A Tale To Tell"), watching a young couple break up ("Ex-Neanderthal"), or just feeling overwhelmingly content ("Happy To Be Alive"), but overall? The weeks passed by in the same way: get up, go to work, come home, spend time with family, work on a song when the family goes to bed, rinse, repeat. On the weekends, there'd usually be a show to play. Nicole and I got a small Chihuahua and named him Meatwad. I was living in true suburban bliss, and for the first time, I had remained in a happy and healthy relationship.

But as I have a predilection towards both manic and depressive swings, things couldn't stay steady for long. I'd gotten back into working at a record shop, but a severe fundamental disagreement with – at first – one employee tainted the entire experience. We all have that person at work that we don't enjoy dealing with, but this guy went out of his way to be difficult. Between recommending obscure psych records to people that we wouldn't even be able to obtain to sell to them, if I dared to try anything of the sort, I'd be taken to task. Once, while I was extolling the virtues of Alice Cooper's criminally underrated *DaDa* album to a customer, he took me aside:

"Why do you always have to like and recommend the albums that no one has ever heard of from artists?"

"Wait, what?," I said. "You're the guy that pushes funk albums that we can't even acquire on people that want to listen to Band Of Horses!"

"Do as I say, not as I do," he said. "And don't try to figure me out. There's nothing I hate more than that."

"But, if it weren't for obscure records, this store wouldn't even exist!"

And a variation on that argument would continue daily. It's all right, though. He later got fired for something that I suspected was going down all along. I eventually parted ways with the shop, though it's still my favorite hole for crate-digging in all of Orlando.

To blow off steam, I'd record silly EPs with my wife while we got drunk on boxed wine (The Glowy Stickers) and make noise rock records as directed by my daughter (*Rocket Speed Is Really Fast*). I'd feel a sense of relief each time I completed something, no matter how frivolous the object seemed.

It was around this time that I attended the funeral of a lady named Stephanie. I'd known her through working with The Rich Weirdoes. She passed away very young, unexpectedly, and kind of mysteriously. When it comes to death, I'm usually a very "Well, their time was up" kind of person, though I will go through the same stages of grief that anyone else might. In her case, it felt jarring because we knew that she had health problems, but none of them seemed life-threatening. She was a joy to be around, and – poof.

The funeral was much like any other, a mixture of sadness and confusion. I would follow my nature and try to comfort people, and as people whispered their goodbyes to her casket? Some familiar notes started playing over the speakers. Those notes belonged to a limited-edition, digital-only live album of mine called *Another Planned Slip*, a record that she not only loved but was in the audience during the recording of. The juxtaposition of hearing people cheering and singing along out of happiness on the album versus the tears and sadness in the room? I'm still at a loss as to how to speak about it.

To say that it fucked me up is only the tip of the iceberg. I put that record out to make people happy. It was an exceptionally fun concert, and we'd captured a better-than-I-had-expected-but-not-perfect recording, so I edited it into a digestible format and let it out into the wild. I didn't know that a simple fringe release could make enough impact on someone that it'd become the soundtrack to the end of their life. On one side of the room, invisible people were singing along with a recorded version of my voice singing "Stuck With Me." Where I was actually standing? People were sobbing in my arms. Obviously, the funeral was not about me, but hearing your own songs in that predicament is something you'll never factor in as a possibility. I was destroyed by it, and I still can't put my finger on why it had made me so uncomfortable.

Mind you, I'd also taken two hours off of work in the middle of the day to attend this unexpected funeral. My wife drove me back to work as I sobbed uncontrollably. I tried to persevere through the rest of my shift, but the owner of the store, a very stoic man named Sandy, urgently insisted that I go home and get myself together. It felt like a selfish thing to be confused about, but I can tell you one thing for certain: that's the moment that I became very, very guarded about what I'd release into the world. I put up a wall. There didn't used to be an "I'm up here and you're down there" aspect of my performances, but I unknowingly built one on that day.

And then I decided to search for my biological dad online. Well, I wasn't really searching for him physically, just sort of looking into what he was up to. I'd been given his occasional internet handle, and I looked it up. I saw said handle fraudulently selling musical equipment that was claimed to have once belonged to me or bands that I was in, but eventually, I came upon a "second life" sort of site that appeared to be him, only a lot younger and with pictures that weren't him.

Now, I suppose that there is the possibility that it was a mere coincidence, and it wasn't him at all. Maybe someone else in an area close by his residence had made one of these profiles with a name very similar to his preferred alias. But that seemed pretty unlikely when I ran across the animated tombstone on the page that contained my name and the name of another blood relative.

It went on to explain that we were raped and killed by a carjacker. This was graphic stuff. And it was written to read as if it had only happened recently, and this was evidenced by all of the comments offering him support during his trying time.

I can assure you that I didn't understand what internal confusion really was until I'd seen this. I tried in vain to contact the service and have it removed. I did make up a profile to comment on the page and tell the truth, that I was indeed alive. It was removed shortly thereafter, and while my biological father had always had a foot in the door of fooling people on primitive versions of the internet into believing that he was something other than what he actually he was, not to mention a heavy understanding of "phone phreaking," I'm not sure that he'd counted on the entire world eventually having easy tools in their reach to get to the bottom of his bullshit schemes.

I knew based off of past experiences that it was likely only a matter of time before he tried to pull something else that would affect me, but now it could also spread to possibly harming my wife or my daughter. I decided to just tell his secrets in song.

DEAR SON:

Here's where it all gets tricky. I know what I saw as a child. But the problem was that I saw it through innocent eyes. As I grew to interpret these actions, one could argue that they became muddied with anger and therefore were unreliable.

For that reason, what I can't do is sit here and tell you everything that I remember my father doing in my youth. But in my songs? It doesn't matter if it's exact. But I can assure you that I've rarely written a more exacting song in my life than "Dear Son." I tried with much difficulty to put myself in my father's shoes, to have to explain to my own flesh and blood what I had done, including legal allegations and explanations as to why he didn't owe me any apologies, even going as far as to insist that I owed **him** one for things that I'd done before reaching the age of 13.

These were secrets that I simply could not hold onto any longer, not while he was out in the digital realm trying to use my fictitious death to illicit sympathy from people that sometimes appeared to be very, very young women.

It had been boiling up through my youth, when people would recognize my last name in San Diego and threaten me with violence based on things that my father had done to them.

It had been exacerbated by my other parent treating me as if I were the one that had wronged her throughout much of my teenage years. Some refer to it as a Madea complex.

Many times in my life, I'd lived out the "sins of my father" cliché in more detail than I could ever do justice to with mere words. And I hated myself each day that I grew to look more like him or, worse yet, noticed traits that I'd had in common with him. I wished for operations where I could have my DNA scraped away.

No part of me could come up with any rational explanation for his behaviors beyond the pure actions of a psychopath. And the Achilles heel of any dangerous psychopath is for someone to recognize their patterns and "out" them. That's what I did in song, but it's only as effective as my memory.

NORMAL BIAS, PART TWO:

I'd spent a few weeks brushing up the rest of the tunes that would make up *Normal Bias*. I traversed through my memories of the squalor we lived in due to that family member who'd pawn my possessions in front of me. I remembered the low-rent neighborhoods that we'd later live in, hoping that we'd be just far enough off an obvious grid that he wouldn't find us, which was never the case.

The real trick was that I needed to actually record this album. All of my four-tracks had pretty much died, but I had a computer with Windows 95 and a pirated copy of a program used for video editing at my disposal, so I set out to commit this album to ones and zeroes before I could second-guess myself.

Heavily inspired by Low's *Drums And Guns* LP, I made a conscious decision to do a lot of heavy panning on *Normal Bias*. I'd have a microphone somewhat pointed at my mouth, another mostly pointing at my guitar, and then I'd pan them hard right and left. This became quite a drag when I'd later attempt to ready the album for its first vinyl release, but I boldly went forth with the idea, and I'm overall happy with the effect.

I completed the recording of the album in three solid days. I took some Ambien and went to bed. I awoke to find out that I'd mixed the album. You do the math.

I sent the completed 10-song album to Chris Zabriskie and awaited his response. He called to make sure that I wasn't releasing a bunch of music (or rather, words) that I'd one day regret. I couldn't make it clear enough to him that finishing this album felt like someone had untethered me from an anchor, and I couldn't wait to release it. I even made copies for a few close friends.

Without pointing fingers, one of those copies made their way "into the wild." I retaliated by recording an extra song a few days before release called "Classic Country Wasn't Multitracked In '61" and slapping it on the beginning of the album. It was my way of saying, "Ha, you didn't really leak the finished album, dickhole," but truthfully, the added song made all the difference, and it became among my favorite records I'd ever made.

Of course, if you'll remember what I'd said about listeners not really "getting" the albums until I'm ready to move on? Well, like clockwork, *Life's So Hard* had become a weird little favorite among my increasingly culty fan base, and *Normal Bias* couldn't have been further away from what they wanted out of me at the time.

I wasn't really concerned, though. I hadn't felt that strongly about having a great album under my belt since *Bubblegum Romance*, and even if it meant that I'd only be able to occasionally sprinkle *Normal Bias* songs into the sets, it'd be good enough for me. There was an ever-increasing divide between what happened at my shows and what went on the albums, and no matter how long the gigs were becoming, I could never fit in everything that people wanted to hear. So why bother? I decided that the albums were going to be their own little sovereign nations.

I'd take any booking that came my way in this period, trying to make songs like "Dear Son" sit next to earlier fare like the misguided-but-very-fun-to-play "Victoria's Girls." Chris Zabriskie was back to backing me up on drums at a number of these gigs, and eventually I'd decided that it was about time that we documented one of these shows. I tapped on a lady named Jen Vargas for a project that was originally envisioned as a sort of documentary, but it grew (or rather, regressed) into a simple recording of a live show.

I'd be very comfortable shifting blame toward the amateur filmmakers for the product that was eventually produced, but what had actually happened was that Jen had sent a friend of hers to shoot B-roll at a gig of mine. Which apparently meant having a cameraman less than one foot from the neck of my guitar for the duration of a show at a very small club named Taste. This hapless individual was only doing what they were directed to do, but they hadn't informed me of how they'd be going about it. As a result, I kept accidentally running into the camera operator because I'm a very physical performer, while the majority of the audience had an obstructed view. It almost seemed like I was doing a bit.

If only.

My sights shifted instead to just capturing one really good gig and releasing the results on a DVD, but the filmmakers weren't really prepared for that type of thing, just as it turned out that I wasn't in the headspace to help produce what they were capable of. In November of 2007, a full show was filmed at Stardust Video and Coffee and released in a practically unedited state, our only audio source being the microphones on the cameras themselves.

It was a pretty good show by my own standards, but I was all too aware that it was being captured for posterity, so I kept my rambling interludes to a minimum. It's actually one of the more scripted performances that I'd ever given but very representative of what the small shows were like: playing very loudly in a room too small for the audience. By the end, everyone was drunk and happy.

Prepping the gig for release was a whole other problem, and if it weren't for Chris Zabriskie's background in film editing and synchronization, the entire thing might have just been shelved indefinitely. Although, they did shoot one more show, and the only thing I remember from it was rolling around on the ground playing my new blue Stratocaster, making caterwauling feedback. I wonder what happened to that footage. It's probably pretty entertaining. One fan said in 2018 that I did this as a response to constant requests for the song "Monkey's Comin' Outta Your Ass," and while I don't remember it that way, it definitely sounds like something I'd pull.

LO-FI IS SCI FI:

Listen, I just can't overstate the importance of Chris Zabriskie in the overall scheme of Marc With a C. Many of my artistic endeavors existed simply because we'd yak on the phone for hours, and I'd eventually be inspired by something. If something was a halfway decent idea, he could immediately see the potential and would support me unwaveringly. If it was a bad idea, he'd shoot it down cold, and as he has mostly impeccable taste – though I never caught his love for Supertramp – I looked up to him as my unofficial editor. And for other reasons, of course.

I'm a little reticent to write this bit out. Once I gave an interview and sort of said "we" in relation to something that Chris and I had done together artistically, and he'd asked me to never speak for him ever again. So understand that anything said in this segment is purely based upon my own memories and interpretations. It does not necessarily reflect how things "actually went down," and it especially shouldn't be looked at as a mini-biography of a specific point in Chris's life.

With that out of the way? Chris was writing songs. Good songs. Great songs. Brilliant songs.

I've often said that Chris is the best songwriter I've ever personally met and known. He'd handed me numerous demo discs over the years under the moniker Soft Rock Champion, and each one contained at least 2/3's worth of material that any singer/songwriter would be proud to count as their greatest writing achievements and would then all but give up, coasting on the sheer genius of their early works.

But ultimately, I saw Chris wrestling with what he wanted to do. And when it came to his own songs, just because he'd agreed to something one week didn't mean he'd be behind it anymore when you next brought it up. As a matter of fact, around this time, he'd been working on various incarnations of songs inspired by Disney's film *The Black Hole*, and I don't think he's ever been happy with it. Or maybe he's so happy with it that he doesn't feel the need to let it be heard? I don't know. Couldn't get a read on him with his own works.

But what was clear is that while I got *Normal Bias* out of my system, he was shedding some skin as well. His religion, his marriage, and basically his entire belief system were all changing or disintegrating. It was being reflected in some absolutely stunning songwriting, and we'd basically come up with a system where we'd flip the script with Lo-Fi Is Sci-Fi: I'd suggest some whittling of song ideas, I'd back him up on the drums, and he'd lead us as a duo with his own tunes.

We were both heavily inspired by Guided By Voices at the time as well as our consistent love for the nine original LPs by The Monkees, with a healthy dose of Michael Nesmith's solo work (special attention being paid to his *Elephant Parts* and *Television Parts* DVDs). The songs recorded for the *We Were Wrong* album were done in Chris's apartment. Minimal microphones and a small portable guitar amp cranked far beyond its intended volume gave the album a tone that sounded like two guys at their breaking point.

I can't tell you how Chris looks back on the album. I can only tell you that I love it, and I find myself saddened by the fact that we didn't really continue the project. A scant few shows were played, and to this day, some people still remember Chris as the frontman for the loudest duo that had ever played at Orlando's BackBooth. (We thought that people hated us there, but it turned out that they were physically unable to come any closer to the stage due to our penchant for volume.)

Ideas were thrown around for the follow-up to *We Were Wrong*, with both of us contributing songs. Ultimately, it didn't go anywhere. Chris seemed to veer off into creating a totally different thing, and almost all the songs offered up for that ill-fated next album were later split between my *Linda Lovelace For President* album and Chris's own *O Great Queen Electric, What Do You Have Waiting For Me?*, which is one of the best albums by anyone, anywhere, ever. If you can find it, do yourself a favor. It's also under the Lo-Fi Is Sci-Fi moniker.

Or, it was made as such after the fact? It's confusing to me, and I was in the goddamn band.

Chris made a video for our song "The Script You Wrote Is Terrible," and the word is that it got played on MTV in ... Brazil, maybe? That's what he told me, and he had some sort of link to back it up, but I just don't remember now. A really cool honor, regardless. This was 2007, and having a music video played anywhere on television wasn't exactly an easy achievement.

However, I did notice some splintering going on.

LINDA LOVELACE FOR PRESIDENT:

Nicole and I got married in February of 2008 at the courthouse in Winter Park. Only four friends and family members were present. It was our feeling that we wanted to get married because we didn't want anything to change, so a big production wouldn't be unnecessary. We got up, got married, ate some Chinese food, and watched zombie movies. No honeymoon. We both went back to work the following day. I might seem nonchalant about it, but it was one of the best decisions I'd ever been a part of, if not THE best. Our marriage has continued to feel like having nightly sleepovers with my best friend.

I'd been so proud of the *Normal Bias* album that I wasn't in a rush to make a follow-up, or so I thought. The change of heart about that mindset came in two ways:

- As per usual, the *Normal Bias* songs weren't always live "barn-burners," so I immediately moved into trying to come up with other new things to play onstage.

- Chris had written two new songs that I loved, which were proposed for Lo-Fi Is Sci-Fi: "Born Vintage" and "All My Drug Use Is Accidental." I'd incorporated them into my shows thinking that I was just promoting the next record from a different project that I was in.

At this point? I felt that I'd taken the lo-fi stuff as far as I could. It was time to move on to making a "bigger sounding" album. I went back and forth with how I'd go about it, but I devised a way to make it happen, despite the few primitive-for-their-time digital tools that were at my disposal.

I feverishly worked on demos and possible tracklists for the album, culling songs from all phases of my career that maybe hadn't really found homes on other albums, plus a few new things I'd cooked up, like the title track, and the painfully honest "I Tried To Die Young." I'd collected around an hour's worth of music, and this record was intended to simply move me into a different phase: a slightly more mature-sounding era.

It might be helpful to tell you that I work best alone. I don't necessarily mean "as a solo act," but, rather, if there's a job to be done, I'm more efficient when there's no one around, and I feel like the last person on Earth. I'll shut off all distractions, completely turn my back on the landscape outside of my workspace, and sink into a headspace that has one end goal in mind: make the art. When the muse takes hold and tells me it's time to do it? Nothing is going to get through to me. I don't eat, I sleep less than usual. Sometimes I bathe, but since I wouldn't really be around anyone else, I wouldn't think to do so until I couldn't stand my own stench any longer.

With this in mind, I took five days off from all my earthly duties. I holed myself up in the small garage I was recording in at the time. Got out all of the gear and gathered piles of cigarettes and bottles of water so I'd only be leaving for mandatory bathroom breaks. I fired up the antiquated computer and settled in to make the first record of the rest of my life, and —

Something went totally screwy with it. It wasn't a virus, and it wasn't quite a hard drive failure. Files of lyrics and demos were simply missing, and each attempt at recording the rhythm track for "It's All Gonna Be All Right" went horribly awry since none of the tracks would stay in sync with each other. I lost an entire day trying to figure out what was going on but chalked the problems up to my natural status as a luddite. It also dawned on me that with the missing files? I didn't have access to the new set of lyrics I'd written for that particular song, which is why I still insist on only writing lyrics in notebooks to this day.

I had no choice but to accept defeat. Technology wasn't going to be on my side, and a nearby four-track caught my eye. I'd decided that since I was already in "album mode," I was going to make a goddamn album. This is how it's done, right? Things break, and you get creative despite the setbacks. Maybe it'll be good.

With that in mind, I hastily scribbled really dumb new lyrics for the song and went to work on recording it, leaving only the barest components in the arrangements. Each song felt like a really dull knife to the chest because I had a huge arrangement in mind for each one, but here I was, ready to embrace bigger sounds but was stuck using only the four-track cassette recorder. I bounced as many tracks as I could on it, but I was losing more and more fidelity each time. I'd run out of space to record the bass on songs where it would have been appropriate and hadn't even considered how to get the vocals onto the album.

Between the last two paragraphs? That was four days of recording, bouncing, and submixing. No real naps or anything, though I do think I ate once. On the final day, I'd realized that I could get at least vocals onto the album by live mixing the album into the computer and singing the lead vocal at the exact same time. Then, I'd be able to send the songs back to a new tape with hardly any generational loss, and I'd have a few slots left open for harmonies. Then, I could send the versions with the harmonies back to the computer, and play another part over it with a digital effect if needed.

It was the most complex process possible for the most lo-fi results one could expect, but that's me in album mode. Something has to get created, no matter what the obstacle is. And 13 songs were finished in that five-day span, though I wasn't able to do much else to the album. Everything had been submixed, so no further changes were possible. If I didn't like it, I'd just have to re-do the song.

The resulting album had some songs that I'm very proud of, but I always hear the record as a complete and total compromise. I do find a few bits that really excite me, like the end of "San Diego Doorways" and the spacey midsection of the title track. On other songs like "Jessica, I Heard You Like The Who," I hear a song that I wanted to be a shimmering power-pop classic but ultimately comes off as twee and lean. I like twee, but it wasn't what I was going for.

But in 2008? I knew what I'd gone through to make the album exist, and being able to play it back felt like a small miracle each time. It was the hardest I'd ever worked on a recording at that point, and I was proud that it existed at all. To release the album, I relied on internet pre-orders for the first time. I didn't have a ton of money to begin with, but the little that I did have was tied up in some civic-level legal cases. To entice people to take part, my wife and I made some T-shirts emblazoned with the cover of *Normal Bias* by hand.

Despite my misgivings about the compromises made during the recording, I knew the songs were good, and I set out doing the biggest round of promotion I'd yet undertaken for a record. I emailed every single blog, venue, and magazine I could find that would accept submissions. Even uploaded the album to some torrent sites to get any available ears attuned to what I was making. I envisioned some type of Guided By Voices-style discovery. I imagined stories about how people had just discovered this chubby DIY guy who made records in a garage in Florida, and that notoriety that I'd never openly claimed to want would come my way. I'd be headlining the indie-rock circuit in no time flat.

I probably don't have to spell out that this isn't what happened. A few reviews appeared, a couple of interviews took place, but after the initial new release buzz had worn off, none of those things had really helped out at all. I was still playing to the same people that had stuck with me for all of these years. I embraced them, but my confidence was starting to be genuinely shaken. I wondered why I was making these albums at all. I enjoyed them, but the actual record-making process was starting to wear on me. I wanted to make the music and write the songs, but in the new landscape full of IDM, the death of regionality due to strangleholds on radio playlists, and the general "music shouldn't cost anything" attitude that was taking over the brains of music fans? I wasn't sure how sustainable it was anymore.

There was a brief time where I considered throwing in the proverbial towel again. Of course, this time, I wouldn't do it in a huge and visible way. Rather, I'd just release stuff when the mood struck me and not really push so hard. That outlook didn't come to pass, but it was a major consideration.

What changed my mind, you might ask? An event called Nerdapalooza.

A few months into 2007 or so, I received a purchase order for every single album I'd had in print. It came with a note, and the general gist was that a DJ named Josh Thew had heard someone play my song "Life's So Hard" on WPRK right before his own broadcasting slot was to begin. He'd just moved to Orlando and was so excited that there was a local artist that he dug.

Fast forward to the spring of 2008. I'm cleaning up while working at the record store, and a flier for a festival called Nerdapalooza caught my eye. It had some very quirky bands listed like Harry & The Potters, and I thought I should approach the organizers and ask if I could play. After all, "Nerdy Girls" was still quite popular locally, I'd been called a nerd all of my life, and it sounded like fun. Trouble was that the flier didn't have contact information, nor did it list the date of the show. Or a venue.

By that time, Josh and I had become friends, and I'd even given him a nickname that didn't stick ("Lucky Monkey Briefs").I mentioned the oddball festival to him. And it turned out that he was working with them, and they wanted to book me.

From the moment that I was announced for this festival, drama surrounded it. Many of the people involved only knew each other from the internet, and being proudly nerdy, there was more than a little social awkwardness at play. Nightly, my email box would blow up with people I had never met having arguments, as I'd now been cc'd on a bunch of email chains for the artists. One particular thread got so heated that a very special individual tried to cancel the event without even being an organizer. At least, I don't think he was an organizer? I didn't really have much idea of who did what with this thing, so I didn't know who to call to see what the deal was.

That evening at around 4 a.m., a man named John Carter (who I'll refer to as Hex for the rest of this book) called me to assure me that the festival wasn't canceled. He also gave me some history on the festival and how it came to be.

We had things in common and talked for a very long time.

I'M NOT COMING HOME:

Let's take a breather for a moment before we continue with the 2008 saga and focus on a song from *Linda Lovelace For President*. The tune in question is "I'm Not Coming Home." If memory serves, I'd written it for a Lo-Fi Is Sci-Fi album that never happened. I thought it would be a good fit for Chris's voice, and it had some subject matter he'd be able to sink his teeth into.

When that album didn't come to pass, I didn't want to let this tune die. I changed the key to better fit my voice and brushed it up into a pseudo-hymnal. And when someone is far enough into my albums to ask me about stuff on the back half of *Linda Lovelace*, this anachronistic song usually makes those folks a bit curious.

I don't always want to directly tell you every single event that lead up to the writing of a song, and often when I tell stories onstage about the songs, I'm embellishing or sometimes just flat-out lying. I haven't really done any of that in the tome you're reading now, but sometimes I'll just have to make something up. I mean, there isn't really anything more to say about a song like "Ammonia", for example, than what's in the song. Ammonia is important, and I didn't know of any tunes about it, so I set out to fill that void. But in the case of "I'm Not Coming Home"? I'll be as candid as I'm capable of being.

All of my brushes with religion have been pretty ugly in some way. I have never felt anything based on religious texts, and any good vibes I've had in a church usually came from powerful speaking married to music. I like many of the things that surround organized religion but not necessarily the religion itself.

As much as I dislike the "I'm not religious, I'm spiritual" statement, it's unfortunately true for me. Might be my imagination, or even a form of psychosis, but I do feel the presence of "something bigger" in my life. An internal compass that seems to implant the difference between right and wrong into my soul. Maybe it's my conscience. Sometimes the presence feels like it knows things before I do.

There are times that I feel selfish, and I ignore the guidance of said presence in favor of doing whatever the hell I damn well please. This presence has a strong influence on my life, possibly as strong as the "muse" I alluded to earlier, but they are dramatically different voices.

I have referred to this spiritual presence as "god", "lord", "it" and any number of nomenclatures, but it doesn't feel like anything that I read about in the Bible. This presence doesn't really seem to give a shit if I openly praise it or not. It just wants me to know that it loves me and everything else. Pretty easy to make peace with.

Now, that's not to say that there isn't *something* to the Christian Bible, or any of the other holy books that I've not really studied, but more that those books are interesting and are full of applicable lessons, though not entirely believable. The Christian one in particular strikes me as some of the most effective fiction ever committed to paper. People love that book so much that they go to weekly conventions for it and dress up in nice clothes to do so. On some holidays, they'll even re-enact scenes from it. The phenomenon makes Comic-Con look positively passive in comparison.

Some factions will even actively try to persuade you to ignore certain passages, considering them to not really be "canon," much like a Star Wars fan might tell you that you should avoid the Holiday Special, though it's quite important overall: you get your first glimpse of Kashykk, and Boba Fett's entire story arc is introduced. But hey, Jefferson Starship shows up, and Marty Balin sings into what appears to be a dildo-shaped lightsaber, so let's all ignore it, right?

Christianity is the biggest nerdy property in the United States, and people have based their entire lives around it because parts of the book resonate with them. It's like a tax-exempt Harry Potter. Sort of makes the people you made fun of for learning how to speak Klingon appear relatively normal all of a sudden, doesn't it?

Anyways, my spirituality is completely internal, so it's hard for me to leave it behind. Even when I ignore it to do things that don't jive with the sensibility of said morality? It forgives me and seems to only ask that I try harder next time. Meanwhile, my brain will beat me up for years when I color outside of those lines of morality.

In the song, I state that "I'm not coming home" because "I never left." I still feel this way. What's inside of me, steering the ship? It isn't really steering. It's just giving me an idea of how I should drive if I want to navigate without hurting others. I'll take that over tithing any day.


LINDA LOVELACE FOR PRESIDENT, PART TWO:

I did two shows at Nerdapalooza 2008. One was a solo set during the pre-party, and one was backed by Chris Zabriskie during the festival proper. The solo one took place on the patio of A Comic Shop, which happened to be in the former location of Hullabaloo. I didn't really know what this audience wanted, so I played around six of my oldest songs with a burst of energy that defied the summer heat in Florida. Shockingly, a good cluster of these audience members knew the songs, and getting a singalong going with "Life's So Hard" was no trouble at all.

During the actual festival, I felt like an interloper in a scene full of outsiders. They all knew each other, but they also somehow knew my music. Some audience members would tell me that they'd paid the 30 bucks to get in just to see me – which was shocking because I'd only driven about 20 minutes from home to get there. We played what I remember to be a spirited set in the middle of the day and left enough of an impression that one would be hard pressed to find a future Nerdapalooza-related event that I didn't perform at in some capacity.

I was starting to feel like playing shows with Chris on drums was the most effective way to showcase the songs. I liked having a backbeat, and I liked having someone behind or beside me to play off of that "got it." We'd close out the bulk of 2008 playing oodles of gigs together, not the least of which was the Athens Pop Festival with the likes of Roky Erickson, Casper & The Cookies, and Fishboy.

I had a good time playing that show and found that Chris and I actually got along quite well as hotel roommates. I envisioned hitting the road more often with him. Two friends crammed in a little car and listening to prog rock albums, doing bizarre makeshift shows, all between shopping for records. My aversion to touring immediately went away after the Athens trip, where bands that I loved and respected liked me back and accepted us as peers. So I told Chris that I wanted to do this: rehearse more often, really get to know the back catalog, and just hit the road together.

He couldn't have been less interested. In fact, our usual daily conversations began to diminish altogether after I'd said this to him. He became unreachable, and I didn't understand it. I felt that we had something special, and he'd begun to pull away, releasing solo albums at an alarming clip, while being more and more reticent to appear in public. My confidence began to dwindle further, and as a man with naturally low self-esteem, I felt that I was (again) losing my best friend (that wasn't my wife). I resolved to keep working, but I found performances without him to be lonely, disparaging, and often aimless affairs.

LOSING SALT:

Due to a misunderstanding of such grave proportions that neither of us would come out looking very good, I quit my job at the record store. I didn't want to, but I felt like it was the only way to handle it, while also feeling that I'd be fired anyways. At the time, this was fine with me because there was a jerk that worked there who'd tried to "out" personal aspects of my sexual life to the other employees for no discernible reason.

With tempers flaring to a point that I'm at a loss for words to describe even years later, I felt humiliated, betrayed, and belittled by the owner's actions, so I quit without giving two weeks' notice. I regret it now, always thinking that there must have been another way to go about it, but I still haven't come up with a better solution than just walking away from unwinnable situations.

And the other jerk there? He got fired for allegedly stealing/flipping rare records from the store. I kind of suspected it, but he was sort of the golden boy at the shop since he was spearheading their entry into vinyl right when that resurgence was beginning to burst forth in the southeastern U.S., so no one was willing to listen when I'd point out that the guy was clearly the opposite of good. He eventually got his, and he can tell his side of the story in his own damned book.

But in a weird way, it all worked out because in the beginning of 2009, I became very ill. My emotional disorders surged, forcing me to seek psychiatric treatment. This landed me on a number of medications that basically rewired my brain but coincided with an illness that went on for a number of months, completely unexplained. Symptoms included constantly losing my voice for no reason, sinus blockage, vertigo, fatigue, chills, and most appallingly? A strange affliction with my ears that caused me to hear a completely differing pitch in each one.

Now, I don't mean that I had tinnitus and heard two ringing notes. An example would be listening to "I've Seen All Good People" by Yes. The first part of the song is in E. My left ear would hear it in E flat, while my right ear would hear it in F. I'd have to turn my head to very strange positions to hear it properly.

I refused every single show offer that came my way for the first time, though I simply could not get out of the birthday show Hex had booked for me at Taste. It wasn't for lack of trying, either. I begged and pleaded for him to please just cancel the gig due to my illness, but he preserved, and I'm not sure why. Two-thirds of Precious reunited for a short set at the party, which did feel pretty momentous, but I was so worn out that I couldn't really do my usual type of gig. I'd been sick for a month, hadn't shaved and had ended up with a bushy, unkempt, and unattractive beard. I could only stand to be in the night air while wearing a heavy overcoat with two shirts and a hoodie underneath, as well as a wool cap to cover my ears from the disparate tones that were coming out of the PA. Tuning my guitar was out of the question, and singing on pitch was a complete impossibility. Still, I was called back for two encores, but upon review of the recording that Ryan Price made of the show? I absolutely cannot believe that anyone sat through that trash. It might have been the worst performance of my career.

As a result, I'd basically given up recording because I couldn't tell if any of it was decent or not. I decided to just release the nine unfinished recordings I'd been most recently working on as an album called *Losing Salt*, though it wasn't easy to promote without shows or actually knowing for sure what it sounded like. Any Doubting Thomas would only need to take a listen to my vocal take of "I Will Repossess Your Heart" to hear what rough shape I was in. I recorded the song while lying on the floor of my garage, doing each part on my back.

A local theater company had asked to use some of my songs in a production called *Sex Times Three*. I was honored, though I wasn't a big fan of musical theater. I instead offered to just show up and play the songs myself. Thankfully, the show kept getting its dates shuffled around, giving me almost enough time to heal from the mystery illness, though I was now abnormally bloated from the psychiatric meds, a poor diet, and the amount of alcohol I'd taken to drinking to get my mind off the fact that I was a physically useless person at that point in time.

*Sex Times Three* ended up being a lot of fun to do despite my physical state and did reinstate some of my confidence. During each show of our run, I'd get to expose my songs to an audience that otherwise would never have heard of me. Plus I got closer to two of the actors that I really liked: Kimberly Luffman (also the producer of the play) and Alex Carroll. I felt good getting back into singing for people and being around people that liked me.

When enough of the mystery illness had subsided, I talked to Chris about doing some more local shows. He agreed as long as they could be as laid-back as possible and would not demand nearly any rehearsal from him. For this reason, Chris took to hitting popcorn tins on stage (the infamous "wuckarnnn") instead of a proper drum set. It made a neat racket, and while it wasn't my favorite way for him to do things, it was nice to have him there from time to time. This is how we played at Nerdapalooza 2009. Afterwards, his appearances during my shows would be spotty at best for a few years.

When I'd cornered him and specifically asked why he wasn't around, he would do his best to avoid the question. Usually I'd get some form of "this is just a hobby for me," and that would be the end of it. But finally, one day around this time I'd gotten him on the phone and demanded answers.

I can't tell you everything that was said, because a good portion of it was of a very personal nature for Chris and would be completely understandable as a reason to remove yourself from public view. Until he added, "And you're SUCH a fucking downer."

My depressive leanings weren't exactly a secret, but that statement cut me to the bone. I'm sure he was stressed out and didn't realize what he was saying, but he ultimately used my afflictions against me, the very ones that I was trying to treat. I tell you this without hyperbole: it was one of the top 10 most heartbreaking moments of my adult life, and I still don't know that I've ever completely forgiven him for it. I wanted to, but it wouldn't be the last time something like this would take place.

On the other hand? I was a total pill to deal with. He wasn't wrong.

By the time of my annual holiday show in 2009, things were at such a low ebb that less than 20 people attended the gig, Chris was a no-show despite being advertised to accompany me, and I needed to do something different. I wanted nothing more than to go back to us having our natural camaraderie, but that wouldn't really be possible for some time. Chris would occasionally make special appearances, but they'd be on his watch, and he often wouldn't even tell me he was coming. I went back to playing at any hole in the wall that would have me. Biker bars, bowling alleys, fly-by-night conventions in towns that didn't seem to have a name, but I was miserable, and I didn't always believe in what I was making. That give and take with an audience didn't work without said audience, and with social media replacing the old "stick a flier on any flat surface" manner of promotion? I'd have to adapt to this new world, and I'd need to do it immediately.

Chris and I both made our respective catalogs free to download on the same day and prepared to march into the new decade together, but separate.

I don't really listen to *Losing Salt* terribly often now. It reminds me of illness, and I'm often taken aback when someone will mention that it's their favorite record of mine. A few less depressing things to note about that album are:

- People having taken umbrage with me using the term "art fag" in "He Left You For A Punk Rock Girl." It was based on a true story, and it was how the "he" in the song described himself to me and others on many, many occasions. It wasn't meant as a slur. It was an attempt at using his own manner of speech to tell the story of a week in his life. I deeply regret it now and will make no further excuses if you dislike me because I'd published a song with THAT f-bomb in it.

- I have been asked many times what "You Do Not Exist" is about. Know that it is not my story to tell, and I was sworn to secrecy by the person who relayed it to me. Also, all of your theories are very good but not even in the ballpark. That's what makes music fun, right?

- The speech at the end of "Magazines" is from a tape recorded by the FBI at Jonestown. It was in the public domain, and I didn't have any more words for the song, so it seemed like a neat thing to place over the run-out. I'm actually quite obsessed with cults, though it was/is not my intention to condone or glorify them in any way.

POP! POP! POP!:

2009 had been such a bust for me physically that I'd hardly even given much thought to celebrating the 10th anniversary of the first Marc With a C shows. Initially, we'd tried to get a double-disc compilation out on the Happy Happy Birthday To Me record label, and while this initially seemed like a go with many long conversations between label owner Mike Turner and myself to prove it, it ultimately fizzled out, and I don't quite remember why. I'm sure if I dug deep enough into my emails, I could figure it out, but it also might upset me. It was far enough along that Katharine Miller had begun making sketches for the album design, and a tracklist that still blows my mind was agreed upon. The set was provisionally titled *Pop, Girls, Etc.*, but it simply never came to be. Instead, we self-released a set called *RetroLowFi: 10 Years Of Marc With a C* rather quietly, and I went back to doing other things.

The "give all the music away for free, only charge for physical products" tactic worked wonders for me. Not nearly as well as it worked out for Chris Zabriskie's burgeoning career in ambient music, but just enough for my happiness. I've never aspired to much beyond making things that I think are good and hopefully reaching the right people with them.

I'd also gone from occasionally co-hosting radio shows on WPRK, that community radio station in Orlando built in a bomb shelter, to hosting an increasingly popular overnight show called *The Real Congregation*. I'd play intentionally off-the-beaten-path material over the air, hoping to inspire some of what left-of-the-dial radio had done for me throughout my life. I tried to do the sort of show that Lana, the host of *The Banana Split Show* all those years ago, might have wanted to listen to.

At every turn, I'd try to turn my overnights into a real and true piece of art. Themed nights, evenings where I'd pretend to be a completely different DJ altogether, and sometimes airing the safe bits of the tapes that inspired "Amy,

It's Kevin" against a backdrop of noise. The staff couldn't stand me, but there was a small yet loyal following that hung on and listened every chance that they got.

One fan that had been won over due to the mixture of freely available Marc With a C material and the oddball radio show that could be streamed online was a man named Domenico Marini from Italy. I cannot overstate the importance of his fandom and support. We started off as pen pals and soon started trading records through the mail. It made me feel really good that someone could get so heavily into my material – with its heavy usage of parodies and satire of American attitudes and general slang – despite a constant language barrier.

I'd been forcing myself to write material as I started to shake off the remnants of the 2009 illness that never fully subsided until the end of that year. I'd also walked away from nearly all prescribed psychiatric medications around the same time as they were more likely to leave me in bed unable to move than the actual illness itself. I'd been spouting tunes into a four-track, adamant that I'd come up with an album's worth of cool material without brushing up any old leftovers, or there simply wouldn't be another album.

This time around, though? The album would be done digitally from the ground up. The world had all but abandoned tape at this point, and my four-tracks were pretty much all useless due to wear and tear. For the first time, it was actually easier to obtain recording software than lo-fi analog equipment. Of course, I'd also learned that a lot of my natural "tone" was coming from cassette tape saturation, and digital recording was pretty unforgiving. It spat out a thinner version of exactly what the microphones picked up. The boon was that there were endless plug-ins and things that you could use to enhance the tones captured by your digital audio workstation, so in a sense, I could fake it.

The recording of *Pop! Pop! Pop!* was a bit of a nightmare simply because I wasn't used to working solely with ones and zeroes. Where I used to rely on room tones and microphone placement, now those things were beginning to be "the enemy" with such clear replication of whatever I sent into the computer. I probably recorded it in about a week's time, but mixing took much longer because I simply didn't understand things like "exporting" and "bit rates." All of this was complete gibberish to me, and as much as I tried to work it into the album, I'm not sure that it wasn't ultimately detrimental.

Still, there were very good songs afoot. Things like "Holly Vincent" (which was about my obsession with *The Banana Split Show*), "Winter Colors" (inspired by the long marathons of *Cops* and MSNBC's *Lockup* that I'd been watching when unable to do much else in 2009), and "The Audience Is Listening," which would prove to be one of the most malleable compositions of my entire career.

I'd send mixes of the files back and forth to folks like Chris Zabriskie and Patrick from Bucket Of Nails, but they kept telling me that it didn't sound quite right. But neither could really point me in the direction of what was wrong, either. Eventually, in a fit of frustration, I released the album as a total surprise online one morning, figuring at some point, it HAS to be good enough. In horror, I realized that the MP3s I'd sent out into the world were at 48000 khz, meaning that many players were either playing them at the wrong speed or not at all.

The bad luck with the album continued as it got unsettlingly mean reviews from journalists that admittedly hadn't actually listened to it in the proper order and an overall sense of "this is different and I don't like it" from many of my most loyal fans.

The main difference with the album was that I exclusively used twangy electric guitars rather than acoustic ones on the recordings, and more than half of the album was produced with a full guitar/bass/drums setup, something I hadn't really done in quite some time, especially not so clearly and unobscured. People were hearing me relatively clearly for the first time in a good long while.

When Domenico and his wife Anna came all the way from Italy to meet me, hang out and see a show of mine? That was a massive confidence booster. Plus, I really liked them. The language barrier wasn't nearly as bad as one would think. When there is genuine affection and appreciation between a group of people, words aren't the most necessary thing in the world. Sounds cliché, but sometimes cliché's stick around for a reason.

While Domenico was a fantastic, funny, and sweet individual, he'd also made it his mission to help me fulfill a lifelong dream: get something out on vinyl. Now, it may just have been that he wanted some of my music on wax and was willing to pay any amount of money necessary to get it, but it was also my understanding that as a massive and lifelong fan of music, he'd mourned being unable to create and wanted to have some stake in putting music that he believed in out into the world. And under the guise of an "angel investment," he put up the needed capital to get *Pop! Pop! Pop!* and a truncated version of the *RetroLowFi* compilation out on vinyl. As a defiantly DIY kind of person, I was unsure about accepting his help at first, but Chris assured me that angel investors were a common thing and that if someone loved the music enough to help produce it, that I should let them do it.

Here's where I should point out that Domenico didn't really want any credit for this, and he expected precisely no return upon the investment. It seemed to be his hope that this would get my foot in the door in the vinyl world, and that each release would finance the next one. That's exactly what happened, and I owe pretty much the entirety of my post-2010 career to him. Also, Domenico helped me out tremendously by loving and believing in *Pop! Pop! Pop!* when very few others did. The bulk of those songs wouldn't exactly go on to be concert standards for me, but he counted it as one of the most important records in his collection, especially loving the song "Winter Colors."

AS THE BOMBS FELL:

My life has mostly been made up of a series of proclamations that I'd later change my mind about, and one of those contradictions has been marriage. In general. You see, I never saw myself getting married, not because I had any problems with commitment, monogamy, or any number of ethical arguments, but rather that I didn't see how being a "lifer" with music could co-exist with the "settling down" aspect of marital life.

It turns out that I just hadn't met Nicole. To know her is to love her, and she is the light from which all good things in the universe radiate. She has supported me through every idea I've come up with, good or bad, and she's always been straight with me in a way that never tramples my feelings. It helps that she's an artist in her own right, starting off as a dancer and eventually becoming well-versed in aerial arts in the amount of time that it might take an average person to warm up a bowl of oatmeal.

Everything she sets out to do, she clobbers and bests her own expectations. I'm floored by her abilities and grace in new ways every single day. And one of my biggest quirks – though you wouldn't know it from my art or reading this – is that sometimes I just like to sit and be quiet for long stretches of time. She can read me on those days and lets me do that.

Around the time that I wrote "As The Bombs Fell," it was just various lines running through my head, trying to come up with a catastrophe so horrific that I wouldn't drop everything if I were scheduled to renew my vows to her. And in a way, I've always felt like maybe we ought to do that. We both have some hearing troubles, and our initial vows were a bit sullied when we both misheard the officiant say "grave mistake" instead of something about "the great estate" of marriage. A part of me has always felt like we deserved a mulligan because of this, but then again, I think we've done just fine.

I once wrote a line that went "All I ever wanted was someone who'd inspire love songs / So I can mean them for once." With Nicole in my life, I often have to check myself to make sure that she's not the only subject in my songwriting because she's endlessly inspiring.

POP! POP! POP! PART TWO:

I made some lo-fi videos for this album, but none were much of anything to write home about. I've never been much for visual ideas but started accepting that it would be silly to ignore the pervasiveness of video in internet culture. I'm still not wild about making videos, so now I mostly leave it to other people, and I rarely give them any guidelines. I figure that if you contact a creative person and want them to do something, it's best to just let them be creative and get the hell out of their way.

I continued doing nearly any gig that I could and heavily featured songs from *Pop! Pop! Pop!* in the shows. I was excited to keep pressing on with new things rather than relying on the old tunes I knew were usually successful in a live setting. Since 2006, I'd only been able to get a few songs that would consistently work in live shows out of each album, so I simply started forcing the issue, intentionally leaving out songs that people seemingly very much wanted to hear at my shows. But I made an exception when preparing my set for Nerdapalooza 2010.

I'd been handed a headlining slot, and, as usual, Chris had been waffling on whether he'd perform with me, making it very difficult to decide what I'd play – numerous *Pop! Pop! Pop!* tunes really lacked fire without a backbeat. So I made an executive decision ahead of time to just do the show on my own and play a nice mix of old and new songs for the occasion.

But I think that enough time has passed that I can freely say that Nerdapalooza 2010 was a fucking nightmare for a lot of people involved.

My recollections are scarce for reasons that will become clear later, but I'll share what I do recall with enough clarity to regard them as nearly factual.

I was asked to help out with sound. Nerdapalooza was synonymous with horrific sound problems at this stage, so I was happy to do it. Unfortunately, the show was running very late because one man had been tasked with setting up mixing boards for two big stages. He'd been at it all night, and by show time, he wasn't even close to being ready, possibly due to chemical influences. He fell asleep very shortly after the show began and hadn't shown me how to work his board, which was a studio board from the '70s. I like analog gear, but this thing wasn't built for this show, and he'd fallen asleep before even giving me a cursory run through of what was routed where. Monitors were a pipe dream, and his parting words before he dozed off were, "Oh, and there's no EQ."

And just that quickly? BAM. Time for Random/MegaRan to take the stage. I did my best to get him going, but he stopped the first song to say, "Hey, Mr. Sound Man. It ain't sounding good up here." And he was right. I had control over only one thing: volume. And here's a few thousand nerds that want to rock out to "Splash Woman," all looking at me like I'm the biggest moron on the planet. Truth be told, I was a moron when it came to that board. Had it been anything resembling a traditional board for live sound, I could have made MegaRan and his DJ (which I think was Projekt Zero that day) sound just fine. Instead, here I was just cranking up this muddy murk as loud as I could, hoping that people would forgive me. I was devastated because I love Ran as a person. I have the utmost respect for him as an artist, and here I was, completely screwing up his show because I wasn't given the proper tools to make it work. I have apologized to him literally every time we've been in the same building ever since, and I'll continue to do so until I die.

During his next-to-last song, I saw a button that more or less enabled or disabled the fabled EQ. I panned all the dials to the center and pressed the button, hoping for a miracle. All of a sudden, I was able to dial in an almost listenable tone for the end of Ran's set. I finally talked the girlfriend of the equipment provider into waking him up.

When he was roused from his slumber, I took Hex aside and rage quit on the spot. I don't regret that. If you'd have been put in my position, you'd have done the same thing.

The schedules had run so far behind that you wouldn't believe me if I told you. It was something like 3 a.m. before The Protomen went onstage. Or rather, SOME of the Protomen went onstage. I think I'd be legally clear to say that their tardiness was based solely on an illness that was brought on by something resembling food poisoning, and it was beyond their control.

On the next day, I was the first of the headlining sets. I was supposed to be on around 5 or 6 p.m. but wasn't on until nearly 8 p.m. People had been asking me what the holdup was. I didn't have an answer for them. I just promised I'd do my best to give them a great show within the time allotted.

Eventually, I went on and launched into "Chicken Pox & Star Wars Guys." I remember being very animated, doing lots of jumps and things that I used to be capable of. And then, after the first line of "Stairway To Rudolph," the stage shifted a bit while I was turning, and then? A "pop" followed by a blackout.

I was probably only out for a few seconds, but when I came to? Everything was in slow motion. I looked down at my leg where I'd felt the pop and saw that my knee looked like a right angle. Something weird ran through my head: "Dude, you can totally fix that."

I don't know what came over me, but I reached down and popped my knee back into its proper place, which probably tore some stuff that wasn't already torn. I saw stars, but again, this all happened in like five seconds. After the knee thing, I think I started sitting up slowly and remembered where I was. Dr. Vern from Sci-Fried was over me saying in a low slow-motion voice "aaaarrreee yyyyyyooooouuuu ooooookkkkaayyyyy"? Apparently, I responded with "get me a fucking chair."

When the chair arrived, I did my best to quickly tune the guitar and pick up from the second line of "Stairway To Rudolph." There was a confused cheer afterward, so I had to explain what had just happened over the PA. I told them that my knee had come out of place, but please don't worry, I've shoved it back into its socket, and I'll finish my set before I go to the emergency room.

I remember that I couldn't get my guitar back in tune at all. I didn't have an onstage tuner for some reason that day, and there weren't any monitors, so I couldn't hear a thing. Keeping my knee bent to sit was starting to prove very challenging, so I asked the audience if anyone had any painkillers – in case you've ever wondered why that joke stayed in my shows – and someone travelling with MegaRan was a nurse and sent some up to the stage. I took a handful of all the various things I'd been handed and stood up to play the second half of the set. That wasn't a smart move from a health standpoint, but my point of view was that a bunch of people paid $30 dollars to watch me sing songs, so I was going to do so until I couldn't anymore.

I think that I was scheduled to play 40 minutes, maybe? The pain was becoming a very real thing, so I cut "Drunk Classic Rock Fans" from the set and finished up with "The Audience Is Listening," "Ammonia," "Life's So Hard," and "Happy To Be Alive." Probably "Nerdy Girls" as well. I don't remember exactly, but what I remember most is that I still kick myself every day for not just playing the whole fucking setlist. I feel like I screwed the attendees out of money for shortening my set. Sorry about that. I hope I can make it up to you some day.

Afterward, the guys from Sci-Fried helped me pack all my things for me while I sat near the entrance waiting for a wheelchair to take me to the car. This was daunting because word had started spreading that I'd somehow faked this. People wanted to take pictures of my bare knee for proof. If you've ever wondered why I have such vitriol towards the "pics or it didn't happen" folks, that'd be a good place to start.

Nicole drove me in a cramped Toyota Corolla to the hospital, and I wasn't even sure I was going to be able to unbend my knee to get out of the car. The hospital took some X-rays, poked, and prodded. I had to be in one of those things that aren't quite a cast but immobilize your leg completely for a few weeks. I got referred to the world's sleaziest orthopedist.

It was the weekend from hell.

My leg is still not the same, which is why I don't move onstage as much as I used to. I've had multiple surgeries to correct underlying causes that may have led to these things happening in the first place. But still? Every once in a while, someone will bring this show up. Sometimes a person will still accuse me of faking it, as if I was going pull some slip-and-fall shit on a festival run by my friends. If you believe that I faked it, you're free to pay my very real medical bills and fuck right off.

But more often than not, if they were there, present in the room and saw this happen with their own eyes? They give me a handshake and tell me how much they liked the show despite the awful circumstances. And those folks? They're the ones I kept playing for. The ones I'm still playing for today.

I spent the rest of that year in bed, not reappearing onstage until my annual Halloween shows at Universal Studios, and I remember them not going terribly well. I capped off the year with a version of my annual holiday show where Chris and I performed the entirety of the *Normal Bias* and *Bubblegum Romance* albums.

While I liked playing some of the tunes we didn't get to play terribly often, it really underscored just how different albums are from live shows. We played well, but the pacing just wasn't there. Plus I just really don't like the song "When You're Not Around," and I couldn't hide it, and I think that sucked all of the life out of the room.

MOTHERFUCKERS BE BULLSHITTIN' PART ONE:

I'd been completely swept up into the "nerd music" scene. I didn't really push for it, but the bulk of my fandom identified with this genre, which I just saw as the logical extension of outsider music, things like Captain Beefheart, Daniel

Johnston, and Peter Grudzien. Oddballs who'd found a way to make their music specifically smell like them. I don't really care what the listeners call the music; I'm just happy there are any listeners at all.

Two drawbacks to nerd music that I hadn't anticipated were:

- All of the performers in said scene were socially awkward in some way.

- Most of the communication to make anything happen took place electronically.

Dear reader, this is what lead to a website called "Nerdcore Drama." It was a blog that – depending on who is telling the story/who you believe – was either created to parody celebrity gossip sites or was just generally built to be mean. And as I considered my fellow performers to be my friends, each story that I'd read would slice me in the chest.

When people look back upon the site, most will tell you that there were fun fake stories, and it's true that there were a few of those. However, there were also very real and serious posts outing people for alleged spousal abuse and the potentially shady business practices of Nerdapalooza.

Regardless, I figured out within days who the culprits behind the site were, and I called them out to their faces. Both of them lied very convincingly, and my gut feelings had a lapse in judgment in trusting their word. Not before a lot of people got very hurt by the site. It was the first time I'd seen people doxxed, and I felt really sick about the whole situation. Not just about the writers and the manner in which they were unmasked, but that select cache of readers that enjoyed these types of life-shaking situations as entertainment. And for the most part, it was all I was able to write about. Reactions. Ways to fix it all.

YOU'RE MY PRINCESS:

I have told this story so many times. If you're interested enough in my life to have read this far, you're no doubt familiar with the origins of the tune: I completed this while on Ambien, filmed the song in a twilight-sleep, and uploaded it to YouTube, not realizing what I'd done until the next day.

Here's some other things I usually don't bring up in the preamble that usually comes before a performance of this tune

- I do have vague recollections of beginning to jot down the lyrics. I remembered trying to invoke the point of view of a heterosexual man that was absolutely horrible at picking up women. I imagined that his words would be delivered over loud music at a meat market-type dance club. Yet, I don't recall finishing it.

- I have seen the video enough times that I feel like I remember the filming, but I truly do not. And truth be told, I did stumble on evidence that I'd uploaded the video the very next day. I just wasn't really sure about leaving it up.

- Around that time, I wasn't in tune with how to properly take my prescribed sleep medication. I thought you just swallowed the pill and went about being an insomniac until the medication knocked you out, and you had no choice but to go to sleep. Instead, it sort of puts your brain into a dream-like state, and you're able to carry on doing some things physically. They didn't sit me down and prepare me for that at the doctor's office, so I ended up doing stuff like this.

The song is lyrically offensive on some levels, but the misogyny really existed to make fun of idiotic men. I think. I'm not sure why the song became so enduring and popular, but I'm happy to leave well enough alone and not really question it.

MOTHERFUCKERS BE BULLSHITTIN' PART TWO:

*The Jerk* is my favorite film of all time. It's a comedic masterpiece, and it's the rare movie that plays with dangerous racial overtones but has still managed to stay relatively timeless. Around this time, I learned that there was a very rare made-for-TV sequel, and I set out on a mission to find it. When I laid my eyes on it, I simply couldn't believe what my brain was processing. It was a brand new guy named Navin, dating a totally different lady named Marie, in drastically different situations. It wasn't in the same universe, and most importantly? It wasn't funny.

While driving to a holiday gathering in 2010 and trying to figure out how to tie together my new songs about technological paranoia, cyber stalking, and general malaise, I posited to Nicole, what if I made my next album a "proper" sequel to *The Jerk*?

That idea was scrapped early on because it was terrible, but a decision was made to make the songs fit together in a tale about people that weren't terribly nice to each other. The main rule of the project was to never change a lyric to further the narrative. If the songs came with inherent contradictions, that'd just have to be the story, full stop.

And I set sail on recording my next album in between playing small shows and hosting my radio show. With this album, a resolution was made: no more cutting corners. Each album would be the best possible art that I was capable of delivering at the time in both content and quality, or it simply wasn't finished.

Friends from my past would pop up at random times during the making of this particular album, people that I was once very fond of. But more often than not, they'd only show up long enough to make me believe that a friendship could be cultivated, and then they'd toddle back to their regular lives, leaving me confused and sad when emails would go unanswered and friend requests were ignored.

This certainly had an effect on my outlook at the time, but the main impetus for the record was often being surrounded by people that were much more socially awkward than even I had ever been. I'd study their actions and ability to screw up situations, and then I'd let it percolate into a further fiction in my head. I found the actions of many of the people in my life to be rather sadistic, and I couldn't help wishing that they had healthier avenues as an outlet for that streak. I'd thank my lucky stars that I had music as an outlet. Without it, I'm not sure who I'd have ended up being.

I recorded the album over a two-week stretch, feeling the beginnings of a bout of bronchitis coming on, so I was trying to beat the clock to get it all done. There was also a part of me that was still getting used to digital recording, and in the process, I definitely didn't treat the bass guitar properly, while compressing the already-bright vocals within an inch of their lives and making more than a few bad calls with phasing along the way. It all added up to an interesting not-quite-as-lo-fi whole, and I came out of the process feeling like I'd made my best album since *Normal Bias*, and I was really ready to work it onstage for the first time in recent memory. My excitement to be onstage is directly proportionate to how well my latest songs translate in a concert, and I knew for sure that at least half of this album was audience-ready. At the same time, with such a growing catalog, I didn't sweat songs I knew I couldn't pull off live, like "I Am Going To Hit You Where You Live." I loved the tune, and it certainly had its place in the story/record, but it wasn't going to light clubs on fire. That was fine, as I had plenty of barn-burners already. And there was always the next album, right?

LOVE MY LITTLE SQUIDDY:

Again, I've always had a fascination with cults. Not just because of near-brushes with things like Heaven's Gate – better left to another book, that story – but rather that it's my belief that everyone will come to a crossroads where they are looking for some type of "answer." If the right person with the wrong intention gives it to them at that exact second? Before you know it, you've given away all of your earthly possessions to live on a commune eating nothing but Bran Chex and worshiping plungers or something.

A particular cult had caught my interest in my studies: The Source Family. Father Yod was at the center of this early '70s commune based on healthy eating, breathing exercises, and tantric sex. And in my voracious reading about them, it seemed that they had the smallest amount of people that were negatively affected by their time in the commune. Sure, some folks were none too pleased about their '70s dalliances upon further reflection, but a large number of these folks seemed to be not only proud of what they'd experienced and had continued to apply Yod's lessons to their daily lives.

But the best part? They made records. Weird, off-the-wall, psychedelic ramblings that would tick off anybody's parents. They were rare as hen's teeth, but when you found one, it was simply the portal to another world. I was especially taken by an album they'd made under the name Children Of The Sixth Root Race. This one was full of sounds that could be construed as "actual songs." The musicianship was killer, and I was especially impressed by their abilities considering the lack of overdubs at their disposal. The record was ultimately just the recording of a rehearsal for a future show, and it hit me at just the right time in my life. I don't agree with all of the teachings, but the tunes that sounded like a mix of psych rock, songs from *Schoolhouse Rock*, and just a tinge of gospel was exactly what I needed in my life right then. I'd play cuts from the album on *The Real Congregation* every chance I got.

One night, after playing their song "Godmen," the WPRK chat room was abuzz. Later, I made some references to a Stephen Colbert joke from the short-lived *Dana Carvey Show*. He was pretending to be George Harrison, lamenting that his skiffle song "Love Me Little Squid" had been vetoed by John Lennon. And the next thing you know? The chat room was plotting a cult for me where the two would be combined. A Facebook event invite went up, with one Emmit Dobbyn at the helm – later a musical cohort but at the time a teenage Marc With a C fan – and it took on a life of its own. I offered up a jokey song that could be played by the cult's band, and the song would go down as one of my

*Marc Sirdoreus*

most popular.

At the first live airing of the track, an enterprising audience member introduced an interactive finger wiggle that would come to be known as "Squiddy Fingers." Most of what went down with the Squiddy phenomenon happened completely independent of me. Fans made a joke, I chimed in and made the joke bigger, and now there's a song that's bigger than any of it was ever intended to be. It doesn't get much better than that.

As of late, I have a love/hate relationship with the song. When it's going over well, it's a really fun experience for myself and the audience. When it's bombing, I can see fingers aren't wiggling in the air, and that'll suck the wind right out of your sails. I'm often leaving it out of setlists unless it's specifically requested – otherwise I can't tell if it's a Squiddy crowd or not.

MOTHERFUCKERS BE BULLSHITTIN' PART THREE:

Just after the completion of the album, I was trying to kick the bronchitis that had shown up at the worst possible time, but someone named Milk Plus kept breathing down my neck to write and sing a hook for a hip-hop collective named Torrentz. He'd sent me a minute-and-a-half demo with one verse, told me it was about cereal, and let me go. I didn't have any other context, and kept trying to put it off until my voice was back at 100%. One day, I did a rough, lo-fi, and barely thought-out chorus about Fruity Pebbles inspired by a harmonic bridge by The Mighty Mighty Bosstones called "Hell Of A Hat." I just wanted the emails to stop so I could get back to healing my throat. I didn't even really like the song.

Unfortunately, the communication had been so threadbare that I hadn't been told that the entirety of the song would be full of cereal **puns**, so my chorus now stuck out like a sore thumb. I also hadn't been told that it was a song ultimately meant for a guy named Klopfenpop. Good ol' Klop had a blast playing the unfinished a capellas of me not at my best to people, laughing at my attempts to do a falsetto voice while incredibly ill. And it wasn't just him drunkenly playing it for people backstage. He turned it into a mini-meme in the nerdcore circles, and making fun of me took up a large portion of nearly any interview he gave at the time.

The chorus got moved to one refrain at the end of the tune, and eventually I had to call him out on it privately. I eventually explained that I had no context, bronchitis, and, on top of it all, I'm a bit hard of hearing, so I couldn't pick up on all the little artifacts that he took delight in raking me over the coals for publicly. I did what I was asked by a third party. I'm cool with Klopfenpop now, but for years, he was one of my least favorite people on the planet. He probably just thought I was a moron.

But really, if you don't want something ridiculous and lo-fi, why on earth would you ask Marc With a C to take part? You don't ask a carpenter to knit you a sweater. A cow don't make ham.

Apart from that, *Motherfuckers Be Bullshittin'* would go on to receive my best reviews in years, and my listeners embraced it in a way that I hadn't seen since *Bubblegum Romance*. Many of the new songs became the backbone of the live shows, and I saw a forward path rather than spinning my wheels. Sure, bits of it were misunderstood. Most commonly, people would assume that the "Brian" in the story was me. I wrote the bulk of the album from an observational standpoint, though a few songs did have personal resonance for me, namely "Good Night Miss Oliver" and "The Kindergarten Steely Dan."

The only really harsh critique I'd gotten was from Chris Zabriskie, who simply didn't like the album and told me so upfront. It stung because I respected his opinion, but in this case, the majority of my listeners were gung-ho about something I'd made, and he was the lone dissenting voice. This made it easy to ignore, except on the rare occasions when we'd play shows together during this period. He simply didn't know/refused to learn the tunes from the record. He liked "Love My Little Squiddy," and occasionally I could get him to do "Since I Left My Baby, I Can't Stop Flossing." But when it came time for the rest of the new songs, he'd excuse himself from the stage. My suspicion is that for the first time, the songs had real arrangements, and Chris preferred to play based on feel and vibe, so these songs simply didn't jive with his drumming instincts. We've never really talked about it, so I'm merely guessing. To be fair, we usually just geek out about The Monkees and Pink Floyd when around each other, rather than getting into heart-to-heart conversations about why he didn't like "Why Are You Keeping Tabs On Me?"

Around this time, I'd branch out again and do some rare shows away from Orlando, and I ran into all of the inherent out-of-town-promoter crap that one would expect. The most important lesson I learned was as follows, though it may not apply to anyone else besides me: if you're a traveling musician, stay at a Red Roof Inn. They have the cheapest rates, and since they charge you for anything at all – use of phone, wifi, the television – you have no choice but to relax, think, and eventually get some sleep without distraction. I like the "last man on earth" feeling, and Red Roof Inns always provide it. Sure, they aren't the cleanest place, but really, what hotel is? All you're looking for on the road is a place to rehabilitate between shows and driving.

We'd also experiment with having an actor onstage with me during this period. My buddy Lando would transform into "Lando The Roadie" for some gigs. He'd lead me onstage with a flashlight and then cater to my whims throughout the night, feeding me water through a straw, toweling me off between each song, and generally looking as bored as possible. Eventually, one of his tasks would be to sing the falsetto verse of "Show Me How To Shine Shoes," and he'd "come to life," overacting and jumping around like the most energetic hypeman ever. And then? He'd retreat back to looking bored on the stage while I berated him. It was an effective joke, and audiences loved him.

Scheduling and his lack of transportation were the only reasons we didn't work together more often. It was something that had first been suggested by committee (if memory serves) from the *Sex Times Three* shows. The first roadie was Kevin Sigman, but he was not available to continue doing the act, and after making sure no one involved would be upset if I kept running with the joke, I would push it far, far past what should have been its limits with Lando, making audiences uncomfortable with just how poorly I'd treat him. I know it wasn't always obvious that I was kidding/acting. The tell should have been that "the roadie" didn't ever do anything regarding the sound equipment, and audiences never saw him until the show had begun.

Though, one show in that incarnation did backfire. I was doing my yearly gig opening for The Rich Weirdoes presentation of *The Rocky Horror Picture Show*, and during the lengthy speech before "Love My Little Squiddy," some particularly insistent audience members were adamant in their requests for "Nerdy Girls." When I stopped the speech to say that I'd be concentrating on new material for the rest of my set, a round of boos started up that continued all the way through "Squiddy," drowning out the song. During the rest of that run, I'd drop "Squiddy" in favor of "Nerdy Girls," but it usually didn't go over well. I learned a valuable lesson in that week: you can sometimes do exactly what the audience claims to want, and they still won't be happy with you. I'd put that lesson to good use later.

RECORDED SOUND:

I greatly enjoyed being on the same page as my listener base with *Motherfuckers Be Bullshittin'*, so I moved quickly to a new EP full of songs that I'd really liked over the years but didn't find their ways onto proper albums. Sort of like a mini-*Linda Lovelace For President* but with somewhat more-capable equipment.

Chris questioned my decision to let quality songs like "Calculator" and "Another Minute Or So" languish away on some obscure freebie EP, but I didn't really see a problem with it.

Also, around this time, my wife and I bought a house. Instead of trying to do all of my recording work in the living room and garage, I'd now have a backroom devoted to recording space, Nicole could have a home office in the back of the house, and the living room could actually be a living room where we'd be happy to have guests over.

Well, we would if we weren't such private and awkward people. Truthfully, we have no idea how to entertain guests. Nicole offers them tea, and I play records for them. That's about all we know how to do. Either way, we liked the house, and I think that we were happier and more productive people with the extra space.

Though I'd greatly enjoyed doing *The Real Congregation* for WPRK, late 2011 was time to move on. My love for what radio can be continues unabated, but WPRK's antiquated equipment made it impossible to do my job. Many people listened online due to the weakness of the transmitter, and often times, our stream didn't work at all. There were nights when you simply knew that nobody was actually tuned in, but you had to sit there and pretend to be a DJ in accordance with FCC regulations, *Wet Hot American Summer*-style.

I had three choices:

- I could continue broadcasting my show through WPRK, knowing it would only be heard sometimes and completely out-of-phase when it did appear for the audience.

- The show could be abandoned altogether.

- I could move the show to a podcast format as part of the Nerdy Show podcast network.

I chose the third option. After a bit of negotiations over dinner, Hex introduced me to Cap Blackard, the CEO of Nerdy Show. Cap was so laidback that I was under the impression that they were a mere contributor rather than the head of the network. Either way, I found Cap to be a fascinating person, and someone I immediately identified with. We were fast friends, and they remain one of my very favorite people that I've ever met.

I threw myself into producing weekly content for the network, but it was a bit more work than I'd anticipated. The good news was that if something failed, it would be my fault instead of WPRK's, and I have no problem taking responsibility in those cases. The bad news was that instead of doing the show live, I had more chances to dick around with the sound, song flow, and rendering. Trust me when I tell you that if you're a DIY recording artist, most of your life is spent rendering files. And these were big files because the show could be anywhere between 90 minutes to three hours. If one mixdown was wrong, you'd have to start the whole process over again, and *The Real Congregation* began to be just about all that I ever did. We scaled back the release schedule a bit over time, but I remember the show as a very rewarding yet heavy albatross.

I think people liked the idea of *The Real Congregation* more than actually keeping up with it. There was more content than anyone could handle, full of bizarre and often impenetrable music, and it sort of cemented how I was beginning to be seen: as an all-around music geek. The workload helped shift public perception of me in a way.

Also around this time, I persuaded Cap that nerdy music needed an online home, a radio station where all of its various subgenres could co-exist together. After all, anyone with an audience ought to be heard. Turns out that Cap and the rest of the Nerdy Show network were thinking the same thing. And so were a few members of Sci-Fried. We got together summit-style and came up with what would become Nerdy.FM. I'm very proud of the station and was even more proud to eventually attempt to hand managerial duties to the station's biggest fan, Lauren Furze.

While I was really happy with *Motherfuckers Be Bullshittin'* being my most recent statement, the further away I get from the release of an album, the harder I find it to focus on how to approach live shows. I had this mountain o' tunes, and without a really new release to anchor a setlist? I'd run the risk of becoming a predictable "play the favorites" kind of performer. But if I ignore the bulk of them, I run the risk of alienating the audience and seeming willfully difficult. That's all alleviated when I have a new album out. People usually think, "Hey, he's promoting a new album" and don't question why they didn't hear a wide variety of songs by the end of the gig.

That is ultimately why I'd continuously create and record. I have no label pushing me for an album/tour cycle, and I have an inborn need to make stuff, which is often followed by a severe craving to make people happy with the music once I've pleased myself with it. That pattern comes with a need for a side-helping of instant gratification, making it a self-perpetuating circle. It's my belief that it takes up the space in my brain where sex and sports would go for a stereotypical man. I also have absolutely no competitive streak – besides when playing a board game – but I have one within myself to constantly make better art than the last time I created something. And that need is muddied with the "you MUST do everything yourself" ethos that I haven't been able to escape since the earlier disappointments of working with outside producers.

The cycle was becoming dangerous at this point. I'd rush out albums full of cover songs to quench the desire to make something and then show off the good parts. In some cases, this yielded results that I am exceedingly proud of. Specifically, an album full of songs made famous by The Monkees called *Good Clean Fun*.

That record was an absolute labor of love to do, as many Monkees songs are much harder to pull off than they may sound, especially vocally. And as the group has always been near and dear to my heart, I worked diligently to not so much cover the songs accurately but to understand each portion of a piece's compositional makeup, and then figure out how to best reinterpret it as Marc With a C. Sort of like filtering the songs into my ears and out of my mouth, mixed in with what the song does to me internally and emotionally.

This lead to controversial decisions like taking the lightweight "Don't Bring Me Down" from their fluffy 1987 reunion album *Pool It* (arguably the least essential portion of their entire catalog), and turning it into a long, slow, and heavy dirge. Or to take a divisive tune like 1968's "Writing Wrongs" and treating it like a Black Sabbath outtake but doing a salsa break in the middle with nothing but synthesizers from the 1980s.

*Good Clean Fun* hardly made a dent anywhere. Even the voracious Monkees fandom barely seemed to take notice, but it remains among my favorite albums I've ever made. The album was also notable for another segment of my life where I'd have to "play through the pain." At some point during the sometimes 20 plus-hour sessions for the album, I'd really done a number on my throat. There was a nagging and persistent pain there, but not the type of hurt one would normally associate with a cold or something. This was muscular, and it sort of stung on the outside of my throat, between the skin and the vocal cords. I kept singing despite the pain, but it started to become outwardly noticeable.

I gained a rasp during speech, while the range of notes that I was able to sing well began to narrow considerably. I found myself tuning down my guitar a full step to get through some songs onstage or even in the privacy of my own rehearsals.

This was the beginning of a troubling throat problem that I'm still fighting as of this writing. Sure, smoking wasn't helping in the least, but the culprit seemed to be a mixture of overuse of those muscles mixed with constant postnasal drip from being allergic to nearly everything that one can name and a particularly debilitating case of stomach problems, with the unfortunate side effect of acid reflux. My poor throat was just caught in the middle, and it was just another annoyance to add to the list of things that didn't/don't work right on my body.

But with that particular case, I was actually directed to go on complete vocal rest for numerous months. No *Real Congregation*, no interviews, no singing, and only talking to family members in hushed tones when it was absolutely necessary. I'm pretty verbose, so it was a special sort of torture. During those mute weeks, I wrote a lot of music, but was unable to truly complete it. Around this time, I also did my first crowdfunded project, a Kickstarter campaign to raise the funds to put *Normal Bias* out on vinyl. I didn't enjoy that type of shameless self-promotion, as it felt too similar to begging for my own tastes, but it had been a very real dream of mine to have that album in particular mastered for wax, and my modest following helped turn the dream into a tangible reality. The inner turmoil of the crowdsourcing venture would inspire my next project, one that was so ambitious that I was actually expecting to fail in public and had mentally prepared myself to fall flat on my artistic face in plain sight.

POPULAR MUSIC, PART ONE:

The concept of *Popular Music* was pretty simple, or so I thought. Collect data from people, turn it into songs, represent said songs on a pie chart, make a vinyl LP look like a pie chart, and the listener could play back the "market research" on it.

Crowdfunding projects were at such a fever pitch at the time that I figured, hey, what better way to represent the mood of 2012-2013 than to let the audience have everything that they claim to want on one record? All they have to do is trust me to filter the information properly, and then on paper? There's no reason it couldn't be a contender for "the greatest album of all time," right? We trust fans with money, so I decided to take it all the way to trusting their ideas implicitly.

Of course, I didn't let on at first. There were simple queries asked from the Marc With a C fanpage on Facebook (or occasionally my personal page). Questions like, What is the biggest problem facing the world today? What's a song title that would ensure that you'd buy a record on sight? What tempo do you think Marc With a C songs should have? Pretty open-ended stuff. I used the answers to inform completion of the lyrics that hadn't been written for musical ideas constructed while on vocal rest

In some cases, pre-existing songs were used because they fit the user data. People really like dick jokes, so "Dickpuncher III" and "The True Story Of Triforce Mike" fit right into what people claimed to want. And of course, like many musicians, I'd grown tired of the "PLAY FREEBIRD" joke that happened at half of my gigs, so I just wrote a song called "Free Bird."

The visual art concept was paramount to the completion of the album. I'd come up with the general idea and then pitched it to Cap Blackard to make it a reality. I'm usually not the type of musician that visualizes an album, but this was a rare exception, and Cap did an amazing job getting my vision across with lots of extra little things I'd have never considered.

Writing the album was easy. Getting it made the way I wanted? That was a whole other adventure.

A few things went awry during the recording process, which I'd decided to document through a YouTube series called *Making Popular Music At Home*. One such situation was that early on, the power went out during the sessions, first day. No big deal, right? Well, when the power clicked back on, for some reason it had set the home stereo amplifier that I was reviewing the mixes on to "bass boost," which I didn't notice for a few weeks, making me believe that everything was much beefier/less bright than it actually was. Understandably, this was problematic.

Another issue was a bit less fun to go on about was the slow realization that to go and promote what I was recording properly, I'd need a drummer at shows again. But when Chris and I got into a room to try to play these songs? Chris was finally verbally open about being taken aback by how much fuller the arrangements had become and how it wasn't really working to just "plug in and go" anymore. No matter how much we whittled down the instrumentation to the barest elements, something still felt lacking.

THE END OF POPULAR MUSIC:

We're all being inundated with so much information and music now that our eyes just glaze over, even when we see stuff that we **do** like in our technological feeds. Social media isn't really built for people who want to tell you a story. People who want to say something that isn't easily distilled into a meme, a silly picture, or a quickie caption. People who believe that sometimes you should have to work for gratification, and the instantaneous variety isn't always all it's cracked up to be. People who want to make and hear albums that get better with repeated listens. People who want to make things that don't fit into socially constructed guidelines by corporations.

Yet, I am an independent musician dependent on the whims of corporate giants to even let you see what I've got to say or let you hear my song. And the main thing that I knew going into the *Popular Music* album was that even if you did everything that the audience claimed to want, very few people would actually hear the final song on the record.

Why? Because albums are dying a little more each day. And that was becoming problematic for me, as I tend to think and plan in album cycles.

Now, let me be clear. I don't think anybody owes me anything just because I make songs. We've really become dilettantes, dabbling in everything. Cluttering up a level playing field with stuff we only half take seriously. Not that things were any better in "the old days." But, there was something about sitting in a waiting room without a cell phone or a tablet, nothing to pass the time. When's the last time you just sat and thought? Not doing anything else. Not driving. Not walking and listening to a podcast. Just sitting and thinking.

There's so much entertainment literally everywhere you put your head that we don't know how to tell it apart from advertising. But believe me when I tell you the following:

There was a period of time in my teenage years where my emotional disorders had gotten the best of me, and I had to go away for a few weeks to recover. The facility I found myself in wouldn't let me watch television, read books, or listen to music. The treatment was basically to cut me off from the artificial things that could provoke emotional responses. I'd been away for about four days, and then the weekend hit, and there was this sort of recreational "music therapy." They'd unlock the cages where percussive instruments and a boombox had been held captive and let us play with it all for about an hour (or less) a day. One older gentleman was having a particularly nasty bout of whatever illness was plaguing him. Don't know what he was diagnosed with, but he'd been there for a while. Blowing his nose into his bare hand and wiping it on other people without realizing he'd done it. I would get annoyed at that kind of thing, and the dude was just "working my last nerve," and I felt bad for being impatient with him.

Anyway, music therapy day rolls around, and everyone is all excited. They flip on the radio to the local generic pop station, and, you know that song that goes "what is love / baby don't hurt me"? That track came on, and this guy started bawling like a baby. He beautifully cried tears of joy for that whole session, sobbing louder at lyrics that really hit him. He was moved by songs that some faceless company paid a kajillion dollars to a radio executive to make sure would be hammered into our heads. Nobody really cared about the quality or emotional resonance of those tunes during that payola process. But to this guy? It was the most beautiful thing he'd heard all week. He lived and died for that hour or so per week when the unexplainable was communicated with 12 notes, harmony, and rhythm.

If we could somehow take a break from sensory overload, any and all music could move any of us that way. That's how it works, even for the "totally sane." We just probably haven't tried to be away from it all for a while.

My second week in that place? I started crying when I heard songs I would have been "too cool" to like as well. And the day I was discharged, I wept in the car at some music in the background of a commercial.

That experience is what the guitar solo at the close of "The End of Popular Music" is about. Yes, the lyrics are important, but it's the only time I've ever tried to say something with a noodling solo. The end was supposed to feel like a real emergency. When you're crying so hard that you can't catch your breath. Nothing's wrong. Everything is right for once because art is hitting you, and there is still mystery and wonder in the world.

Right now, the music just can't always cut through the din.

POPULAR MUSIC, PART TWO:

The second phase of crowdsourcing *Popular Music* was actually raising the money through IndieGoGo. At the time, Facebook was in the middle of one of their crazy algorithm shifts, but I didn't know that. I could post links to the campaign all day long, but the social media platform wasn't letting people see them. I took to writing individual letters to fans asking for their monetary support in producing the album.

There was a very real period toward the end when I truly did not believe we would meet our goals. I was discussing it with my wife, and, before I knew it, I had tears streaming down my face, which was puffy from far too much alcohol consumption to dull the thoughts that crept in at the reality of having an unrealized piece of art. I'd kid myself all of the time, assuring myself that since I was only having maybe one or two drinks per night, it just wasn't a problem.

But they were really big drinks, and alcohol tends to bloat me a bit more than it does the average person.

I'd only drink at night, right before bed, usually around 4 a.m., when my liquid numbing agent wouldn't bother anyone else, but my body wasn't reacting well to it. A whole new set of problems were creeping up on me physically. It also didn't mix well with a pre-existing blood disorder called hemochromatosis. Overall, my body was becoming a real mess.

Regardless, the monetary goal was met, and now I had to set out on a course of finishing bonus rewards for those that had helped out with their hard-earned cash. Alex Carroll had shot the bulk of a long show at a favored corner shop sort of venue called Sleeping Moon Cafe on his HD camera, so we offered it to backers as an official bootleg on a DVD, as well as some albums you couldn't get otherwise: a collection of outtakes called *Unpopular Music*, and a disc full of many of the working demos for *Popular Music*. The latter is notable because I slightly prefer the demo versions of "Proper Amount Of Snare" and "Whack Jite" to the finished versions that made it to the album. I'm cool with the versions that are commonly known, but sometimes that initial excitement is most present on the first recording, flaws and all.

Along the way, I would find rarities and offer them up to backers as freebies as a thank-you just for believing in me. In one case, I wanted to do a one-off cover of a song by The Little Girls called "So Hard To Be True," but felt that it could really benefit from the voice of a lady harmonizing with me. And it just so happened that a lady named Leslie Rising had been posting a bunch of videos recorded from her iPhone where she was singing on various social media platforms, and I told her that I thought she should sing more often for people. She agreed and eventually after posting about looking for vocal work, I asked her if she'd like to come and sing on this cover song.

Not only did she take me up on the offer, but she knocked it so far out of the park on the first take that I had to invent reasons to do safety takes. She barely needed EQ on her voice or any treatment at all. Her voice was just the type that could blend in anywhere with anything. I felt more inspired by her singing than I had by anything else in a good long while. That one cover song quickly turned into an EP of covers by our newly made-up little band called Claire and The Potatoes, a name my wife had come up with when Benjamin Bear and I had considered starting a psych side-project, for which we wrote one song and then promptly never saw each other again. Why waste a good band name?

I'm sure that I did a lot of work upon the proper release of *Popular Music*, but it feels like it all pales in comparison to the work that it took to make the album a reality. I did shows, but promoting an album that was secretly about the death of the album format proved to be a tricky format for a live show. And again, songs that I initially thought were built for the stage most assuredly were not: "Slick & Unused," "DJ Danny Treanor," and "Brand New Thing" first felt like the cornerstones of the next wave of concerts but ultimately felt clunky and directionless when performed in front of people. The lack of glue that could only be provided by the bottom end of a bass player wasn't something we could do without any longer.

I contacted Emmit Dobbyn. He'd been a fan of mine since he was around 15, and he really combed over my albums as a listener, not just a pedestrian fan of the most obviously fun tunes. He'd become a pretty good bass player, and his travels had moved him from Australia to the USA, eventually settling near Tampa. It wasn't exactly convenient for him to pop over for rehearsals, but he was fervent about wanting to be the glue we needed, and his excitement for the material – not to mention his dedication to understanding and bettering himself at his instrument – really lit a fire underneath me the same way singing with Leslie had.

Emmit and Chris became The Expansion Pack, a duo that would back me up on selected gigs. We'd sometimes be augmented by Leslie for backing vocals as Chris was singing less and less on the stage. A mixture of drum parts that needed more attention and his seeming dislike of his own voice necessitated such a move. It was awkward at first, especially for Leslie. She'd have to take the night off of work and wait for us to get a song right, and then we'd see where she'd need to sing. Often, she'd just be standing at a microphone long enough to sing two lines, and then had to sit through numerous run-throughs of other songs, waiting for her services to be needed again. She didn't last long in the lineup, and really, who could be expected to do that every week for free?

Reception to *Popular Music* was exceedingly positive for those that had the ears for the rather post-modern concept. I felt great onstage playing with the band, despite some burgeoning physical discomfort, and after a period of really delving into The Soft Boys and ABBA, I began to realize that sometimes music could be realized better by the merging of personalities, The Expansion Pack wasn't built for that. Chris still saw it as a hobby, and his ambient albums were really picking up steam. Luckily, Leslie was itching to do some musical work. She didn't fancy herself a musical writer, but she did have a gift for interpreting music though her own ears and lungs, and a bunch of creative bells went off in my head.

HAVE AN OKAY TIME WITH CLAIRE AND THE POTATOES:

The Brill Building songwriters of yore would often have a man write something attempting to tap into the feelings of young women, and then they'd have a real live young woman sing it, and it would become a product. These songs would then appear to be a glimpse into the psyche of an average lady of the time, though rarely actually having the input of anyone of the female-identifying persuasion – Carole King being an obvious exception.

I wanted to experiment with that sort of songwriting but with one major difference: Leslie would tell me something she wanted to sing about, and I would exaggerate it for a completely different persona: Claire. Claire was the mean average of a mostly heterosexual woman navigating the divide between the moral values of 1950's Americana (get married by 20, pop out a kid by 21, etc.) and the ability to live lifetimes worth of relationships through the technology of 2013. Claire would be overwhelmed by the choices in front of her and the way that they battled with the demands of her family. Now, mind you, the character was not based on Leslie, but many of the attitudes and more blunt nature of Claire's statements were.

What I found most inspiring about Leslie beyond her voice was her complete lack of pretension when it came to music. She just liked to sing. She didn't care if it was cool to like or dislike, say, Lynyrd Skynyrd or Fleet Foxes. If she found it fun to sing, then it was a-okay by her. Plus, each round of applause greatly excited her, while I was a bit jaded by now. So each bit of kudos that we'd receive? I might initially brush it off, but it would be new and exciting to Leslie, and that excitement would rub off on me and inspire me to do more work toward the Claire project. When it came down to it, Leslie was a great singer, but she just didn't have any songs to sing outside of karaoke bars. I wanted to provide them.

I'd written a few songs for the project and threw in a couple of tunes that I'd been holding back for another Marc With a C album, (e.g., "A Different Take On Faith," "Honey You"). Leslie and I started doing shows as a duo. Quickly, it became apparent that these songs would be vastly more effective with a band. But who would that band be? Who could I call on to basically let Leslie and myself sit in the driver's seat and be happy to simply act as backing musicians for this unproven idea?

I'd received a CD by a local group named Milk Carton Superstars during my stint at WPRK. After a few listens, I decided that they might be the best group in Orlando that no one was aware of. Jim Myers was the drummer, and he'd reached out to me for some possible gigs. I'd been unable to help in that regard, but I liked his playing, so I decided to give him a call and see if he might like to join up with us on a for-hire basis. He thought it'd be fun to try but explained that between his day job and MCS, his time would be limited. I decided that limited time was better than no time at all, so an audition followed, and there was no doubt that Jim was "the guy." Plus, I liked him and his wife a lot as people, and that doesn't always coincide when musicians can gel tonally.

When it came time to find a bassist, a lady from The Rich Weirdoes named Amy had offered her services but ultimately didn't answer her phone. Jim suggested we give the other half of MCS a whirl: Guy Larmay. I was told that while Guy was the guitarist for MCS, he was really a bassist by trade, and that he would really understand the retro vibe we were going for. I trusted Jim implicitly, so we gave it a go.

Leslie and I made our way to an antique mall in Mount Dora that Guy co-owned for our first rehearsal as a four-piece. Guy had really dove deep into the first Claire EP and seemed to know it pretty well. He was just a little clumsy with his bass lines (to be expected for a first rehearsal) and played excruciatingly loud, but these seemed like things that could be worked through. During a smoke break, Leslie and I decided to give him the thumbs-up, and that was the solidification of the lineup.

Understanding Guy is impossible, but it's very important to explaining the Claire story. Guy seemed like a complete space cadet when you talked to him, but he was very smart, artistic, and well-read when you figured out how to interpret him. Thoughts just got lost somewhere between his brain and his mouth, but it would all come out through his fingers when playing. So when things were going well, and he was happy, he'd play right in the pocket with the rest of us. When his life was in turmoil, his fingers and melodies would become convoluted, unpredictable, and impossible (for me) to play around. The latter ended up being the case more often than not, as he was at the beginning of a long and slow divorce process. This meant that three members of the group would know the songs inside and out, but we'd have to play the songs over and over while Guy tried to get a certain "feel."

But how was Guy to feel? I wasn't giving clear directions. The demos I'd hand him were bare bones, and he'd go into the stratosphere looking for a bass vibe that worked for everyone. And I don't know that he found what he was looking for. I was in the unique position of not wanting to tell him exactly what to play, as I didn't want to undermine or lessen his creativity. All I could tell him was that I didn't like what he was playing. I was a tyrant to him. But I think it would have all evened out if he would have at least agreed to play at a volume that allowed the rest of us to be heard too. I love The Who, but I think that he got it in his head that I wanted him to be John Entwistle.

What we eventually had to accept was that Guy's nature is to overplay, and that it's just highly unlikely that he'll ever play something the same way twice. Basically, if he wrote something, he could understand the inner workings, but it seemed to take him a longer time to understand someone else's creation, or at least any of mine, I felt. Also, he was a big fan of The Rolling Stones, and he was partial to their more shambolic moments. The rest of us were trying to create a tight pop band, and the two didn't always play together well, but we eventually came to create "the Claire sound."

And having a sound meant that this was becoming a real band, which none of us had really anticipated. It had always been my intention that I'd do this concept album that would masquerade as a band, but it'd still ultimately be a Marc With a C project. Basically, the follow-up to *Popular Music*. Instead, it met somewhere in the middle: a real band that portrayed a fake band, with me writing the bulk of the material and Leslie acting as "the face" of the band. We had an identity crisis from the day the four of us entered a room. Despite that, we all shared a mutual love for one another and laughed through our rehearsals. I believe that Leslie felt like the odd one out, as she mostly just sang what she was given, while the rest of us were free to create our own parts. I tried to quell that, reminding her that without her voice, none of us would be in the same room making these songs at all.

The four-piece proved to be very popular in a few ZIP codes and gained a small but loyal fan base with ease. We won local popularity awards without even trying or without having played very many shows. We'd gig anywhere, and there were times where Guy just simply didn't show up for various reasons. While there was that distinct love between all of the band members, and we had a certain "one for all, all for one" gang mentality, usually at least one of us was making things rather untenable. That person changed depending on the week.

For a period of time, it was me. We had to take a few months off while I got multiple corrective surgeries on both of my legs. They were swelling due to certain veins being too big. By the end of a day, nearly all of the blood in my body would pool in my knees and feet, leaving me lightheaded and hardly able to move. Sitting for long periods didn't do well, and standing wasn't any better. The only time it wasn't a problem was when I'd lie flat on my back, or maybe with my legs raised above my head. This was apparently something I'd inherited from other family members, and once when I called one to ask about it, they'd imbibed some substances and weren't speaking too clearly. They used the word "lymphoma" when they meant to say "lymphedema." For about a week, I thought that I was going to die fairly quickly.

After a few months off, we went back to preparing for what would become the *Have An Okay Time With Claire And The Potatoes* album. I'd hit a few brick walls trying to complete the project, and Jim started offering up some lyrics that I could write music around. Guy even pitched a tune that Jim whipped into shape called "A Shot At Love," which turned out to be one of the best songs from the project. But to really understand all of the characters at play in the album, each time I'd try to lose myself in "the vibe" of the situations inherent on the record, I'd inhabit a mental state that was a bit similar to method acting. Except none of that came naturally to me, and without proper training, I often found it very difficult to leave those headspaces.

I was finding myself driving Leslie back and forth to rehearsals. If the band wanted to rehearse, it was a minimum of four hours in a car every day just to do that. If someone wasn't at their best while I'd devote all of that time and energy? I'd snap quickly and without mercy. Jim was a great peacekeeper in these moments. I stand by the fact that in our situation, if it had been possible for everyone to pull the same amount of weight that I did for the Claire project, we'd have been an indestructible force.

The long and short of it is that the making of the album landed me back in the care of a professional therapist, and I will have to refuse to elaborate on that any further. I was at the end of my rope in a situation that I had created on my own to try and get in the proper mindset, and if Jim hadn't come through with great tracks for us to flesh out as a band like "The Real Enemy," we'd likely never have completed the album.

I loved playing with the band and wasn't expecting the amount of love that was returned to us by our audience so quickly. I also wasn't prepared for some fans of Marc With a C to dislike the project simply because I wasn't the lead vocalist. It was basically two different groups of fans that I was trying to please simultaneously, and I was absolutely cracking under the pressure. Thankfully, the pressure was relieved without much of my own say-so.

EXACTLY WHERE I AM:

During the Claire project, I was still playing Marc With a C gigs with The Expansion Pack. One day, Chris wrote a very nicely worded letter to me that spelled out in no uncertain terms that he could not continue playing the drums for me. I didn't want to stop playing with a band, but Chris was not exactly a replaceable cog. We had undeniable chemistry as a trio with Emmit, but Chris hadn't taken so well to rigorous rehearsals that were necessary to keep a band tight and above even a mediocre level. On top of that, he had a full-time job, his ambient music continued to take off, and he had a family to take care of. The least important thing in his life was hitting things while I played the guitar, really. He promised to finish out 2014 with me, but his demeanor onstage sometimes suggested to me that he'd already checked out.

Shortly afterward, Leslie informed us she'd be moving to North Carolina, making future work with Claire and The Potatoes nigh on impossible. I understood her need to move on, as she'd found love and happiness with her boyfriend, but it did sting to have really overextended myself for an album that had only been out for a few months that was now officially dead in the water.

In the meantime, I put an end to *The Real Congregation*. The Nerdy Show network was moving toward a distribution model that wasn't terribly conducive to what I was doing any longer. Plus, I was just exhausted from trying to keep up with the show and attempting to not sound tired on the microphone. I was rehearsing two days a week, recording/writing two days a week, and usually gigging on the remaining days. I didn't have a lot of time to listen to records anymore, let alone gush about them. I let the listeners host the final show via call-ins and voicemail messages, and it was probably the best episode in our five-year history. Of the first run, anyway.

If you want to properly put bands to bed, you've got to do "final shows." And they'd better be good. You don't want to go out looking tired and listless. So off both bands went, rehearsing more often than ever just to end. I loved playing my guitar with all of those friends, but these rehearsals would often make me feel sad. To keep my head somewhat straight, I started fleshing out and recording new ideas. Now, I wasn't really setting out to make an album, but recording and playing back my ideas is extremely therapeutic when I'm not really looking at the "finish line."

I'd also decided to quit smoking tobacco with the help of an e-cig. Those things get a bad rap from people, but I can tell you that many of my vocal troubles subsided within days of my last cigarette, and after a few short weeks, I'd gained back a massive amount of the upper range that I'd assumed that I was losing due to natural aging. Shortly afterward, I'd also decide to just sort of eschew alcohol. Not as a hard and fast "never again" rule but mostly because I didn't really enjoy the effects anymore. Both of these things happening in tandem had a very positive effect on my overall health and outlook. With so much coming to an end, I knew that there was a real chance that I could lose myself in various numbing agents, but I opted instead to just, well, feel it all for the very first time. It made me feel better than I had in years, strangely.

During a show in early 2014, I'd asked the bar for a glass of water from the stage. I'd emphasized that I'd prefer that it came to me in the largest receptacle available to them. Before I knew it, a giant crystal glass arrived in front of me in the shape of a boot. The World Cup was being shown on all of the televisions, and that's when I decided who I was rooting for: Bootwater. It just became a running joke through the night. But it did sound like it could actually be the name of a real small town in Florida.

THE RIGHT TO BEAR ARMS:

One night, back in Mascotte, Florida, sometime around the beginning of the new millennium, I was working the graveyard shift in a convenience store just around the corner from my house. I didn't like the job at all, but as it was basically a small truck stop, there were a lot of transient folks making their way in and out at all hours, so you never really had the chance to get bored at least.

On this particular evening, a pickup truck was in the parking lot and hadn't budged for a number of hours. Now, this wasn't too out of the ordinary, as OTR truckers slept in our parking lot all of the time. The odd part was that there was a man in the driver's seat who was wide awake and intently staring at the highway in front of him. While I was outside, sweeping and smoking, I pushed my broom up toward his open window, and the following exchange took place:

"Hi there. Everything okay?"

"Oh, it's gonna be okay," he said. "When she gets off work."

He then reached over to the passenger seat, lifted a towel, and exposed a gun to me. He followed it up with one the most chilling grins I've ever seen. The sort of smile that says, "The world will see my actions as wrong, but my God will reward me for doing the right thing." It's still hard to explain years later because I was so terrified that all of my memories go a little bit fuzzy at this point.

I remember sweeping my way back to the front door and trying to covertly call the police. It wasn't hard to do because the city hall was literally next door, one of the positive aspects of small town life. Cops filled the parking lot in less than two minutes, and he sped off into the night.

These police officers came into the store all of the time, partially to check on our safety, partially for the free coffee that I always kept fresh for them in respect to their vigilance and protection of the shop. (This was a store in the middle of nowhere, surrounded by very few residences. If something had happened to me, there was a good chance I wouldn't be found for hours. Those police officers diligently kept me safe and were quite protective of me.)

Usually, these folks of the badge-wearing persuasion would chew the fat with me about their adventures as long as it was a case that they could speak about. But for some reason, they would always change the subject when I'd bring this event up. No one spoke of it, and I never saw or heard of the man with the gun again.

Years later, I'd try to make sense of the situation in a sort of therapeutic "make a song out of what you know" way, trying to connect the dots to try and reach peace with what seemed to be a brush with the ugliest aspects of humanity. The truth is that I still don't know the outcome, and that it still chills every cell in my body to recall those events.

EXACTLY WHERE I AM, PART TWO:

The final Claire and The Potatoes show was performed in November of 2014, on the heels of the release of a tune called "The Final Single." Jim Myers had written the lyrics, and I'd written some rather smooth and out-of-character melodies and grooves to go with it, mostly inspired by off-the-cuff jams we'd have at rehearsals. The show was emotional, as it became clear that our sole album had connected very deeply with some listeners. We heard cries of "I love you, Leslie!" coming from the crowd, and some attendees openly wept while having us sign their memorabilia. It felt great to have connected to all of these people in conjunction with my friends, but I also felt a mountain of pressure leave my shoulders when we called it a day. We had accomplished quite a bit in a very short period of time, and I can only chalk it up to a chemistry that made us greater than the sum of our parts. Or, if not greater, at least "somewhat more effective." We amicably went our separate ways.

The final Expansion Pack show was a very different beast, as I knew that it wasn't my last gig, and that I had no plans to stop performing with Emmit if I could help it, but it was the proverbial tolling of the bell for Chris and I as a performing unit. In my opinion, we didn't perform very well that night, but that had to do with me being very on edge.

Emmit was exceptionally late to the gig, and as he'd accidentally bent and ultimately broken his phone while in the car, he was unreachable. I became convinced that something very bad had happened to him. He arrived safely, but those nerves never really went away, and I found myself jittery and short with people throughout the night. Chris looked to me as if he was completely disconnected from the music, something that audience members would ask me about relentlessly. Due to his (allegedly unintentional) demeanor, many believed that the Expansion Pack was disbanding due to friction between the two of us. While it's true that there had been arguments and tussles, we were actually pretty harmonious during this period. He just wasn't interested in playing the drums because it took him away from the things that needed his attention more, as I understood it. There was no actual drama in that breakup, and we remain good friends, though I completely understand how it must have looked on a stage.

Before I knew it, I'd recorded enough material for an album. Many of the songs were based on the my experiences with the scarier sides of small towns, and I tied them together as the "Bootwater Suite," sort of a view into the seedy underbelly of one night in a fictitious town. Side one was populated with slightly less esoteric material and felt like it might be a little less impenetrable to the average listener.

I tried to release *Exactly Where I Am* with a long mysterious buildup. Each day, a new photo of me taken by Emmit would be released via social media with the caption: "You have _ days left. Can you guess exactly where I am?" This would lead people to try and calculate the exact location where the pictures were taken, which was Mascotte, Florida. One especially studious fan figured it out, which was quite impressive, but all someone would have had to do to answer correctly? Answer "exactly where I am." It probably frustrated more people than it had impressed.

The album was released to much fanfare from those that bought all of my work on the day of release, but did not seem to ignite much of a fire in those that weren't die-hard fans. Though it seems the album was a slow burn, it started catching on months afterward as people had time to digest this rather dark album that wasn't at all made with the listener in mind.

*Exactly Where I Am* is one of the rare occasions where everything sounded exactly as I'd envisioned, and I didn't feel that I'd made any concessions or compromises along the way. Again, this can probably be attributed to the fact that I hadn't actually set out to make an album. I was just recording for fun.

Shortly afterward, Jim Myers would join Emmit and I in doing shows as a band, and it was a very nice pairing. Beyond being a fantastic, intelligent, and smooth gentleman, he wasn't your average club-fisted rock drummer. He really understood dynamics and could play any variety of feels. You could tell him,

"Play that part a little quieter," and he could do it, where most rock and roll drummers would simply start leaving out parts of the beat, giving more space instead of less volume. We whipped ourselves into a tight little power trio in what seemed like no time flat.

INTERMISSION - JUNE 2015:

And my friends, that brings me to the present. Unfortunately, the present isn't actually the present in relation to when I expect to let a person read this memoir. I have a long way to go, and a lot more that I want to do before I tell my story. From here on out in this book, I'll be telling the rest of the tale in the form of journal entries. It's hard for me to remember emotions and idiosyncrasies of each event, but I can take care to note some day to day goings-on of what I do in the coming pages.

I don't do this because I believe that my life's work itself is important enough to be documented in painstaking detail but rather because there are a million DIY artists out there. The stories of just how deeply we live our art usually isn't told until we pass away, and even then, it comes through third-party assumptions and conjecture. I'm sharing mine because my American life is not traditional, and it may be interesting to someone, someday. If you're reading these words, I hope that it has been so far.

# Part II: Diary

7-29-15

Today, I woke up to the whirring of a weed-wacker just outside of my bedroom window. I wasn't mad. The lawn guy was doing his job, and as it was around 1 in the afternoon, I couldn't exactly take him to task for maintaining my lawn at a poorly chosen time of day. Of course, I didn't go to bed last night until around 6 a.m. Insomnia, sleep medication that only works half of the time, and getting far too into my umpteenth screening of *Raiders Of The Lost Ark* were surely the culprits for my late rising. Or possibly that I'm just a late riser by nature. Always have been, if I can get away with it.

My morning ritual consists of walking to the kitchen, taking my thyroid medication, and downing a cup of ice cold coffee that my wonderful wife has lovingly made for me. (I like cold coffee.) I then walk to the cell phone with a lump in my throat, terrified that people have been trying to get in touch with me for hours while I've been dozing. Today? There is no correspondence on the phone. I leave the ringer off as usual, keep it plugged in, take my e-cig from its charging source, and head to the other communications box.

The computer in my office looks like a lo-fi NASA terminal. A desktop computer far larger than the technological demands of 2015 call for, surrounded by mixing boards/studio monitors and littered with cups that I can't be bothered to take back to the kitchen. When you look at it from far away, it looks like a makeshift skyline of cups and glasses, and I've grown rather fond of Cup City. I wedge my spot of frozen joe into the debris and check all of the various social media things that help me communicate in this age: Gmail, Facebook, Twitter, tumblr (though I really don't feel like I fit in with that one), and then back to the phone for Instagram.

Gmail ends up being the only one with anything terribly pressing. The only truly pertinent cable is from my wife who is telling me that I've placed second in the *Orlando Weekly*'s yearly popularity contest in two categories: one is Best Open Mic, and the other is Best Singer-Songwriter.

As for the open mic? I've been hosting that at The Geek Easy for nearly two years now as a favor to the owner Aaron Haaland. I love that venue and the community, but hosting the open mic isn't terribly enjoyable for me. (Editor's note: Due to unfortunate circumstances, as of August 2019, Marc is no longer associated with The Geek Easy.) I could give you a laundry list of reasons, but I'll just say that it isn't my bag and hope you'll take that to heart. But people seem to think I'm very good at hosting and arranging these things, and I'll admit that it beats digging ditches for a living.

I'm actually on the cusp of leaving those hosting duties behind. I've been training a local musician known as AJ in Evolution to take my place. I produced an EP for him, he's well-liked by the community, he enjoys this type of work, and he's a fan of mine. The latter is important because it means that he's likely to respect the way I've run the event, which is what I believe has ultimately made it successful, while alternately really upsetting other people because they can't "game the system" – I don't allow people to sign up in advance. They have to be in the venue at 7:45 p.m. when the sign-up sheet goes out. They sign up in numerical order instead of for a specific time slot. And that's that. But people tend to complain about it, especially the comedians. The room isn't always hopping.

Still, I'm glad the show exists for the community because there are very talented people in this particular group of Orlando-based nerds, and I like that they have a stage to show off what they do. Without open mics, I couldn't have honed what I do as Marc With a C, so it's been nice to afford others the same opportunity on a level playing field without playing favorites or giving special billing/treatment to anyone. It'll also be nice to not do it anymore because I just don't have a great time arranging what amounts to a last-minute miniature festival over and over again. I'm happy that AJ is excited to take it over.

Now, coming in second for Best Singer-Songwriter? You'd think that's a major blow to my ego, right? Only second place?

Quite the opposite. First off, the lady that took first place, Kaleigh Baker, is wickedly talented, and she plays more shows locally than I do. People love her, and she works hard to make sure her talent is heard. Secondly, I didn't campaign at all. People voted for me of their own volition. Considering how weird some of the stuff I make up can be, the actions of those that "get it" genuinely mean something to me, whereas awards usually don't matter to me in the least. I've won awards through campaigning before, and it always felt a little dirty. The ones where I shoved the voting process down people's throats always felt tainted and unnatural. This year? It just happened on the heels of an album that wasn't really built to please anyone but myself, so I do feel quite honored.

There isn't really an awards ceremony associated with this. If you're lucky, the *Orlando Weekly* will send you a plaque, and sometimes they'll contact you and invite you to their party. The party usually happens on the same day the results are made public, so you can't really plan for it. It often takes place in a very large dance club. The music is far too loud, there's a limited-time open bar, and local restaurants cater it. I don't really drink anymore, so it basically feels like I won a sandwich. (That's not snarky, either; I really, really love sandwiches.)

I probably won't go, though. Both of my current band members are unavailable, and my wife has to teach a dance class, and I wouldn't enjoy going alone. I might just stay at home and listen to records. Or maybe I'll work on making more music.

I can't help but see the irony in being invited to a party for winning an award that wouldn't have been possible if I went to a lot of parties. But the sentiments of those that voted for me aren't lost on me. They wanted to show love for the things that I make, and they did so in force. That love is more than enough of a reward for me today.

8-10-15

I've spent the last three days at Orlando Nerd Fest, which is sort of the successor to Nerdapalooza. Not a replacement but a similar type of event. There's a pre-party and a post-party, both held at The Geek Easy. Both are daylong events featuring multiple acts. This year, the main portion took place at the Orlando Science Center. I was slated to go on at 4 p.m. on the main stage in the room with all the dinosaur stuff in it. Looks great on paper, but in actuality, I was playing a loud rock-and-roll set with Jim Myers and Emmit Dobbyn backing me up in a room full of kids, and we'd have to play one of the cleanest, most G-rated sets of my entire career. I'd done "toned down" shows before, but few that would have to be THIS tame. And of course, don't let the word "nerd" fool you. This is still a music festival: people show up to drink, meet a possible sexual partner, dance, and get rowdy (not listed in order of importance to the audience, of course).

We'd rehearsed our set very carefully and knew we'd have to leave out things like "You're My Princess," but for certain audience favorites, we'd merely modified the lyrics to fit the gig. The plan was to have some fun with it all, and take some jabs at the flat-out absurdity of what was expected of me; the guy best known for songs like "Motherfuckers Be Bullshittin'."

Scheduled at 3 p.m. on the secondary stage was Allie Goertz. Allie is one of my fave raves at the moment. She made a fantastic album under the name Cossbysweater – named before the nasty situation with Bill Cosby had become THE hot button issue, of course – and this was my first chance to work with her. Trouble was that we basically needed to be setting up in the other room while she played. As luck would have it, I had the chance to quickly meet her on her way to the stage and present her with a gift: an 8-track tape of Steely Dan's seminal *Can't Buy a Thrill*. We both have an unhealthy amount of love for that band, so I hoped it'd be a nice icebreaker. She seemed pretty happy, hugged me, and went onstage. I was lucky to see her first two songs, have enough time to run back to the main stage and soundcheck, and then come back for her closing numbers.

When we took the stage, we had a pretty okay crowd. Ended up playing to the same amount of people that most of the headliners would perform to. The trouble was that the stipulations about what could/couldn't be said during our set became increasingly clear as the show went on. Things seemed okay at first, opening with a rare reading of "Your New Voicemail Message" that went into "The Sometimes." We all had a good laugh as I introduced "Motherhuggers Be Bullmittens." In the breakdown of the aforementioned edited version of the tune, I held up a bottle of Bawls, which is an energy drink whose company was sponsoring the event. Promotional signs for the beverage were up everywhere in the room, so while holding a bottle of the sugary concoction, I did a mock commercial/call-and-response game with the audience where we chanted "I wanna dip my Bawls in it" back and forth to each other.

Apparently this greatly upset some parents in the room, and the staff of the science center were having a meeting near my merch table that Nicole overheard about whether should pull the plug on me. We kept going, though. And it's a good thing because, musically, as a band? We were catching fire that day, and I'm my own worst critic about this kind of thing. Also, we made the Bawls company very happy, as they sent a bunch of bottles up to the stage. Happy sponsor = happy event, as far as I'm concerned.

An audience member (later to be revealed as Twill Distilled) had shouted out

"BUKKAKE" as the answer to a question I'd asked. In saying, "No, not bukkake," I realized "OH MY GOD I JUST SAID BUKKAKE IN A ROOM WITH A BUNCH OF KIDS IN IT." I felt terrible, and even the host Dick Steel ran up to the stage to tell me that I couldn't say that word. It was a pure slip-up, plain and simple. Hell, you can probably get away with saying it on the radio, so it's not that big of a deal.

But again, more parents complained, and my feeling is that if you understand the meaning of the word "bukkake" and are still offended by it? That's your hangup. Still, kids were there, so I owned the fuck-up. I kept the chatter to a minimum for the rest of the set while we blazed through "Free Bird," "Terror Song," and an especially fiery take on "99 Pounds" by The Monkees. Even got an encore and played The Who's "Long Live Rock." We played especially well, and since we're on the brink of a break for a few months, I'm quite excited that it's the note we went out on.

People haven't stopped talking to me about Bawls and bukkake since. I sort of wish that'd gone a different way, because I'd rather that they noticed how hot the band was, but this isn't my first rodeo, so I'm shrugging it off for now.

Later in the evening, Professor Shyguy and I got to perform our duet of "Red Light Special" again. The premise never changes. We bring up a volunteer from the audience and serenade them with our chip-influenced take on the TLC classic until we get so caught up in each other's gaze that we break away and ended up grinding on each other and ignoring the volunteer-turned-victim entirely. It's pretty funny and always a blast to do. On this particular evening, we were honored by getting to sing it to Allie Goertz. She didn't really know what to expect, and her background in comedy really came in handy as Allie often stole the spotlight without the aid of a microphone, just silent reaction. Toward the end of the tune, I handed her a bottle of Bawls, which she swigged from, punctuating what had turned into a running joke through the festival's duration. Silent acting is a genuinely admirable skill, in my eyes.

Many had suggested that our musical threesome was the highlight of the festival, and I had so much fun doing the number that night that Shyguy and I had talked about possibly retiring the bit after that performance. It's going to be hard to top, really.

MC Chris closed out that night's show, and he dropped so many f-bombs that Orlando Nerd Fest should've charged attendees by each contract-breaking word. They could've donated the proceeds from this "swear jar" to a charity and raised enough money to cure a horrible disease forever from Chris's set alone.

I was so exhausted upon returning home that I'd literally fallen asleep while sitting straight up, waking up at two in the afternoon, missing a good portion of the third day's events. Age is creeping up on me. This baby face may not last forever.

8-16-15

I've spent the last week working on the vinyl reissue of *Life's So Hard*. The recent resurgence of love for vinyl has made it possible for me to reissue some of the more important albums in my catalog on their anniversaries. Of course, this rekindling of vinyl lust also means that all of the pressing plants around the world are backed up, so if you want to release something on a certain future date? You might as well just send it off for duplication when you have the money, art, and materials in order. Turnaround times are a myth at best now. The worst-case scenario is that the album is just sitting in my closet or storage space when I'm ready to start the promotional cycle.

The last release was a reissue of *This World Is Scary As Fuck*, and it'd hit #1 on Bandcamp's vinyl charts, which was pretty mind-blowing for me. It's a lo-fi album about depression, finding love, and trying to understand BDSM, but it was somehow selling better than it ever did in its first run. I'm the opposite of unhappy about it, but it's still puzzling!

There's a fair amount of reconstruction that goes into these vinyl reissues, too. Of course, many of the multi-tracks are long gone partly because I didn't know any better at the time and partly because if I didn't take away my option to pull a "George Lucas" later on, that's exactly what would have happened. I would have constantly changed things every time I got a new recording toy or something.

Instead, I have the two-track digital masters to work with. Often, these things are digitally clipped and out of phase because, again, I didn't know what the hell I was doing when these things were first made. I've found shortcuts to put things back into phase that doesn't take away all of the tones, but it leaves me with a sort of duophonic sound, though there are still semblances of stereo separation. It just took months of behind-the-scenes work.

There's also visual art to think about: Chris Zabriskie had made the art for CDs way back in the day, almost as an afterthought, because I'm not visually minded and don't consider the visual components until the last possible second most of the time. Often the images had to be stretched well past their peak resolution to even look right on a 5-inch cover, and now it's gotta look great on a canvas more than twice that size. He probably goes through the same things with the art as I do with the music from 10 years ago: we question the artistic choices of our youth and then make them as functional as we can, hoping it holds up. At least, I imagine it's like that. The two of us mostly get together to listen to prog albums in 5.1 as of late.

*Life's So Hard* was an exceptionally bright and out-of-phase monster of an album, and I liked getting the chance to deaden some of those excruciating highs. I don't have the best hearing in the world, but in those early albums, I'd often secretly master the albums with far too much treble so that they'd sound right for my wife's hearing disability.

It's true. And now the secret is out. Scandal.

I don't currently plan on actually putting this reissue out until around January, though waiting isn't my strong suit, so we'll see. And according to the plant I'm using now, it'll be here in October. So that's a lot of sitting on product, but you have to be really good at that sort of thing if you want to survive nowadays. I'd rather be putting out stuff constantly than to be nudged all the time about when my next thing is finally coming out.

And on Tuesday? I'll start laying down bits and pieces for the next album of new material. It's scary because I usually have the entire album mapped out before I start recording, even if it changes somewhat. This time? I have a lot of ideas and an unsure-if-this-will-work direction that may take years to fully realize. My intention is just to record all of the ideas and then decide what makes sense together later in a multi-year project. I think I've earned the right to seem a little aimless while I get the project going.

But it isn't aimless, really. I want to make a record, but for the first time in a long while, I don't really know what that record will be. I know what I'm hurdling toward in general, though. Best not to think about it too much right now. Because after I'm done listening to a Guided By Voices record, I'm taking the rest of the day off: my wife and I are planning on lying in bed all day and watching *The Simpsons*. If we get hungry, we'll order a pizza. We've both earned a day off.


8-22-15

I've done some tinkering with recordings for the next album, which I'll probably name *Unicorns Get More Bacon*. My daughter drew a picture with that title that's just begging to be an album cover, so that pretty much cinched it.

So far, I've been successful in completing the recording of "Anything But Plain" and "Long Distance Dedication." And yes, these are older songs, and I'm redoing them with the intention of placing them on the next album. The former never really ended up with a good enough home or a version that I'd call "definitive." The latter is one of the first songs I ever wrote for the Marc With a C project, and it has a special place in my heart for numerous reasons, but mostly I just really like the song. I think there's another direction that the song could go in besides the one you may have already heard.

But it's been tough going, internally. News broke this week that hackers dumped all of the information they'd stolen from Ashley Madison onto the internet for anyone to take. By the time anyone actually reads this, it'll be boring old news. Everyone will have long-formed opinions about whether people who had considered cheating on their spouses through the website deserve to be "named and shamed."

I don't know what the future holds for this information or what will come of it, but I can tell you that in my circle of friends – which are mostly just co-workers and people that listen to the songs that I make up, admittedly – it's been almost universal schadenfreude. It broke my heart and triggered a bit of a depressive cycle for me. Not because I have anything to do with the website but because I do not believe that a person should be able to infringe on the civil rights of another human being just because they disagree with their life choices.

If you're surprised people cheat on each other, I can't wait to show you how exciting rock and roll is.

It's my hope that everyone will look back and think, "Geez, we all did a really awful thing by invading the privacy of those people," but I don't know if that'll be the case. Right now? People are just having a blast looking up the email addresses of their friends and loved ones and making judgment calls.

Of course, here I am making judgment calls about that, so I don't suppose I have a leg to stand on. But I had assumed that we'd be further along by now. Like, we could have all just learned how to be nice. Or at least try being nice for an extended period of time, because what's the worst that can come of it?

Usually when I start recording an album, I'm pretty good at blocking everything else out and just quickly banging away and making serious progress upfront. This time? Not so much. Every little thing that goes wrong with Nerdy.FM, my family, or while watching a television show to blow off steam? Feels like a knife to my liver. I wish I could do something about it, but there's just a general malaise hanging over these sessions that I can't pinpoint. Maybe it'll go away as I get a little more warmed up.

Or maybe if I weren't seeing so many doctors all the time, I could focus. Sometimes my throat doesn't do what I tell it to, and that has increased in frequency for the last few years. Of course, no one has any idea what the deal is, or why I feel pain exactly where I do, but that's the deal with these appointments. Eliminate every possibility and hope for the best.

9-4-15

I'm spinning side three of George Harrison's *All Things Must Pass* as I'm drinking my cold coffee today. Last night, I listened to 11 rough-but-pretty-much-almost-finished mixes for the next album. Right now, there's 40 minutes of completed material in front of me, which is enough for an album, but it doesn't feel like an album yet. Plus, I have many other pieces that I want to touch up and record, and then I'll either be whittling those down to a single LP, or stretching them into a sprawling double LP.

I'm leaning toward the latter right now, mostly because I've never done a double album as a "new statement." Also, very little of the material that fits together intersects with the other songs thematically. My gut tells me to take a "white album" approach and just do a big and slightly incoherent double-disc set that's a bit of "Here's everything I do in one place." There are silly songs, very short songs, long and drawn out ballads, acoustic tunes, angry things, and then a fair amount of tracks that are really just me asking "what does this button do" and then seeing if it holds together.

I can also see a benefit to holding back some of the material to let this arty idea I've got all unfold over time. What's the rush?

I successfully handed the monthly open mic over to AJ and got to watch the show as a spectator for the first time. Right now feels like a very in between time for me, so I'm trying to keep my head on straight to make the most out of my creative time. That guessing game of not knowing whether I'll want to stand behind the work later on is palpable and real. I usually quell it by telling myself that people are free to make sense of it when I'm dead. What matters is the impetus to create. The end result is what matters to whoever might be reading this. My job is to act on the urge to make things and complete them.

9-18-15

Mixing this record has proved to be very challenging. Doing this type of thing yourself in 2015 means you have to straddle a line between mono summation of the bass frequencies for vinyl while keeping the highs crushed, but you also need it to be loud, bassy, wide and bright for digital consumption. Just when I get a mix right for one format, I have to completely turn my brain inside out and start all over from the opposite end of the spectrum. In these cases, my thoughts turn to wishing that someone else would do the heavy lifting.

I'd wanted to take this album at a much more relaxed pace than usual, but with the crazy turnaround times at vinyl pressing plants as of late? Not an option. This went from a record that I thought I'd complete around November to an album that needs to be done in a week and a half. Good thing I'd sliced and diced the running order to a single LP and let the rest play out over the next few years. Poor Katharine Miller. She's also feeling the time crunch as well, I'm sure, having to finish the visual layout with practically no time to do so.

So, overnight, with a few interesting guidelines from the pressing plant? This went from a let's-make-a-fun-album thing to an oh-my-squid-this-has-to-be-done-yesterday thing. And so I return to the state where I hardly sleep or eat. I wait out bathroom breaks as long as my bladder can stand it. I work until my ears are fatigued, and then I listen to the work on a different stereo to pretend to rest them. I snap at people constantly if bothered. And sometimes when I'm not bothered at all.

Tonight, I laid all of my problems on my daughter over dinner, just complaining about all of the doctors and album woes, but I'm reminded that what I should have capped it all off with was, "But I'm glad I'm here with you because you make things better." Instead, I complained and then waited for a response. She's friggin' 15. She shouldn't have to care about this at all. But that's how these recording holes go: I do my job, but I'm only ever thinking about it at the expense of those around me. I do this day in, day out, but people mostly want dick jokes out of me.

I played her what I thought were particularly problematic tracks in the car, and she thought they sounded fine. The moral of the story is that you shouldn't aspire to be an audiophile. Keep music fun for yourself. Let things just sound "fine."

Actually, that isn't the moral of the story. There is no moral right now.

These are the joyless parts. Sometimes you forget that other people will actually listen to this stuff. Or you hope that they will, at least.

9-24-15

On Monday, September 21 of the year 2015, I did something I haven't done in years: I admitted to myself that I was completely in the weeds with *Unicorns Get More Bacon*. I'd heard the mixes I was happy with around 300 times but was still not getting any closer to figuring out the missing "mastering glue." The thing that would make the album feel and sound whole.

A series of phone calls to my friends in production ensued, where I found myself looking for any suggestion at all that might help me get closer to what I was hearing in my head. This continued into the middle of the night and wound up with me actually making an international call to the Abbey Road studios mastering department.

This is the path that would lead to living-legend Mark Kramer mastering *Unicorns Get More Bacon*. Kramer is the man who mastered albums by Ween, was in The Butthole Surfers, and basically discovered Low. (I think.) When the chance dropped in my lap to work with him, I simply couldn't say no, but upon further reflection, this gentleman has mastered stuff by Daniel Johnston, so I was going to be on the more "normal" end of the spectrum compared to some of the projects that this dude has taken on.

Within a week, a finished master dropped out of the sky. This freed me up to do some work on the "Frankenstein's Bastard Daughter" seven-inch, which will accompany the pre-orders of the album, though no one will know that until it arrives in their hands. After hearing Kramer's work, I'm not sure I will want to go forward without working with him at this step in the process.

Now I begin the readjustment period. I get back to household duties, periodic rehearsals (by myself at this point), and interacting with people socially. I get to listen to music that isn't mine again. It's like I'm on vacation before the real work begins, but that's far from the truth. I return to performing onstage next week, and I still haven't found any new solutions for my throat. Maybe just general rest helped out? I don't know, as I haven't sung for any long stretches for a while now. I'll start rehearsing again this weekend, and then we'll just hope my throat has had a nice enough break to kind of work for a little while longer.

10-5-15

Just a few nights ago, I returned to performing onstage after a few months off. Really great gig opening for MC Lars and Random Encounter. It was an extra special show, as it was the last time that Careless would be fronting RE. The venue was packed to the gills, and it was an emotionally charged evening where there were simply no barriers between fans and performers.

The love sent my way during my opening slot really made me feel welcome. I premiered the title track from *Unicorns Get More Bacon*, Careless joined me for a rare reading of "Show Me How To Shine Shoes," and we had one of the loudest singalongs in recent memory during "Life's So Hard." Add in the general joy that occurs anytime MC Lars is in a room, and you've got one special evening – not to mention that Random Encounter pulled out all of the stops and put on one of the most amazing shows that may have ever taken place in the confines of Orlando.

The *Orlando Weekly* wrote up a fairly condescending piece about the show that amounted to "this isn't art, but whatever, they're selling tickets." To be fair, they did call my set "quite decent," so I got off a little easier than the other performers, but Random Encounter and I have consistently placed in (at least) the top 3 in our respective categories in that magazines popularity polls every year, no matter how hard the free magazine tries to make us seem like a passing fad.

And they might be on to something: nerdy music as a genre might be a fad, but some of the artists within those confines are just making music because they want to and would be doing it anyways even if we didn't belong to any genre at all. Hell, I don't even really fit in with "nerdy music" when you get down to the nuts and bolts of it. I just happen to get booked on those shows more often than not.

The club was slapped full of people that knew all of the words, and they seemed to read us loud and clear.

'm not mad about it, though. I've been more upset that a fan of mine passed away from an alleged heroin overdose. Her name was Madison, and she'd always smile and sing along loudly at my concerts. Always very kind to me and relentlessly supportive. It seems that her addiction got the best of her, and she died in her car, not to be found for an entire week. Broke my heart, so I went out and bought a bunch of toys for the bunnies, the cutest version of retail therapy I could come up with. I'll feel the sting of Madison's passing long after the critical drama passes. Haven't seen her for a few years, and now I'll never see her again. Songs like "Love My Little Squiddy" seemed to get her mind off of her troubles for a little while. I'm glad that I made a troubled soul happy sometimes.

10-14-15

The good thing about making records is that it never becomes predictable. The bad thing about making records is that my anxiety prefers a certain level of predictability.

10-24-15

Last night, I did the first of four shows opening for the local *Rocky Horror* shadow cast, The Rich Weirdoes. These shows in movie theaters are always a little odd. The benefits are that you have a captive audience of at least 400 people that can't go anywhere. You are their focal point and the only entertainment available. The bad part is that they came to see something that is not you, and they bought props at the door to throw during the film.

How'd I end up opening for movies, you ask? Simpler than you'd think: The Rich Weirdoes were celebrating their first anniversary, and they wanted a musical guest to open to celebrate. Someone – not sure who – brought up my name and mentioned that I did *Shock Treatment* covers sometimes. This was around 2003. The people that I remember being in charge at that time were Ofir and Keely. They brought me in, believed in me, and gave me an audience sight-unseen. It went well enough that a yearly Orlando tradition was born.

This was the 12th or so year I've done these gigs, As usual, the times for being able to get into the theater changed every few hours. This is tough because I have to park in what is in actuality the world's largest parking garage, and then push two dollies full of my PA, merch, and other necessities through theme park crowds, though some nights I'm lucky enough that my wife comes along to help out. That may not sound like much, but I'd invite you try it sometime and get back to me. Then I have to actually be admitted into the theater in enough time to set up my stuff. Again, doesn't sound like much, but getting a movie theater to understand that the functional needs of a musician are different than that of a patron is always an ordeal. And of course, no matter what you do, you'll never get it sounding right – those theaters are built to absorb sound. You can't rely on any reflective surfaces, so by the time the audience enters the building, they absorb more sound, and you end up producing a distorted mess. Never mind that you were attempting a soundcheck while an entire stage was built around you.

The above reads as whiny, I know. I love doing those shows, but I cannot pretend that it isn't a total headache. The setting up/getting into the venue part is the drag. Performing is a blast. Though last night's show was almost a catastrophe. A mixture between a frazzled director and a non-compliant theater staff made the audience 40 minutes late to enter and sit down. Many had gone and asked for refunds before even being allowed to come inside. And when they entered? I'm the first face they were going to see. Not the lips that open that picture show they love so well. I expected a furious audience.

I was happily wrong. I did have to chop off a song ("Liana") in the interest of time, but they were my favorite kind of Rocky audience, and that is the type that came to take in the spectacle, not to create it. It's true that the film is an interactive experience, but I enjoy when the audience doesn't fully know how the Weirdoes do it, and sort of sit back, take it all in, and join in when prompted.

They listened, seemed to really like the new song I opened with (phew), joined in with the call and response parts of "Motherfuckers," clapped and laughed in all of the right places. No one threw anything at me. Merch sales were nice afterward. One particular fan was there who really likes me – she has a tattoo on her ankle of the title of my song "Anything But Plain." Bit of a megafan. Every time she comes to a show, we go through the same thing: she looks over my merch table and gloatingly proclaims, "Ha, I already have all of this stuff." This time, I came prepared with the first vinyl copy of *Life's So Hard* for sale, put aside especially for her. She was very excited and surprised.

If they could all be like tonight, they'd be the best run of Rocky gigs I've ever done. Three more to go.


11-3-15

The last of The Rich Weirdoes shows wrapped up a few days ago. Leslie from Claire and The Potatoes was even there on the next to last night, though I didn't know that until afterward. Unfortunately, we weren't able to do much hanging out, but hopefully we'll make time for that next time she's in town. She still has family here, so it probably won't be long until she returns. The last few shows were good. Hopeful about the future.

Major family stuff started going down in the last few days, and it all has me pretty shaken. Had to cancel some things and get "off the grid." Still have to do tomorrow's rehearsal, but before and after that, I get to go back to being the sort of gatekeeper of the familial drama. Nearly impossible to concentrate on anything at all.

## 11-12-15

Up to my ears in *Life's So Hard* mail. It's the top-selling pop vinyl for the week on Bandcamp now. Of course, I completely ran out of cardboard mailers, so now people are going to have to wait a few extra days for their stuff to arrive. I hate that, but I thought I was sufficiently stocked up. Simply wasn't prepared for this glut of attention. Especially since this time I haven't done any press whatsoever.

At the band's last rehearsal, we went through stuff that hasn't been played in years, namely "Laura, I Need Medicine" and "Well Fucked Sailor." I haven't played the latter for about 10 years at least, so the band is about as familiar with it as I am. The latter is so personal, but it's personal for the individual I used to be. The good part about singing the song now is that I'm doing so as a person that doesn't relate to any of the lyrics anymore, and I'm singing it for those few people in the audience that might need to hear it. This is brand new territory for me. Usually once a song ages past a certain point, I just retire them altogether. Resuscitating older material in a "song, not the singer" manner is foreign land, and I hope it comes off that way in concert. I'd hate to sing the line "attracted to the most fucked up girl / In any given room" and have a bunch of eyes dart to Nicole as if there's trouble in paradise or something. Nicole is the bulk of the reason I don't relate to the song anymore, and she saved me from being the miserable sod that I truly was in those first few years of Marc With a C.

I'd write here about how impressed I am with my current band, but I don't know how to put it into words. I tell them after particularly good run-throughs of songs "good job," and I'm afraid I come off like a boss giving kudos. Instead, I'm doing it because it's only slightly more appropriate than bursting into spontaneous applause at the end of every tune.

11-22-15

I'm not really prone to migraines, though they run in my family. Monday, I got one so severe that during practice, I wouldn't have made it through if Jim's wife hadn't opened her medicine cabinet to me, and I hadn't also worn the thickest earplugs known to modern civilization. All work has ceased. Last night was spent in the emergency room, after some of my motor skills had stopped functioning properly.

They shot me up with Reglan. The combination made my body twitch and convulse. In comparison, the headache was livable. I begged to be let go. They told me things that sounded like, "You have a broken bone from constant sinus infections" but proceeded to give me a useless drug for the migraine. The twitching continued through the night, as I fell on a pile of my own sealed records, making them unsaleable. I can hardly control my body right now.

I come from roughly six generations of migraine sufferers. Mine only showed up this year. I've seen the fights my family have gone through to have their symptoms taken seriously. It's all but killed some of them. I now know why they couldn't describe it to me. It's as if your body and brain have parted company, but you look capable to the outside world. I'm not mincing words: I'm not suicidal, but this makes me want to die. It wasn't far off from what the beginning of a stroke might feel like. Terrifying.

First CD print for *Unicorns Get More Bacon* came in – looks good. Wish I could concentrate on it more.

12-2-15

I have not slept well for the last three days or so, which really does a number on my head. With the hospital visits and such, I have to be really careful about this sort of thing. Unfortunately, Meatwad doesn't know that. He's a Chihuahua. It's in his nature to bark at everything, even those things that don't exist. I'd only really been asleep for about three hours. Before that I was just lying there and pretending to do it, trying to show my body how one might go about resting, but the mailman came. Meatwad wasn't having it.

He seems to try to tell these people: "My dad has real trouble sleeping, and if you don't pipe down, all 6 pounds of me is going to have to teach you a lesson. To further my point, I will now yell at you for the next 20 minutes until

I can be assured that we can all get some goddamn peace and quiet around here."

Wife is at the doctor, took all the phones in the house with her. Partly as a preemptive measure, making sure that nothing has a chance of setting Meatwad off, but also in case vital prescriptions are filled while she's out, and bless her heart, she wants to pick them up for me because she thinks I am sleeping. It's 10:44 a.m. I'm usually not up this early unless someone has either just been born, has just died, or I haven't been to sleep yet.

Emmit and Jim are getting scarily good as a rhythm section. If there's ever an upset between us as a trio, I think they could do really well to just replace me and get on with it (with different songs, of course). Importantly, I've never felt such camaraderie with a backing band. I feel like we're on the same page, we all like the songs, and we all understand our common role: serve the song. I don't think this has ever taken place for me!

Mentioned a crazy idea to Jim that I'd been toying with, provisionally called Olivia and The Potatoes. Basically, Claire's daughter would try her hand at rock and roll, stealing her mom's backing band and living in her mom's shadow. The Claire and The Potatoes concept itself was so deeply rooted in rock and roll cliché that a sequel would only make sense if we took it to unfathomable extremes. He agreed with me that it sounds interesting on paper, but we wouldn't want to make Leslie feel unimportant. It's a fun idea, but ultimately, our time could be better spent elsewhere.

(Importantly, this "Olivia?" I'm not saying that she's the "Olivia" in the song "Olivia Rules Everything Around Me," just that it was *a possible path* that we could follow, if we chose to do so. I've heard plenty of guesses about who/ what Olivia supposedly represents in said song, and you're all wrong. Sorry.)

But you've got to admit, having Claire's daughter sing "I Wanna Be Your Shadow"? Meta beyond words. I refuse to entertain the idea further until I have some songs written that would be worth the concept. I'm not jumping at that chance. I want to do at least two more Marc With a C records first to complete what I've begun with *Unicorns Get More Bacon*. Right now, I'm just having a good time playing with these two people, and I'm really excited about the album for 2016. For once I'm just going to enjoy that and not think too far past those events.

Otherwise, I'm liable to actually give myself that stroke I thought I was having.

12-4-15

I am so pregnant with album that it hurts. Emotionally, though. No physical pain.

I can't imagine that this phenomenon is specific only to me. Try to imagine all the hurry-up-and-wait that it takes to do an album "the right way" in 2015, or rather, 2016. Oh sure, you could release each song as you come up with it, and then you could compile them all at the end of the process into a saleable whole – and that works for some people – but as a creator that still thinks in terms of records? Doesn't work at all for me.

I come up with ideas that I think are really good and hope that others will agree with me. I have to wait months to find out, though. And once it finally is unleashed to the small pockets of the world where Marc With a C songs are played, I have to wait for them to sink in. By the time that happens? Well, truthfully, I might be in the middle of another "pregnant with album" scenario. Though that may not be terribly likely.

Haven't been writing as many songs lately. Came up with some lyrics, but it was so close to the *Unicorns* vibe and the songs I'm holding onto that I stopped short. And I don't have any other ideas gnawing at me to express at the moment besides furthering the narrative that I began on the newest record. A couple of zygotes of ideas, but nothing substantial enough to get a whole tune out of – and that's saying something, because I love to explore minutia. It isn't writer's block, though. It's what happens when I am pregnant with album. In the stage where I can hear it, hold it, but can't show it off. My creative juices stop flowing completely until I can publish the baby pictures, as it were.

Plenty of stuff to tackle, if I wanted to. Scott Weiland died last night, there have been more mass shootings than days in this particular calendar year, and my personal life has seen better days (wife and daughter excluded). But I don't want to touch on it. I'm trying to keep the new album fresh in my frontal lobe and trying to balance knowing the back catalog like the back of my hand for the upcoming shows.

Today, I did some work in giving Jim his Christmas present: I'm getting parts of the Milk Carton Superstars discography published on streaming sites for him, with his blessing. Emmit's present was easy: I got him the new Frank Zappa DVD, the one shot at the Roxy in 1974. I don't know what to get anyone else right now. I tend to give people musical gifts because that's how I think, but I'm afraid that by the age of 37, I should have grown the ability to consider what people genuinely love and want that doesn't quite speak to my sensibilities. I'll keep trying.

12-9-15

Throat is absolutely on fire. Wanted to go out tonight to see Larry Fulford's *Life's A Gift* show, but being in public means talking to people. I need to conserve my voice for the upcoming shows. Got really croaky during last night's rehearsal, and I'm kind of surprised that I held up.

Actually, if I'm telling the whole truth, before rehearsal, I took a prescribed non-narcotic-but-still-pretty-addictive-anyways painkiller for my throat and some of the "real deal" Sudafed? And then I just felt like a rubber band. I know how that reads: "Sudafed, eh? Wuss." But seriously, that stuff reacts with me like I assume crystal meth makes other people feel. I only take it in extreme cases of sinus pressure, and I was feeling pretty rotten yesterday. So this Sudafed makes me feel super speedy, and the painkiller does relax me just a touch. But when they were combined, I felt energetic and invincible, but I was ultimately just high at rehearsal. I should feel guilty about that, but based on how my throat feels the day after? Those drugs were necessary. I'll just repeat the process today while I heal and shut the fuck up.

Got some Iron Maiden in my headphones. Got some excitement brewin' for getting back to shows. Looking like everything is on track for the rest of the shipment of the new album to reach me before the end of the month. Today is a good day despite feeling like I gargled broken glass.

I don't get it. I can do warmups and can sing from my diaphragm. I can pace the set so I'm slowly warming up throughout the night, gorge myself on room temperature water for maximum throat lubrication, do everything exactly as the professionals tell me to do them, and I'm still unable to do my job without some serious pain. I've been singing my entire life, really. This is still a relatively new development that I just can't wrap my head around.

Guess I'll keep singing whenever I can while I still can. At this rate, there's just a few years to go before I can't hide this anymore. I hope it's not noticeable to audiences. I don't have a typical voice anyways, so maybe that's enough to throw them off the scent of something being wrong.

12-13-15

Last night was the annual holiday show. Good room. Not slam-packed, but most seats were filled. A lot more hecklers than I've had in recent years, but I think that I did okay at brushing them off. The music started at 8:20, and we didn't finish until around midnight. Three short set breaks, but otherwise continuous music. My throat is on fire. Well, not my throat, but really more the muscles around it. Didn't really start giving me trouble until the encores. Partially due to having to have my voice really low in the monitors to prevent feedback, and possibly also due to the fact that I was singing for much longer than human beings are probably meant to at one stretch.

I always feel very guilty at these shows. I'm juggling putting on a good show, conserving my voice, and trying to be friendly to everyone that wants to chat. And I really do want to chat with everyone, but sometimes time won't allow for that, so I end up hiding to save my voice or looking as if I'm playing favorites with the few folks I do speak to. Last night, one longtime fan was heading right for me as soon as we were done with the last encore, but my throat had almost swollen shut, so while making eye contact, I ducked out of the room. To her, it must have seemed like the ultimate dick move. I'll send her a letter later to let her know it was self-preservation.

Emmit and Jim were great. I wish I could afford to have them at every gig. We've come such a long way in a short amount of time, and I feel like if we can keep this lineup together, we'll be a pretty unstoppable rock band. Though I'm primarily known as a solo act, my heart has always been immersed in rock and roll, despite my increasing feeling that genres are meaningless. I think that with all of the windmills and rock poses I tend to do onstage, that may have been clear, but some might be surprised. I think sometimes people assume I'm doing them ironically.

Onstage last night, I could hear every bum note. Every dropped beat. Every time I went out of tune. Right now I'm reviewing last night's show on headphones, and I think that it all melded together to make for "our sound." And like Roger Daltrey once said? Rock is a bum note and a bead of sweat. I certainly had us taken care of in the sweat department, and I know that I dropped quite a few out-of-tune moments into the mix.

These marathon shows are such an endurance test, and Jim and Emmit were more than up to the task. I can't express my elation. After years of false starts, I'm in the band I'd always secretly hoped to have. A band full of best friends that really get the dynamics of a rock show, with everyone mastering and understanding their role. I bring in the music and control the albums, but these guys are fans of those things, so they help me wade through it all to make the best show we possibly can. There have been ups and downs, but right now,

I'm happy doing what I do, and I truly love everyone in the organization.

On a more personal note, everyone who spoke to me last night kept saying, "You look good." I've been replying with "YOU look good, too!" I'm doing that for two reasons:

- I'm not really used to hearing that.

- They do look good.

The things I've changed about my lifestyle are pretty simple. I don't smoke tobacco anymore, and I don't drink. Well, once every six months or so I might have one beer as a celebratory thing, but that's it. I suppose I also am not eating like a jerk anymore. Not much fast food or what have you. Plus, I'm just not eating unless it's absolutely necessary. Most days, I'll subsist on a protein bar or two, or some trail mix, and I'll end the day with a nice and nourishing dinner. It's not really something I've set out to do, it's just how things worked out.

My wife keeps insisting that we should go and buy lots of new clothes, since I look like a bag lady in these rags that are clearly too big for me. But after dropping nearly 70 pounds in two years, there's a part of me that just keeps thinking it'll all come back one day. Then I'd feel like a total asshole. If we went and spent a few hundred on new clothes, and then I put the weight back on? Oh man, what a terrible pill to swallow. I'd rather wear the too-big clothing and spend the money on records instead — both for listening purposes and future releases.

Since I plan releases very far in advance, I'm currently considering devoting 2016 to the promotion of *Unicorns Get More Bacon*, eschewing the "anniversary cycle" for how I've been releasing the older albums on vinyl and just putting out both *Linda Lovelace For President* and *Losing Salt* in 2017 as a stop gap while I work on the following albums of new material. The completist in me sort of wants to reissue *Human Slushy* on vinyl, but the part of me that doesn't love the album isn't interested. It'd take a lot of work to make that album work on wax, and it isn't something I want to spend a few months concentrating on. All we have are two-track masters that are already heavily compressed. We don't have much wiggle room to do pretty much anything with the sound, so it seems pointless. But I can't argue with the fact that I'd feel pretty fulfilled to be able to point to a row of my complete discography of full original vinyl albums on my shelf.

I'm really just thinking in text right now while I wait for a file to render. Glad I haven't had to speak today. Next show is on Tuesday, and that's just a simple half-hour gig, so I think I'll be on par for that. Should probably start thinking about the setlist for the gig, but who knows? Maybe I'll just go up and wing it. Haven't done that in quite some time.

Got an offer for a new year's eve show out of state, but they've been very slow with communication, and I don't think I can commit based on the notice they're giving me, let alone promote. Nicole has a private event going on that night. There's a superstition that whatever you're doing at the stroke of midnight into the new year represents what's to come the following year. I've never really seen that to be true, but if it is? At this rate, my new year will be rung in by my wife doing all kinds of amazing stuff while I sit at home alone listening to records.

Maybe that's not so bad. She's definitely the more talented one in this couple.


12-18-15

Doesn't look like a New Year's Eve show is going to happen, which makes the gig I played on Tuesday the last show of the year. It was just as I expected: playing a show in the courtyard of a sex resort. Folks hardly even noticed that I was on, and I just played for my contracted amount of time. You'd think I'm pretty hard to ignore, but if people just want to drink and talk, I don't really have the fight in me to dissuade them right now. I think I played well considering few were listening, and that the setup has all of the speakers so far away from you that there's a 3-second delay between you playing something and the audience hearing it. I got paid, kids got presents donated for Christmas, and people came to a sex resort and got drunk. I think it was successful overall, if not artistically so. Voice held up, though.

Last night, I went with Nicole and Juliana to see a private early screening of *The Force Awakens*. Nicole wept. I smiled for 130 minutes straight, and all Juliana could say for nearly half an hour afterward was, "That was awesome." I'd say that the filmmakers did their job pretty well.

Also received my tickets for Duran Duran in the mail today. This has been a good week for 5-year-old Marc. Thirty-seven-year-old Marc is very happy as well. Nothing wrong with nostalgia when it leaves you walking on air for a few days, if you ask me. And you did, because you're reading this.

1-1-16

I spent New Year's Eve cleaning the house while Nicole went out and showed off her increasingly amazing lyra skills. Saw some video of her show and have only now been able to pry my jaw off of the floor. Meanwhile, I made the house so spotless that every single part of my body aches today.

This is the day where everyone takes to their social media accounts and either talks about how hungover they are, or their hopes for the future, or why the previous year was good or the opposite of good. I used mine to promote that I'm having a 15% off sale on all of my merchandise. Truthfully, I can't make sense of years too well. I mark time by album cycles.

For no good reason, I was thinking about my first band today. Not the high school one I talked about early on. Actually, there was one before that where a bassist and I ripped off Black Sabbath songs. We weren't good. And before that was The Past, a duo where I played second banana to a pretty misogynistic guy who wanted to be Robert Smith but refused to learn how to play his keyboard. But the one I'm thinking about came way before any of those.

I was around 8 or 9 years old. I wasn't yet at the age where legal guardians were cool with me coming home and bumming around the house all by myself, though I would have behaved. Hardly had any friends, and none of my parent's stuff interested me besides the food and records. So, each day after school, I'd be sent off to Karen's house. Karen was a lady in her early 20s who seemed to embody heterosexual relationships in the '80s: she married a guy named Milton who knocked her up, and there didn't seem to be any real love between them. She was rather plain and very sweet, and he was a chubby and somewhat slow dude that would forget that kids were in the house, so he'd fall asleep in less than pants quite often. Like many ladies of the time, she was obsessed with *Dirty Dancing*. Beyond that, she basically didn't keep up with popular culture unless a topic was brought up on a sensationalist afternoon talk show. And to make ends meet? She'd babysit. And she didn't interact with us all that much. Not like we were neglected, we just did our thing while she watched television in the living room.

One of the kids she babysat was a gal named Cassie. She came from a family that appeared to be similar to that of Karen's, though I believe that there was much more love in their house. We didn't have very much in common besides two things: we were about the same age, and we loved The Monkees. I know that it may be hard for some of you to believe, but in the mid-'80s, The Monkees had a massive resurgence in popularity. MTV ran reruns of the show constantly, and Davy, Micky, and Peter had reunited to do numerous sold-out stadium tours. I was totally swept up in the second wave of Monkeemania, and while I enjoyed the show just fine, my obsession leaned towards their music. I still stand by the unpopular opinion that their recorded catalog between 1966 and 1970 might be the finest pop output of all time.

Cassie and I loved The Monkees so much that it was practically all we talked about, and we were reminded by adults who didn't take them seriously that "they didn't play their instruments." I was too young to argue that The Beach Boys didn't actually fucking play on *Pet Sounds* either, but it's a moot point (and only even semi-accurate for the first two albums of their original nine-LP run). We figured that if The Monkees could be a band that simply pretended to play instruments and sang? We could do it as well.

We dubbed ourselves Thing Of The Past, which is still a really fucking good band name. Cassie had an acoustic guitar, I had a toy keyboard, and we did gigs all over our neighborhood. And by gigs, I mean we'd pick a corner, pretend to play and sing completely made-up songs at the top of our lungs. Cassie had a knack for the made-up melodies, and I still get this one line stuck in my head often: "Blue / Blue / Is there something to do / Blue / Blue / How about you?" We'd record all of these shows on my Walkman with the built-in microphone and call them "albums."

Of course, these tapes are long gone now, but just today I was realizing that it was the true origin of Marc With a C. Can't play? Keep going anyways. Don't have a song? Just make one up. No studio? Who cares, just capture the sound and worry about the presentation later.

I couldn't play drums at all when I did the *This World Is Scary As Fuck* album around 2005, but I kept bashing away until I came up with a beat that wouldn't be too noticeably bad when you put some guitars and vocals on top of it.

Cassie and I never really questioned what we were doing. The band "broke up" when I moved yet again. I'm willing to bet dollars to donuts that if you put us together in a room now and tried to get us to make something that pure and unpretentious again, we'd fail miserably. There'd be pride to deal with, worry over how our friends and relatives would perceive us, and who knows if we'd even get along?

What I'm getting at is that it'd be unlikely to work while "adulting." But I think that this year I'm going to strive to regain that purity in my songwriting and musical ethos. At least somewhat. It's the complete opposite of what everyone else is doing at the moment, but it's probably the happiest I ever was when making music. The less fucks you give, the more fun the songs are.

Well, sometimes. Now I have this new type of happiness when I've, say, performed "Music Can Heal" very well and gotten a lot of applause for it.

Maybe I can find a cozy place right between the two. Being really good at purity in writing? Hah, seems like a weird thing to strive for.

I'm probably talking out of my ass, anyways. How in the living fuck am I supposed to measure purity, anyways?

1-12-16

Yesterday, the band played at the wedding of two fans. They had hired me just to do a long version of the Marc With a C "rock show." The gig took place in the middle of nowhere, literally. A small town in the woods called Paisley. We played for about two hours. Some liked us, some did not. But every time the show felt like going through the motions, I'd see the bride happily singing along to every song, and that'd give me a much needed jolt of energy.

I think that the band played fairly well under the circumstances. It was below 40 degrees, and we were outdoors. Your fingers don't really work properly, and you lose a lot of dexterity in that type of weather. I think Jim and Emmit did a great job, but we were all battling the elements to play decently. It was two days' worth of work for an okay paycheck, but ultimately? When the bride came to us afterward and gushed about how blown away she was to have her "favorite" playing at her wedding? That's what it was all about. Made my night, and despite my voice really giving me trouble in the dry cold air, I felt electrified internally.

An interesting moment came during "Life's So Hard." The second verse is basically a parody of melodramatic teenage journals and ends with the line "I denounce God." As the lyric approached, I realized that the holy man that had married the couple was standing right in front of me and listening. Now, I've made my feelings on religion/spirituality pretty clear, but my mind started racing. I was thinking, Come on Marc, you cannot look this pastor in the face and make a mockery out of his life's work for a cheap laugh. I quickly changed the line to "I denounce MOM," as Emmit and Jim cracked up behind me, able to watch my entire thought process unfolding before their eyes.

Came home to see that the bonus seven-inch that secretly goes out with pre-orders of *Unicorns Get More Bacon* had arrived. Unfortunately, the plant pressed it at 33 RPM, and I'd specifically ordered it at 45 RPM. This just means that the fidelity is not all that it could be, but as I intend to announce the pre-order next week, there is simply not enough time to recut the entire run. I don't suppose that anyone can really complain about it, since it's just a fun surprise that they'll be receiving with the album. On the other hand, the actual LPs for *Unicorns Get More Bacon* did show up, and they look and sound fantastic. Really proud of it. Katharine really outdid herself as far as making this one an eye popper.

Physically? I feel completely run down after the hurry-up-and-wait of the last two days. The best part for me was spending so much time with Emmit. Really love that guy, and I don't have many close male friends, so our growing bond really does mean the world to me. Also, being so inundated with work meant that I was unable to really dwell on the death of David Bowie, which is for the best. Everyone is writing eulogies to him right now, and I don't suppose that anything I have to say would be all that important. I love his art, and I have nearly everything he'd ever released. I was lucky to see him in a club that held less than a thousand people in 1997, which just happened to be the longest concert he'd ever perform. I mourn for his loved ones and the loss they are dealing with, but he had given me so much art and inspiration that I couldn't possibly ask for more from him. I just hope that my gratitude for his gift is clear.

1-15-16

After reviewing some video for a possible upcoming YouTube series, I've noticed that I'm coming off very short with people lately. I think I seem cold, sarcastic, and as if I can't be bothered to talk to them. This was a complete surprise to me, especially when looking at footage from rehearsals because I'm so thrilled to be around Jim and Emmit.

The only thing that I can think of that might trigger these reactions in me is a massive bout of anxiety I'm always experiencing, knowing that time is always limited, and you have to make the best of "now," no matter what the circumstances of "now" happen to be. I'm often rushing so I can do so much more with "now" than I had initially hoped. And then I'm reminded that I'm mortal, and I get a bit mentally and externally dour.

It's an accident. I love nearly everyone I'm around all of the time. Whoever happens to read this in the future? It's not you, it's me. I'll try harder to be nicer.

1-21-16

A lot of good things happened this week. The pre-order of *Unicorns Get More Bacon* went to #1 on the Bandcamp vinyl pop chart despite some awful issues with PayPal tacking on extra shipping fees all willy-nilly. I got to see my buddy Steve Poltz (which still reads weirdly to me, since I grew up idolizing him). Everyone seems to be giving the new music a positive reception.

Today, I woke up to an email from Katharine wondering why I hadn't credited her for the artwork on every single press blast. I had sort of assumed when she took her last name off the artwork, made herself impossible to tag on Facebook, and told me she was bowing out of design that she didn't want that kind of attention. Then I noticed that she'd been subtweeting about me all week, and now I feel absolutely devastated that I could make her feel "less than."

All the good stuff doesn't even percolate for me because I unintentionally hurt one of my favorite people on the planet. It's shit like this that makes me want to quit completely. Playing songs for people is nice, but hurting the ones I care about isn't worth it. It's taken everything in me to not do drastic and stupid things. Felt the immediate pangs of a depressive cycle. Have to try to ignore it. Have to right my wrongs and continue doing promo/press work even though I hurt a friend and don't deserve positive attention right now.

1-26-16

This is tough. I know I'm supposed to be chronicling my day-to-day experiences as a DIY musician in a no-holds-barred sort of way here, but I also know that I can't name names when it comes to really incriminating things. Or rather, I'm completely able, but it isn't really the right thing to do. So when I approach this current situation with kid gloves, please understand that it hurts me to even have to broach the topic, and also that I can't just talk about the whole thing outright.

The marketing strategy for *Unicorns Get More Bacon* isn't terribly complicated. I know many people currently just want MP3s to slap on their phone, but I feel that everyone involved has made a really cool piece of art that deserves to be appreciated as a physical piece. So, we opened the pre-orders early, where, yes, if you buy the CD or vinyl, you get an immediate download. I didn't want to do it this way initially, but a few experiences during the pre-sale for *Exactly Where I Am* made me feel that this was the right move. Every time I send out a download code, it's done in an email that all but begs for people not to share the album until the street date. After that? I don't really care. I just want people to have the chance to experience this as a physical object before reducing it to a pile of ones and zeroes. Those are "the artist's wishes" — just wait like five more weeks to share it, but after that, go nuts.

This backfired last night when a musician from a fellow nerd rock band decided to share the album in full in multiple formats on a well-regarded private torrent tracker. When I caught him and explained how he'd just given my marketing strategy a major handicap, he became very apologetic, and he admitted he has made a mistake. I refuse to go any further with our relationship – either personal or professional – until he can manage to get the files removed. They've only been shared around 20 times, and the damage may have been done, but the slap in the face being undone would move mountains for me emotionally, and I'd be able to at least consider forgiveness.

I know that in 2016 nothing is sacred online. Everything is fair game to be shared and probably will be. That's not news to me. Here's why it hurts so much:

At one point, this person had some very, very exclusive demos by a Band That Might Be Huge. He saw people in that fandom acting quite elite because they possessed recordings that others did not, and it represented some imaginary class system for him, so he took it upon himself to "liberate" said recordings. But not before he had two separate long conversations with me about the implications. I stressed that the artist had specifically requested that these particular recordings were not spread, and if he was a fan, he might consider trying to respect this group as human beings with feelings. But when we had our second conversation on Skype about it while I tried to dissuade him? I saw a sly smile. He seemed to feel power in being able to "liberate" something. There was a sense of entitlement that the music should be shared: if it's good enough for a few folks to hear, it's worthy of being heard by everyone. I felt kind of curious as to why I was even asked as, like, an arbiter of morality or something? But in that conversation, I made clear to him that I couldn't care less if someone "leaks" my music, but only after it is available to the general public at large. Because really, if such a thing were to happen, at my level? It wouldn't drive sales at all but rather cut my throat.

That's the part that hurts the most: if some jerk in Wyoming shares the album without knowing my sales strategy, I can't really be upset or surprised. That's how things go right now most times. This was a friend, someone I had shared secrets and laughs with, and a person that I was beginning to consider as one of my best friends. He's apologizing profusely and trying to get back into my good graces while the album continues to spread. I don't know that I can trust him again just yet. He didn't see a problem until I found out about it on my own and — don't you hate when that happens?

I've lost far more friends than I've made in this line of work.

On the opposite side of things, I seem to have done enough to ease Katharine's anger towards me. And thankfully, tonight I'll get back to work with the band so I'll have distractions from the heartbreak. This means I'll be spending the bulk of the afternoon writing chord charts of the new songs for Emmit. I'm glad I have something to do beyond sitting and stewing. Maybe today will exhaust me to the point where I'll sleep tonight for more than four and a half hours at a stretch? That'd be nice. Hard to face this stuff without much rest to speak of.

1-30-16

Nice to be home and relaxing. Right now I'm sipping on some just-in-case-I-need-it kombucha and enjoying a live album called *595* by Karate.

The leak of my new album seems to have been stopped, though the leaker was threatening suicide apparently. His girlfriend was frantically messaging me about how he'd cut himself up after I'd gotten mad at him. Had to break my silence, call him, and beg him not to self-harm. It was hairy, especially since it coincided with an interview that I was supposed to be doing for The Nerd Groove. Unfortunately, I couldn't drive out to do that interview in person because I'd woken up with something in my left eye that I couldn't remove. Said eye kept watering and as such? Driving was an impossibility. Had to settle for doing the interview via Skype and hoping it'd turn out okay while also being concerned about the well-being of someone who had wronged me. He leaked the record before the release date, and that was wrong, but he didn't deserve to friggin' die over it. He scared the living hell out of me. At the end of the day, these are just pop songs, and a life was in the balance because I got mad and wouldn't talk to the dude. I suggested to his girlfriend that they look into serious professional help because the next time I get involved in that kind of situation, I'm calling the police.

I'm aware that the last paragraph was a total jumble, but it's actually more coherent than actually trying to juggle self-care, keeping someone from hurting themselves from several states away and also trying to "turn on" the Marc With a C personality for a podcast interview. The best news is that he lived, the interview was probably okay, and my eye was fine after a long nap.

Tonight I did an interview on WPRK FM with Christopher LeBrane. I just like that guy a lot. We have such similar taste in music and art that I wish he'd just come over and listen to records with me some time. But doing the appearance was fun despite not feeling so hot physically. He always rolls out the red carpet for me. We played radio edits of a few songs from the new album, and I performed "Celebutantes" and "Pinball Wizard" live in the studio. Made sure to give as much credit as possible to Katharine and video-auteur Tim Labonte for their help in making the visual side of the album what it is. Probably bent over a little too backward and sounded like I was overcompensating. Which I was, of course.

Tomorrow is an interview for Fandomania. I am excited for this one because Chad is a big fan of what I do, and I think he really likes the album. He's always got interesting questions for me because he really, really listens. He'd actually written a review of *Popular Music* that nailed the album in ways that I would have never been able to describe on my own. My interest level in his reading of the new album is very high. And I just like him in general.

Then we've got a house guest coming to stay for a bit. It's our friend Amialya, and she's coming down from Washington D.C. to hang out for a few days. I like her a lot, and she's one of Nicole's closest pals. And Nicole is feeling extra low and stressed lately. Her job is sucking the life right out of her with unrealistic expectations, and she deserves/needs a few days to sort of relax and hang out with one of her friends.

I'm spread pretty thin while she's here, so I'll only see her here and there. I think Nicole and Amialya might hit up a theme park on Sunday, but it may be the only day off I've got for a few weeks, so I'm not sure if I'll go. Might just be best for those two to go on their own. Plus, long lines make me cranky.

Last rehearsal was great. Really dove into the new album, and all of the new songs we've tried are sounding pretty good so far, but the real star is "Epic Fail." Jim found a way to just really push that one ahead, and it kinda tore my head off the first time he did it. I really love the *Unicorns* album as it is, but the more I hear what the band can do with silly stuff like "I Hate This Song," the more I regret that we were unable to record this album as a unit. But that's surely improbable: Emmit is in like six bands, and Jim is overwhelmed with Milk Carton Superstars. Can't expect them to devote any more time to my songs than they already (generously) do, but if they could and we could somehow solidify this as *the* Marc With a C lineup? We would likely do some damage. I don't think I'm underestimated, but I think that the band as a unit definitely is. Can't wait to show people what we can do with this new stuff.

Time for me to finish this album I'm listening to and get some rest. The dose of cough syrup I drank to make my throat feel less on fire is actually making me a little spacey.

2-2-16

Here's a bit of a potentially interesting tidbit about the song "Staying Dormant," which is one of my very favorite songs I've ever made up: I once explained a little bit about what inspired it at a show at Will's Pub once, and afterward? An audience member told me that I was wrong. I was flummoxed, so I asked them to give me their interpretation. They gave me a long spiel about how it was from the perspective of a writer of indeterminate gender orientation deciding to transition into the opposite of the owner of the genitals that they currently had. I was surprised because it wasn't my intention at all, but it made for a more interesting song when I thought of it that way.

This is why I love to listen when people want to talk about my songs. I'd rather hear what people get out of them than tell the truth about what inspired it. Sometimes to "sell" the song live, I'll just make up some total bullshit. The bullshit is often coming from a truthful place, just not actually applicable to whatever I'm about to play. Mostly, I tell the truth. Most times people can't tell the difference, and that's good, because I'm doing my job correctly. Making up songs is one of the only careers you can have where it helps to be really good at telling lies with a straight face. No matter what, the song will be *someone's* truth.

That's probably why I'm pretty good at being honest in most other facets of my life. I have an outlet to lie, exaggerate, and indulge in behaviors that would seem otherwise uncouth. I'm pretty fortunate on that front. I'm just incredibly tired of all of the information being tossed my way. I want to think at a normal pace again, and I hope that by the time I'm able and ready to make a social media exit that others will have decided to do the same. Maybe phone calls will come back into vogue. We've had a vinyl resurgence, now I just want people to start speaking to each other again.

2-8-16

Interviews. Also some interviews. And then? More interviews. I find these things a lot more fun than I used to, but I'm not seeing a huge uptick in pre-sales due to them. Have to wonder if the more effective way to sell an album in 2016 is to just shut the fuck up and stay offline. Definitely have that in mind as I head into whatever the future holds.

Got some cool records in the mail today. More excited to play them than my guitar, but I also just did a trade with Emmit: he got the fretless bass I used on the bulk of *Unicorns Get More Bacon*, and I got his Fender Strat. One of the few electric guitars that immediately felt like home when I played it. But I've been neck deep in promo work, so actually playing the guitar for fun hasn't really been on the list of priorities. Definitely one of the drawbacks to being a DIY musician. The time where you can just play your instruments for fun is dramatically decreased, instead deigning to pick up a guitar unless you're going to get paid for it at some point.

Screw it. I'm making some time to play that guitar tonight.

More rehearsals this week, which we sorely need: "Ethics In Gaming" isn't clicking for me with the band just yet. Waiting for it to become second nature is hard. So many of the songs are immediately gratifying for us to play, and the ones we have to force usually don't stay in setlists for very long, no matter how popular they are. See "I'm Gonna Miss You" and "All My Drug Use Is Accidental" for reference. The songs from the album we haven't worked on are "Falling Sometimes Down," "Where's My Giant Robot," and "Long Distance Dedication." The latter two feel like mistakes because they seem to be favorites right off the bat. Goes to show that I was at least a little right about "Long Distance" in particular: I knew the song was good and capable of more.

Haven't shaved for days. I haven't had to appear anywhere visually for a while, so I haven't thought about it. Or felt like it. I get a lot done, but it's always at the detriment of self-care. But really, is shaving self-care? I don't really care if I have a weeklong face shadow. Do other people? I spent so much time trying to unlearn how to care what other people think about my appearance that I don't know how this shit works anymore.

Been sleeping very well lately. Like 10-12 hours at a stretch. Need to sleep a little less and go out a little more. These records aren't going to sell themselves. And if the records are unsold, the songs can't make people happy. If people aren't happy due to songs I've made up, I've wasted my life.

Note to self: sleep just a little less. Somehow.

2-13-16

Settling in and enjoying a Kinks compilation record. Just relaxed and played with the bunnies (Alice Cooper and Tammy Faye Bakker) in the kitchen for a little while. Set up a new record player in the office/studio. Generally relaxed day, but still productive, especially with adding things to Nerdy.FM.

New stuff is coming along nicely in rehearsals, though this last one was rougher vocally than any in recent memory. Around 8 p.m. every day this week, my voice has started getting raspy and then just going out completely. Absolutely due to the dry weather, as I'd tried a bunch of different combinations of variables, and nothing had any impact. I can chug a gallon of water, and I'll get my voice back for about a minute, and then it disappears again.

Earlier, I went over to Jim's place to do some vocal work on the upcoming Milk Carton Superstars album. Leslie was also there for the same reason, having drove in from North Carolina. Still not really sure why she's here. Apparently she's just been laid off at work, but that still seems like a long way to drive for some unpaid session work. Probably just needs to see some friends and decompress a bit.

At the session, there wasn't really much hanging out or goofing off, everyone had their work hats on, which is my preferred way of doing things most times, but having not seen Leslie in a while, I'm wishing that things had been a little looser. Apparently Guy was sick, so that stopped it from being a fully-fledged Claire reunion, though it'll technically be one on the MCS record. I like the song, too. Also listened to Leslie hit it out of the park on the harmonies of another new song that I can't recall the name of. She's supremely talented, and to my knowledge hadn't done any recording of note since we did "The Final Single" about 16 months ago. Some people just have it.

2-20-16

Going without one of the medicines that I'm prescribed for my throat is proving to be really difficult. I feel very loose and ungrounded. When I walk, I know how to balance, but I feel like it's only by chance that I haven't fallen. My body feels like it's going at speeds that are faster than I'm intending. Time speeds up and slows down quite a bit.

Woke up today to find that the interview I'd done for Fandomania had gone live. Took hours to listen to it because something kept coming up every few minutes. It's actually a fairly dark interview, and it reminds me that I shouldn't talk to the press unless I've been up for at least four hours. My sleepy-time meds mean that I wake up much slower than the average person, and it takes me a while to get into the headspace of "fun Marc." At least the interview isn't boring.

Had to quickly leave the house with little notice because my sister-in-law gave birth to my beautiful niece, Piper. I was really excited to meet her because I love babies, and they usually love me. I relate to babies. We both like breasts but tend to only be attached to one pair at a time. We both feel like screaming when we want food. We don't really like lying in feces. And ultimately we both just want to sleep. I could seriously just be a nanny for newborns and be perfectly content.

Well, I don't know, actually.

But people tend to be surprised at how much I love kids and how well I get along with them. Ticks me off, too. I've always been good with kids. Once people see it in action, some folks treat it like a superpower, and it wouldn't stick in my craw so sharply if it wasn't such a weirdly gendered thing to say to a man. It shouldn't be impressive that a guy likes to hang out with kids and in turn that the kids like them back, you know?

Anyways, back to Piper. She's beautiful and perfect and a little bundle of crankiness and lots of hair and rainbows. I hope that the world is nice to her. Even if it isn't, I'll be good to her. I think I was born to be the cool uncle. I certainly have the record collection for it.

Since there was no rehearsal this week, I set aside some time last night to just play guitar and sing for a bit. Improvised a really dark song about killing someone with a shovel, just to practice in case the government came to "take our guns away" and you needed other weapons to kill with. Should have been running a tape, I probably could turn it into something worthwhile. But then again, I don't really want to answer for that type of lyric for the rest of my life.

Thinking about recording a live album with the band if they'd be into it. I think that we do some pretty hot versions of songs from the back catalog. I bet if we went nuts and booked a long marathon-type show, we could capture enough for a record that would just be a total blast to crank up loudly. I think my discography could use a loud and sleazy rock and roll record, warts and all. Making something like this has been on my mind for a while now, and I'm going to pitch it to the band pretty soon. I'd want to just sort of emphasize what we're good at, rather than making a "greatest hits" type of affair. Though there's still a bunch of tunes that I really want the band to know. Right now, we can probably do around 60 songs from my various records and such, but I don't think that we even know a single song from *Normal Bias*. Occasionally we run into a tune that doesn't catch fire for this lineup, though you'd think it would – "Popular Music" immediately comes to mind – but then there's others that I think are true highlights for this lineup that one might not expect, like "The Right To Bear Arms" or "Epic Fail."

Overall, I just think that this band deserves to be immortalized on wax, and I don't have any immediate plans to record an album with them for logistical reasons. Such a release could be really cool, like the interpositive of *The Real Live Sound Of Marc With a C*. Could call it *The Real Loud Sound Of Marc With a C*.

That's not a bad idea. Let's see what the band thinks when I run it by them.

2-28-16

I am feeling exceptionally lonely lately. I still don't really know anyone that I didn't meet through doing Marc With a C or family. The family is bound by blood or legalities to at least pretend to like me, really. I still have one friend that knew me before this became all that I did with my life, and that's Heather. I think that I glom on to her a little too hard for that reason, and she gets sick of me. Hasn't said as much, but I can feel it. Had a new pen pal for a while, but she stopped responding to me a few weeks ago, though I see that she's plenty active on Facebook.

This is probably why I pine for the lost friendship of the pal that partially helped inspire the whole *HRG* saga. She liked me for my personality traits and didn't really even seem to like my music, which means more to me than I can explain. And sure, Nicole is my best friend, but I need a separate friend. Someone removed from my family and my job. I desperately want to feel like my company is welcomed and that talking about those songs that I make up and stuff? Well, that'd just be me going on about work.

Friday was an early-morning interview. Good thing the show was bizarre by design because I was fighting a serious case of the "I just woke up" crankies. Tonight is a Skype interview for a radio station in Canada. I like Canada and want to go there soon, if I can ever make that record with Jordan Zadorozny from Blinker The Star, which I should probably talk here about fairly soon. Anyways, this Canadian show is called *Thunder Geeks*, and I heard one episode, and I can't quiiiite hang with their nerd knowledge. Hope they'll take it easy on me. Feeling fragile.

I have a lot of love in my life, but I'm constantly fighting feeling alone at the moment. That's bipolarity for you. Time to go back to pretending otherwise. I'll just keep distracting myself by listening to these old Who 45s and then maybe I'll go play with the bunnies before the interview. The bunnies don't give a shit if I make up songs or not.

3-1-16

While we should all consider our actions, I certainly get blindsided with a case of the overthinks. Today is one of those days where it's especially out of control, so I'm going to write here for a while. I'll be talking about a few things that I'd been meaning to get to in this book but hadn't brought up until now.

- I wrote a song a long time ago that I've pretty much disowned called "Blowjob Queen." Here's the story for posterity. Years ago, my ex-best friend (Ska Steve) was dating what seemed like a perfectly nice young lady. One day as I was getting ready to go out, she called me out of the blue. This was odd because they'd just broken up, and she'd literally never called me before. I'm not even sure how she got my number! After a few minutes of mindless chatter, she started going on (unprompted) in great detail about her abilities when it came to providing oral sex for a partner. I figured that this must be some sort of not-very-well-thought-out trap to try to make her ex jealous, as I'd most certainly bring the phone call up to him, so I joked that I'd just write a song about it because there was literally no other reason for me know any of this. She giggled and said I oughta do that. I told her that if I did so, I'd put her full name in the song. She laughed harder, and that's exactly what I did. Even played it for her. She had no problem with it at all, suggested that I put it on my next album and even laughed at that.

  Until I started performing it in public. That's when she threatened me with legal action, though that all happened via third party. I asked her if I could replace her name to continue playing this tune that was starting to be requested at the shows, and she suggested that I do so with the word "cunt," and that's how it got entered in the song at all. I used to think that the word was funny – I no longer do, obviously – so it worked. And many agreed that the word was at least a little bit funny as the song was a longtime request at my shows. I phased it out slowly, and I hate being known for the song, but I made stupid mistakes in my past. Definitely a moment where overthinking would have come in handy.

- I've been recording experimental tones, sounds, and noise under the name Natural History Museum. So far I've released two albums under that name that no one knows about. Unfortunately, right afterward, another band started releasing material under that name, and it'll probably get ugly one day, though they'd have to find me first. Just about to release another album under that guise, too. It's just a therapeutic outlet for me to capture sounds and make art without pressure. I don't know when I'll tell Marc With a C listeners about it. Probably before you read this. If not? Surprise!

- I've got so many records that I've had to instate a process so I'll get through them all. Each day I play one album (decided by alphabetical order) in its entirety. I have to make time for this one LP, no matter what. And if the next thing in the collection alphabetically (by artist) happens to be a single? I have to hear that as well. I have to make some time to be influenced by things that I may not necessary be in the mood for. If I were listening for my own tastes, right now I'd probably reach for an R.E.M. record that I've heard a billion times. Instead, I'm hearing this really cool La Luz album. Fate worked out better than my own wants today.

When I was on Canadian radio a few nights ago, I slipped up and said "fuck." I've never done more interviews in a stretch than I am doing at the moment, and I think it's wearing on me a bit — I certainly know better. Still beats digging ditches, but I forget that when answering the same questions over and over. Talking about my music is supposed to be fun. Maybe I'm just having a low week.

Rehearsal beckons. This is the best because I get to go make loud rock and roll noise with two of my best friends. It's becoming the highlight of every week.

3-7-16

Album comes out tomorrow. Stomach is doing flip-flops. I'm either very nervous or I ate something that didn't agree with me. I'm leaning toward the latter.

Nowadays, the release date means very little. It's all build-up, and then hoping that on the day of release that the album is strong enough to keep people talking about it. Either that or you have to do the surprise album drop. This time was the "surprise announcement with build-up to actual release." We'll see how this one turns out. I've done about all that I can do — now I just have to hope that it's enough.

Had some setup work done on the backup guitar I got from Emmit. Picked it up on Friday, and saw Guy from the Claire and The Potatoes days at the shop. We talked for a while in the parking lot. He seems to be happy and in a really good headspace. Realized how much I missed him and just how inside-out he must have felt during the Claire period. His life was in turmoil, and a small part of me wishes we were able to give things another shot with him as he currently is. But I also don't think that my head could take another go-round with the Claire concept. I just couldn't survive it, and I think that it'd be one of the rare times that Nicole would put her foot down and demand that I recant. If a project lands you in therapy, it might be very, very good musically, but you have to be concerned about some manner of self-care and your quality of life. Guy being happy is great to see, and I'm thrilled that all of the band is on good terms with each other. We rightly could have ended up completely estranged, but there doesn't seem to be anything but love between all of the members.

The Marc With a C Trio did the record release party for *Unicorns Get More Bacon* on Saturday night. I was jumping out of my skin at the show because while Uke-A-Ladies were turning in their amazing opening set, the venue was only a quarter full. I started to get very concerned. We'd already sold tons of copies of the album at my stealth birthday show and enough copies online to go to #1 on Bandcamp — why would anyone come to this show other than to hear the new songs live?

By the time I went on, the venue was possibly three-fourths full, and that's about where attendance stayed. I opened the show a bit differently. Instead of doing an introduction, I launched into a quiet solo version of "Long Distance Dedication," and the audience continued to talk over me, thinking it was all a soundcheck. I had to stop the song in the middle to ask everyone to be quiet because I couldn't hear myself. Didn't look classy, and I don't think I'll ever do it that way again.

After that, the show went quite well. A rather quiet audience, too, to the point of uncomfortable silence between songs. Maybe to make up for the way it all kicked off? Biggest reactions were reserved for favorites like "Squiddy," "Life's So Hard," and "Dickpuncher," though there were surprisingly loud responses to "Make You Better" and "Epic Fail." One of the best parts for me was watching an audience member I've never seen only sing along with the songs from the new album while not seeming to know the old stuff. They were especially excited that we played "Celebutantes," too. Seeing someone like that in the crowd keeps me going.

The song that I was a bit surprised by the clunkiness of was "The Ballad Of Dick Steel." I felt like that song was built for the stage, but maybe it just wasn't ready. It's probably the one we'd worked on the least, so it'd make sense. People chanted along in the right places, but it didn't come off as the barn-burner I'd expected. As a unit, the band played with a fierceness, and besides the occasional new song hiccup, it might have been our best show yet from a technical standpoint. Haven't really reviewed the tapes yet, but that's certainly how it felt.

Everyone was very nice except for a pushy-and-drunk media person that had confused me with a roadie and then begged me to get on camera upon realizing that I was the main draw for the night — and then begged me to have the band set back up and play more after we'd already torn down. They had only shown up for the last song and hadn't caught anything on film. I denied this request, as they'd never asked for permission. Camera crew even followed me outside and tried to ambush me as I was loading my gear into the car. You can't say "no" enough times to some people. I would have said yes to an interview if they'd only been polite or realistic.

Someone from my past keeps trying to get my attention, and I don't want it. Things ended on bad terms, and I wasn't in a good place when we met to begin with. She just brings back bad memories. Anxiety has been the name of the game every time she comes around. The person from the past that scares the hell out of me didn't show up to the show, thankfully. She messaged the Facebook fanpage about how she didn't go because she "didn't want to make me uncomfortable." I blocked her there, too. I don't know how many places I'll have to block her before she gets the message. I don't want to fall into the typical trap of saying she's got a mental illness or something, but apparently she's been looking at Nicole's pages online as well. Her ability to respect obvious boundaries appears to be pretty low, and I am increasingly uncomfortable.

I was supposed to do a co-interview with the band Pulled From Panels for Nerdy FM, tonight, but my head has been so focused on me-me-ME that I couldn't come up with any decent questions for them. Begged Lauren — my replacement as manager for the station — to do this one on her own. I think it'll be better this way. I like their two EPs, but she understands their source material better than I do. She's a great interviewer and doesn't need me in the least.

Tonight will be spent doing all of the email blasts about all of the places that one would be able to find my new album. I have to wait for Spotify links to go live before I can do that, but I can write up skeletal things in the meantime. I got an armload of new records in the mail today to listen to while I sit and nervously wait: a Bowie bootleg, the mono Monkees boxed set, a bunch of the scarce D.I.Y. compilations on Rhino Records, and most importantly? *New Adventures in Hi-Fi* by R.E.M., which rounds out my collection of their studio albums. Have a great soundtrack to the day, and now I just wish I weren't jumping out of my own skin.

3-12-16

Today is the last night of my "three-day, one-city" promotional tour. I'll be appearing at a faux-late night talk show. I'm not terribly excited about it, but I feel that it's such a bizarre concept for Orlando that it could be very cool. I've never seen Steven Seidman actually do one in full, but I'd seen when he'd try to workshop them at my old open mic. It has promise, and if nothing else? I'll get to play one of my new singles to a crowd that wouldn't have probably heard it otherwise.

This week was more interviews. I thought they were over for a while, but that was a miscalculation on my part. It's cool, though. One of them was especially fun, and one turned into a critique of the new album that actually seems to be selling some copies, which makes me quite happy. Slow and steady wins the race? I'm not trying to win, I'm just happy to be able to run.

Last night I played a short set at a burlesque show thrown by Skill Focus in Orlando. I think that this was the first time they'd brought a musical act into the show, and it felt really good from the stage. The year is young, but so far that's my favorite set of 2016. Great audience participation, as they continued to sing "Life's So Hard" long after I'd left the stage. Wasn't a big moneymaker, but it did wonders for keeping my spirits high. Afterward, I found some money on the ground that I thought I'd dropped, but when I did final counts at the end, it didn't belong to me at all. Emailed my contact for the troupe and let him know that if someone came forward having lost some of their pay that I'm happy to send it to them. It'd be easy to keep it, but it's easier to sleep if I make sure that another starving artist can buy some groceries with the money that they rightfully earned.

Thursday was a last-minute solo show at Will's Pub. I was on really early and played to around 10 people. I just played new songs and got the heck out of the way. Mostly wanted to see Steve Garron's new band. Joe Panton is the bassist. Joe and I are at peace now. We even joked around during load-in, and he invited me back to his place to kill time before soundcheck, an offer that I had to decline — I'm allergic to cats, and he now owns four of them.

Steve's band was fantastic. Felt like a really natural progression for him, and I can't wait to see where they are headed. Steve has had so many near-death experiences that I'm happy to see him able to play at all, let alone walking and talking. Ten years ago, I would have put all of my money on him not being around in 2016 for any number of reasons. A true survivor.

I have a young fan with cystic fibrosis named Aubree. Emmit knows her pretty well, I think. I've only met her a few times, but she's such a gentle and kind person that I ache thinking about her quality of life. Found a GoFundMe where people can donate to help her afford the medicine that will keep her alive, and I want to give it a signal boost, but I'm a little unsure about turning that leaf. Also, it's spearheaded by her mom, and I don't want to embarrass this young lady. She seems a bit shy, and I don't want people to come up to her at shows and corner her and ask questions while she's trying to have a good time and forget her troubles. I'll talk to Emmit about it and see what he thinks the best course of action is. I want to help, but I have to do it correctly for everyone.

Band rehearsal is called off for next week. We didn't have one this week either. After tonight? I think I need a few days off from thinking about Marc With a C. Beyond sending out some albums? I think I might be able to pull that off for a few days. Or at least, I can try.

Spinning R.E.M.'s *Document* right now. File under fire, indeed.

3-17-16

Last night, I picked up a cassette four-track from Chris. Or rather, he dropped it off with the wrong adapter, and it smelled like it was on fire. I brought it back to him thinking I'd killed it. He found the correct plug, and all was well. Though we did have one of our classic misunderstandings: I said a joking comment, and it came out very badly. He chased me out to the car demanding clarification, and he was right. I have a real habit of sticking my foot in my mouth with him. Wish I didn't. I love him so much after all these years that I still get nervous and tongue-tied around him.

Recorded a reworking of a new song that means a lot to me on the tape machine: "One Of These Are Gonna Be Your Day." The tones felt like coming home, and I really love the sound that this box makes. Keeping a good amount of decent tapes at my disposal will be the real trick. I hope people like this song. It could sound like "just another Marc song," but these sentiments come from a very different place.

The new song is going on an EP that I'm recording with the band on Tuesday. We're just doing some "live to tape" versions of a few favorites from my catalog, and we're going to release it as a digital EP and give the proceeds to Aubree. Now that I know how sick she is, how expensive her medicine is? I can't let this go. She's a nice person who should have her whole life in front of her. As far as I know, she's only 20. I want to raise some money, even a small amount, that helps her to see 21. That GoFundMe campaign that her mom kicked off doesn't seem to be getting much traction, but sometimes people give me money to sing. So there's the plan: release an inexpensive EP where all the proceeds can continuously go to her, and maybe I can do a positive thing for someone in need. The band seems really excited to do this as well.

I know that in some ways I'm shooting myself in the foot by putting this EP out so quickly after *Unicorns Get More Bacon*, but here's the fact: she's sick NOW. She needs help all of the time. My fiscal strategies don't line up with the reality that this young lady needs medicine, so screw it. I'm going to do my best to have this EP out and able to be purchased in two weeks' time. Once I had the idea, I couldn't ignore it. If something happened to her, and I'd waited to try to help until it was "convenient?" I couldn't live with myself.

### 3-28-16

I've been trying to write here a little less because I feel like I'm doing just as much chronicling as doing anything at all. I have made a few demos of new songs to finish the next few records but very little that I think deserves to be fleshed out and made suitable for the public sphere. I would very much like to clean up my office and make it less cluttered. To just let some songwriting ideas flow through for a few days. I don't see a chance for that this week.

We released the *Songs For Aubree* EP over the weekend. I think that the EP itself meant a great deal to Aubree and her family and, really, the cystic fibrosis community. I've received a few calls and emails about doing further work for various foundations. I'd like to do that. I'm happier being selfless than self-reflecting lately.

I've chatted with Aubree quite a bit since the EP came out. She's a remarkable young lady. Relentlessly sweet and positive. I have tended to view her as a fan in an unfortunate situation, while she's looked at Nicole and me as friends. I'm starting to see her as a friend as well. Even going to go and surprise her with a hospital visit that her mother has orchestrated later this week. Going to bring her some music to listen to, as well as a card game, so maybe we can have some fun instead of being reminded of the heaviness of her convalescence. I think the role of a friend is to raise your spirits when you are low, so I'm going to give it a whirl. I want to do it right. My hopes are that she'll be thrilled by it.

The EP hasn't even raised $200 as of this writing, and I know that it may not have been a great career move: to push this so heartily less than a month after the official release of *Unicorns Get More Bacon*. Both the muse and my heart told me that this was the right thing to do. There's a price to be paid when you follow those instead of the time-honored traditions of "How To Promote An Album 101." I never much liked following musical rules anyway.

In other news, the date where Lauren Furze takes over Nerdy.FM looms ever closer. I couldn't be more thrilled by this because I really need the time I'd invested in the station back for my own creative endeavors. Lauren and I did an interview with [NAME REDACTED] last week, and I thought that one of them was a little rough on me, and I'm pretty sure [NAME REDACTED] was aware. I don't know why. It hurts me more than just someone not liking me. Rather, this one stings because I love the records they make, and I more often than not agree with their politics and try and apply them to my own life. It stings when I don't feel like a peer or ally and instead feel a bit maligned due to my mere presence. Sometimes I think they'd be happier if they never had to deal with me.

I got pretty bent out of shape about it this weekend after they had told their fan base on a livestream about how they had made me very uncomfortable during the interview because they are "a misandrist" – their words. I think it's in my best interest to avoid them unless we simply have to work together. They won't have to put me in my place, and I won't have to have hurt feelings. Still can't bring myself to listen to their records for pleasure anymore, though I love what they do musically.

Speaking of Nerdy.FM, we usually do a pretty big thing for April Fool's Day. In the past, we've played different versions of "Stairway To Heaven" for 24 hours straight. Last year, we devoted the station to nothing but Adam Warrock songs. This year, I was going to pretend to be a megalomaniac and play nothing but my own songs for a whole day. Ultimately, I think that since we have a big announcement to make with our staff changes, I don't want people confusing the actions, plus I don't want any reason for our listeners to think we're kidding. So instead? I'm going to level with them and just play a recent recording of one of my own concerts on April 1. Seems like the smartest way to go.

Tomorrow, the band is going to help me record an intro and outro – since it's a show done with Emmit and Jim, this feels right – sometime during rehearsal. Also, rehearsal will be interesting as we're going to start doing half-acoustic/half-electric practices so we can be ready for some upcoming things. I haven't played a ton of acoustic guitar recently, so I'm excited for this.

I got some criticism from a piece of fan mail over the *Songs For Aubree* EP. They were bewildered by the song selection. They claimed to enjoy the new song but felt the other song choices were uninspired and not representative. I found this interesting, as this is a fan from Hamburg that has never seen me live and seems to only collect my colored vinyl. I explained that a few of the songs were specifically Aubree's favorites and that myself ("Epic Fail"), Jim ("Jessica, I Heard You Like The Who"), and Emmit ("'Til You Come Home To Me") each took turns picking our current favorites songs to play, hoping to end up with spirited performances on a very last-minute decision. I haven't heard back from them, but this wasn't meant to be a "best of." It was just supposed to be a reward for helping out a person in need. Critical analysis of that type of thing really smarts.

4-3-16

Finally saw Duran Duran last night. Nile Rodgers opened up and blew them off the stage. I finally fulfilled a childhood dream by seeing Duran Duran, but the setlist was too heavy on the new album, which I simply can't connect to. Also, there was a tacky Bowie tribute in the middle of "Planet Earth," which was a total boner killer. The best part was spending time with Nicole. The bad part of going to shows with her is that when there's so many people around and so much going on – especially between acts – I feel so inundated by all of the sights and sounds, all of the hustle and bustle, that I just end up clamming up due to being totally overwhelmed. I'm afraid that she takes this as me not wanting to talk to her, but in reality, I feel completely unable to communicate in these situations. I often end up watching the music completely stone faced, and I'm sure that it must look to people like I'm not enjoying myself at all. That's not the case. Again, I'm just trying to focus on something – anything – when so much is vying for my attention.

Last night was a pretty bad medical night for Aubree. I spent the night on the phone with her. Her breathing was really troubled due to some adverse reactions to medications, and she was scared to go to sleep. Her mom was staying up with her, but I called and kept her awake on the phone until just after six in the morning so her mom could take a nap. I had offered to drive to Gainesville to keep an eye on her through the night, but we all agreed that the phone was an easier solution. Caring about someone with CF is already very exhausting, so I can't imagine what it must be like to have to deal with it on a daily basis. Trying to strike the balance of "manage an unpredictable illness before it manages you" and all. I care about Aubree and her mom very much. I want to make it all better, and I feel powerless that I cannot.

4-10-16

Just had a good crying jag in the shower. I've struggled with bipolarity and depression all of my life, and it's either winning the fight today, or something else is very wrong.

I feel like an abject failure. I set out to make people happy with music. And if not happy? At least to feel something when I make patterns of sound. Whatever people want to hear nowadays, a large portion of the world has made it very clear that I am not "it." The "making people happy with music" thing sometimes works very well when I'm in a room with an audience, and all of the attention is on me, but beyond a few tattoos and a couple of nice stories, I don't know that I've done any lasting good. I don't know that the climate of how we consume art will allow me to do any better than I have up until this point.

The *Songs For Aubree* project is something I have worked on very intensely and sincerely. We've raised a whopping $235 for her as of today. That probably wouldn't even buy her a weeks' worth of any of the medications that her insurance refuses to cover. I threw myself into it, it's barely making a dent, and now I feel completely worthless as a human being. This isn't a fucking game: she has 20 PERCENT LUNG FUNCTIONALITY. She needs more support than my stupid fucking songs can provide. And while I did not create her problems, every time she gets exceptionally sick I'll now forever have it on my conscience that she can't get her medicine or the proper medical treatment because I'm not popular enough as a public personality. And no one else cares enough about her issues to do much of anything else to help.

So, what's the fucking point? Why am I really doing this? Those dreams of making records that will matter to someone, someday, when they find it in a dollar bin long after I'm dead? That doesn't help right now. Obscurity is not beneficial to me in the present, and I'm all too aware that I can't have it both ways. I can't be relevant and an outsider artist at the same time. Achieving even the level of "obscure" is pretty much the highest that my sights were ever set. I'm there, and it doesn't always feel like the right fit.

Listen to all those cautionary tales about being careful what you wish for, kids!

My wife and I hardly see each other. She spends her days at a 9-to-5 job that she doesn't like, and then spends evenings doing aerial arts. She comes home exhausted. I have a bizarre sleeping pattern, and I'm finally really ready to start my work day in earnest at around 5 PM. I'm peaking right as she's falling asleep. I work until I realize that I have to medicate myself into more restless sleep. There is no alternative: it's either this way or nothing ever gets done on my end.

I've been oddly lucky that I've had no choice but to throw myself into work for Nerdy.FM work, getting the library in shape for Lauren's takeover. It's about all I'm going to do until it's "done."

I want to make music. Music is a massive problem because it isn't doing enough for anyone while demanding too much out of me. I have identified as a songwriter my entire life. I am not good enough. I am not effective enough.

I sometimes can ignore these realities with the proper medicine. It doesn't really make me happy, but it reminds me that I'm very lucky to have anything at all: relatively good health, a few listeners, a loving wife, a roof over my head, awesome pets that we're able to provide love and shelter for, a daughter that I have not completely alienated, etc.

While writing out that list, I knew that I should be happy right now, or at least content. Today, my insides won't allow for it. If I dove into writing a song about it, the Nerdy.FM work wouldn't get done as I'd endlessly tinker just to get a demo that I like.

I'll keep fighting today. All of the fight is only contained in my body, which is very small when you take an aerial view of my neighborhood. And if you pull the lens back further, you can't even see my house, let alone the city that I reside in. If you pull back far enough, you can't even pick out the floating rock that I'm typing this on. If my heart stops beating, does the internal conflict ever stop in my soul? Do I carry it over into wherever my consciousness goes next?

That last sentence is the reason I've kept myself alive.

4-20-16

I noticed something interesting at last night's rehearsal. When I used to present songs to Chris or Ryan for possible concert material, there would always be a hint of reticence to the proceedings. I think it often felt pointless to learn so many of my numbers when in all likelihood, we'd play the bulk of them once in a while at best. Chris specifically didn't enjoy it – he seemed happier just getting behind the drums and bashing away, rather than going over things with a fine-toothed comb. But with Jim and Emmit? They're fans of the records first, so I'll bring them a song, they'll already have an idea of how it goes, and then they're excited to put their own spin on it. In the second half of our allotted time last night, we worked out "Song Song," "DJ Danny Treanor," "Stairway To Rudolph," and "Pinball Wizard" – all to the point where we'd all be comfortable playing them onstage today. I feel confident with them. It's really comforting, and I'm having a really good time with them, instead of rehearsals being a chore. Though it still tears my throat up.

Nicole is out of town for her job until tomorrow night. I'm using a portion of this time to put together her birthday present behind her back. She's loved Janet Jackson since she was a little girl, and I'm trying to track down every LP of hers that she doesn't have as well as every DVD of videos and performances. I know that she used to watch these things and memorize the iconic dance routines, and I want her to be able to reach for any of that stuff and relive the good memories at absolutely any time. She'd never buy it for herself, so it's up to me. I'm doing this while she's out of town in hopes that she won't notice the weird bank transactions, as certain Janet titles are ridiculously expensive on vinyl. I hope she'll be happy with it. I'm also considering putting together a hi-fi turntable setup in her office that's attuned specifically to her hearing, and even though her birthday is nearly two months away, I have to really space these transactions out, or she'll be able to figure out what I'm doing.

Recorded some Duran Duran covers recently. Did "Girls On Film" and "Shadows On Your Side." I'm highly considering doing an album's worth of their songs, but I don't feel like I'm in a rush to do it, as I have so many other things scheduled to come out that I don't know when I'd even have time to release it without going into overkill mode. But it is on the docket for now. Good way to blow off steam. The only thing that troubles me is that I don't really want to sing anything post-1988, which doesn't seem fair, but I can't control which material of theirs that I connect to, you know? I'll keep thinking about it. As far as I know, I have plenty of time.

4-28-16

Been far too busy to write here lately. The Nerdy.FM transition has taken up far more time than I ever dreamed that it would, and there are some family problems which I can't really talk about here.

Last weekend, the band played at a mini-festival called Orlando Overdrive. We went on second out of eight acts. I really didn't want to go on so early, so I went out onstage with a weirdly competitive mindset. Sure, I wanted to entertain, but I mostly wanted to blow every other act off of the stage, making people rue continuously giving me such low billing. This is completely unlike me. And it's true that we played a pretty blistering set, but I found myself getting cocky afterwards. I don't like that side of myself and would very much not like to explore having that attitude any further. Besides, I watched my friend Chris Allen/EyeQ lay waste to the same audience with an improvised set, so why am I competing with my friends? This is supposed to be fun. I have to keep that in mind.

I'm writing this from the waiting room of a CentraCare. I stepped on a broken drumstick a few days ago, and the swelling still hasn't gone down, so I figured I should have it checked out in case I need antibiotics. Only hurts when I stand on it, but that doesn't seem like it'll work for tomorrow's show.

## 5-10-16

I've spent numerous days mastering *Linda Lovelace For President* and *Losing Salt* for vinyl. A real test of will. Due to the conditions they were recorded in, they were often out of phase, tinny, and kind of a total mess. To get them functional, I actually had to pull some maneuvers that would ultimately change the tonality of the albums. But truly, it was either change the overall tone (which came with the territory of centering the low-end and narrowing the stereo image to fight the phase problems) or just never put these on vinyl. If I were a wealthy man, I'd have hired Kramer to do it for me, but I do not believe that these reissues will generate enough interest/money to warrant that sort of special treatment.

*Linda Lovelace* doesn't sound all that different, just a bit less bright. *Losing Salt* got a total makeover. I now like it so much that I can actively enjoy listening to the album possibly for the first time. It's a strange little 28-minute trip, and I'm actually very proud of it now. Sounds like the work of a person who is not me. I'm excited to get this one out, but it probably won't happen until January. Just hope that everyone is okay with the changes in EQ and compression that had to take place.

I've been slowly working on more Duran Duran covers. I've been asked on more than a few occasions why I don't have a Patreon. Now, in case you're reading this at a time when that service is not on the tip of everyone's tongue? Patreon is a website that allows you to donate money to artistic types on a regular basis. You can set it up so that every time you give those backers a song, you get a buck from each of them, for example.

I've fought against doing one of these for a very long time. One reason is that

I feel that it's a very slippery slope. It would be very easy to just give people a throwaway track just because you need some money, and my credo has always been "make music despite poverty and not because of it." But as people are pressing me to make one, I feel bad saying, "No, you can't give me money." Instead, I've recently begun to think that this would be an interesting way to clear out some unreleased material. I record about 75% of my concerts, and this seems like a cool way to offer some of them to the die-hard type of fan that might want to hear, say, me promoting *Exactly Where I Am* in front of a crowd that didn't want to see me. I'll just have to find a way to make it clear that these releases are only for the hardcore, and that if you're looking for material on par with my main catalog, you're in the wrong place.

I could really use that extra income. This hasn't been a great year in terms of Marc With a C money – partially because of streaming paying out far less money than physical sales, partially because I shot myself in the foot with Aubree's EP – and I feel like I have to explore every possible avenue right now.

Getting back to band rehearsals tomorrow after a two-week break. I really need this. I am growing to thrive on making music communally with friends. It feels less and less solitary lately.

In other news, I had to extract the half-inch piece of drumstick in my foot all by myself the other day. The doctor basically told me it was all in my head. If that doesn't explain the state of medical care in America in 2016, I don't know what does.

5-16-16

Woke up today with a very scratchy throat, a head full of mucus, and lots of drainage. As the band will be spending the next two days rehearsing and recording for the *Cark* tape, I really hope that I'm able to knock this out of my body quickly. I am armed to the teeth with kombucha, ibuprofen, and extended-release cough syrups.

Saturday was the recording of the Nerdy.FM "unplugged session" for the band. I suspected that one particular attendee was sick but hoped they were telling the truth when they attributed their coughing fits to lifelong sinus problems. Then again, I was around a lot of cigarette smoke, which I'm not used to anymore. Gah, shouldn't even be dwelling on it. Hopefully it's just a weird allergy thing today.

The session itself went pretty wonderfully. The usual issues within me still went down: I get so focused on working that I am terrified that I'm coming across as dour or unhappy, when it simply isn't the case. The small audience was made up of truly hardcore fans, all armed with requests I couldn't have seen coming a mile away like "Counting Down" and "Americana." But the band played well. We only had to do second takes of "Unicorns Get More Bacon" and "Make You Better." We should have done a second take of "Pinball Wizard," but I couldn't really hear just how off Emmit was. It happens. We had to do the retakes because of my mistakes, so I couldn't exactly be upset! It'll be the only song cut from the special.

Speaking of Emmit, he's finally dating Aubree. Everyone knew that this was the natural progression for them, but they'd been so timid about it. I fail miserably when I try to play matchmaker, but in this case I really pushed for them to date because they are both so obviously head over heels for each other. Very happy for them.

I'll spend the evening getting chord charts for "Already Dead" and "Where's My Giant Robot" ready for the band to play. Cleaning up the house a bit since Emmit is crashing here between sessions, and I'm trying to rest so I don't push myself too hard and end up sick.

It's a shame that my body is acting up like this. Have a cool idea for a song, but I'm scared to try and write it because my voice is so ragged, and I have to conserve it for all the usage over the next few days. But it's nice to have ideas for new songs again. Soon!

## 5-17-16

And just that quickly, all plans for the recording sessions are squashed. Jim and I got very ill with a terrible cold. If it had just been me, I would have pressed on. I could have simply overdubbed my vocals later. At first, I was terrified to call the band and tell them because they both had to request time off from work to do this cassette. Turns out that Jim looked at the cancellation as a blessing because he wanted to spend the day in bed.

## 5-20-16

Only have a little writing time before I must run off to watch my wife do some aerial art. Those venues are always so punk rock. Just imagine converted warehouse spaces with a couple of folding chairs, piles of unfinished insulation everywhere and a folding table where they sell some snacks. That's pretty much it. And I think it's really cool. It's people doing their chosen art by any means necessary. Exactly how I started. They're honestly the types of venues I might be almost too jaded to play now, but I always feel differently once I see one of the shows she appears in. Plus, she's been working very hard on a routine based around an Alex Winston song. I helped her make an edit of the track that would fit her needed performance length. She's going to steal the show, as always. I've been plunking away at a one-person show idea that'd tie a bunch of stuff together for years, and I'd love to put it on in a non-traditional venue just like that.

Last night I surprised my daughter by taking her to see Micky Dolenz and Peter Tork touring as The Monkees. The band has been a fixture in her life since she was little – I certainly saw to that – and now she's appreciating them on differing levels as she ages. She was mostly upset that they didn't play "Can You Dig It?", which is a rather obscure tune from the *Head* soundtrack – my daughter, folks – but otherwise was elated at the surprise. We had a great time together, and I worked really hard to hide the fact that I felt totally miserable from the diagnosed early stages of acute bronchitis. DayQuil and inhalers kept me going. It was cool to hear deep cuts like "Steam Engine" and "Don't Do It," but not quite as neat to watch Micky forget the words to "Saturday's Child," a song he has no doubt performed thousands of times. Time waits for no one.

If you subscribe to the spoon theory? By today, most of my major symptoms have subsided, but the complete lack of energy hasn't. I'd like to regain those specific spoons very soon. I have a lot to do. Many songs that I want to work on. I am the last act of a festival in just over a week, and I haven't even begun to consider my setlist. It's probably just as well that the band couldn't work on the cassette. I was kidding myself about how rough I felt during the prep work or writing chord charts. I looked over the chart for "Already Dead" and couldn't believe what I was about to hand to Emmit. I must have either had a serious case of medicine-head or been thinking about a different chorus altogether.

Nicole just texted me to let me know she'll be going on next to last. Now I'm not sure when to leave. I'll continue as planned until given further instructions, I suppose? Don't want to be disrespectful to the other performers even though I'm clearly only there to watch my wife.

Back to the lack of energy? Today, all I've been able to do is open a package of records that I ordered – rare titles by Eugenius and Jonathan Richman – change a light bulb in the bedroom, sweep up the shards of a drinking glass that I dropped, and send out this week's packages at the post office. Usually I'd have gotten that all done by the second hour of being awake. Today, it's taken hours. Hope nobody is waiting on the edge of their seat for my next move. They might be uncomfortable for a while.

6-12-16

What's being referred to as the "worst mass shooting in U.S. history" happened in Orlando this morning, merely 10 miles from my house. At this point, we know very few concrete details, though speculations and arguments are running rampant. Today, we have heard that around 50-60 people were shot at a LGBTQ+ club called Pulse, and at least 50 more were injured.

The day before, a young singer named Christina Grimmie was shot and killed while signing autographs after her show at The Plaza, also in Orlando.

I am a pretty staunch opponent to guns being everywhere, and while these events reinforce my initial attitudes, even without the guns themselves, the hatred that would move someone to take lives in this manner will not go away. While I know very little about the motivations behind both tragedies, one could certainly not be blamed for believing that you don't intentionally lay waste to a night club and then figure out halfway through that it was an LGBTQ+ establishment. Likely purposeful. But again, I know next to nothing right now.

I've done a few things as a reaction. First, I temporarily removed some of the more violent songs out of Nerdy.FM's rotation. I paused all of the paid online advertising for the new pressing of Bubblegum Romance and Tim Labonte's fantastic new video for "Where's My Giant Robot" because the salesman hat doesn't feel like it fits right today. I messaged the band to tell them that "The Right To Bear Arms," "A Shot At Love," and "Terror Song" will be taking a hiatus from the setlists. I can't donate blood due to my hemochromatosis, but Nicole can, and all of the facilities for donation were overrun, so trying to help out in the short term didn't work out. Local promoter Kent Ward and EyeQ were talking about putting together a charity show to benefit whoever needs benefiting. I immediately volunteered to play.

I love Orlando, and the last thing I want to see as an outcome would be innocent folks that are scared to go out and enjoy all of the neat things and places that this city has to offer because of awful tragedies. The longer we wait to get back "out there," the harder it will be. As a community, we need to embrace each other and the melting pot of culture that we are so lucky to have. I want to help. I'd love to get on a stage and sing "Music Can Heal" right now – even tonight, if possible.

I mourn and grieve for the victims and their families, but I also am incredibly hesitant to let these atrocities define the place that I call home. I want to get back out there and sing songs that make people feel better as soon as possible.

With the heavy reminders that life is short, fleeting and precious, my wife and I needed a break from all of the stormy moods. We stayed in for the night playing records that make us happy – platters by James, Imperial Teen, Kirsty MacColl, David Bowie, and the soundtrack to *Walk Hard* – and playing silly games like Scrabble and Uno. We needed something lighthearted to do. We have to take advantage of those little things that we experience together. They are the things you'll miss when they are no longer available, and nothing is forever.

Meanwhile, all the other stuff I was up to this week seems trivial now. It all seems like fluff in comparison to the slaughter of the patrons of Pulse, a club that many of my friends and fellow performers frequent. The only thing that feels right today is keeping my loved ones close.


6-14-16

Members of the Orlando community have wasted no time in putting on an event at The Geek Easy with money going to the Pulse victims. It'll happen Saturday, and right now there are over a thousand RSVPs less than 24 hours after the event was announced.

Originally, we were to record a Milk Carton Superstars live session for Nerdy. FM on that day, but as soon as the event became a confirmed thing, we all dropped our plans to offer our services. At this point, there's talk of all of the Claire members getting together to play "The Real Enemy" during the MCS set. Even that one song took a little bit of negotiations, as all of the members wanted to go about things in a different way, but for the most part I think we're all trying to keep our egos in check to just pull out something heartfelt for the event.

Tonight my regular band will resume rehearsals. I do this with a heavy heart, remembering those that can't carry on with their lives, but also out of respect – letting no perceived threats scare us into hiding. It's times like this that I remember the love between myself, Jim, and Emmit. We're a good team, and sometimes I feel like we're brothers that don't really fight.

If I'm nervous about anything? The Geek Easy is about to have a lot of attention thrown its way. You can maybe cram 300 people in there if they are all holding in their breath. It has two exits and one bathroom. I don't know if the building is ready for all of this love. But on the performer side of things, this looks to be an event that's coming together with no egos and all heart. We just want to carry on and celebrate the good things about Orlando and to show the world that we have not been defeated. I hope we make it clear and that our attitudes are contagious.

6-20-16

I feel a little relieved after taking part in the Pulse charity event, but I know that our work is far from over. It's really got to be ongoing: until the LGBTQ+ community doesn't have to fear for their lives and rights simply because of who they are, until minorities aren't marginalized, and until the world becomes a kinder and less dangerous place? Our work will not be finished. It may never be done, actually. What matters is that we fight in any way possible.

Over $5,000 was raised that day for the victims of the Pulse tragedy, but it's a drop in the bucket compared to what is actually needed, I'm sure. And money only goes so far. There are still stubborn hearts and minds that have to be changed.

Also worthy of note was the Claire and The Potatoes reunion that took place with about 24 hours' worth of notice. It turned out that every former member was already involved with the event in some way, so it felt a little "now or never" to me. Not to mention a worthy reason to do it. We met up at Jim's house and went through "The Real Enemy" on the night before the show as if we'd never been away. Also tried a few other songs, but those were not as successful. We'd really only planned to do the one song at the end of the Milk Carton Superstars set, so that was just fine.

Leslie asked me afterward why I spoke with such animosity about the Claire era, and I came clean about my resentment toward the running-to-stand-still nature of the project, as well as my own personal turmoil from that time. Before we went onstage the following day, I got us all in a huddle to apologize for any hurt my sour-puss nature may have caused and assured them that I would try not to be so stuck up about it anymore. That doesn't mean that there are plans for the future, either. Most of my stoic grumbling comes from the fact that I did not choose to end the Claire project; Leslie did. I took it as my job to keep the gates closed due to having a "final performance." I don't want to toy with people's emotions. If it's dead, let it be dead. I do have love for those three people, and if the right occasion came up to play some more songs together, I probably wouldn't be as deeply opposed to it as I was in the past. Though I also wouldn't chart it very high on the list of probable turns for my career.

My own set at the Pulse event was very therapeutic for me. Songs like "Music Can Heal," "Happy To Be Alive," and "Motherfuckers Be Bullshittin'" took on a very different poignancy at this show. I was especially surprised at how malleable the latter song has become. It's oddly become one of the songs I'm most proud of in my entire career. Folks came up to me after the set to tell me how much "Music Can Heal" meant to them, and I'm still shocked every time. It's almost as if my music of the past caught up to what (some) people want to hear today. An odd intersection for me, especially since I consider myself to be a current artist with plans to make more music. Just not today. I've got a few new songs now, a few that I'm wild about.

7-9-16

Today, I'm listening to the first McCarthy Trenching album and trying to take it easy. The world has lost its mind with shootings, protests have turned into riots, and people have Pokemon apps for their phone. Alternately, every few months, someone I'm related to will completely lose it, and a ripple effect will make its way through the family. That's happening right now, too.

I feel guilty writing songs with all of the confusion. I feel guilty for not writing songs amidst all of the confusion. I can't remember a time where I've put more pressure on myself to finish an album, actually. I feel that if the album is a dying format, my next statement – or rather, the one I'm in the process of making that began with *Unicorns Get More Bacon* – had better be absolutely fantastic to even have an excuse to exist. With that being said, I really need today's journal entry to be lighthearted. No nitty gritty stuff today.

I accidentally stumbled on a song that I wrote and must have squirreled away called "I'm Glad It's Not Your Birthday," but I'm not sure when it was written. Probably before the Claire project, as it reuses part of the chorus of "Empirical Arguments" – the "I just want to have something to do" portion that I'd been trying to shoehorn into a song for a few years – and likely after 2010, as the demo sounds like a digital recording. Interestingly, the song has a bit of promise, and with some retooling, it might be a contender for future release. I have to come up with a better system of archiving demos because this is a common thing. "I'm Gonna Miss You" was mostly written in 2003, but I didn't stumble upon the demo again until 2012 or so. This happens more often than I'd like it to, but it's also like I'm giving myself a present when I stumble on a good one.

Nicole ordered a Monkees Blu-ray set for my birthday. It contains the entire series restored to HD standards, plus their movie, TV specials, and almost every commercial they appeared in from the '60s. My birthday was in January and that was when it was supposed to be released, but it'd been pushed back until now. People are reporting damaged boxes, missing discs, torn lenticular covers, but I seem to be the only person that got it as intended/advertised. Last night when I should have been restringing all of my guitars and working on new music? I was drinking Ecto Cooler and watching episodes from season one.

I'm also drinking Ecto Cooler right now. Can't be good for me, but it's delicious, and I've been pretty conscious of my diet recently. I'll allow it. Today.

I've recently been on a huge kick for the band War. I saw them at a free concert when I was about 13, and they turned a simple free gig into a full-on downtown dance party. One of the best shows I've ever seen. Since then, I have had the major releases: *All Day Music*, *The World Is a Ghetto*, *Deliver The Word*, etc. I sort of lose interest in their music just after 1983, but I'd recently discovered that there were tons of albums that I didn't have. Soundtracks, albums under the moniker The Music Band, and early stuff with Eric Burdon – I thought they'd only made one album with him. Since there isn't much interest in the group lately, I've been able to pick up all of these albums pretty cheaply. I'm especially digging an album they did with Bobby Womack called *The Other Side Of War Warms Your Heart.* Kind of a soul record for rainy days. Also digging one called *The Music Band Jazz.*

They are so underrated, but they've tarnished their legacy with versions of the band that only contain one original member. Unless they bury the hatchet, and the remaining living members play together again to remind the world of what a killer bunch of groove creators they are? They'll likely just be remembered as the cats that did "Low Rider" and "Why Can't We Be Friends." Not a bad way to be immortalized, but they are so much more than that, and they deserve better.

It does sort of strike me odd that a band with such a rich, fun, uplifting, and rewarding discography like War can languish in obscurity. Meanwhile, the world-at-large picked, say, Foo Fighters to get really into. Nothing wrong with the Foos, but why them? Their music is no more interesting than the War albums to my ears. And Radiohead? Cool band that made some records I genuinely love, but I don't hear anything in their LPs that hadn't been done multiple times over by Brian Eno. I'll never understand how we choose who we're gonna love en masse.

Since there isn't any real meat to this journal entry, I'll tell you a pre-Marc With a C story. Gather 'round.

I was a teenage Nirvana fanatic. I didn't just love the lyrics, liner notes, T-shirts, rhythms and whatnot, but I'd actually pick apart blasts of feedback on the albums, trying to figure out what that mistake might have communicated. I was in **deep** with those records. Maybe deeper than I've ever been with recorded music? (That's a real possibility, as I've heard those albums so many times that I haven't felt the urge to hear them in about 10 years as of this writing, I feel like I know them so well that they've ceased to be entertainment.)

You'd be correct in assuming that I was emotionally destroyed by the death of Kurt Cobain. And you'd also be correct to assume that when I found out that Dave Grohl was carrying on with Pat Smear that I decided that this band would not only "carry the torch" but possibly save rock and roll and all of the world's problems. That didn't occur, but Foo Fighters turned out to be a pretty good rock band.

I went with some friends to see Foo Fighters in 1996 when they came to Orlando. I was more interested in the Nirvana-by-proxy aspect of the gig than any of their actual music, but when I found out that Kim Deal would be opening with her new band, The Amps? Nothing could have kept me away from that show.

I'd heard that Foo Fighters were doing a cover of Tubeway Army's "Down In The Park." I had just discovered Tubeway Army from a Marilyn Manson b-side, and this was arguably the most exciting prospect of the show for me. Plus, my teenage band was known for covering "Down In The Park" at the time, so that would be extra cool to see Dave Grohl do it in concert.

By the time they came out for the encore, they still hadn't played that song, and as I was right up front, I started yelling obnoxiously for them to play it. Somehow, it worked. I started rocking out and was definitely bumping into the people sandwiched next to me against the barricade. Dave tapped a security guard on the shoulder and pointed at me. I was sure I was being thrown out, but instead? I was pulled onstage and planted in front of a microphone to sing the song with Mr. Grohl. My memory goes black at that point, but for many years afterward, I was recognized as "the guy that knew Dave Grohl," and it certainly didn't hurt my old band with bookings. I don't have a recording of the show, and the only souvenir I had from the night was a T-shirt that the band signed backstage for me.

Unfortunately, I'd given the shirt to Ska Steve back when he was referring to me as his best friend and brother. I didn't have much money for his birthday, so it became a gift. He really loved the band, so it made me happy to do at the time. If I'd have known he'd eventually cut me out of his life for daring to criticize his treatment of women, I'd have kept it. Live and learn.

I'm not against pulling a Muppet-style caper to retrieve it one day, though.

7-16-16

Today I played at a cystic fibrosis benefit, and it wasn't a good time. Even though the event was happening adjacent to a building with a stage and a PA inside, I was on an outdoor stage where the people outside simply did not come to hear music. They didn't love or hate me; it was just the worst possible reaction: indifference. If someone yells "you suck" or "fuck you" when I'm doing a gig, I can work with that. I mean, I wouldn't be happy about that, but I'd have circumstances to overcome. There is a chance I can win them over. At this particular show, the few people milling about didn't even half-heartedly applaud between songs. Just continued their conversations.

Those "indifference" shows are incredibly disheartening. You forget every compliment you've ever received, every award, every standing ovation, every word of encouragement, etc. All you can think about is running as far away from the show as possible and never touching your instrument again. Even though I know deep down that I'm a pretty okay recording artist, my brain is telling me how much I suck at my profession.

The whole day was a real wash. The organizers had put the wrong address on their Facebook event invite, and people were being sent to the location of a closed down building with an empty parking lot. The hot weather was oppressive to say the least, and by the time I left, I was breaking out in splotchy hives from being overheated. Aubree and her mother came out to show support, but it turns out that this CF organization has apparently refused to help them in any way, and if I had known that from the get-go, I never would have signed on. When it became clear that the only people listening were Aubree, Terrie and Nicole, I just ditched my planned setlist and started playing stuff that I liked, like "Winter Colors" and "Pinball Wizard." No records or T-shirts were sold. Didn't seem to make a single new fan out of what was purported to be around two or three hundred people spread out over a field. I can't help but to take that pretty hard.

Heck, since it was a benefit? I can't even say to myself "at least I got paid." Hope the next show goes better. I don't take mediocre receptions very well. I liked hanging out with Aubree, though. She's one of the sweetest people I've ever met, and her mission in coming to the show was just to make sure that I didn't suffer alone. That's a good friend, right there.

Recorded a few new demos this week, including a brushed up version of "I'm Glad It's Not Your Birthday." Dropped the reused Claire lyric, and now I think the chorus needs a little something extra, but beyond that, it feels like the most "Marc" of the new batch so far. Also finished up a cover of Duran Duran's "Chauffeur," which is the fourth tune of theirs I've recorded this year. Sometimes I feel as if I'm working toward a tribute album/EP for them, but something in me keeps saying "it isn't the right time," so I'm unsure what to do with the recordings now. I'll just take my own advice and keep making stuff when I'm inspired.

7-30-16

I'm midway through prepping the songs for the next album. Jordon Zadorozny has agreed to produce it, and this is massive for me. I'm envisioning building the album from the ground up with his advice about arrangements and general ear candy. His albums as Blinker The Star are full of some of my very favorite tones committed to tape in my lifetime. Few could currently know the gravity of what this album represents for my career and life, and interestingly, as I don't know when these words will first be released to the public, I am not sure that I can explain it here. I can say that I have a plan that started as a whim, but I haven't been able to shake it for years. I fully made the decision around the time of *Exactly Where I Am*, and it's what I feel I am constantly working toward. So why not make the most important part of the process with a producer that I absolutely love? Let's go back to the beginning of Marc With a C: have a producer guide me, but get better results. I'm excited, and Jordon seems to be as well. We've been trying to make this happen for a number of years, but it had to wait for the "right" record. Now that I know the trajectory? It's time.

I was supposed to be doing a photoshoot with a person named Vikka today, but the week had really gotten away from me, and I hadn't gotten permission from all of the locations. Also, Meatwad had congestive heart failure a few weeks ago, and while he's heavily medicated, he still flips out when new people come over. I'm not sure that his little ticker is ready for having a portion of the photoshoot taking place in the living room with all of the records.

Tomorrow I'm slated to play for about an hour at LAMECon in a town called

Land O' Lakes. It's nearly two hours away, but I'm excited and optimistic about it. Fun aside about the gig: it's yet another show where I've been told that I can't swear, yet the organizers have specifically requested that I perform "Stuck With Me." That song says "fuck" four times. I've got a good and relatively clean setlist written up. Just hoping that the gig goes well. I really need a positive experience after that horrible benefit show. I think I underestimated just how deeply it had shaken my confidence. Each time I've picked up my guitar since, I've considered putting it right back down, with a voice in my head reminding me that no one wants to hear my stupid bullshit songs anyways.

There's more stuff that's gone on this week, but it's mostly been related to fighting my own self-esteem to try to work on new material. That's all that I feel I can do. Just keep playing, even if no one will care or like it. If I'm happy with the results, then I've made successful music. Besides, now that I have a bunch of Marc With a C stickers, I've got to keep going so that people will want to stick them places, right?

8-6-16

Everything hurts. Played a Tampa gig. Odd setup. I opened with an hour of clean material, Uke-A-Ladies played for around two hours, and then I did an hour of the more "adult-oriented" material. That's the basic premise, at least.

The reality is that the venue was a glorified sports bar, and the patrons really didn't feel like listening to music. There was a leak in a pipe above the stage, leaving puddles everywhere and soaking a lot of our equipment. You really didn't feel very safe on the foot-high stage. Every member of Uke-A-Ladies was very ill, and the stage/PA situation was kind of a joke. Before we loaded in, I told them that if they decided that they wanted to cancel, I'd walk out in solidarity. There just didn't seem to be any chance of the show being rewarding for any of us. Obviously, the show went on.

There were roughly eight really big fans that came to see me, and they'd staked out their places in front of the makeshift stage. I could see the waitress being alternately surprised and frustrated that they weren't ordering food and had just come for the show. This pub clearly wasn't a place where people came to watch concerts. Music is atmosphere here at best.

In my second set, the eight fans were right up front, and there were scattered people through the venue watching the Olympic opening ceremonies on television. My chatter-filled set wasn't vibing with what the people in the back had shown up for. Probably just wanted Sublime covers while they drank expensive beers. But taking a page from the book of Zappa, I decided to offer the attendees an "evening of completely personalized entertainment," using conversation to lead me into stories, with stories leading to songs, getting the listeners to supply rhythmic support, stealing their cell phones while they chanted during "Dick Steel," then giving them back to the wrong owners during the second chanting section. They sat there for hours waiting for me to come on, and I felt like it was my duty to give them a Marc With a C show unlike any other that had ever existed. I think it worked. Each one of them walked out with merchandise, thanking me for coming to their town.

I can say that the pub had really good fish and chips. Emmit came by since one of his other bands was playing just up the road. He tried to order some chips and gravy from this British-themed place, and the waiter looked at him like he was speaking Klingon.

I'm trying very hard to take this weekend off. Besides writing these thoughts, taking a shower, and playing some records or reading, I really need to not do anything for a few days. My body is feeling the effects of stress and overuse, and I'm mentally taxed while alternately not feeling excited about anything. Since that could be a dangerous combination, I need a few days of simplicity. If nothing else, my body could really use a few days to recuperate.

8-13-16

It's barely been a week since I wrote here last, but it feels like years.

In preparation to record the fabled live-in-the-studio cassette that's had a bunch of false starts now, I was mapping out where each of the eight channels used to capture the band's performance would be sent, and in some cases doubled up and submixed. The gravity of the project started to really set in, and at that very moment, I looked at social media and saw that Bob Hershberger was offering up services for mobile recording.

I've known Bob for about 10 years. He's been a local bartender, sound guy at plenty of my hometown gigs, he's opened for me with his Bob On Blonde project, vice versa, etc. We have a healthy respect between us. I made the 11th-hour decision to hire him to bring his rig down so he could engineer and capture the performances. This meant making a bunch of frantic calls to Jim and Emmit about why this was a good idea, and why the newly raised price tag for the project would be beneficial. My argument was that, yes, I can record it myself, but we're going to end up with distracted performances as

I'm keeping one eye on the dials, hoping that the snare drum isn't clipping, for example. Or I can just bring Bob in, have everything set up in a professional and trustworthy manner, get handed the files afterwards, and then make us sound like we actually sound in the ensuing days.

Bob really was a pro. It took an abnormally long time to get set up, though. We planned to meet at 1:30 at Jim's place for setup and to be playing by 3 p.m. This'd leave us plenty of time to do extra takes if needed. Around 2:30, Bob realized he hadn't brought an absolutely mandatory cable that was also completely obsolete – couldn't just run to a store to buy one. He scrambled to call people and find one, and Emmit and I had to drive to get it, getting caught in one of the horrific afternoon storms that Florida is famous for. When we returned with the cable, not a single microphone had been set up. It was interminable, and there's little that I detest more than hurry-up-and-wait.

We finally started playing at 5 p.m. and had five hours to get satisfactory takes of 40 songs. The first set was acoustic, and only "God Save The Queen From Navy Seals" had to be redone, which wasn't a song that I expected to make the final cut, but Emmit really wanted a copy of us playing it, so it was mostly done for our own archives. Ended up getting such a fiery take that it could make it to the tape after all.

The first electric set didn't fare as well. "Popular Music" is a real nemesis for Jim and took three tries before we got a take that we liked. And then there was "The End Of Popular Music." That's one of the most difficult arrangements we have because the numbers of bars in each connecting piece change every time they are played, and it becomes very easy to get lost. While trying to capture it, Bethany (Jim's wife) came home and had brought us sandwiches so that we didn't have to go out, which was nice of her. Unfortunately, it made their dog Tigger lose his mind and bark his head off. Bethany kept coming in and out of the room we were recording in, and it was really distracting against a complex song. Each time, we'd get almost to the home-stretch of the tune and something else would happen in the house to throw one of us off. The third time that we train-wrecked in the exact same part of the song, I lost my cool, threw the Fender into its stand, and walked out to collect my thoughts.

I was ticked because the sessions now weren't free, and we were trying to beat a clock, plus the more we played, the more strained my throat would be, making later takes "less than." I had to keep reminding myself that we were in Bethany's home space, and that she could go wherever she damn well pleased whenever she wanted because otherwise there's no reason to have a house. Jim and Bethany volunteered the space for rehearsals and recording, and I can't be upset if they needed to take their dog out in the dead center of one of the hardest songs in our catalog. A few hits from my e-cig and I calmed down. Bob came out to check on me, took a few tokes of his own, and reminded me just how much we'd accomplished in a short amount of time. I mellowed out while everyone else ate dinner.

The third set was relatively sedate, as the Rickenbacker gives off more calm and controlled tones than the Fender, but also might have been the best of the three for this very reason. While the point was to capture us "as we are," a recording is still very different from a live performance. You're trying to make it sound like you're jumping around and having the time of your life while standing or sitting very still. This is where some manners of acting come into play. In these situations, I might throw in a few extra vocal tics than I usually would for that hint of extra personality. Or "putting the eyebrows" on, as Zappa might have said.

We wrapped up all of the actual playing at around 10 p.m. and commenced to dismantling all of the equipment. Much easier than the setup. We were all so bushed from the sessions that I didn't have the energy to thank everyone as warmly as I would have really liked to. Considering that we set out to record 40 songs and captured 39 in five hours of playing? I can't help but to be proud of everyone's efforts. We're a pretty fuckin' good rock band.

I've spent the bulk of the week mixing the sessions. Bob gave me great and well-miked individual tracks to piece together, so thankfully I could merely focus on EQ and imaging rather than "fixing" things. In truth, I did fix a few things. There were roughly two songs where Jim played an extra beat, and I faded those out. Emmit was noticeably late on one crucial note in "DJ Danny Treanor," so I copied the note from earlier in the song and plopped it into place. I punched in precisely two vocal lines of my own that I simply couldn't live with, but I won't tell you which ones. I'm willing to bet that you wouldn't notice, but also, I only remember what one of them was.

While mixing, I ran over the cable from my new pair of headphones with my office chair and killed them. One casualty. I'll pour out a tall cold one for it later.

Now the mixes are done, and I've uploaded all of the songs to the rest of the band. We now must go through each track separately and decide what we like the best. We have two hours of recordings, but the tape is to be an hour long. Severe edits will have to be made, and I think that some feelings will be hurt in that stage. I already have my own personal list of "I hope this doesn't make the cut" tracks, but I don't want to tell the band what those are, as I want them to have equal say in the final tracklist. I'll tell you that I'd like for the recordings of "Make You Better," "Jessica, I Heard You Like The Who," and "The Right To Bear Arms" to stay under wraps. You can compare my list to whatever the finished tracklist is to see if I got my way.

This is a lot of work for what is ultimately a fringe release. A cassette-only, live-in-studio recording of the current lineup playing songs from all over my catalog? What a rehash, right? Maybe to some eyes. And I don't suppose I could blame you for thinking so. But this is an important release for me on a personal level: my excitement for playing with Jim and Emmit is only equally rivaled by playing live shows with Chris in the *Bubblegum Romance* days. Every other lineup is a runner-up for me. This feels like home, just as much as playing solo. It is important to me to capture this and show it to people. This is a major phase in my career, but it's being represented in an odd way. Should something happen to this lineup's ability to perform together? I'm just going back to being solo all of the time. Neither of these guys is replaceable. I don't want to play with musicians that aren't them for Marc With a C performances, and this is the way to best show that off.

Plus, putting it out on tape means that no one has to feel like they are buying anything for the billionth time. If you don't like the idea of buying this tape? Fine. Don't. We're making this for us, and for the burgeoning cassette resurgence market. People who want tapes should have an option at the merch table that's just for them. Alternately, I didn't want to just reuse older recordings for a tape compilation. Would have been too easy and a total throwaway. If we're making a tape for the first time, we're going to build it from the ground up.

On top of recording and mixing 39 songs this week? I also finished and sent the masters for the *Linda Lovelace For President* and *Losing Salt* albums to the pressing plant. And did a few more videos for the "unboxing series" I'm doing for the Get It On Vinyl website. I'm worn out. (The unboxing series is exactly what it sounds like: I get records in the mail, open the box on camera, and talk about it. It's like ASMR for people who like to open mail that does not belong to them.)

Today, I'll review the tape mixes in the car. It's my sister-in-law's birthday, so we're going to a dinner for her, and then if we get out in time, we'll go to see the new Zappa documentary in Winter Park. Sure, I've already seen the screener, but it was fantastic, and I want to see it a second time, and I'm hoping against hope it'll help Nicole to understand where my Zappa obsession comes from. Maybe she'll even start to dig some of the recordings? She's tried, but aside from a few songs on *Joe's Garage*, I don't think anything stuck. It takes a very special person to understand Frank. Nicole is special, so fingers crossed.

8-16-16

Haven't been up for long today, already in a crappy mood. I'd secretly been asked to go to a wedding in another state and play "Long Distance Dedication" at the wedding of some fans that really like the song. I was making enough money from the appearance to have a financial backbone for a small run of tour dates. I'd been told by the groom that it needed to be a huge secret, and that I wasn't to talk to the bride about it under any circumstances, otherwise I'd ruin the surprise. The first correspondence I saw when I woke up today was from said bride telling me that she was sad that it couldn't happen.

These fans are very nice, so I decided to just walk away and not talk about it any further with them today. If they can't make it happen financially, I can't be mad at them — that'd be a fool's errand. However, a few hours of conversation had been spent planning it all, and I was scheduling my fall concerts around it. Without this gig, there is no tour. Without a tour, I now have weeks of wasted correspondence when I could have been making other plans. I feel like a jerk for being upset about it. It's their wedding, after all. I have to conduct myself like an adult. All smiles. Happy fun Marc. That's what people want.

Spent a few days mixing the *Cark* tape, but I've run into more issues. I'm not convinced that the whole thing doesn't need one further remix, but I might rest my ears today. Jim has the brightest snare and cymbals that I've ever heard in my life, and while it sounds really cool onstage and in the room, it isn't friendly for mixing. My current task is to hand the band a version of the cassette that they can just press play on to give me a yay or nay on the tracklist. I'm now to hand them the version that I would have made if they'd had no input at all, and then they are to tell me what they'd have excluded/ included instead. I was up late last night making the tracklist, but side two is still 10 seconds too long, even though I've scrunched all of the segues together as tight as possible. I'm probably going to have to drop either "Song Song" or "Stairway To Rudolph." The former is one that we like to play. The latter is one that will help sell the tape. And that's assuming that the band even wants those versions released.

I should probably get myself together enough to go acquire that haircut I've been meaning to get for about a week. And I still have to bring a thumb drive back to Bob.

8-26-16

Have absolutely no idea what to do with myself. Nicole is performing at a festival in Atlanta over the weekend. Took her to the airport at 4 a.m. As soon as I woke up around noon just to get a drink of water, Meatwad had very noisy and labored breathing. He couldn't walk to me. When I picked him up, his paws were freezing cold. It appeared that he was having congestive heart failure – again. Through tears, I called the vet and explained the situation, and they had me rush him over. He's now on oxygen, and I'm just sitting and waiting for the phone to ring.

For obvious reasons, I'm flipping out. Another less obvious reason is that Nicole is going to call at some point. She's going to ask how I am. She's going to ask how Meatwad is. She's going to hear in my voice that something is wrong. I cannot have her freaking out and panicking about the health of our dog while she needs to concentrate on doing aerial tricks. Usually, performers get sent home when there's a personal problem because it compromises their safety and concentration.

I don't lie to Nicole. I don't hold back. That's not our relationship. I had to call family members to ask how I should approach this: do I tell her or just avoid her phone calls until I know something concrete? I'm not programmed for this. I'm worried about my favorite little dude, but I'm also worried about treating Nicole in a disrespectful manner, wrecking her show. If I don't answer the phone when she calls or texts? She'll panic knowing that something isn't right.

I have a short set tomorrow at The Geek Easy – they are throwing a party for the second place winners of the Best Of Orlando poll, where I've placed without campaigning – and I've agreed to drop by and play "the favorites" for about a half an hour. "Life's So Hard," "Dickpuncher," etc. Even asked Leslie to drop by and sing "A Shot At Love" with me. I have put on a brave face for performing plenty of times, but since I'm the only one that can care for our dog at the moment, I'm not sure if I shouldn't cancel.

My initial plans for the weekend were to go full-on bachelor: clean the house wearing only boxer briefs, set up my amps, and just fuck around until I got some ideas recorded. Instead, my best furry friend is possibly at death's door again, and I have to find a way to break it to my wife. Marc With a C might just have to wait. The next call from the vet could potentially change everything.

8-28-16

I've got my headphones strapped on, have a Joni Mitchell LP on the office turntable, and I'm doing my best to wind down after a stressful few days.

Meatwad is home. He doesn't seem like himself, just appears to be completely exhausted and unexcited by anything. Since he came home yesterday and is fine besides being worn out, I finally broke down and told Nicole a smattering of what happened. I didn't get into the gory details, but I think that it was better to let her know what was going on once I could lead with the fact that he is home, safe and resting.

I was an absolute basket case. Haven't driven while crying for a very long time, and I can't say that I missed it.

Tonight I felt like the worst puppy parent in the world: I had to leave him alone to go and play that show at The Geek Easy. Talked to some friends about Zappa for a long while before the show which helped me relax quite a bit.

My set was pretty short by design. There was an odd mood in the room, though. More folks than normal just talking over my set, and I eventually just sort of laid into them in the middle of "Motherfuckers Be Bullshittin.'" I couldn't hear myself over them at all, so I pointed out that I didn't care if they didn't like me, but that they'd need to shut the fuck up for the people that came to listen. It worked, and I was called back for a totally unexpected encore. I wasn't prepared, so I asked for requests. Someone yelled for "Free Bird" from *Popular Music*, but I decided to just play the entirety of the Lynyrd Skynrd version. I stumbled on the words in the second verse, so I made up some new lyrics about how you should be careful what you request. And where the solo should have gone? I just shouted Minor Threat lyrics. It was a really fuckin' strange night.

9-1-16

The more I think about that Geek Easy show, the more I wish that I could have been in a better mood. I think I was nice to everyone I spoke to individually, but when I addressed the room, I believe I was too harsh. It had everything to do with being mentally preoccupied, but that's really no excuse. If people choose to give me even divided attention, I have to deliver all that I can and be happy to receive it. Some people that make up songs don't get any attention at all. I shouldn't be taking mine for granted.

Meatwad is doing great. You wouldn't even know that there was anything wrong to look at him right now. As long as he gets his medicine at the exact right time. I'm so lucky that Nicole understood my motivations for all of my actions. She's holding together and being exceptionally strong for him, which isn't her natural reaction. In cases like this, she usually defaults to being a factory of tears, but she knows that her attitude will rub off on him, and she is doing the same as I am: cherishing every day we get with that snarky little dude.

He's used to being the center of attention now, though. I was holding our bunny Alice Cooper last night, and he just flipped out. Whined, cried, couldn't handle it.

In other news, I'm slowly putting together the materials for the Patreon campaign that I don't really even want to run. Shot a bunch of footage for the introductory video last night, but I hadn't been sleeping well, and the panda eyes are especially noticeable. Hope it won't deter anyone from supporting me. I still feel strange about it, but I'm being pretty clear that I'm not really changing what I do or kowtowing to demands with the Patreon: you simply have the option to give me money every month for what I'd already be doing anyways.

And I need it. Because, look, we all knew streaming was going to fuck us up, but the reality is that my mail-order business is basically kaput unless I have JUST released a new thing. It doesn't live on without hype. Otherwise, I mostly sell physical items at shows, and the mail-order stuff is often found by people willfully looking for something very obscure (and if you're one of them, I cannot possibly thank you enough). I don't have the money to tour to play more shows to sell more items. Instead of buying vinyl and CDs, people are streaming the music, even the curious collectors of obscurities. I am thankful that anyone is listening at all, but the money I make per stream is laughable. I have as many listeners as I ever did – hell, probably more – but it's bringing in less income than it ever has. I either have to go the route of asking for money to be Marc With a C or go and do something else completely.

Went to Jim's house with a massive headache to help him out in planning the vinyl release of the upcoming Milk Carton Superstars album. I was a little surprised at how Kramer chose to master the album – not with sound, but he left a few steps for the cutting engineer to do, which is the opposite of mastering. Unless I'm mistaken, the master should equal "everything is done except for the plant sticking it on the right format." I could be dead wrong, though!

Regardless, hearing that new MCS album was pretty inspiring. Orlando doesn't know what they've got right under their nose with that band. They don't get called for the sweet opening gigs. They don't win awards. They don't hobnob with the people you're supposed to be friends with to get ahead in this town – they just make better music and wait for the right people to find them. Such a good album, and I'm so proud to appear on it, even briefly.

Today a hurricane is passing over Florida. Orlando is just getting the outer bands, but it's basically just overcast and gloomy outside. Looks like a Morrissey video. I find this inspiring. It reminds me of what the sky looks like during cold weather. Cold weather inspires me greatly – I usually do all of my best writing bundled up in a hoodie. I want to write some more new songs, mostly to wrap up this next album. I think my big stumbling block is that I want to say something very "final" with this trio of albums. Each time I put pen to page, two things cross my mind: is this subject important enough to deserve space on a new album, and what is the more important thing that I should be covering in case I die tomorrow? It's creating a writer's block of sorts, but just for songs. Usually there's nothing to do but to just get on with it and write the song, even if it sucks, but I can't stop second-guessing myself long enough to even write something terrible.

9-18-16

Patreon is launched. Almost at $200 bucks per month. That's not quite wrinkly-old-white-people money, but it'll help out a lot. Tomorrow, the backers will get to see the new video for "Epic Fail" a week earlier than the general public. Tim Labonte did a great job, and when I inquired about further videos – maybe something to push along the upcoming reissues – he came clean with me about a health problem that might sideline him for a bit. Had I known that he was going through a rough patch, I might've just paid him for the video and decided that fourth single wasn't nearly as important as his health. I didn't know until I saw the finished edit. I hope he's okay. I also don't know what this means for future music videos.

It used to feel good to write songs just for the sake of writing. Now when I put the pen to page, I know that I'll need to sing a bunch of melodies to try to form it into a song, and it's probably going to ache after about 15 minutes. I now associate writing songs with physical pain, and if it keeps up, I may have to go and seek even more therapy.

The *Cark* tapes should be here by the middle of next week. I found this plant very nice to work with when I finally got ahold of someone – had to call them via Skype to get some answers. It just so happened that the week we decided to push things through was the same week that most of their staff went on vacation. My luck in a nutshell. My own tape deck is on the fritz, but it's lived quite the life, so after much careful searching, I bought a used but minty JVC deck from eBay.

Y'see, I'd tried to buy a tape deck from someone on Craigslist, and once I made sure they weren't a serial killer, Nicole and I drove to a shockingly nice neighborhood in Apopka to make the transaction. Turns out that it was just a little old lady selling off things she didn't use, and this tape deck looked like it'd never been touched. I handed her the $24, and we hit the road. It didn't work, and my vocational training in electronics didn't come in handy, as it was a frozen belt issue. Didn't feel right to go and pound on the door of the nice lady and demand a refund. She probably needed the money more than I needed a tape deck. She'd actually brought a police officer over to watch the transaction take place. How cute is that?

9-23-16

Just woke up, but it's right back to work I go. This week I've done one demo that I like, one halfway done song that I'm very "meh" about, and a silly cover done to blow off steam. I'd talk about what's going on with that "meh" demo, but it's stupid tonal stuff. It was a good idea in my head, but it didn't work in practice.

*Cark* tapes are in. For the first wave of release, we've teamed up with Park Ave CD's for their celebration of Cassette Store Day. The album will be released for one day, October 8, and if you don't get it that day, you'd have to wait until December to buy one. When I first played the tape, my heart sank a little bit. After working so hard on the sessions and the ensuing mixing? The tape made it sound so muddy and hissy, and it sounds so inferior. But that's just a normal bias cassette for you. Despite the small cassette resurgence, I don't see many plants offering the superior option of chrome tapes, but I also feel like they transferred it at a very low volume and that contributed to the low fidelity.

I'd told Patreon supporters about it, and immediately I was asked for a digital version – of course, we're going to do something along those lines, but the point here is to do it on this older format first. I don't like telling people that they can't have my (publicly released) recordings for any reason, so doing this type of "exclusive" release will be a real test of patience for me.

One of those Patreon backers seems to be a bit of an audiophile. We frequent many of the same "sound nerd" message boards. You'd never know it to listen to my albums, but I'm quite big on audiophilia. Though I'm not looking for perfection in tone - I want music to sound as close to the artistic intent as possible on consumer-grade equipment. I don't feel that I need to spend a few grand to hear music "properly." I just wanted it to sound like it oughta.

My current living room rig isn't that impressive: a 1984 Marantz amplifier, a

Pro-Ject Debut turntable with a Nagaoka MP-110 cartridge, some Bose Phase II speakers, and the new JVC tape deck I just procured. For CDs and whatnot, I merely use my DVD player. I don't even have a port to run an iPod or a computer into it. This stuff is all priced and aimed at the average consumer. And for most things, it sounds pretty good. When something sounds crummy on the system, I know that it probably sounds that way for everyone else and that someone fucked up along the line.

An infamous example was a Muffs album around 2014: I plopped it on the turntable after a lengthy session with AJ In Evolution, and we couldn't believe the garbage that was coming out of the speakers. Just this horrible midrange mess. This is a punk rock group, and the digital version of the album sounds fine (brickwalled, but fine), so I know that anyone else's copy of the vinyl is probably the musical equivalent of listening to the sound of baseball stadium dirt. That's it. My ears aren't special. I just want music to sound like it was supposed to when it left the studio. Usually vinyl is the most forgiving way to receive that, but the tides have been turning about that lately.

Some think that this attitude makes me demanding and snobbish about musical products, but I'd remind you that every single piece of gear (besides the turntable) was bought used for under $50. It's not that expensive to make music sound better, and it might improve your quality of life just a tad.

But not the cassette version of *Cark*. It sounds exactly the way I remember tapes to sound, and I'm not thrilled about it. Maybe it'll sound cool on boomboxes. Maybe people are just buying tapes for the download code. I have no idea what that market is all about.

10-2-16

It's late at night, and while my heart is full to bursting with emotions, I can't find the hook to hang them on when I'm working on lyrics. I believe that this is partially because I feel very low about the gig I did yesterday; EyeQ makes hip hop records, but a few years ago, he was just "my buddy Chris." He's grown by leaps and bounds as an artist while still being an unbelievably sweet and grounded guy. When he asked me to play a set at his public birthday party, I was happy to accept.

The audience was just not terribly present for the first half of my set. I probably started things off on the wrong foot. Just two lines into the opening song, a gigantic fog machine that was about 4 feet from my head thrust out a loud gust of synthetic cloudiness that completely engulfed the few that had come up to the front of the stage, and as a result, I completely forgot the words to "Unicorns Get More Bacon," a song that has opened nearly every show I've done for the past year. It took nearly half of the 40-minute set to get the room to respond to me in any way. Oddly, "Music Can Heal" was the song that turned it around. From there, I think I pulled off pretty good but cursory run-throughs of "Squiddy," "Life's So Hard," and "Happy To Be Alive." I still like performing the latter, but again, it felt like a gig where I was really working to connect and mostly failing.

Today, I find myself very sore all over my body. I did all of the prerequisite stretching that one is supposed to do, but I still feel like the guy that lost the fight. I was pretty excited to get back to playing shows, and now I'm left to wonder what I'm doing wrong. Truth be told, I'd let EyeQ pick the setlist as a birthday present, and he just happened to have picked a bunch of songs I'm terribly bored with at the moment (besides "Epic Fail" and "Music Can Heal"). It could just be that since I wasn't terribly connected to the songs, but there wasn't much way for the people in the room to do it either.

I'm looking forward to returning to the Universal Studios Halloween gigs because, despite the general confusion and stress that goes with opening for The Rich Weirdoes at a theme park, I'll mostly be playing songs for them I have never done in that building before. I really need that change of scenery right of now for performing. I can honestly say that I would have been better off if my touring plans had panned out for this year. Even financially. Funds are at a low ebb, and with the constant state of motion that touring places you in, it's a good reminder that "if you're not playin', you're payin'" or whatever Mike Watt used to say.

Overall, it's just a low-energy period for me. I keep trying to make things happen, and they simply aren't. The mood of the country is also pretty hopeless. According to the rules of drama that I heard someone make up on a YouTube video once? That just means I'm in the middle of Act II.

10-3-16

Wow, I was a real whiny-pants yesterday. It's a wonder that any of you have any patience at all with me, let alone interest in what I do.

Today I'm delivering the download codes to Park Ave CD's to go along with the limited-release of the *Cark* cassette. They'd also requested a CD copy for in-store play without any f-bombs. At first I was a bit dismayed at all of the cool songs that would have to be left off, but I got over that pretty quickly.

Also, I'd felt pretty back and forth about the situation, sometimes excited that the tape would happen, sometimes not crazy about the music being "held hostage" on a format that few are actually playing. Now I just think it's pretty cool that it exists.

There's also that "halfway between new albums" malaise and panic that's always a big cycle for me. Being unsure where I will end up creatively this time next year always does a big number on my head and attitude. One way that I might fight it? I've been writing a lot of songs that would be "perfect for the album I want to make," but in between, I'm not really writing anything that will bring joy specifically to me. This means that I'm treating nearly every aspect of creativity as a job, each idea as "saleable product." I need to make some stuff that gets me off without really being concerned about what to do with it.

I always "lose the plot" just a little bit when I know I'll be making more things soon, but I have to wait to birth it. Everything is fine. I can write any time I want to. I can (usually) play whatever I'd like during shows. I have no label that can reject my recordings and still charge me for the sessions. Compared to any other musician that might go through the bullshit tortured artist clichés, I'm actually doing pretty well, and it'd serve me well to remember that.

Something I've never talked about publicly has been popping into my head lately, and I'll share it with you now:

Years ago, in the middle of being in my first "real band," I'd given very rough cassette demos of numerous songs to the fluctuating members of the lineup so they could pick and choose what we'd learn. Not all of their playing skills were at the same level, so I wanted them to point to the songs they'd feel most comfortable building on, right? One member who was a budding visual artist had chosen 10 of these song recordings, seemingly at random, and put them on a cassette tape. They'd made an illustrated cover that looked pretty neat, called it *Experimental Serum* and handed me a copy, like "look, we can sell this." And I didn't see why we couldn't. I didn't (and still don't) think that the tracklist was representative of the best I was capable of at the time, nor did it seem to even inhabit the same world of what the band knew/would learn how to play, but sure enough, it looked like a low-budget local release, so why not?

We drove around to the local shops, looked at the local sections and decided to price the tape well under whatever the others cost to buy, ensuring that someone, some day, would walk into the record shop, only have a few bucks, and be looking for an impulse buy to check out. And to my surprise, this worked. The tapes always sold out. As we often were not playing shows in the towns where the tapes were moving, and the release had pretty much no radio support at all, we really had no clue who would be taking these things home, let alone what they'd make of the tape. There was a true divide between artist and audience.

Fast forward to 2002. A young lady calls into a radio station after they've just played "Why Don't Girls Like Me?" and demands to know where she can get the new album by Moloko Plus (one of the many names that this old lineup would use and discard). The DJ had no idea what she was talking about of course and said, "No, that song is by Marc With a C." Though my voice on the two recordings couldn't have been more worlds apart – if you think my voice is whiny on *Human Slushy*, you can't even imagine how squeaky, whiny, and gritty it was on that old demo tape – she somehow figured out that after years of searching, I was in fact the guy singing on that mysterious tape she'd bought years ago.

In 2003, she sees in a concert listing that I'm playing near her. She shows up, introduces herself, and hands me a CD-R transfer of that old tape, explaining how much it meant to her and how excited she was to finally hear/see those songs live. I tried my best to explain that I not only hadn't chosen those songs, but I no longer performed those songs – let alone knew how to play them – but I promised to try to resurrect one or two for that night's show, just for her.

The show began with me singing an embryonic version of "Liana," and after my very first line, she and her sister cheered like this was an arena rock show. I tried my best to play versions of the silly teenage songs like "Tell The Lies" and maybe "Stick Figure" — I don't recall, exactly. I do remember that those songs stuck out like a sore thumb next to the more fully realized material that would come later in the set.

I'd asked her if she'd had a good time after the show, but I'd gotten the distinct impression that she was a bit dismayed at the newer direction. She didn't seem to like the new mix of expletives, humor, and super poppy melodies. I'd see her at a few future shows over the next year, somewhere in the back, and she'd disappear before the end of the show, presumably after realizing that the days of the teenager spewing his diary over hissy recordings were long gone.

I've always wondered what she saw in those early tapes, as I recently dug up and archived her CD-R transfers. They were as bad and embarrassing as I remembered, but those songs meant a lot to one person. And all I can come up with was that these songs were honest. They certainly weren't "good," and it was even more lo-fi sounding than you're guessing. But if you pressed play, you just heard a confused teenager trying to work it all out, and I think that she related.

All of those songs were written for myself. Maybe I had hoped that someone else would like them one day, but those were really and truly just for me. It might not hurt to try that again sometimes.

10-8-16

The one-day-only Cassette Store Day promotion is over now. I won't know what the actual sales are for a few days, but I had to go and replenish their stock after a few hours. They'd begun turning people away when they sold out of the first batch rather than just calling me to ask for more. Still went pretty well. A few people were frustrated at, get this, having to call a number and interact with a record store. I think they might have missed the point, but I also don't want them to go without some of my music if they want to have it, so I had to make exceptions for a few people. Didn't thrill me, but I've done enough releases now to know that sometimes it's easier to just go ahead and bend a rule than to deal with a bunch of fallout when disappointed folks talk smack online. Keep the customer satisfied and all that.

It's telling that I probably could get more attention from letting a fan down than by helping each one that reaches out to me the way that I do, but I just don't want the headache, nor do I want to let myself down. I just hold myself to a higher standard than that. If someone wants to give me money in exchange for what I made, I'm determined to help in any way that I can.

While jutting about town, I listened to the first half of the Claire and The Potatoes album in the car for the first time in about a year. Was really shocked at how well it held up for me. I'd even sort of forgotten how some of the songs went. Found myself really floored at "I Wanna Be Your Shadow," which simply has to be in the running for one of the best pop songs I have ever written. We made such a potent product when all was said and done. I wish that things were different and that we could have done more.

A few days ago, Professor Shyguy and I did "Red Light Special" in concert just one last time. We'd wanted to start doing "The Girl Is Mine" by now, but we just couldn't get it finished in time. We got as far as the skeleton of the music and my vocals on a demo, but didn't have time to finish Shyguy's parts – plus there's some ear candy and backing vocals buried in there that you don't really notice until you don't hear them. My throat really hurt that day, and I felt bad that I had to brush off every single person that wanted to chat before showtime so that I could keep it together to perform only one song. We did it just fine, but the gimmick has worn thin, and it's time to move on.

Compiled an hour-long disc of demos that are all potential contenders to be on the next album and listened to it with Nicole. Out of the songs that I feel are unquestionably forerunners, there are still plenty of lines that need tweaking. And there's a few that just bored me overall. Some are in such an unfinished state that they almost can't be considered songs. It's odd to think that there was over 60 minutes of music on that disc, but I couldn't carve THE album out of it yet. That said, Jordon is especially jazzed about "One Of These Is Gonna Be Your Day," "Terribly Popular," and "Maybe" (a working title for now). I like all of those, and I have two songs that I think would go together nicely to end the record. One is "Please Don't Let My Art Die," and the other is currently nameless. They both mine the same territory lyrically, but I feel really strongly about all of the sentiments. There's probably a way to combine the songs, as the keys could work together, but I'd rather make more tunes before I start whittling down existing ones.

Juliana was off seeing the first concert that she picked out and went to with friends – Pierce The Veil. She kept excitedly texting me all through the day, and it really warmed my heart to see her so happy. It's her favorite band of the moment, and I remember how important that teenage gig that you look forward to for weeks is. Even better, she left happy and called it a "dream come true." Nicole got to work as an aerialist for a little girl's Star Wars-themed birthday party. They both got to do rad, rad things. I was peddling a cassette tape all day. We're all doing some version of living our dreams today, so I can't say this has been a wasted Saturday. We just had a hurricane narrowly miss the state, Donald Trump has a bunch of controversy following him after an old tape surfaced of him suggesting that he could do anything he wanted to women because he's a celebrity, and Meatwad is having an exceptionally buoyant day.

All things considered, this is a pretty nice weekend. There's bad stuff too, like the death of my beloved iPod, but I'm personally getting back into CDs, so it's all balancing out.


10-14-16

A few days ago, Alex Trebek called nerdcore artists "losers." This doesn't really bother me because even though I've erroneously been referred to as nerdcore in the past (which is usually a term to describe nerdy hip hop), it's actually turned into a bit of controversy that is translating into decent publicity for the genre. TMZ is covering it and everything. Pals like Mega Ran are getting heard by the mainstream as a result, and he's one of my favorite MCs I've ever heard, let alone met. It's good for them in a bigger picture sense. Of course, the genre is made up of people with varying degrees of social anxiety, and I don't like that they are getting called a "loser" by someone they probably grew up watching on television. Always a cloud with every silver lining.

Just woke up from a dream that I thought I'd share with you. Usually my dreams take place in one of two locations – I'm either in the hills and backroads of Jamul, California, lost and trying to make my way to my aunt's house; or I'm on another planet similar to the one we inhabit but spliced with various attributes from science fiction properties. A hint of *LOST* here, a pinch of Star Wars there, etc. Last night's dream took place in the latter location.

There had been a robot that received calls every few hours featuring messages from invisible entities that would give out crucial messages for the survival of that planet. These robots would wordlessly enact whatever needed to be done, and people didn't really question it. Just robots doin' robot stuff. But something had happened to the robots, and I was deemed the one that should receive the messages now. I wasn't in danger of having the secrets stolen because if someone else were to listen in, they'd merely hear silence. I'm the only one that had ears to hear it – probably a leftover remnant of adults telling me that I was "special" when I was younger, I'm sure.

One message was crucial: it contained a statement that would save the planet I was inhabiting. I was to give the statement to the correct person at six seconds after 7:50 p.m. I was told that I would absolutely know who I was supposed to communicate with. Some people had dragged me off to what appeared to be a renaissance fair, and I sat at a picnic table, trying to figure out who I was supposed to talk to. Everyone was either in costume or just there to buy a corndog. Nothing caught my eye. Each time I'd want to wander off to find the right person to talk to, the people I was with would remind me that they'd set me up for a guitar lesson with a special teacher, and that I really shouldn't leave. The time came and went, and I started to get very nervous. At 8 p.m., my old pal Jeff Nolan showed up at the picnic table, ready to give me my surprise lesson.

I told him that I was late to give out a message to save the planet and read it aloud to him. He responded with, "Wow. I really wish you would have told me that 9 minutes and 54 seconds ago." And then I woke up.

10-20-16

Last night, I hosted a screening of *Shock Treatment* at The Geek Easy. Turnout was low — either due to lack of interest or the competition of a presidential debate. Those who did come were really enthusiastic, which was fantastic. I bookended the movie with sets of songs from the soundtrack. Lots of singalongs. I really needed that gig. I'd felt like the last few shows were so hit or miss, and the focus of just playing songs from the movie really helped. Though EyeQ did demand "Love My Little Squiddy," and it was actually really fun to play this time! About 80% of the audience knew the words, so it felt celebratory. That song can be such a slog when the attendees don't "get it." All smiles last night, and now I'm ready to "get back on the horse."

That sounds like slang for deciding to resume a heroin habit. Not what I meant. Hopefully obviously.

This week has marked the three-year anniversary of the final Nerdapalooza. The difference in this anniversary is that a bunch of people figured out that the court records related to the demise of the festival are searchable. Nobody comes out looking very good in those black and white documents. Said documents don't include oral contracts, aspirations, hopes and dreams, etc. I've been watching the gleeful social media posts that have enjoyed a fair amount of character assassination. Mostly people throwing shade at Hex for "lulz." I owe Hex a good amount of thanks for my career. He's also pissed me off immeasurably by crediting my wife as the editor of *Alan*, his book, but did not actually use any of her edits, making it appear as if Nicole had left that thing as a hard-to-read mess. So while I have reasons to be wary, I've never seen him as malicious — rather just a guy who is too excitable for his own good and has questionable business sense.

I'm doing it, too. Everybody has an opinion after reading those documents. I feel crappy for everyone that had their lives ruined by bad business practices. I also can't thank the creators enough for all of the good times and wonderful things that it did for my career. While I've skimmed the court documents, they're actually pretty standard lawsuits for the most part and not really terribly interesting. They're just complex and involve a very big-name band, so people who have ever had anything to do with nerdy music all have some opinion on this thing. I'm in the vantage point of having seen the lows and highs from behind the curtain and the audience. My opinion is that most who are treating this "drama bomb" like WikiLeaks are in the period where they are looking back at what they did in their early 20s and cringing, and it's easier to laugh at legal misfortune than remember that the community wouldn't have existed without true fervor. I mean, someone had to actually like that stuff, right?

It's all had me in a fairly bad mood all week. I haven't been very productive, and I've felt disconnected from the things that usually bring me joy. Only polished off one new song, an instrumental with a working title of "Billy," but I don't imagine I'll do anything with it until I slap some words on it. Words are the problem lately. Everywhere I turn? More words. All of them either say nothing or are obscuring their true meaning. I'd like to see more people walk it like they talk it while still retaining kindness and poise.

10-24-16

Just finished mixing the Milk Carton Superstars session for Nerdy.FM. Though I showed up happy and ready to work on the night it was recorded, my patience wore thin quickly. A bunch of gear didn't work properly, and very little was ready to go when I arrived. My job was simply supposed to be hosting it, watching it, and then mixing it later. I ended up as more of a go-between in the middle of the band and Chuck Silver, part of Nerdy.FM staff as well as the guitarist in Sci-Fried.

Some attendees would just get up and leave at inopportune moments, dragging what amounted to 65 minutes out to nearly four hours. I thought they were rude. They probably thought that I needed to lighten the fuck up. I wouldn't argue with that.

At the end, all of the members of Claire were present, so we strapped on some gear and tried out "A Shot At Love" and "The Real Enemy." By this time, attendees in the studio audience were just staring at their phones, so it was pretty masturbatory. Thankfully they weren't paying enough attention to hear how rusty we were.

That new MCS record is stupidly good, though. I haven't been able to get "The Ban On Pre-Sliced Bread" out of my head for a week. I hope that it does well for them. Jim is such a fantastic lyricist, singer, and drummer, and it's obvious in the songs that he really poured himself fully into this album, possibly in a more personal way than ever before. But I'm all too aware that working really hard and being very good doesn't always equal a just proportion of listeners. I hope that their new album can cut through the muck and touch some people. Even though I just sing on one or two cuts and helped them with the vinyl pressing, I feel oddly protective of the album and any possible reception. Likely because I love Jim so much as a bandmate but first and foremost as a human being.

I woke up a little miserable today because I had to fast for a physical. This meant that I had to get up earlier than normal and forego caffeine until my blood was drawn. It was worth it, as I learned that on the surface I'm apparently healthier than I've been since high school. Bloodwork could reveal something very different, of course, but I'm happy staying under the impression that I'm *bordering* on healthy for the first time ever. As long as I keep up with the medications.

After the physical and some WaWa coffee, I had to pick up an ungodly amount of vinyl from UPS. The shipments for the first-time vinyl issues of *Linda Lovelace For President* and *Losing Salt* were in, but I couldn't promise that I'd be home to sign for them, so I just arranged to have them held at the distribution center instead. Joyful glee overtook me as I loaded the boxes into my Scion. I couldn't help opening them to take a look. They both look so cool, and after play-testing both of them, I'm happy with the way that they hold up. The only possible gripe is that for some unknown reason the pressing plant didn't shrinkwrap *Losing Salt*, which means that I have to buy a surplus bulk of protective sleeves that can be sealed shut. Hopefully the plant will hook me up with a discount or a rebate, as I've now technically paid for protection for that record twice.

Today I sent Jordon Zadorozny another demo for the album I'll finally be going to Canada to make with him, this time for the song with the working title of "Broken Heart Surgery." I'm on my third draft of lyrics for it, and I'm still not sold on the words or the subject matter. It feels like the kind of thing that I should just start over from scratch. I love the music and the arrangement, but I feel like the words are too on the nose. I haven't had any feedback on it because I've been so precious about keeping it all to myself, but for all I know Jordon will hear the clichés and say, "Ahhh, finally some normalcy." It's the most obvious rock song I've done in years, and that might be a good thing. It's oddly reminiscent of Tom Petty, which is strange because I've hardly ever delved into his work.

It's a pretty good day overall, though. I'm able to put 90% of my "core" discography on my record shelf and feel somewhat complete, as if I can finally gaze upon my life's work. *Human Slushy* is missing, but I'm getting closer and closer to just writing it out of the canon altogether. I doubt that anyone would accept or alternately argue such an action, but I also can't fathom someone putting that album on and going, "This is totally prime Marc With a C material." I was sifting through it the other day, and it dawned on me that it's really the album that my teenage band probably would have made if we'd ever gotten it together to finish something. But as none of the on and off members of that collective appear on the songs, I can't really consider it as such. I wish I could just say that it all really starts with *Bubblegum Romance*, but I'm pretty sure that my audience has figured that out on their own by now.

Still might do a very short run and bare bones vinyl pressing of *Human Slushy* one day, but it would only be for my own sake, satisfying the completist in myself. Not because I think that anyone would reach for it all that often, nor would I want to encourage them to do so. Maybe it can be a bonus item to go along with another release one day? Or maybe I could let it die. I have a hard time letting go, even when I don't like something.

11-2-16

The last week felt excruciatingly long, but it was also over so quickly that I kind of don't believe that I could take Friday off and just clean the house or something. Or wait, maybe I can't. I just got an email about an interview I might have to do on that day. We'll see.

Friday and Saturday was a return to Universal Studios to open for The Rich Weirdoes presentation of *Rocky Horror*. This time, I brought Juliana to help me out with equipment and merch. Both were fantastic audiences, but the cast — I can't describe it, but there seemed to be a lot of tension backstage between members. I try to keep my show separate and not get in their way. The bulk of the audience is paying to see them, so it's not really my gig. Juliana didn't "get it" at first, but she seemed to really enjoy the second night when she could watch the show from the audience's perspective. And though both audiences were excitable and fun, I watched them all leave, walking past my merch table as if the CDs and vinyl I was selling were ancient artifacts from a bygone time. Very few things sold, but I think I made at least a few new fans.

Sunday was my first livestream for Patreon backers. YouTube simply would not cooperate with my video encoder, rendering the stream completely unwatchable for anybody. It was such a stressful hour, and I took it very hard. These people were paying to support me, and they deserved entertainment on time. Not only did the technical problems make me very late, but when it finally did work, it would buffer every few seconds, and you couldn't watch at all. As I watched the number of viewers dwindle to zero, I kept playing on the off-chance that YouTube would at least properly archive the show in case those supporters wanted to try to watch it later – it didn't – and I was too choked up to properly sing. I sunk into a deep depressive swing that I'm not fully out of. If I cannot deliver entertainment on time, I'm wasting their money, and I don't deserve their support. Problems like that keep my almost-ego in check. I'm reminded that I'm lucky that anyone puts up with my bullshit art at all.

The Monday show at Universal didn't feel right. I was still in a highly depressed state but trying to plaster on a fake smile to again deliver "entertainment on time." Eventually the thoughts caught up with me halfway through performing "The Ballad Of Dick Steel," and somehow all of the lyrics were wiped out of my brain and replaced with "YOU SUCK, NOBODY LIKES THIS." I choked and just had to stop the song to level with the audience that I'd massively fucked up. The set never really recovered after that. A positive thing was being able to shush insistent hecklers that thought they were being clever with cries for "Freebird" by playing my original song by that name, but I could also hear the murmuring through the 400 attendees – they were just sort of done with me. And again, I'd watch hundreds of people pour past me on the way out, not picking up a single thing – not even free stickers.

I'm having to just accept that I'm doing an outdated thing. Rock music still exists, but it isn't growing. It isn't dangerous, it doesn't threaten the status quo, and even if it did? People would take to their social media devices to claim their outrage at having their own norms questioned. I'm getting easier to ignore, but I also don't have it in me to shake people up and force them to notice anymore. If people don't want to hear me, it isn't because I've made myself unavailable. My preferred canvas is a record. Now records are so normal that they are easy to walk past again. They don't catch your eye any longer. The CDs might as well be 8-tracks. Meanwhile, my Spotify plays continue to go up, but the money that I make from those services do not. This just isn't sustainable, but I have to stay the course. I have to make it to at least 20 years. The most important thing is how you wrap up, if you have any say-so in the matter. Would The Beatles be as revered if *Abbey Road* wasn't "the last word," and instead it was, say, the soundtrack to *Yellow Submarine*? It's hard to argue that more people know how Kurt Cobain died than actually are able to hum you a Nirvana song these days. It feels like my aim right now is working toward a really good ending. I just have to be strong enough to not compromise what I'm making in the meantime.

Today was relatively easy, as I went to WPRK to do an interview with the *Local Heroes* show about nothing in particular. They had me sing some songs in the studio and give my websites a plug. As I got home, I started feeling a nagging pain in my left ear and my throat, so now I'm just hoping that I'm not catching a cold. Everybody around me has gotten sick at some point in the last month or two, and a bunch of The Rich Weirdoes were apparently doing the show with strep throat, so I'm holding out hope that this is just a weird thing that'll pass.

Jordon just sent me a message about the new demo of "I'm Sad It's Your Birthday." I think he might like the song more than I do. I think it's pretty okay, but I thought that it was sort of a "bottom of the stack" type of tune compared to some other new tracks. He'd written out different vocal stacking he wanted to try in certain passages and everything, so this might end up actually being an album contender. I'm trusting him implicitly because he isn't in the business of making bad records. He'll be able to bring cool stuff out of songs that might seem a bit drab or boring in demo form. Imagining the ideas he wants to implement already made me dig the song even more!

11-6-16

I have to handle this carefully: I'm not in a great place, and it's because of the behavior of a fan. That fan is not yet legally an adult, so I can't be terribly blunt with or about them. The short version of the story is that after they'd seen Juliana in passing at the merch stand last week, they'd decided to send her an invitation to "hang out." This was after said fan had blown up my Facebook messenger, and I was just too busy to respond as often as they'd seem to want. I told them that they'd crossed a massive line. My daughter is just off-limits until she's an adult and can make up her own mind as to which of my fans are people she'd like to know. And as I've apparently never stated it anywhere officially, I took to all of my social media outlets to say, "Can't believe I have to say this, but liking my songs doesn't give you the right to contact my family members." Most people were also pretty shocked and appalled by it.

Presumably in protest, the fan decided to withdraw their Patreon support, and I decided that they were being a bit too invasive for my own level of comfort. When I went to "unfriend" them on every site I could think of, I found that they'd left a sort of suicide note on their tumblr.

I didn't know what to do. I felt that it was attention-seeking behavior. If I gave in and called the authorities out of concern, they would receive the attention they were all but demanding of me. If I ignored it, and they turned out to be fine? It'd be a clear indicator that I was correct in my assumptions that my daughter should not be allowed anywhere near them. With as stuck as I was, I texted Aubree because she usually keeps late hours and asked if I could call her. And like a beam from the heavens, Aubree helped me to realize that literally anything could have set this person off, and I might have just been an excuse for their unhealthy behavior. I don't know what I would have done without her bringing me back down to earth that night.

A part of me feels cruel for having not called the police because this is a human being, and this is not normal and rational behavior. The other part of me feels that if this is their reaction to being called out for invading my privacy? I was completely right to keep a distance to protect myself and my family. I feel terrible for having to make that decision in the first place.

To be completely honest, I don't know what they did. They might have tried to harm themselves. I hate being in this position. I'm such a small part of the universe, and I've never been anything but nice and respectful to this person on a musician/fan level, but it's ludicrous that this is a reality of the life of the guy that wrote "Love My Little Squiddy." My empathy is off the charts, and it's my instinct to try and help. I can't be assured that it won't do more harm than good. It makes me sick to look at my guitars right now.

11-9-16

It's just turned into the day after election day. The results aren't officially in, but Donald Trump is very likely going to be the next president. I have rarely, if ever, made governmental politics a part of my music and entertainment. Actually, I take that back. I did say some political stuff in "The Problem Is Me."

Somehow, my friends list on Facebook is a big echo chamber and not by design because I don't really have a lot of close friends. I befriend nearly anyone that wants to be my pal but use my personal page for "branding" just as much as I would any "official" site. But I'd been under the impression that Hillary Clinton was going to win, hands down. America certainly wasn't going to elect that smug billionaire star of reality television, were they?

Resoundingly, yes they were and are and did.

This is a guy that threatens any criticism with lawsuits. I actually am concerned that writing about him will one day be a reason to be sued into oblivion or worse. And that's one of the last good things about American life: you can say stuff about people in power and not face retribution.

Tonight the band got back to rehearsing – and boy, we were rusty – but during our 9 p.m. break, we saw how tight the presidential race was. Emmit is crashing at my place tonight because Aubree is in the hospital in Orlando, and together we saw the sad reality come down via numbers and predictions. Nicole was genuinely freaking out. I have no idea how to comfort her when she wakes up.

There is little that I can say about the awful person that Donald Trump is that can't be said more eloquently by someone else. I can say that many of the people I adore are part of the LGBTQ+ community. They are Muslim. They are women. They are people of color. They are ill. They were not born in this country. And they are all people that Donald Trump has made light of in some way. They no longer feel safe in their country of residence.

For years to come, people will pontificate how this happened. I cross my fingers that those that feel unsafe will behave like scared animals backed into a corner: unpredictable, striking wildly and ready to survive by any means necessary. I will do my best to protect them if that's a thing I can do, but we may be beyond repair.

For the first time in my life, I understand why someone would be unwilling to accept someone as "their" president. And for the first time in a long while, I'm genuinelyfuckingterrifiedoftheworldthatmydaughtermustbecomeanadultin.

11-16-16

We've had a little bit of time to accept the fate of the nation. I can't really bring myself to dwell on it right now. When I see injustices occurring to those that I can actually help, I'll do my best. I cannot get sucked into the national paranoia right now or I'll never get anything done. That's what the retirement home years are for – shaking your fist at whipper-snappers and the like.

But I did let it affect me a bit. I didn't send Jordon a demo this week. I was a little too shaken up to complete any of the projects that've been in various states of flux. Really need to get back to it. Especially need to shine up "Please Don't Let My Art Die" as well as an untitled mammoth that'll probably close the next record, "Broken Heart Surgery," and "You Do You." And those are just the ones I've bothered to record so far.

Good rehearsal last night; the band is getting back into shape. I think Jim is too overworked to do much more past the holiday show, which is not an ideal situation. I can't create more hours in the day for him, but I wish it could be different. He's so stressed out, and it's palpable. If he told me that he needed to quit the group in the interest of self-care I wouldn't be surprised, nor could I possibly be mad. I just hope that it doesn't come to that. If he has to leave, I'm not replacing him – it's just back to solo shows for me.

Went to see Aubree in the hospital – she has pneumonia in one lung – and surprised her on one specific day: I'd seen that she was sad that she couldn't go out and photograph the supermoon, so I made a bunch of calls and convinced the hospital to let me sign her out for a little while. I brought my Nikon CoolPix – not as cool as her camera, but it's the best I've got – and I pushed her wheelchair around in the parking lot, trying to find good angles where she could take a few snaps. Couldn't live with myself knowing that my friend was hooked up to machines while an event that might only happen once in her lifetime went on outside of her window. She loves to photograph nature, and I wanted to help her do it. I'm starting to feel very big brotherly toward her.

Brought back *The Real Congregation* for Patreon backers. A few folks seem to be really happy about it. I had a good time recording the new episode because

I knew that it was only going to be heard by people that would "get it." And that's been on my mind this week. I saw a review of *Unicorns Get More Bacon* that called it "painfully boring." I can see not enjoying what I do, but I never once thought it wasn't at least interesting in some way. Am I hitting middle-of-the-road stride? I mean, I suppose it is the most normal album I've made in quite some time, but just had a bit of a complex about it.

There was a great thing that happened last weekend, though: a bride named Chelsea had contacted me to have me pop into her wedding reception to do a surprise performance of "Life's So Hard." Her husband-to-be is a big fan, and the song holds a place in their heart as they have fond memories of hearing it together on their second date. Though it was really hard to stay hidden in a stealthy way for many hours in that very fancy hotel, it was worth it. Sure, it's the least likely song to ever be played at a wedding, but I'm flattered that I made up a melody that a couple can sort of consider to be an important part of their development. Those things really flatter me and during tough weeks like this one, they keep me going.

I still don't enjoy weddings very much. I doubt that'll ever change, but I feel really good about myself when my music is being used in them.

## 12-1-16

There's a high chance that Jordon and I will be narrowing down the tracklist for the new album very soon but leaving the door open for me to pitch any special new songs that come down the pike. I'm excited to be standing at this corner because too often right now, I'm very rarely writing just because I want to say something since I already know what I **need** to say. I've taken special care on this album to only try to say things that I mean to complete the saga I've already begun, and I think that it could end up being pretty alienating for that very reason. The salesman in me is definitely noticing a potential lack of singles. The teenage punk rocker in me is happy that there aren't. I don't know what 2016-era Marc wants, really. Mostly I like when the phone doesn't buzz.

We've seen a prominent torrent tracker shut down in the last few weeks. In general, I support piracy. In my case, it doesn't lead to me buying less music, though I can't speak for how it might devalue art in the eyes of others. But I did notice an interesting development: Juliana is really into The Weeknd right now. We were up late as Thanksgiving turned into Black Friday, which also happened to be the release date for his latest album. Of course, Juliana couldn't wait to hear it, so we piled right into my office to turn up my studio monitors and hear it as well as Spotify would let us. Sure enough, the album went live at midnight. The next day we went to two record stores to buy it. No one had received the CD. The vinyl will not even ship out until February. You can release a headline-making album without having any physical representation at all, and that makes me fall out of love with the process. Nothing against The Weeknd or anyone else that chooses to do that with their art, of course. I just don't think an album is an album until it can be held. I'm in the minority on that, and it hastens my wish to just walk the hell away from an industry that I no longer understand.

There were some nasty family problems in the last few weeks. I was able to somewhat diffuse them by having some patience and coming up with measured responses. I'm not sure that anyone would have put money on me becoming the level-headed one in my bloodline, but that is how it has seemingly worked out. I went into a protective mode and eventually "let's solve it logically mode." I think things are merely copacetic right now, but many people that I'm bound to by blood are highly combustible folks. I seem to be one of the few that is happy to just keep to myself and not spread everyone's business. For once, I also seem to be among the healthiest people in my family.

I was interrupted while writing the above paragraph by more family drama. Perhaps I spoke too soon. Thankfully, I can just throw myself back into music. Got some Nerdy.FM work that should keep me busy for a while tonight.

12-8-16

Today I'm writing this just after waking up. I like to do this when I can because I tend to be a little less guarded, a bit more blunt, and I often don't remember what I've written later on. This means that I'll get to read this portion at the same time that you will, most likely.

If I think back to older sessions and rehearsals, I can often remember that there was some drama afoot, but I usually don't recall the specifics. There's really only two that I remember:

- Leslie and I had a falling out during a Claire rehearsal. She wasn't feeling well, and I was mad that she was continuing in less than great health. I yelled a lot.

- Ditto for Emmit, though his was because he forgot the notebook that has all of his bass cheat sheets. I have roughly a kazillion songs, that's a pretty necessary thing for him.

I remember lots of tension between me and Guy during sessions for the Claire album. I recall that it was happening while we were tracking the bass guitar. I don't remember what it was or who thought that the other one was at fault. And there were far more arguments between Chris and myself than I've listed in these pages, but that's not how I remember our overall time playing together.

I say this because when I think about what makes for an interesting memoir from a musician, I have few of the typical hallmarks: sex, fights, and people screwing me out of money. In the interest of keeping this tome juicy, I thought I'd tackle each one of these subjects bluntly.

Sex? I've probably had far more of it than any person that looks like me should've. But it doesn't really have anything to do with my job, and I haven't had sex with anyone that isn't Nicole since 2005. You'd probably feel awkward knowing about our ongoing sex life, wouldn't you? Maybe if I'd had physical relations with a person of some cultural stature? But overall, unless there's a point where I'll be entering a set of activities with you where my pajama pants will be off, I really can't find the benefit in any kiss-and-tell stories.

Fights? I told you about the ones that affected the records. There have been others: legal, romantic, familial, and personal, but again, they have so little to do with Marc With a C output that I shouldn't waste either of our times. I'm a tyrant when it comes to arguing, too. I don't relish fighting, but you'd rue the day that you got into a row with me. When someone is mad at me, I tend to want to crumple into a ball and flee. There usually isn't much in between.

Money? As an independent musician, a very, very, very small percentage of the world thinks that I deserve compensation at all. Many people believe that I should be doing what I do while also keeping a food-service job at the very least. This would take time away from my creative output. If that were to occur, between cries of "come to Ohio" and "put out something new," the irony is that the very same folks who'd say those things would likely also prefer that they didn't have to pay for the music or concerts. I think that this is simply a product of that very American attitude: "hold on to your hopes and dreams, but work on them on your nights and weekends."

The very fact that you're reading this many words may be confusing when I say this next part: I think I've said most of what I want to say. I just need to wrap it up in a nice little box. I could conceivably just walk away, but there's a few things I feel the need to do first. Those are to finish this last album for this trilogy with Jordon, giving listeners (and myself) the satisfaction of the curiosity over what might happen if I made a "properly produced" album. Then I need to take the show on the road, at least for a little while. And then I need to distill it all into a 20th anniversary package, part of which I'm writing for now.

What I truly need afterward is to just write for myself. There may come a time when I have plenty to say, but it won't be of this "era." I've chronicled my life in intimate detail, setting it to melodies. I often waste entire days waiting for that promiscuous inspiration to arrive. Or as I've done this week? Avoided the world, nursing my throat so that I can go and sing for many days in a row. I don't want to live under those circumstances forever; I'd like to talk to people more. To not always be near a pen and a notebook "just in case." I will always make music, but I'd like it to eventually be a hobby. I don't know if I'm wired that way, though. I need to find out.

In the coming week, I have a radio appearance and three shows. That's probably more than my voice can handle, truthfully. The spaces between will be hermetic, hiding so I don't have to talk. That is not how I want to spend the rest of my time on Earth.

12-14-16

The public gigs for 2016 have wrapped up as of last night. I don't feel very confident about any of them, but I'm trying to fight the malaise. I only ever feel as good as my last performance, so it's easy to get bummed out when things don't end up the way that I've hoped.

The annual holiday show was an especially odd duck. Lower-than-average attendance mixed with a crowd that was half-talkative and half-docile. We'd play a big favorite like "Dickpuncher III," hear people singing along, and then complete silence where the applause should go. Sometimes I couldn't hear myself speaking to the audience over the people that insisted on playing board games loudly in the back. Such a strange gig. We played around 40 songs, but the strange vibe in the air kept throwing me off. I was forgetting lyrics left and right. We played well on average, but the stuff that went over best were the things that we'd premiered: a cover of "1979" by The Smashing Pumpkins and, of all things, the first performance of "Falling Sometimes Down." I assume that the latter is a little boring for Emmit to play, but it's a pretty intense track that I'd like to do more often. I felt awful because I had to really conserve my voice to make it through the entirety of the show, so I couldn't talk to people yet again, and it makes me feel bad, as if I come across as stuck up. On nights like that, I want to be everyone's buddy. I still haven't balanced being the entertainer and a social person at the gigs.

The next day I was playing at a DIY art fair outdoors. I had to do a family-friendly set, and I think I'm starting to get the hang of them. The shame was that very few people got to hear it, as it rained during most of my set. I was performing for vendors that were stuck at their booths, mostly. I realized that I had no business playing "Laura, I Need Medicine" about halfway through the song – not only is it basically a laundry list of drugs, but it's got some pretty randy lyrics. It dawned on me that I shouldn't sing the "I just wanna know / Does the carpet match the drapes" line – and not just because the lyric is exceedingly dumb. I quickly replaced it with "This replacement lyric / Is totally kid-safe" at the last possible second. Only during the closing "Happy To Be Alive" did the rain (thankfully) let up so I could do the song properly. One fan gave me their painting of a giant robot after the gig, which made me feel good. It's a really nice piece of art, too.

Last night was the yearly set at Parliament House. For a toy drive at a sex resort, it doesn't get terribly rowdy. I gamely played my 30 minutes while people talked over me. Best reactions came from songs from *Shock Treatment*. I broke a string during my final song – the humidity was out of control for an evening in December, and it really mucked with my guitar. Overall, it was a nice night. I know I'm just hired to be atmosphere, but it still stings to be ignored.

And today while running errands, I compiled a possible sequence for the next album out of the existing demos. Right now my gut is telling me to drop "First Time Collar" (previously known as "Broken Heart Surgery") to place it earlier in the trilogy's running order. When Jordan intimated that we were "almost there" with the songs he'd already been given, I wasn't sold, but when I assembled this facsimile of what the album could possibly be, I was certainly impressed. It's light on "singles," but if the aforementioned song was dropped, I'd be crazy about pretty much every track and saying exactly what I wanted. I never get goosebumps from my own material, but the one-two punch of "Please Don't Let My Art Die" and "Why" really did me in today. I've got another somewhat "on the nose" idea for a song percolating right now, but beyond that, I think the songs are ready.

Been really into The Smashing Pumpkins lately. Loved them as a teenager and am not sure why they are flipping my switch so much right now. I suppose that I do feel a little bit silenced. A little bit like the world isn't really interested in what I have to say/want to make. Though obscurity is the path I chose, I relate to the tension in their albums. And it's actually the stuff from after the *Mellon Collie & The Infinite Sadness* album that's got my attention as of late. I feel strange being nearly 40 and relating to it so well, but if music sounds good to you, I don't believe you should fight it because of perceptions of what's hip. Also got a really amazing package from Katharine full of handmade art, jewelry and knitted caps. She's so good to me, and I don't feel like I deserve her friendship. My self-esteem is low right now, and I don't feel like I deserve much.

But on the other hand, I feel like the art I make is better than it's being given credit for. Is that entitlement? Does it mean that I need to work even harder to push it into the faces of those who'll "get it"? When those folks come to shows, there's not a lot of wild cheering and such anymore. It's getting so sedate. Are we sick of guitars? What's the deal? I usually think I'm pretty good, but swearing off live performances for a while is starting to look more and more enticing.

12-26-16

Unless something drastic happens, this'll probably be my last entry for 2016. On one hand, I don't expect any huge Marc With a C developments to happen. On the other, I'd like to put my nose to the grindstone for a week or so. I'll come back to that in a minute.

In the last few months, I've gone through some personal upheaval in my family. Not only does each day with Meatwad have to be treated as if it's going to be the last one – really, it's a miracle that he's alive at all – but the most gentle way I can say this is "there has been some family drama." I feel a little bit bad saying it because I try to make a point to not air dirty laundry here unless it directly relates to the stuff that I create, but in this case it actually kind of does. Without pointing fingers, there have been actions by some parties where I've lost entire working days with literally no decent explanation. I had to put the kibosh on many plans at intermittent times to play referee between familial relations that were not gelling. I'm watering down the situation greatly, but it seeped into every single day, as things became so unstable and unpredictable. In truth, as much as I tried to concentrate during all of the December shows, I was distracted with being terrified about what I might hear the very next time the phone might ring. I feel like I haven't been at my best, but I've tried mightily to exceed expectations. If we are awarded points for trying, I feel like I should have a number of those imaginary things.

My finger hovers over things but can't be placed on any one of them to describe the odd disconnect I'm feeling from my past. I like performing the music from my catalog of songs, but I don't want to feel beholden to any particular song. I also like playing new songs, but I don't want to ignore older songs at the expense of the "now." Oddly, I feel like I should be proud that I went so heavy on the new material at the 2016 gigs, but now that I'm at the other end of them and see just how few of the songs really caught fire? I feel like that wasn't the best move.

Attendance has been diminishing, and it just cannot be ignored. That would have been an okay realization if I'd ended up with a bunch of things that make people happy at the level of "Love My Little Squiddy," "Nerdy Girls," or "Life's So Hard," but I think people like the title track to *Unicorns Get More Bacon* well enough, and "The Ballad Of Dick Steel" seems to be well-liked. Beyond that, I spent the year working "Ethics In Gaming" and "Epic Fail" to death because they are fun to play, plus I deeply believe in what I'm saying in them. But are they anyone else's favorites? There's not a lot of rapturous applause for them. People don't shout for them at gigs. It's so odd to have a well-received album from your fan base but not really have any particular song really take off and stand out from the pack.

Does that mean that the people that show up to gigs just like me and are ready to sort of follow me wherever I'm heading? I don't think it does. I tried a monthly series of "art installation" shows called Anything Goes, where I'd have to play different setlist each month with no overlap. The third one became the finale as I performed the entirety of the *Motherfuckers Be Bullshittin'* album to roughly 12 people.

You know how you can be really into an artist, obsess over their b-sides and scandals, consider getting their lyrics tattooed on you, have shocking thoughts about the self-harm you'd inflict should anything bad happen to them, etc., and then one day, you just wake up and stop following along but don't realize that it's happened until you go and see them, realizing that a lot of stuff has gone down while you were doing other things? I think that's happened with a number of my fans.

Importantly, I think it happened to me with my very own music. I still like it, but I don't really have a bunch of drive on how to best present it with the connection between myself and the audience. It hurts to admit, but I think I've actually lost the plot a bit as 2016 has gone off the rails. Even now as I write this, I'm being honest, but is that even entertaining? Why am I putting it out into the world? Have I lost the ability to think and create without considering where the words will eventually live?

Though I know where I'm going with my next album, I feel like I have a bunch of time to kill until it can be unveiled, and I have to find some kind of direction for sustenance between now and then.

I quickly released an exceptionally stupid song on Christmas Eve called "All

I Want For Christmas" that I literally shat out in a few hours. Had the idea around 4 p.m. wondering why the song didn't already exist. By 6:30, I started jotting down words figuring that this just wasn't going to enter the world unless I rolled up my sleeves and did it myself. By 9:30 p.m., I had released the recording with sleigh bells and all out into the world.

So I think that over the next week, I'd like to see how many truly dumb songs I can come up with in a short span of time, recording them all quickly and rather lo-fi, and maybe just rush-releasing a 10-inch EP for the center of the trilogy, possibly? For all I know, it could take a sharp detour away from stupidity and end up being kind of serious or maybe even good. I think it's also a good excuse to get "First Time Collar" out of my system. It doesn't fit the next proper album, and I'm not sure how I feel about the song, but something about it won't let me cast it aside. This 10-inch could even BE the bridge between *Unicorns Get More Bacon* and the album I'm recording with Jordon. Actually, this'd sort of solve a lot.

See? I'm already working out my next move right here in front of you. What would I do without these outlets? Would I even make songs anymore?

Back to the personal stuff. Christmas Day was good but overwhelming. There was a lot of confusion in Nicole's mom's house, and I'm pretty sure that everyone had at least their own miniature version of a panic attack at some point during the day. Juliana made out like a bandit, thrilled to have the soundtrack to *Rocky Horror Picture Show* on vinyl. She also recently saved up her own pocket money to upgrade her turntable, which made me proud. We capped off the night by watching *Heathers* and looking forward to a day with very little pressure ahead of us. Or at least, we hope that'll be the case.

And then? Let's see what writing without concern for quality can yield. I've got to get back into letting things flow without calculating each move as a business strategy.

1-3-17

So far, it's been a pretty quiet new year. For me, at least. I dove into recording that EP and ended up recording five full songs. A few simply need to be finished, and I'd have a new thing I could release. Writing and recording has been easy, though the usual throat problems have sprung up.

The problem has been actually liking any of it. Last night I decided to listen to the projected openers, "Long Time Listener" and "First Time Collar." I'm at a weird crossroads where I need to finish the EP to see if I like it more once it's all stuck together and is better than the sum of its parts. I guess there are worse fates than having more stuff that didn't get released because it wasn't up to snuff. The bad part is that, to finish it, I'll have to devote myself to some work that I'm having trouble believing in. It's probably me I'm having trouble believing in, though. Actually, that's definitely the problem. You get enough hate mail for having been born, and you'll start to believe some of it, eventually.

The seeds for my doubt were planted shortly after my last entry. I looked into some pricing for 10-inch records, and it's actually much cheaper to do a short run of 12-inch vinyl. That changed the figurative shape of the project in my head. A 10-inch record says to the listener, "I'm just a small object, not here to be taken too seriously." A big ol' 12-inch, even with less songs, still looks like a "statement" because it takes up as much room on the shelf as, say, *Normal Bias*. Never mind that it might be 20-minutes long and play at 45 RPM.

When it wasn't cost effective to do a let's-bridge-the-gap-for-fun EP, I sort of lost interest before I'd really gotten going. I'm loyal to many things, including my own ideas. This means that I feel honor-bound to finish the recordings. If I don't bring them to life, the ideas die, and it isn't the fault of the idea, right? On the other hand, it's sort of like mindless busy work that your boss gives you during slow days at work: if it probably won't matter, it's pretty hard to stay focused on something that only exists to occupy you.

I should be looking into passports, but I'm recording surprisingly angry and depressing songs. Of the five that are completed right now, I most like the short "I Don't Love You." It's to the point, I mean it, and it sounds neat. As there is a gem in the pile of uncertain audio, I can't give up. Took two days off to rest my throat where I mostly mixed what was already there, but I think it's time to get back to real work now. If I don't keep recording, I'll start feeling bad that my 99% of my peers are all performing at MAGFest while I'm stuck in the unseasonably warm south working on an EP that I'm having a hard time believing in. I might even turn to socializing. If I socialize? That's less time spent working. Can't have that.

1-13-17

I sure was cranky in that last entry.

Beyond one small and easy mastering step, the EP is finished. It probably won't change anyone's world, but it's quite fun, and bits of it were very cathartic for me. I think it's also neat in the way that everyone will have one favorite song, and the rest will just seem like seven generous B-sides. That song will change depending on the listener.

Katharine has to create the art without having heard it. I'm trying to give her the same chance I had: to just be creative without constraints. That's what we all need, maybe. An outlet that the government can't take away. The morale of the United States is very poor at the moment, and it's rather contagious. Everything feels hopeless, and I feel as if the only way to get through the muck is taking every possible chance for some escapism.

Last night I did a "personal" livestream for a person that backed my Patreon at the highest level. He's a very ill man. I Skyped in for almost an hour, as he and his mother/caretaker asked me to play songs from *This World Is Scary As Fuck*. This man was hooked to tubes, on a pretty high dose of morphine, and he wanted to hear me sing "This Is Hopeless." It should have been heartbreaking for me, but instead I felt good – I made him feel happy at a bad time. Or maybe the songs I sang said things that he was unable to say himself. He would try to sing along with "God Save The Queen From Navy Seals," though he had a breathing apparatus shoved into his throat, while I sang lines like "hospital machines pumping juices into me." These songs take on lives that I couldn't possibly predict.

Booked a real and definable tour date. I'll be going to Minnesota to do a show with Judy Tenuta at a convention called MarsCon. When I announced that I'd be doing a show outside of Florida, my email box blew up with people demanding information so that they could book flights. This set will only be 30-minutes long, and for obvious reasons I'll have to stick to the sillier songs, but it's a nice step in the right direction. Need to get my dick wet with some tour dates again if I'm going to be ready and able to push the next full album properly.

My birthday present to myself will be going to see Dweezil Zappa with Nicole and some friends tomorrow night. Couldn't pick a better time. I need Zappa's music right now, and so does the rest of the country.

1-18-17

I write this while procrastinating from some long postponed housework. Often I'll think "I'll just clean this all up as soon as I'm done with the recording," but then I get into the intricacies of post-production, which usually involves staring at a computer screen for a very, very long time. Thanks to this tunnel-vision, I rarely notice how messy things have gotten in the area where I've chosen to work/molt.

In a real catch-22 situation about this EP. On one hand, yes, it'd be a cool stopgap between the two releases, but on the other, I know it isn't an earth-shattering piece of art, and releasing it in the fashion that would best suit it would put me a few thousand dollars away from the goal of going to Canada. And in truth, that's going to cost so much money that I haven't even come up with a needed dollar amount. I just keep taking things as they come. "Can I afford to get a passport today?", etc. The EP would probably be enjoyable to my listeners but not so enjoyable that I should lose sight of the goals that are bigger and more important to me.

For a number of years, I'd release almost anything that I deemed "finished," but there wasn't nearly as much at stake financially. I was thinking globally and acting locally. And with technology giving everyone the same opportunities with music at the exact same time, it's got to be nothing but global thinking now. This EP was cathartic, but what I really needed was to actually make it, yet I don't really have a burning and fiery need for people to hear and understand it. It's odd.

In other news, the vinyl reissues for *Losing Salt* and *Linda Lovelace For President* went to #1 and #2 on the Bandcamp vinyl pop chart before I'd even made an announcement about it. *Losing Salt* is outselling the other title by only a little bit, and in some ways, I'm not surprised. The people that took to it really "get it" on a level that even I can't quite share with them. I like that the record seems to have almost its own cult following.

I'd gone to Philadelphia a few years ago to play a private birthday party for a person named Reed, and they just got a tattoo of the title of "Music Can Heal." That makes for the third tattoo from that song and the fourth Marc With a C tattoo overall that I know of. I feel alternately unworthy and flattered. Not even alternately, really. Both at the exact same time.

This year's birthday show was mostly a cluster of songs from *Normal Bias*, *Linda Lovelace For President*, and *Losing Salt*. A small-but-mostly-attentive audience was there. A few people decided to mess with me by requesting "Blowjob Queen," and I tried a new version where I'd replace the subject with my own name, but I had to abandon it. I didn't even remember it well enough to make fun of it! Overall it was a pretty good show, and playing it made me happy.

I need to get back to cleaning now. It helps me work things out in my own head, and there's some stress outside of the music that I've got to turn into something constructive. Sitting around won't solve anything. Neither will cleaning, really. Just more of that mindless busywork, but that busywork keeps me out of trouble.

1-30-17

This has been a difficult month. Everything you've read since November of 2016 has been the product of my attempts to work despite a massive problem: by the legal definition, I have a stalker. This stalker has made numerous threats against me, my wife, and my daughter. Having this stalker has ultimately been a full-time job, as they would take up entire days with harassment. I had to cancel promotional appearances and ignore making further musical plans because I didn't know what I'd be capable of actually delivering on any given day. They have leaked my phone number and home address online, inviting all of my fans to my house at a specific date and time. They have made statements that can be construed as death threats. They're close enough for me to fear real and lasting damage.

Thankfully, local courts were quickly able to produce an emergency injunction to protect my daughter. I had to go to court to get my own injunction. The judge really rushed me through the process, and as I wasn't able to fully explain the issue, the protective order I was granted only covers six months. I was pushing for a permanent one. I hope to never, ever hear from them again for the rest of my life. I'll have to deal with them again when I accompany Juliana and her maternal grandmother to court in about a week, as I possess a screenshot where they admitted to having stalked my daughter at a bus stop. I may be called upon as a witness, so I have to attend a very early court session. I'd rather be doing pretty much anything else one could name instead, but my terrified daughter needs me, and everything else will simply have to take a backseat, including my own sleeping schedule.

I've gotten very little done as a result. The mental toll this has taken on me has been immeasurable. Every time I've seemed like my head was somewhere else in the past few months? That's where it was. Wondering if we'd all make it through the night without incident. Being concerned that someone would show up to the gig to pass out fliers with my name and address on them. It gets pretty hard to concentrate on lyrics when you've got that kind of fear in the back of your mind, when you're always scanning the room and weighing everyone mentally by their potential for danger as well as their intentions. Worrying that literally anyone in the room could be a plant sent there to do something nefarious to you.

Today, I write this with the knowledge that if they contact me directly or indirectly for six months, I'm legally protected, and they'll likely just end up in jail. I don't want them to go to jail; I just want them to stop.

Though it might seem like a cakewalk, what I do takes a tremendous amount of concentration (for me, at least). That concentration had been broken due to safety concerns, but now I'm determined to get back to work and make up for lost time. I want to play harder, more often, and more intensely just to prove that I can't be broken that easily. Really, I only need it proven to myself because I'm actually pretty damn fragile.

## 2-17-17

There's sort of a ceiling that one can hit where you haven't necessarily woken up on the wrong side of the bed, but you only have a certain amount of fucks to give. If you're as naturally empathetic as I am, you tend to often have a surplus of fucks. There are days where your supply of fucks dwindles, and by the close of the day? You're out of fucks. Can't even borrow them from a neighbor.

It would probably be overkill to say that's where I am, but I'll finish out this sentence for the cheap seats.

It's odd. Picking up my guitar and singing felt like a chore today, but I still got things done. Finished the mastering for the *Half Kidding, Half Serious* EP, got the video for "Long Time Listener" as close to finished as it's going to be, and finished the negotiations with the printing press to get this EP produced for a little less than the princely sum that they were asking.

Tried to hook up a compression and gating unit to my home studio setup, but I found that it wasn't phantom powered, rendering half of my usual microphones useless. And after numerous trial-and-error sessions with it, it seems as if I'm still going to have to use a number of VSTs to get the combo of limiting and noise gating for my voice that works best in this room. This begs the question of why I need the thing at all. It'd just take up space.

I'd been chatting here and there with a younger fan that had just discovered *Bubblegum Romance* and reached out to me. They said something to me in Spanish. I responded with the only thing I know how to say in that language, which roughly translates to "Where is Pepe's house?" I was then told to "stop being white."

Let that sink in: "stop being white."

I get the anger directed at white dudes. We've been responsible for a lot of reprehensible shit over the years. I'm certainly not a "white pride" person, but guilt by association does sting. I kindly told the fan that I had to go and that I didn't feel that what they'd said was okay. They apologized. I can't let it go for some reason. When I think about how upset I am about it, I turn the anger inward because this shouldn't be bothering me: no one is wrong about me being born with a certain amount of privilege.

It wasn't just those things that contributed to my mood today. As my depression and crankiness grew, I was reminded of many things said by the person I had to take legal action against. I should tell you that they were in a position of massive influence over me and that few people in the world knew me better, at least up until they stopped listening to "please stop" altogether. In the middle of the harassment, there were things stated about whether I should have ever been born. I felt like righteous Teflon about it at first, but now that things are calming down on the home front, I'm realizing just how far they got into my head.

Maybe if I were working a bit more than I currently am, I wouldn't have so much time to dwell. Alternately I'm afraid that if I had to do public things right now, I'd be party to behaviors that I'd soon regret deeply. Things like this didn't pop into my head during this week's rehearsal, but the slow depressive swing started when a friend got an anonymous harassing and quite stalker-y voicemail.

Now I can't shake an anger that lurks below my surface and the scent of hopelessness that seems to permeate off of every action I try to undertake. This had really better be temporary. It doesn't feel good and I'm doing nothing positive for the world by feeling this way.

2-22-17

Didn't sleep well. Up much earlier than usual and just getting back to work instead of laying around wishing that I could sleep.

Last night was pretty slammed. Recorded an interview for Nerdy.FM with Jim concerning the about-to-be-released Milk Carton Superstars album — I am actually editing that in another window while typing this. Then I set up extra stuff at rehearsal, as it was my friend Kim's night to come in and try out playing the solo to "Free Bird" on her flute with us. Felt really bad for her. I could tell that she could play, but that flute hadn't been used in a long time and kept going completely out of pitch with the stringed instruments. She'd start in B, but by the time she'd make it up the scale to a high B? It was giving off tones like when you're bending a string to be sliiiiightly out of pitch with the rest of the band. As this is a wind instrument, I assume that such a thing shouldn't really be possible. She's going to have some new pads thrown on the instrument, and we'll try again next week. I know she struggles with a low self-image, and I wish I could have made it clearer that I wasn't disappointed. I've been struggling with a different guitar setup for the last two rehearsals, so I understand when your tools refuse to do the job. I hope she feels okay.

Afterward, Emmit and I drove around so he could listen to the demos for the Canada album. He seemed to like it. I think he's a bit too close to be objective, so I haven't really heard any reactions from someone that won't be invested in the record in some way. And when I got home I talked recording dates with Jordon. May 21 looks like the arrival date at the moment. Excited and terrified, but more on that some other time.

I have a new single coming out in a few days. It's a number that I wrote in about 15 minutes called "Song For The Sad Girls." If the album is dying as an art form, I felt that I should at least toy with the idea of standalone singles, so I threw one out into the wild that isn't necessarily representative of how most people might perceive my output.

Might do some more. The other day I was looking through an older hard drive, which I do my best to avoid unless I'm trying to archive something. I ran into two interesting things:

- I found a 2010-era demo called "Anyone But Me," which was pretty gruesome and cruel, but it has potential. I have no idea why I abandoned it. I may try to whip it into shape as another one-off single.

- Found the multitrack files for the title track to *Motherfuckers Be Bullshittin'*, and it turns out that I may have exported it without the bass drum. The recording has been out in the world for six years, and I've only now realized why the "oomph" was missing. It was supposed to be muted for the first half of the first verse, and then come in fully when the bass guitar also does. And it was never unmuted, somehow. Toyed with remixing it and trying to put it out for about an hour but decided I shouldn't pull a George Lucas. The recording might be an erroneous mix, but that's the one that people are attached to. Maybe I'll futz around with it for a later compilation?

That's why I try not to root through the hard drives. I want to go back and change everything. Not a healthy past time. I get mired in "improving the past" far too easily.

Been starting to come to terms with just how rattled I actually am in the aftermath of the "stalker" situation. There was one day toward the middle of January when I was trapped in my house, and I wasn't completely positive that I'd make it through the day alive. I tried to be stoic for everyone else's sake, but now that the imminent fears are (somewhat) alleviated, it's all sinking in. All the destructive and hurtful words resonate in my head. The feelings of being confined to a small bathroom comforting my dog while his congestive heart failure was being drastically tested by the constant noise, shouting, and banging on doors and windows. Trying to email a neighbor to film the events and get them to call 911 because they hadn't responded to my first two calls. All of that rushes in when I close my eyes now.

Do I have a new lease on life? No, I don't. I find myself becoming less patient with people, less willing to put up with behavior that makes me uncomfortable. I don't feel invincible. Instead I have this notion that I'm one hurtful statement away from shattering like a cheap snowglobe. I try to keep anything that could disrupt my generally steady mood as far away as possible. That's meant turning away from my usually lenient and compassionate attitudes to simply shutting folks down as soon as I feel the slightest bit uncomfortable.

3-4-17

I'm writing this from the lobby of the Hilton I'm performing in this weekend. I'm sipping coffee at nearly midnight because I have to sing again in a little while.

Did pretty well on the plane to Minnesota. Not much motion sickness, which is a big change of pace, as air travel doesn't usually agree with me. Some kids kicked my chair for the duration of the three-hour flight, but it wasn't a bad traveling experience, all things considered.

StarF has been helping me get around town in St. Paul. Picked me up from the airport with the patience of a saint. We went out for hot dogs, and he took me to a cool record store. I didn't buy anything, but I convinced him to buy a William Onyeabor record for himself that I hope he'll like.

The weather is dry, cold and windy. Light snow falls on factories that look as if they've been closed for 40 years. It just appears to be a bleak place, but I have only seen a small portion of the state – basically the highways that connect the hotel, The Weinery, the airport and Electric Fetus Records.

Mikey Mason was a tough act to follow last night. The audience seemed to know all of his songs, and his set was one big singalong. And then, me. Trying to just do the more ridiculous of my material in front of 90% new faces.

Right before I began, a security guard came in to explain that he was sorry to those that felt harassed or something? I didn't get it, but it brought the jovial atmosphere to a halt. My literal introduction was preceded by an apology for the apparent abundance of harassment at the convention. At a comedy show. So I jumped into "Unicorns Get More Bacon" and hoped for the best. Played kazoo while strumming the guitar behind my head during "I Can't Remember Your Name." It ended up going okay. I thought I'd really screwed up by playing "Amy, It's Kevin" due to the utter silence where the uncomfortable laughter usually goes, but afterward? It was the only song people asked me about. How weird is that? Not "You're My Princess", "Dickpuncher," or "Life's So Hard."

Instead, the clear winner in the battle of "which song went over the best" was an obscurity from my third album that I was determined to wedge into the set for any hardcore fans that might be sick of what was a relatively predictable setlist. You just simply can't plan for what's going to work for an audience on any given night.

And then of course, Devo Spice came on and made us all look like amateurs. His comedy rap has just the right balance of self-depreciation and skill. I'm always impressed by him. I like him a lot as a guy, too. Ditto for The Great Luke Ski, who not only booked me but is a large part of why nerdy music ever even ended up happening at many nerd-type conventions (at least, if my understanding of his history is correct.)

A bunch of the performers hastily put together a *Rocky Horror* tribute concert. Rehearsal was this morning at around 11 a.m., and I'll be singing my one and one-tenths of a song in less than an hour. I don't think that all of the singers have been in the same room as the band all at once yet. It's likely to be shambles, but I'm hoping for a good type of shambles. Turned out that two of the vocalists are on reality television shows (*King Of The Nerds* and *The Quest*, though I'm not familiar with either one) but are here to promote their fun parody group called The Library Bards. They were very nice.

Actually, everyone here has been pretty nice. I hope I've been nice to them. I've felt a lot of anxiety from all of the confusion inherent with conventions, travel, and concerts that run long and late, but I've been working hard on trying to keep smiling in those moments. Not metaphorically, either – actually keep smiling no matter the situation when in public. Don't want to add to the sadness, anxiety, and fear of the times.

The lights in the bathroom in my hotel room are very, very bright. I switched it on and could see every line and wrinkle in my face. I look old. I look sad. I look tired. I hadn't seen myself in that type of lighting for a very long time.

Wasn't expecting my reflection to look like that. As most people assume that I'm still in my 20s, I was really surprised at the face I've been walking around with lately.

3-12-17

Feeling very sore. I may be reaching the age where every largely exaggerated move that I make for the stage stays in my muscles for days afterward.

While leaving Minnesota – literally while the plane was on the tarmac awaiting takeoff – a person contacted me that had run across a videotape that was purported to be of a Marc With a C set from 2003. I had many reasons to believe that this was factual. Here's the history:

Back in the early 2000s, there was a local Orlando show called *Bootleg TV*. They'd go around town and film concerts, playing the standout clips on a late-night show. It was really cool. Around 2004 or so, I got an email from a fan that had discovered me through the show, but the trouble was that I had no recollections of anyone filming any gigs for television, nor was I aware of any broadcasts. I lost touch with this fan but started trying to track down the *Bootleg TV* folks to get a copy of the show.

Fast forward to 2012. It was the 10th anniversary of the *Human Slushy* album, and I didn't really have much in the way of ephemera from the time. The few shows I did have on video had completely blown-out audio and suffered for one reason or another. We snagged some footage from dilapidated VHS tapes and showed off a little bit of what those days were like but they were all very hard to watch. I suspected that there was something which was almost broadcast quality from the aforementioned TV show, so I went about trying to find it. Tracked down the cat that probably shot the show, and he had no memory of me. Told me he'd keep it in mind. I didn't hear anything back, so I just assumed it was gone, and that didn't break my heart because, as you have probably surmised by now, I have very little love for the recordings from that period of time.

That person from the television show contacted me to communicate that he had not only had found partial footage, but he wanted me to pay him for it right then and to pick up the tape later, which didn't include transferring, as I'd have to figure that all out on my own. I agreed that I'd come and pay him as soon as the tape was in my hands. Unfortunately, he'd filmed some other group on the same tape, so he wasn't willing to just sell me the master. And even less fortunately, it was shot on a mini-DV, which is antiquated by about a decade.

As my friend Alex is a movie buff and quality geek, he just happened to have all the right stuff lying around to transfer the tape. I had assumed through context that the show was one with Joe on drums and Chris on bass, and also one where we played surprisingly well despite not getting along and being furious at having our 9 p.m. set moved to around 1:45 a.m. We all had to get up for work, and the people that had come to see us were leaving in droves. We were pissy and took it out on our instruments and each other. We had a good audio recording from the soundboard, but as it had been slightly edited and seemed to run a few cents too fast, it wasn't worth the trouble to sync it up to the video. No matter, though. The tape had aged quite well, even if the banter and some of the lyrics hadn't. Sound wasn't bad with all things considered.

I haven't fully decided what to do with the footage, but it was fascinating to see the things that had changed and the things that hadn't. It was clear in my demeanor that I didn't want to be on that stage for one reason or another, but it's also clear that I still wanted to play. The odds that I've always fought internally are on full display here. There was so much negative energy rolling off of me that it's a wonder anyone even listened to anything I had to say back then.

It was poetic to see moving pictures of Marc With a Bad Mood just days after a show where I also felt miserable at a gig. A few days ago, I did a show with MC Lars and MegaRan. The performance itself wasn't stressful at all. I love playing with them, and the type of audience that the bill draws is always a pleasure to sing for. Very responsive, very sweet. It's all the crud that happens before the band goes onstage that tends to go awry, and for this show? It all felt very, very wrong.

This particular promoter believes in presale tickets. And mostly in having the opening bands push them. Now, one would think that a headliner would be enough of a draw where folks could make up their own mind on whether they wanted to see the concert, but these cats seem to set up ticket sales with online vendors like TicketFly, slap a few posters up at their venue, and then breathe down the necks of the opening bands to sell a certain amount of tickets or they not only won't get paid, but they also won't be asked back. So there I am, hustling for a gig where I'll be onstage for 25 minutes, but all the money goes to the headliners, venue, and promoters. I find it lazy, cheap, and only a few steps away from "pay to play." This promoter has even insisted that all local acts do not have fans but rather "friends." This promoter obviously doesn't understand that I hardly talk to anyone at length about anything, and the few folks that I'm close to outside of my household don't really come to see the shows. I do, in fact, have fans – however few in numbers – and he's simply wrong.

Because he wants to keep you on your toes and pushing the show? They don't tell you when you are going on until you get there, usually based on which opener sold the most tickets, which makes planning for a set length impossible, not to mention planning to be at soundcheck, or if all of your bandmates can get off of work in time for the show. And that's precisely where it all started going wrong.

At about 5 p.m., Emmit called to say he'd been stuck in traffic for two hours and was still in Tampa. Since he was supposed to be loading in at that very moment, and we still had no idea of when our set would be, we couldn't guarantee that he'd make it in time. I publicly announced that the Trio wouldn't be performing, but I'd still be doing a solo set. The promoter (who hadn't arrived until an hour later) finally messaged me to say we'd be on at 8:20 after seeing that, which meant that the band could very likely arrive in time. I had to go and recant my words immediately. This all could have been avoided if he'd have just said, "Hey, you're on at 8:20" in the first place, but if he'd have done that, we couldn't have had people showing up early to drink alcohol with nothing else to do, I suppose.

In the interim of trying to track down bandmates and get my gear inside, my car almost got towed for inexplicable reasons. I'd parked on the side of the building like a million times before, but somehow a tow truck driver had hooked himself up to my dad-ride while I was on the phone around the corner. This meant that I'd have to park in a parking garage and make six trips up and down four flights of stairs to unload my gear and merch. I was exhausted long before doors opened.

Once it was all done, and the confusion finally subsided right before the audience was let in? I saw two of the promoters arguing about curfew times. It sounded pretty ugly. They couldn't seem to agree on anything at all, and any time I had a question, I'd get a curt and short response from them. Most of my help had come from Joe, the soundman, who was truly invaluable to us. We learned more about what was happening at the show from him than we did from the people that were supposed to be running it.

Peter Pepper was the first opening act. They brought more gear than the rest of us combined – for a 20-minute set. I couldn't make heads or tails of that. Once we finally got on the stage to play, I was certainly ready to beat up my instrument. And all those folks singing along to my songs? All the folks in the crowd in Marc With a C shirts? The promoter saw them as friends. Probably thought that I'm just super well-connected because he doesn't seem to take local acts seriously. And the truth is that I'm not "local." I just happen to live in Orlando. Those loud audience members also sang along to MegaRan and

MC Lars songs. Before, after, and during the show? The promoter acted like he was doing me a favor while I did most of the street team and hustling work.

Despite that? The 25-minute performance was good. The anxiety fueled a tight and angry performance for the band. Jim was getting over a cold, but you'd have never known it from the crowd. Merch sales weren't huge because many of the attendees already had a lot of Marc With a C memorabilia, but some sales were made to brand new fans. That 25 minutes is why I allowed myself to be treated like a second-class citizen who didn't even belong in the club. Weeks of planning and dealing with people that don't even see you as human? All for 25 minutes.

## 3-28-17

Meatwad suffered another attack on his congestive heart failure today. Nicole found him this morning, and he couldn't catch his breath. I had to upend a ton of stuff to be here for him, but he's family. That's what you do. This also consisted of moving rehearsal for the next gig until literally a few hours before we perform – which is really bad for my throat – but we simply don't have a choice. Meatwad nearly died again today. The band was really supportive.

They didn't have to be. Saturday night was home to a catastrophic misunderstanding. The trio was opening for the Milk Carton Superstars album release party, but the audience wouldn't shut up. I was kicking things off with a few solo numbers, but the crowd was so loud I couldn't hear myself. After a revamped "Nerdy Girls," I took the microphone and walked offstage to the table nearest me to chide one of the loudest portions of the room. Could not see them, but I could hear them just fine.

The plan was to do the old "Marc versus a heckler" routine, and just as I started? When I got close enough, I realized that it was Jim's wife. And as she was running a raffle and the merch booth? Out of all the people in the room, she had every right to talk. I sheepishly mumbled something like, "Could you please be quiet, and can I go back to the show now?" but the damage was done. It looked to everyone like I was targeting Bethany. Heck, it would have looked that way to me. If I'd have been able to see that it was her, I would have walked to any number of other offending tables to do the bit, which does alienate some, but works about 75% of the time.

Jim was really pissed off at me, and rightfully so. Since I knew that it wasn't intentionally targeted at her, it never dawned on me that it would appear otherwise. When that idea finally sunk in on the drive home, I felt really low.

Sure, Bethany and I don't always see eye to eye, but she's still my buddy, and I wouldn't ever try to humiliate her.

I made some frantic apologetic calls on Monday, and I hope that they know just how unintentional it was. I was actually in a great mood until I got onstage and couldn't hear myself over the conversation. The audience was so bad about it that I've decided to take another small hiatus from performing.

I just don't have much fight in me right now. Maybe the legal issues drained it out of me. Maybe I feel like it should be a given that performers should be treated with a modicum of respect, and I'm tired of trying to educate folks about it. Whatever the reason, I just can't go on doing this. Devoting hours upon hours to rehearsals for a show that can't be heard by everyone that came. Watching people that drove for hours to see the show get frustrated that they can't hear the songs. It's just not something I have the will to try and combat anymore.

I have two more gigs to go. The last one is a mini-fest that I'm headlining. I want to really make it count, and frankly, I'll be lucky if Jim wants to stick it out with me. Bethany understood and accepted my apology. Jim accepted my apology, but I'm not sure if the sting will go away as easily for him. It happened at his record release show to his partner in public. I probably wouldn't forgive me terribly quickly either, no matter how accidental the circumstance.

I want to start trying to create some cool stuff late at night. Something very different from Marc With a C or even Natural History Museum, as the latter hasn't really excited me lately. Did a whole album for that project that I don't feel strong enough about to release. But maybe if I can do some more melodic experimental stuff, I'll feel different. I need another outlet. One where the only judge is my own taste. I need to just create for myself again.

3-31-17

It's been an eventful few days since I wrote here last, despite precisely no music being made in that time.

On Tuesday, I started feeling a strange bit of vertigo. Nothing like "drunk spins" but rather more like I felt as if I was tumbling, feet first, heels over head. This happened every time I'd turn to my right, and unfortunately it dawned on me while driving. I figured it was just an anomaly, so I kept trying to ignore it. Wednesday gave me another long drive, and I kept feeling a sensation not unlike that which you might have if your car was about to roll over. This kicked off about 20 minutes into a 90-minute drive.

It got worse through the day. Tried some home remedies to clean my ears – this has happened before and is usually coupled with wax buildup – but that just made it worse until I could not hear out of my right ear. And my equilibrium had shifted. And now I was slurring. I probably looked like I was having a stroke to the naked eye.

Drove myself to the nearest emergency room, but after two hours of waiting while my hearing got worse in my right ear? They assured me that I'd only have around four more hours left to wait before I could be seen. My life and career flashed before my eyes, and as people vomited around me, and no workers came out to help with the mess? I weighed my options. Sure, I could wait, but people who might be worse off than me aren't being treated, and they don't seem to have a single bit of staff ready to help. Of course, if I drove to another emergency room I could endanger the lives of others because I really shouldn't be driving. Bad balance. Dulled senses. Feeling angry. All of those things put together equaled a lot of reasons that I should stay put and hope for the best.

So of course I rage-quit the shoddy waiting room of [HOSPITAL NAME REDACTED] and drove until I found another emergency room.

By the time I entered, I was having to keep my hand on the wall to support myself. I couldn't hear the questions being asked at reception and before I knew it, they plopped me into a wheelchair and immediately checked me into a room.

It'd turn out that I had infections in both ears, and the balance issues were caused by a mixture of a buildup of cerumen, pus, and mucus. They did their best to irrigate me, handed me a ton of antibiotics and steroids, and sent me off into the night at least somewhat more able to walk a straight line. I'm lucky I didn't get pulled over. I must have seemed positively hammered.

During this whole issue, I was glued to the phone, as BackBooth had double-booked the dates for the Orlando Overdrive festival. As I've been told I'm the headliner, I had a vested personal interest in solving this issue. BackBooth wanted to move the show to the following day. I couldn't let that happen because Jim and Emmit had already requested that specific day off from work. And as I'd signed a contract for a performance on April 22 with The Marc With a C Trio? BackBooth screwing the little guys in favor of keeping their gig with a bigger act was also going to put me in a fairly precarious situation.

I suggested that we just move the show back to Geek Easy. Sure, we've been having some trouble with that venue's patrons, but heck, at least they seem to want to have us there. BackBooth as a staff has been treating me like crud for quite a while now, and I'm not alone, The Geek Easy always tries to put the artists first, even on nights when the audience isn't reacting favorably. We're bringing the show "home," and a bunch of people bent over backwards to make that happen.

4-5-17

Last show was probably the most sedate I can remember being while on a stage. Had to stand pretty much stock still so the vibrations didn't knock me over as this vertigo still permeates. While I'm feeling much better now while I'm typing this, I probably shouldn't have done Sunday's gig.

When we walked into this hole-in-the-wall bar to set up? I turned to my right, assuming that the stage was being set up in the big quiet space. Emmit and Jim went to the left and surveyed a stage in a separate room in the front of the building where tons of people were. My suspicions were right: the venue had chosen to put us on in a place where patrons do not go.

We played to somewhere between five and 20 people, depending on the song. For the best, though. I wasn't really capable of doing all of the jumping around and windmilling. I almost fell over when I tried to play guitar behind my head. There wasn't really any pain with these ear infections, just a bunch of balance issues, and each time the fluid in my head moved, it felt like an earthquake.

I could tell that something was bothering Emmit, but I didn't want to ask until after the set. Sure, I didn't want bad vibes present while we played, but we already had enough hurdles to jump just to get on the stage for that 45 minutes. After we loaded out, he told me that he and Aubree had broken up while he was driving over. I love both of them, and I was more upset that I had to go to work and couldn't spend my time consoling them like a good friend. Instead? Had to be focused and sharp so I could play "Unicorns Get More Bacon" again.

I did make it home and talk to Aubree via phone for over three hours. I offered to come over with a bunch of junk food and stupid DVDs for us to watch, but she wasn't having it. I feel very big-brotherly and protective over her, not to be confused with me feeling any different toward Emmit. I think that their breakup was a matter of circumstance and not the product of wrongdoing on anyone's part. Which makes it more painful, as it just doesn't seem like it could have been avoided or ignored.

On a completely different note, I'd been putting together a multimedia experiment called "Pepsi Is Bae." It required the involvement of numerous visual artists and was going to be interesting at the very least. As of yesterday, Pepsi put out a rather offensive commercial where Kylie Jenner "solved" a protest by handing a police officer a soft drink. Weeks of planning went out the window. You just can't account for scandals. I'll have to start working on something else instead while I wait for the new EP to be pressed.

Not been in a great mental space, and I haven't been able to defeat it to get work done. I still accomplish goals, but the inspiration for new things isn't there right now. I think it's a byproduct of all of the hurry-up-and-wait concerning going to Canada. And now I'm overthinking that whole album: do I really like "I'm Sad That It's Your Birthday" all that much? Should I try to write another song to replace it? What would work well between "Terribly Popular" and "Low Rent Truman Show" instead?

I currently have questions, distrust of my own instincts, but few extra new ideas waiting to fill in those gaps.

4-10-17

This is really happening. Passport arrived in the mail. Went to see my doctor today about getting enough medication to last the duration of my trip outside of the United States and some for a "worst-case scenario" cache. Next steps are buying the actual plane tickets and paying Jordon.

Still not really sure about one of the songs from the album, the "birthday song." Think I'm going to write another song that could possibly take its place and see if Jordon wants to record it as a backup – if it's any good, of course. I feel like I should be really sold on every song for this album, and while this tune is probably among the most immediately identifiable as "Marc," I like it the least. Also thinking about running "Song For The Sad Girls" past him. Something just keeps gnawing at me with the tune, that it deserves better than it has gotten. Wouldn't hurt to have a few session outtakes, at worst.

At the highest Patreon tier, people get to choose a topic for me to write a song about. They are forewarned that no matter what they choose? It'll still go through the Marc With a C-filter and might end up being about something completely different, but I'll at least use their subjects as a jumping-off point.

One fan is named Ken. He's really, really ill. His mom had even befriended me on Facebook, and most of her posts have been about the way that Ken is barely hanging on at the moment. I took longer than usual to deliver his song – just sent it to him last week. I don't know that he's heard it. I don't know what kind of mindset he will be in if he actually gets to play it. The song took so long to complete because I just couldn't connect to the subject matter, and once I finally found a lyrical angle, his health seemed to be taking a turn, which I didn't know. Until I'm sure he's gotten to hear it, I won't let anyone else hear the tune. It feels like the only way I can internally make peace with it.

I have a very, very full week ahead of me. Surprisingly little of it has anything to do with playing my guitar until Friday. I guess I should probably warm up a bit here and there for the upcoming livestream show for Patreon backers, but I don't like playing guitar by myself much lately. I'd better hop to it because I still have to figure out a setlist for that Orlando Overdrive festival and get it ready for the band to practice this weekend.

4-15-17

Literally minutes before I played today's livestream for Patreon backers, I learned that Ken passed away. The one that I just completed "Japanese Starship" for. His illness made its way to his brain. He fought valiantly for 31 years.

I was really shaken, considering he was in the Patreon tier where he was eligible for the livestreams. On top of that, today I was supposed to focus half of the set on songs from his favorite album of mine, *This World Is Scary As Fuck*. I even had "This Is Hopeless" on the setlist, and that was pure serendipity as I have not performed this song since 2005 (other than performing it for him on a private livestream). About four or five songs in, I explained to the viewers what had happened. I literally found out as I was turning the camera on, fully expecting him to be tuned in and viewing. I think I caught some fire about 30 minutes into the set, composing myself a bit, and going ahead with a "show must go on" attitude. I considered canceling at first, but I could not do that. This gentleman battled worse odds than I ever have for three decades. To cancel would have probably disappointed him greatly. I went on when I probably should have at least postponed by an hour just to get myself together.

I've been doing this long enough to become somewhat close to some fans and to watch them pass away. I'm not getting any better at handling it. I hardly knew Ken, but he inspired me greatly.

4-25-17

Feeling pretty sluggish today. Actually, I've felt sluggish for the past three days. Ever since the Orlando Overdrive festival, I've had to fight for every bit of energy I can. It's not coming naturally right now.

Just before I left the house to perform at said festival, I saw that the respondent that I had to get a protective order from thought that they'd found a loophole to contact me. Emphasis on "thought." They did succeed in reaching me, but it still broke the order, and in turn it broke my mood for the day. Knowing that there was very little I could do about it, I decided to let my mind and body have its little anxiety-ridden-freak-out session in the car while driving to the gig, but after that? I was going to need both the mind and the body back to do my job.

With nine very, very loud acts on the bill, it was easy to temporarily be distracted from the pressing issues at home. I had to check in at the show around 3 p.m. and stick around until roughly 11 p.m. to play, and then a few hours after to get paid. On the way, I went to a secret hidey-hole that'll hold Record Store Day releases for me, and, as relatively few people shop at this store, I get to skip the lines. The shop seems to like doing this for me because I'm a guaranteed sale; something that comes in handy when you're rolling the dice on non-returnable merchandise geared to one day's worth of promotion. I picked up a David Bowie live album, the reissue of Evan Dando's sole solo album, and a Frank Zappa 10-inch record. Took great care to insulate the vinyl from the heat as they'd be living in my car while I did the show. I seem to have done a decent job as they all seem to play just fine.

The show itself went a lot better than it should have. When folks wanted to talk to me, I had to shout to be heard over the music. That'd left my voice pretty weak by the time we eventually went on around midnight. Just as I'd suspected, most of the audience had cleared out by then, but the cluster of people that stuck around were the die-hards who knew every word to every song we played. They treated me better than I deserved. I had some guitar troubles that plagued me through a good portion of the set, but they all sang along and danced as if it wasn't an issue. Emmit and Jim played exceptionally well, too. There were loud and excited singalongs to "Where's My Giant Robot" and "I Hate This Song," which really surprised the band as a whole.

It was one of those shows where the vibe and audience were better than the performance. They carried me and made a fantastic set, and it became something bigger than what any one individual was up to. Just goodwill and people determined to have a good time after waiting all day to see us play. A few folks told me afterward that it was exactly what they needed after a rough week. I suppose that after the way my day kicked off? I needed it as well.

The very next day I had to call the authorities and report the broken protective order. The police reassured me that I was doing the right thing, but I wasn't crazy about the way they said they'd deal with it. I just have to protect myself and my immediate family. The moment that I let something small slide past? That might lead to a bigger thing happening because I did not react or report it.

I saw my doctor again today. I've had some issues in a specific location that might be predictable for a male at my age, but more like oddities rather than anything painful or non-functioning. And he didn't really understand it either, so he gave me a diagnosis that he assumed was a possibility as well as some antibiotics in hopes that it'd get things back to normal. Everything I've read about this diagnosis says that it is usually caused by things that simply aren't a part of my lifestyle, so I'm left with more questions than answers. The main reason I went was because there's a history of cancer in the males on the matriarchal side of my family, and it usually presents in, erm, "a tender location." After a checkup that involved a lot of touching that I usually reserve for at least the third date, my doctor said that my bigger fears didn't seem to be founded. At the moment.

Between these things, I've been mixing the recordings of the Orlando Overdrive sets for broadcast on Nerdy.FM. James Dechert recorded each set from the soundboard, with each instrument on a differing channel. This means that I can make each set sound pretty good for broadcast, but it also means that I'll have a lot of work to do. Nine sets at a minimum of 35 minutes a piece, with up to 16 individual instruments at a time to mix. I'm glad I spent a lot of time away from the stage because I'll be quite up close and personal with this gig.

And when I get a chance, I still have to transcribe all of the new songs from the demos to paper. Played "Maybe" live on WPRK, so that was the first premier of some new stuff. No one complained, so I guess it wasn't awful. Chris LeBrane filmed my appearance with a few cameras planning to make a live video for the internet from it. It's hard to be visually interesting while also concentrating to make sounds that make for good radio. With an unamplified guitar, you're stuck to the microphones and cannot move around too much. Can't imagine that'd be much fun to watch. Chris has a good eye, though. He can make it cool.

5-3-17

The last few days have been spent transcribing songs from the *Half Serious, Half Kidding* EP for the band to learn. Jim told me that he didn't feel comfortable singing the harmonies to "All I Want For Christmas" – which I found surprising, but that's an unspoken rule in the Trio: if someone has a moral objection, we don't do it. As a result, we haven't even attempted the song yet.

Spent a bunch of time coordinating a video shoot for that song regardless. It's a simple one-shot of the band miming the song, but we're going to have my friend Tera lip syncing the song instead of me. She's the star of the "Longtime Listener" video, and, as that song is about impostor syndrome, it made sense to have the follow-up single use an impostor in place of yours truly. And then there's a video she's going to appear in for "Selfies," but I'll start making calls for that treatment after I'm done writing this entry. Tera is the running thread for this trilogy of videos, but it helps that she looks really nice on camera and is really good at silent acting, and she's had plenty of practice at that with The Rich Weirdoes. I'm pretty sure she's kind of a ham anyways, so I hope she'll have fun with these concepts. She certainly isn't doing it for the money because I don't have much of that.

Everything I've done recently has been very time-consuming but not terribly interesting to talk about. Hasn't left much time for sustenance and inspiration. To the outside world, this might appear to be a period of inactivity, and as a result, people have been dropping off of the Patreon left and right. What I'm really doing is all of the non-glamorous behind the scenes stuff, and that's when I need the support most.

I'd released the "Song For The Sad Girls" single a few weeks ago, and it was a complete flop. Actually, it was so resoundingly ignored that the word flop intimates that someone even listened at all. Last night on a whim I reposted it on social media, and, while it wasn't viral or anything, it finally got some spins and some positive feedback. That's the deal now. If you don't make it clear that you like something, us artistic types have no way to gauge reactions anymore. We need that enthusiasm. To further my point? Last night, I brought eight new songs into rehearsal – or rather songs that were new to the band – and I decided that we'd drop "Sad Girls" completely, not even bothering to work on it. After a number of folks mentioned that they liked the cut of its jib, or that they related to it? Now I have to recant and make the band learn it. It's just that topsy-turvy. If you've released around 300 songs, the only way you can gauge what to play live is either only performing what you, the artist, is in the mood for, or playing songs that people have made very clear that they enjoy.

Nearing completion on my long-game Zappa project. The project was as follows: Frank claimed that if you played each album end to end, back to back? It's one big and long composition with reprises, recurring themes, and whatnot. I couldn't find proof that anyone had ever listened to and reviewed it as such, so I thought I might as well be the guy. He's his own damn genre. Never thought I'd get sick of him, but here I am, sort of excited that I'm taking a breather from his works. In truth, I found that the *You Can't Do That On Stage Anymore* series was a bit more than I was ready for, and that's when it started grating on me. I have three more albums to write about, and then I go through some cleanup work to try and sell the piece.

5-12-17

Slammed is the word of the week. Video shoots, another wave of demos for the Canada album, and a lot of driving.

The band did our last rehearsal before our planned regrouping in late June. So far, I'm unhappy with the progression of "Longtime Listener," "First Time Collar," and "Selfies." Jim still isn't thrilled with "All I Want For Christmas." The first two might get better with some retweezing, the current arrangement of "Selfies" doesn't feel stage-ready, and Jim's reservation about the Christmas tune seems to lie with being uncomfortable singing the harmony lines, so, easy, we just won't have harmony.

Tera canceled on the video shoots with less than a day's notice. There was a loose lineage, a sort of storyline for all of these videos, and now it's totally gone. Kimberly Luffman stepped up to the plate on no notice at all for the "All I Want For Christmas" video and did wonderfully on a first take. I tried without success to schedule with Tera to still involve her in the "Selfies" video, but her texts became so non-committal that I just decided to spend that time finding people that actually want to appear. The concept is shot to hell now, but I'm not going to twist anyone's arm to work if they don't feel like it. I think the videos would have been better with their original scripts, but they were dependent on the initial actress appearing in each of them. That's the life of a DIY musician: use who and what's available to make the best art that you can. Tera's having a bad time, though, so I'm not mad. I'm not just saying that, either. I don't think I could put up with an hour's worth of her current daily struggles. Strong, strong lady.

Tonight I'm taking Juliana to see The Weeknd. He's her current fave rave.

I'm not very well-versed in what he does, but maybe coming into his show a bit cold will be a boon to my enjoyment. Tomorrow I'm doing an on-camera interview and performance for a variety show that I know precious little about. They're shooting at Retro Records. I haven't got much time to prep for this at all, but oddly? I'm looking at playing a few oldies like a nice "break." My world has been focused on the forthcoming EP and the about-to-be-recorded album. Even stopping to perform a song from *Unicorns Get More Bacon* feels like a day off at this point.

The Geek Easy got robbed last night. I'm supposed to be on a hiatus, but the owners called to ask if I'd do a benefit show for them. I gave them my dates of availability and hoped that they can work something out. They've had my back when my ideas have flopped. I can take a few hours out to sing songs if it helps them, for sure.

5-24-17

Writing this from Canada, resting on the couch in Jordon's studio. I've been here for a day and a half, but we've already gotten all but one drum track down. It's helpful that I'm not the drummer on this album for the sake of time management, as Jordon is a drumming beast, and my silly little pop songs have been easy for him to tackle. He's out with his kids at the moment, and I'm listening to King Crimson on his record player.

The flights were the easy part, but all of my travels began right as I'd usually be going to bed. There were excruciatingly long layovers, and while the actual customs formalities were much simpler than I thought they'd be, the general air of confusion and long lines sucked the fun out of that new experience.

Jordon and I have gotten along famously so far. We understand 99% of each other's musical references, either in production talk or casual conversation, and he's been entertaining me with tales of working with the likes of Carole King and other famous people I admire.

This studio is a pretty wonderful little crash pad. Very homey and cozy. Great record collection to check out in my off time. Kind of feel as if I should be using the spare hours to see a land different from my own, but that's unlikely as I have no transportation and am literally in the middle of nowhere in Pembroke. There seems to be a Canadian Tire and a Walmart a few miles away, but that's about it. Love the place so far, though. Already a bit homesick.

The last-minute benefit gig I did before I left was a pretty loose shindig, but I think that really made my set better than average. An attentive audience with few expectations is a lot of fun. As I had to leave early the next morning, I had to jet right after I was done performing, so I'm just left to hope that a good amount of money was raised for The Geek Easy.

5-27-17

Today has been kind of a day off in the studio. Jordon's kids are over, so they've been at the center of attention. Last night they chose to watch the Doctor Who miniseries called *Pyramids Of Mars* over *Guardians Of The Galaxy*. This morning, they chose *Mystery Science Theater* over cartoons. It's safe to say that I'm pretty much "ride or die" with Scarlet and Sidney at this point.

Most of the electric guitars are done being recorded now and about half of the bass parts. Some of these songs are so basic and simple that I felt like a total heel when I'd fuck up a rudimentary part in front of one of my musical idols, but things like that get balanced out by Jordon turning several shades of red when his 8-year-old son would innocently tell me things like, "When daddy was 21, he wrote a song called 'Hunting At The Fucking Zoo'!" I think I'm bound by honor to mention that Jordon seriously regrets that tune.

Pembroke is a beautiful place. Tried poutine for the first time today. We walked around a gorgeous lake, and I was able to see some local color. This place is like a bigger than average "small town" in America that somehow has a pretty progressive attitude. People don't seem as on edge in this country. On days like today, I feel like I'm on vacation rather than making a record in a studio.

Still a week and a half to go, but many of the basic building blocks for an album are in place. We've been playing a Robert Palmer album called *Clues* over and over, which was new to both of us. Inspiration comes from things I don't always expect. With the new surroundings there has been a different energy in the recordings, a "new fun," so to speak. I'm intensely excited for the sounds to take further shape.

Of course, the eternal fanboy in me was equally excited that Jordon showed me some new Blinker The Star material. Life is pretty cool right now.

**5-29-17**

Jordon woke up today and promptly cranked up an AC/DC record. We're hoping that sets our tone, as we want to work hard today, hopefully finishing the recording and spending the rest of my time in Canada doing some mixing. The finish line is almost in sight as far as actual recording goes.

Last night we must have spent hours doubling gang vocals on "Terribly Popular." As in, we both only said the words "I'm terribly popular" over and over for a chunk of the day. We also miked the crickets outside for some atmospheric moments we hope to use. We're far enough along to start taking some risks and just trying out things that seem interesting to us.

After tracking harmonies on the newly rechristened "Your Goddamn Birthday," we had a long heart-to-heart chat about painful issues we'd lived through, and last night felt like the moment that we really bonded as friends. I'm going to miss him when I go home, but I'm also eager to get back to my family. Yesterday there was an emergency, and I had to find a Western Union to send some money back to Florida. Felt bad being away and doing my job instead of being accessible. Soon.

**5-30-17**

Halfway through yesterday's session, my biggest fear about this trip was realized: I got sick, and my throat gave out nearly completely.

Thankfully, I only started feeling that tell-tale pinch when there were two harmony vocals left to go. I told Jordon in no uncertain terms that this was the last day we'd be able to do anything vocally. He seemed to understand the gravity quickly. We not only finished all recording but have finished mixes of three songs!

Jordon's mixing process is really interesting. Many people working with ProTools will just sort of bounce the mix they're happy with to two-track stereo, no muss, no fuss. Instead he sends the music out of the computer and into something that's called the "nicerizer," which is a heavy piece of analog gear that emulates the old Neve boards. A mix that sounded good the first time around sounds so full of life and buoyancy after being routed through this gear. In fact, these mixes sound so good I almost cringe at the idea of what the mastering process could do to it, but I know it must be done.

I believe that while I'm crazy about what we've done, this is absolutely going to be a "love it or hate it" album for folks that have followed me for a while. Regardless, this is the album I needed to make, the album I clawed through life to make, and I'm not really sure how much else I have to say musically after this piece.

But I say that after every album.

Jordon and I are getting a bit silly and loopy from all of the work – or we are just getting more comfortable. Spent some time last night putting LP covers next to each other to see which art could match others and make a bigger piece. The clear winner was the merging of an album each by Nazareth and Weezer. You had to be there.

Hopefully I can kick this cold soon.

6-2-17

Only two things left to do before the record is "done" on our part: Master it. Commission the art.

That's it. I listened to the finished mixes yesterday while laying on an air mattress with a head full of Canadian cold medicine and was thrilled. It's a Very Good Record.

Why not great?

It becomes great when it merges with your ears. When you receive it, and it's functional for you. To call an album great on my own would probably be overshooting and just a means to set myself up for disappointment. What if I'm super attached to it, but everyone hates it?

On a technical level, it's the best record I've ever made, bar none. On a songwriting level, it's the best record I could have made right now. I've communicated all that I want to. I feel as if I've found a tasteful way to get all of my current feelings across. I feel like I have a mental blank slate. If I were to sit down to write more right now? I'd be forcing it. There's nothing left to say. I know what the central theme is, but it's something more effective if the listener discovers it on their own, for sure.

We've just been killing time now while I wait to go home. Nothing left to do. I have the 24-bit mixes. I have MP3s for reference on my iPod. I'm just in a holding pattern. Last night we watched documentaries about space until bedtime. Each night we've gone out to look at the stars through a telescope. There's no light pollution here in the Canadian countryside, and there's one specific star – or at least we think it's a star – that bounces around, flashes different colors, and changes positions in the sky ever-so-slightly each night. It isn't a plane or a satellite, as both of those things move quicker. This object changes positions each day, but only bops around in a small radius. Curious.

6-4-17

As we've been finished with the record for days, I've just sort of been sitting on my hands here at the studio. Due to the horrendous cold, I've not felt well enough to spend the free time seeing the Canadian sights. Mostly just lying on the air mattress in the control room, listening to Lisa Germano on headphones, and reading one of the books I'd brought with me.

On Friday, we ventured to a small record store where I found a copy of the Robert Palmer album we'd discovered to bring home and call my very own. Even that short trip sucked all of my remaining cold-ridden energy away.

A few days ago, the first shipment of the *Half Serious, Half Kidding* EP arrived in Florida. Nicole sent me pictures and videos so that I could approve the pressing in a rather lo-fi manner. It sounds huge even through tiny speakers, which excited me greatly.

I think I'm going to spend most of today keeping a low profile. Besides making art, Jordon and I are naturally introverted people who can go for days without speaking. For two straight weeks, we've been roommates, and I can feel that we both need to "shut off" for a bit. My own manner of introversion is that I need an amount of "me time" that is directly equal to how much time I have to spend being "on." I suspect that it's much the same for Jordon but probably a bit more difficult for him as I'm in his fortress of solitude, so to speak. There's no abrasion or anything of the sort; I think we both just need some space. I've wondered if I should get a hotel room close to the airport for the remainder of my time here, but if I could afford that sort of thing, I'd have coughed up the $200 needed to catch an earlier flight home.

I'm going to miss him. I'm going to miss the kids. But I really need to be home. Two weeks is almost enough time for me to start cracking, and it's been a helpful reminder as to why I'm not spending my life on the road. New environments don't play well with my body. I become sick, miserable, and unable to do the most basic parts of my job. And I miss my family terribly. It's just better for everyone if I stay home and work, but I wouldn't have traded this experience for the world.

6-11-17

Since I've been home, I've done nothing but work on *Obscurity* as well as the release prep for the *Half Serious, Half Kidding* EP. I launched that latter pre-order the day after I returned home, and it went to #1 on Bandcamp's pop vinyl chart again, which kind of blew my mind. I know that this EP is merely a bridge between two albums. It's not top-tier work, but it puts two things together very nicely. Despite this (and trying to make it clear in all of the press blurbs), I've seen people treating it like "my new album." This scares me because, well, it just isn't. It's really two EPs on one red 10-inch: a jokey one and a deathly serious one.

Kramer is midway through mastering the new album. I've heard the 24-bit masters of each individual song and approved them, but there's been a few disagreements over general minutia. Things like how to index the tracks, where crossfades need to be – really piddly shit that makes all the difference in the world to me but probably no one else. Kramer's a quirky dude, and I knew that going in, but I am too, and I want the album to flow correctly. Conceivably, I could just cut them myself because I know exactly what I'm after, but I feel like it wouldn't be fair to credit him if I did that. Mastering may not seem like much to the average person, but it's a crucial step that can make or break the sound and feel of your album.

I've sent all the components to Katharine so she can get started on the artwork. Or at least, I think I have. I'm so close to this thing now that I can't remember general things sometimes, like "how many pages go in the CD booklet" and whatnot. I told her as much, so I expect plenty of questions for all of the information I neglected to include. Really wish I could have visited her while I was in Canada, but that 5-hour drive is no joke. Also, I wouldn't want to have gotten her sick.

Though I've done nothing but work and make trips to the post office since I came home, I also feel like I'm slumming it a bit. Really just trying to get back to normal. Trying to remember to do household chores and get back to my daily "required listening." Jumped back into Pink Floyd when I resumed that alphabetical-listening-journey today with *The Endless River*, which isn't as bad as people made it out to be. It's exactly what it should have been: David Gilmour, Richard Wright, and Nick Mason just jamming and sounding like Pink Floyd. They weren't the primary songwriters, so why bother with actual songs? It's a great mood record. Perfect for a day like today, where it's just constantly pissing rain.

I feel like I've been so busy that I haven't even had time to have feelings or form opinions on things besides the current administration in America. What a shitshow. Hopefully I can keep making songs that get people's minds off of the grossness, at least for the few minutes that they're listening.

6-20-17

There's a current trend in vinyl, and I can't wait for it to pass. Lately, many folks are pressing 12-inch records at 45 RPM. With shorter records, I almost understand – take advantage of the higher fidelity that a quicker spin might afford you – even though this is mostly happening with indie and garage-type groups. Or sometimes? LPs will be stretched over two discs because of the whole 45 RPM deal. One notable example is *Indie Cindy* by the Pixies. Now, it's not exactly a fantastic album, but it's nowhere near as bad as the buzz that you've heard about it. It's a fine rock record. I mean, "Bagboy" is pretty annoying, but beyond that, it's pretty cool, right? But here we are, flipping the record every 11 minutes. Could've been a solitary record at 33 RPM at around 22-ish minutes per side – which works, no matter what pressing plants tell you. Please see *Dark Side Of The Moon* for reference – but maybe the pointless platter-stretching turned some folks off. On top of that, it's mastered pretty loudly, so you're not really gaining any "better" sound quality by having it play faster. I just don't get it.

Katharine gave me some mock-up art for *Obscurity*'s front cover. I love her general idea: she's using the pantones of the last two albums but mixing it with the "northern lights" and a reference from a Rush album cover for the Canadian connection. I like it in general, but I really didn't flip for a specific font she used. I can't explain it. It just grated it on me. I hate giving her criticism because I know that I don't really have much of an eye for visual art. Also, it sucks to say, "I can't tell you exactly how to fix it, but make it better." A part of me feels like I'm being precious about the album because this really, really has to come out of the gate properly, or it'll never be received well. At least that's what going on in my head.

Heard a few songs from the finished master in the car today. Firmed up my decision to make "Low Rent Truman Show" the lead single. Tried to call Tim Labonte to see what he might have in mind for a video. Or if he's even available? But it's hard to tell people what I want right now. The timetable for release is in so much flux. I've thought about November, but that feels like pushing it. I could also hold it back until February, but I fear being sick to death of the album at that point and not wanting to promote it at all. But I could also line up so much promo in that time that —

You know, never mind. You're just watching me work this out in my head. I'm gonna run it by the band and see how quickly they think we can learn the new songs. That's the ultimate question, really. No point in putting out an album we can't represent in live shows. We should be rehearsing today, but both Jim and Emmit are sick. I'm surprised they aren't ticked at me – I totally fucked up with a double-booking that was my own fault for the first time in my history, and honestly, other than just getting tighter with the songs from *Half Serious, Half Kidding*, there's not really anything we're prepping for.

I'd like to get back to shows, but I'd like to feel confident about it first. Got a crummy review of the EP that was also factually incorrect, and it's been in the back of my mind. I can stress as much as I want that this EP is only meant to be a 20-minute slice of entertainment between "real" albums, but it hasn't stopped some from gauging it as "my new statement." It's not how it was intended, and when you look at it through that lens? Yeah, it isn't very good. But as a little clutch of pop songs, it's pretty cool. As a bridge? It's just right.

7-8-17

It was somewhere in the 16th run-through of the song "First Time Collar" with Jim and Emmit where we were continuously "looking for the groove" that I just said, "Let's shitcan it." I mean, really. Who cares? I don't mean it in a whiny way, either. Truly, no one is going to care if we know how to play that song and bring it to them. Though I went through at least three vastly different rewrites before it ended up on the last EP, and despite the fact that I've probably spent more time working that song out than any other in the last year and a half? Doesn't matter. The song isn't great. It's good, but not great. And why waste our time on songs that are just "passably good." I can't fit all the songs into a show that people might like to hear and that's an awesome problem. Needed that reminder that we just can't play everything.

I'd like to insert here that I like "First Time Collar" in the four-song suite that it lives in. But that's where the song works best. Out of context, it's just kind of boring, maybe.

I've been up to quite a bit, but I haven't made much time to write here. The vinyl edition of *Obscurity* is off at the presses. Tim Labonte is begrudgingly working on the video for "Low Rent Truman Show" – he isn't in love with the track and doesn't think it's strong enough to be the lead single. And he might be right, but this album doesn't have a ton of obvious singles, and that tune is the most immediate to me and Jordon. Though if Tim would offer a substitute idea, I'd be happy to hear it out. He only got a copy of the album last week, but, since he'd gone through some surgery, I highly doubt he'd had time to listen to it. Probably my fault for not giving him the album upfront. If he'd have heard it as a whole, the song might make more sense as to why it stuck out? But that's not good either. Oh, crap.

By the time you read this, the non-disclosure agreements will be null and void, but right now, I'm waiting to see if some of my *Shock Treatment* covers will be used on the film's upcoming Blu-ray release. If they are, then I have to drop everything and immediately get that sucker out on vinyl as a tie-in. I was supposed to have confirmation roughly nine days ago. It isn't here. I can't go and pay for all the rights to do this if I'm not going to have a promotional bump from Twentieth Century Fox. I can't pay Katharine for art if the album doesn't need to happen, etc. We're in such a holding pattern that I've decided to simply put off releasing *Obscurity* until February. This isn't as painful as it sounds; it's more time to get things right. More time to book shows. Interviews. Podcasts.

I did two interviews last week. Nearly every interview I've done in the last few years is always prefaced with, "I've never heard you, but I've heard you're really good" or some variation thereof. Alternately, said interview is usually followed by some kind of statement of surprise at how "articulate" I am. I don't get this. I'm thankful for it, but I'm also seeing interviews becoming less helpful in convincing people to listen to my songs. One of the interviews was on a show called *A Corporate Time With Tom & Dan*. A really good time. Everyone involved was super sweet and professional. Their fan base is massive and loyal. I talked with them for two hours and didn't see a single uptick in people listening to songs, watching videos, or doing much of anything concerning me. Meanwhile? I got a lot of texts and messages saying, "Great job on *Tom & Dan*", which sounds to me like, "You weren't a prima donna, so good going." If no one is convinced to listen to the music, how good of a job did I really do?

Recorded two covers for Patreon in the last week. One was a cover of Spinal Tap's "Gimme Some Money" for obvious reasons, and the other was a take on "Tamagotchi" by an Australian singer named Meri Amber. I ran the rough mix past her just in case she'd take umbrage with the facelift I gave the tune. She seemed flattered, gracious, and even a bit playful in our correspondence.

Besides interviews, I haven't done anything in the public eye. No shows for a few months. Just admin work, really. It bears repeating that I really don't end up playing my guitar terribly often lately. It's mostly promo and behind-the-scenes crud just to keep things afloat. I'll be in public a bit more on Wednesday when I'm trying my experiment on Facebook called Listener Appreciation Day. The idea is that through an event invite, I'll release free downloads, bargain sales on vinyl, and eventually cap the day off with a livestream.

That day happens to coincide with the third anniversary of the release party for the Claire and The Potatoes sole album. I found some unpublished footage of that show and ran it by Jim and Leslie to see if it'd be okay to release. They dug it. It made me a little wistful and reminded me how good of a band we were. Even made me a little sad that those days are never coming back, but I'm so much healthier and happier now that I can't be too upset. Better to have once been a Potato that to never have Potatoe'd at all.

7-9-17

I really didn't want to write this, but the sooner I do, the sooner I can be done with it.

Last night, I went out to The Geek Easy to see Danimal Cannon and catch up with some friends. Was having a pretty good time and feeling very little of my usual "leave me alone, I'm watching a show" reflexes. It was nice to just get out for a little while.

I was around 10 minutes away from home, and my phone kept buzzing. Nicole was texting to tell me that Meatwad was acting strangely, coughing and wheezing constantly. I couldn't respond because I was driving, and when I got inside? He seemed fine. Or as fine as a dog battling congestive heart failure can be. Usually there's three things the vet has you check in these cases before you panic: color of gums, bowels movements, and appetite. If those three things all seem normal, you're probably going to be sent home. And they did.

When I started doing some web-sleuthing, it dawned on me that it could be a brand new problem altogether. I hadn't been home 10 minutes, but I found myself driving him to the emergency vet as quickly as I could put my shoes on.

Everyone was optimistic at first, because again, gums, stools, and hunger seemed in place. They slapped him in an oxygen tent and put him on some heavy diuretics. I gave them a bunch of money for the projected treatment, and they started on the usual exams. We'd been down this road before. A few hours in the oxygen, a few grand less in the bank, and we'd be on our way.

I appreciate that the veterinarian did not mince words when she came in to tell me that it was worse than anticipated. His heart was so enlarged, and his lungs were so filled with fluid that his trachea was being squished. He couldn't get enough air in, and he couldn't get the lung fluid out. She told me that it was "time." And if we didn't make the call, nature would be doing it for us very shortly, but he'd be in a lot more pain until that happened.

I drove home to wake Nicole up and tell her the news. When we returned to the vet, I fed him one of his favorite snacks and brought him the stuffed Jawa that he loved to cuddle with. The vet heeded my request that we dope him up to the point of being completely oblivious before his last injection was made. He died in my arms while Nicole held his face, looked him in the eyes while telling him he was a good boy, that we love him, and ... good night.

He was our best friend. Nicole had spent all day in bed with a migraine, and he just laid there nursing her with kisses. And as I sit here knowing that the whole intention of having this "diary" is to share everything that connects the dots, my story, etc? Though Meatwad was a huge part of my songwriting canon, my wife and I have spent all day crying. Loafing around the house. Seeing things that remind us of him and weeping. It's hard to say much because there's been a death in the family.

He was only around 7 pounds when he passed away, but his personality was so big that he completely filled this house. The same humans live here, but now this place feels overwhelmingly and imposingly empty.

I have two days before I have to sing for people again. I have to pull it together.

I miss him. He used to lay next to me while I wrote these entries to you.


7-14-17

It's late at night, and I'm spinning Robert Pollard's *Normal Happiness* LP. On some days, it's my favorite of his solo works. On other days, my favorite Robert Pollard album is whichever one happens to be playing.

I feel wrecked emotionally. Losing Meatwad did me in much more than I feel that it's okay to let on about. Because to be public about the depth of grief that I feel? I'm afraid of the "but he was just a dog" backlash. Afraid that I can't show how genuinely vulnerable and breakable I feel. I'm not a terribly manly man, but to some people I represent a certain amount of strength and perseverance. If I let on, what will they think?

That's how wrecked I am. I care what you might think about my personal feelings.

We raised Meatwad much as one would raise a child. This was easy to do because of his higher level of intelligence than one might associate with a Chihuahua. Due to his small stature, we treated him like an eternal puppy, and he reflected this in his behavior and demeanor. He felt young because we'd never treated him as if he wasn't. He was even happily chewing on things on his last day. We knew that we were on borrowed time for the better part of a year, but if you'd have seen him on the last day of his life, you'd have thought he was only a few years old with a naturally grey snout.

He followed me everywhere. He yelled – literally yelled – at me whenever I'd leave a room. This had me convinced for years that he didn't like me. He actually didn't like men at all, except for Emmit and a select few members of Nicole's family. And Domenico from Italy. Eventually me.

Well, Nicole says he liked me all along, but I felt that he loved me but didn't "enjoy" my presence. He got comfort from me that he used to be very protective of Nicole. We were in a constant power struggle to be the head of the pack, and he never let up on that fight. I have endless respect for the stubborn nature that he clearly learned from me.

They say that animals only learn what you teach them, that pets only come with a certain amount of pre-programming from their breed or DNA, but the personality is up to you. In this case, I believe that a male (or possibly numerous males) were terrible to him before he came home with us. And we taught him that chicken was awesome, how to wave to people, and that after the initial "you cool?" period, you never let anyone go until they were already gone.

Ultimately, we put a lot of sweetness into him. My favorite memory of him will always be the night in 2009 that I was freaked out about a legal matter that I'd have to attend in the morning. He was fast asleep between Nicole and me. We were watching television, and eventually I just burst into tears because I was terrified of what the morning would bring. I couldn't pretend to be strong and stoic anymore, and the tears, mucus, and fear poured out of me loudly and probably shamefully. Meatwad woke up immediately, went to find one of his favorite toys, brought it to me, and tried to get me to play – he was sharing things with me that made him feel better.

That might seem like a silly Hallmark story to most of you, but it's more kindness than most human beings have shown me when I've felt weak. He truly was my best friend that I wasn't married to. There's no replacing him.

I feel like there's a huge hole in my chest. I also feel terribly selfish about that because after beating congestive heart failure three times, his failing body isn't hurting him anymore. I'm conflicted by several stages of grief all happening at once. They should bump the "seven stages" up to eight and throw in a "general confusion" step, because that's where I am. I can't cry because I'm all cried out, but I can't feel a lot of true joy, but also? I'm happy he doesn't have to be in pain. Because we'd all want that for our best friend.

The Listener Appreciation Day was a wonderful and welcome distraction. I think that the little livestreamed show from my sweltering home office made a lot of people happy – at least that's what they typed. I'm not in love with performing to a camera, and getting delayed reactions because reading comments while strumming a rhythm and singing in a potentially different meter is tougher for me than you'd think. I got used to performing onstage after numerous years, but this new "virtual stage" just sort of showed up a few years ago, and you can't really practice it. You can't plan for the numerous ways that your trains of thought will be derailed by the feedback. You can't just tune out said feedback because that's part of what people seem to enjoy about these little intimate online shows.

After some wacky one-day sales, though? Somehow *Pop! Pop! Pop!* and the *RetroLowFi* compilation went to #1 and #2 on Bandcamp's indie pop vinyl chart seven or so years after their release. Oodles of copies were sold, but there's still tons left to sell. Every time I walk past an unopened box of unsold vinyl, I feel like I should be working harder. Or that it's just a bad record and that I should try again. That kind of thinking leads you to a pretty massive discography.

But it's supposedly the motion of the ocean.

7-22-17

Still on a Robert Pollard kick because I have to be. That's how this alphabetical journey works. Tonight's record is *We All Got Out Of The Army*. Starts off super creamy and then gets progressively more strange. At first I didn't really want to hear this album, wishing that instead I could play the new Japanese Breakfast album again, but now I'm quite glad that it's on.

Mysterious finger pain came and then mostly went away, so I'm chalking that up to "I'm getting old, and things are starting to randomly hurt." Voice has been giving out on me at the exact same time every night. I can set a clock by it at this point. I had to run through some songs to warm up a bit for the

Patreon-backer livestream I'm doing tomorrow, and doing so in the afternoon was a good call. It was the first day in the last week that my throat didn't give out halfway through the first song. Maybe it needs to be stronger? I am noticing some distinct tonal changes even when I'm not struggling. I'm going to have to find a way to stay on top of this.

This week's work turned out much differently than I had anticipated. Just after my last journal entry, I saw that it'd been officially announced by The Shock Treatment Network that some of my cover songs from that movie would indeed be on the Blu-ray. I knew that the second I found out, I'd have to be ready to drop everything and put it out on wax. Even had Katharine on standby, ready to do some of her art-magic at a moment's notice. We worked fast and hard, but it's ready for vinyl. I have the rights to the 12 songs. I remastered them with a light touch, just to get the songs into phase so the needle wouldn't jump out of the groove. This was tough because I really want to give the whole thing a facelift and re-do nearly every single note, but that wouldn't be very nice to that small cult of people that this record means something to.

Hours after we got the necessary work done? Shock Treatment Network had tons of my fans sharing the news and super excited that I'd be Rocky Horror "canon." And that's when they announced that they'd jumped the gun, and that truly, they had no idea which bonus features would actually make the cut after all. But here I was, having already acquired the rights – which was no mean feat, as I had to get kind of creative due to a pretty clear publishing error – and getting the licenses cost money. Had to be able to somewhat recoup the investment, so we went ahead with beginning a pre-order for the vinyl edition. There's simply never going to be another point in time where it would make more sense to do this.

The pre-order went to #1 on Bandcamp within hours, but then sales just sort of stalled out. As I type this, I'm just a few hundred bucks away from being able to press it. It's such a specific type of release that I can't imagine it's going to move much. I've spent most of the last few days doing interviews about it and sending out press release after press release, hoping for any coverage at all. It's relatively easy for me to reach my own fan base. Reaching the people that love the sequel to a cult film is proving much harder to do. I'm hitting the promo pretty hard out of necessity, meanwhile I'll likely have no idea if I'm even on the Blu-ray until I receive the copy I've pre-ordered for myself in the mail.

The mood of Orlando became pretty grim in the last 48 hours. Billy Manes passed away. That name might not mean much to anyone that doesn't live in Central Florida, but he was ever-present here. He was a journalist and an activist. You couldn't forget him, and he worked tirelessly to spread what he wanted to say, and he was an empowering figure for the LGBTQ+ community. We'd been in the same room numerous times, but I only recall having met him once, and if my memory serves? He seemed kind of cranky about me. But that's par for the course: he wrote for *Orlando Weekly* for years, and they were infamously flippant about me until somewhat recently. Right now, many people are descending into the park at Lake Eola to hold vigils for him by candlelight. To many, he was the voice and face of Orlando. It's sad to have to see a city in mourning yet again.

As usual, I'm coping with loss by pushing myself into more work. But how I'll do it is kind of a mystery to me. After the *Shock Treatment* pre-orders have made enough money to be sent off for pressing, I plan to just lay low with putting out new stuff for a while. Besides the occasional Patreon goodies, some interviews and the shows that I've got lined up, I **really** need to not release any music for a while. I have to not inundate the nice folks that listen to the songs I make up with so much information for the rest of the year. I have to start building anticipation for the Canada album. Trouble is that I don't really know how to be creatively idle. I'll have to learn.

8-1-17

As of today, Cap and I had to make a decision on how to proceed with Nerdy. FM. All the costs were spiraling out of control. Domains, hosting, servers, app renewals? All these things were doubling (at the very least) in price. The trouble is that there's been no growth in the listeners in the last year. If there was some sort of upward trajectory, I think we could have made an argument to keep it running. Lauren had been just as busy as I've been lately and wasn't terribly available as a manager. Dr. Vern took it pretty hard, and I had to stay on the phone with him for an hour to make sure he wasn't going to hurt himself. He was already down, this was just the proverbial straw for the camel.

There's more, but some business has to stay at the meetings.

I'll miss it. Eventually. Right now I'm sick to death of it. Much as the listener base hadn't really expanded, neither had the majority of nerdy music. The acts that sprung from the genre that are doing the best are the ones that don't completely tie themselves to it. They're just making music, but it happens to have nerdy overtones sometimes. Those are the folks that are probably going to make it (should they want to "make it"). I could name a bunch of acts that I think are especially good, but I don't want to get caught up in favoritism. It's easy to tell the lifers from the hobbyists, though. A lot of genuinely great music has sprung from this genre. Of course, nerdy music is so firmly rooted in nostalgia that the peaks and valleys will be rooted in the phases of what pop culture is into at that time. Right now? Pop culture isn't into us. That could change within seconds.

I've taken the reins back to put the station to bed. I'll make an announcement next week, but I'm leaving a gap so we can make sure that we're doing the right thing. As much as I have sort of mentally checked out of the usual station duties, this is something I've been intimately acquainted with for a number of years. You only get one chance to say goodbye in a classy way. If you botch it, you end up coming back year after year, trying to do it correctly.

Of course, for all I know, the nostalgia might demand that the station come back, and numbers might support such a possibility. They'd have to find someone else to do it, though. I don't think I can keep spreading myself so thin for what is ultimately a tiny blip on my own radar. I'm mostly doing the work for it because otherwise it won't get done.

I'm going to ask Nicole if she thinks it'd be a good idea for me to take a staycation for the remainder of the week. I could really use it. I'm mentally taxed, and as I'm about to get back to work with the band in a few weeks and beginning to truly line up all of the stuff that'd go with the release of *Obscurity*, I feel like this is the last break I'd get. She's overworked as well, so I feel like a total dickhead for even approaching the idea. Maybe, though?

8-7-17

Making the Nerdy.FM announcement later today. No staycation went down. Was initially going to go to a Disney park with some friends for a birthday shindig, but that was canceled. It worked out, overall. Nicole wasn't feeling great, so I hung with her, and we binge-watched a TV show. I still did some work, though.

Ambien has another side effect (besides the "make you write offensive lyrics" one). That side effect? You're going to eat like you've never eaten before when it is kicking in. I've been on the drug for years now, so I just don't even fight it any longer. Instead, I eat more than sensibly through the day but always very, very light meals, since I know I'm going to binge while being half awake. It's odd to be so groggy but completely able to hypnotically eat everything in the cupboards. Scares me that I could conceivably choke and be unable to do much of anything to save myself – motor functions aren't usually at their height during Ambien impairment – but I guess with as much time as I spend alone, it's not worth dwelling on.

Anyways, a filling popped out while I was eating last night. Now, it's just turned into Monday, and I'm still awake because when the air hits the tooth, it's super achy. I'm trying to get my mind off of it by catching you up on a few things. I don't have a regular dentist, and even if I did, they mostly don't work on Sundays.

I'd like to tell you two things while I hope that the eight ibuprofen I just swallowed make a dent in keeping my mind off the whole mouth thing.

I used to be really into bashing musical artists that I didn't care for. If I felt that their art was some type of affront, I took it very personally and got irrationally mad. There are few groups that I've had more ire for than Led Zeppelin. For some reason, people like to pit The Who against Zep, and while it's an unfair comparison because the groups are pretty diametrically opposed, it's put me in position where I've had to defend my Who fanaticism to broken-glass Zepheads. These arguments get pretty heated, but there's never a winner, with art being subjective.

Since you've asked by continuing to read, I'll tell you my whole deal with Zeppelin. As I understand it? In 1968, Jimmy Page wanted to basically rip off The Who. Like, actually run off with Keith Moon and John Entwistle, be the star guitarist that wrote the brilliant songs like Pete, and get some eye candy for a frontman. As it happens, in that particular year, The Who's fortunes weren't doing too well, so John and Keith considered it. But eventually Keith said that the idea would go down like a lead balloon. Jimmy just recreated the band with other people.

Of course, Led Zeppelin ended up being a very, very different group despite Jimmy's early attempts to carbon-copy The Who's formula. But for said formula, he'd often just run off with other people's ideas. Period. They'd take blues songs and credit them to the four members of Zeppelin. In famous cases like "Dazed and Confused," they nicked riffs and lyrics from a Jake Holmes song called ... "Dazed and Confused." And "Stairway To Heaven"? Well, it'd be easy to say that the song's passing resemblance to "Taurus" by Spirit is mere coincidence if Zep hadn't toured with the group. These aren't isolated incidents. Somehow the band not only got away with it, but their fans passionately defend the group's right to plagiarize.

(Though I myself have inadvertently ripped off other songs, I know it wasn't intentional on my part. The biggest offender is "my" song "One Hit Wonder," which uses a huge portion of Pete Townshend's "Keep On Working" chord progression. I have NO idea how I didn't catch it for years. Sorry about that.)

I'm not really down with it, myself. Most of what I hear in the band is a very good rhythm section fronted by two guys that "recycle" other people's music. Those two guys up front do look cool, but Robert Plant had a shaky voice at best (after the first few years, but it's not like I have any room to talk), and Jimmy Page could rarely recreate his studio wizardry on stage (ditto the last parenthetical statement) – that's perfectly acceptable, but he didn't even try to get around it. He was just sloppy as hell while everyone pretended that he was some kind of deity.

Something I have to make clear is that I can't like something halfway. If I'm in? I'm in with the passion of a million oompa loompas hell-bent on singing the same song with new words every time someone leaves the room. Ditto for hating something. I can be only ever occasionally be "meh," but when I'm on either pole of love or hate, I sort of let it identify me.

Which is why it's a **complete existential crisis** that I'm getting really into Zep's album *Presence*. "Achilles Last Stand" is 10 minutes that doesn't seem derivative, Plant doesn't do all the "ooooh, push, push, BABEH" stuff, and Page doesn't overplay just because he's got the ability to do endless retakes. Like, on its own? It's everything I was promised that Led Zeppelin would be. The same goes for everything else on that album - except "Nobody's Fault But Mine," which they stole from Blind Willie Johnson but gave themselves the songwriting credits for.

And "Boogie With Stu"? It's a tasteful track (from a different album) with a really interesting rhythm loop, some cool acoustic work, and it'd be among my favorite Zep tracks if Plant didn't just screech some bullshit clichés he stole from "Tutti Frutti" and "Ooh My Head." Don't even get me started on my irrational love of their rather obscure tune "Down By The Seaside."

As of this writing, I've found three LP's worth of Led Zeppelin songs that I actively enjoy and I feel like **this is my own version of a midlife crisis**. Have I heard so much music that I'm now reappraising music that I previously dismissed? Am I just getting more tolerant of things that I once perceived as mediocre?

I don't identify with any one political party. I don't have a specific religion. No allegiances to any particular set of "here's how to live" rules that I think are better than the next list. One could say the most rock solid thing about my identity was that I'm just a dude that really, really hates Led Zeppelin.

But now I don't. "When The Levee Breaks" popped up on the radio two days ago while I was in the car, and before I realized what I was doing, I'd cranked the volume.

I no longer know myself.

On a totally different note, I've found myself relating less and less to songs I've written. The lyrics are probably who many people think I am inside. They were probably sometimes right when the song was fresh. Someone who has just picked up *Normal Bias* for the first time might think that I really want to watch a town burn down or something. It's not in line with my feelings, but I can kind of live with all of the words in my catalog, even the misguided ones – and there's plenty of those to go around.

But the line that I often regret writing most might surprise you.

In "Bounce Bounce Bounce," I sing a fun song inspired by watching my daughter jump up and down on the bed. There's not really much more to it than that. If memory serves, everything in the song was absolutely true when I wrote it.

The line at the end of the bridge: "the only reason I haven't shot myself was to be her dad."

Okay, listen. Staying alive to be there for your child is not a bad motivator, but the pressure that must put on Juliana is likely the opposite of fun when/if she thinks about it. Like, "I fought my suicidal ideation for you, so don't fuck up." Really?

I certainly just went for the easy line to shock in an otherwise perfectly good song.

I've had suicidal ideation tendencies for as long as I can remember, with emphasis on the word "ideation." I don't recall feeling welcomed or wanted by my family. Sometimes there were clear statements made about whether my existence was a mistake. Most times, I'd just sort of be in the same room while my parents did other things. That's my recollection, at least. I suppose they're free to write their own book if they want to complain about me, but that'd really just further my point.

Some people feel as if they were born in the wrong body, the wrong gender. I feel like I should have been born to the parents in the next room over in the hospital. I've always been aware of being a burden to the fun that my parents would've been having if they weren't legally bound to make sure I didn't starve to death. As that eventually broken home didn't go for many bonding exercises, I never felt much like a part of anything. Not at school, not around relatives. Nowhere.

When suicidal thoughts pop into my head, it's not a reaction or a response. It's not "I'm sad, and I know how to make that stop," nor is it "the world would be better off without me." It's sort of like this ever-present "you shouldn't have ever been here." Knowing you weren't planned and that few ever really warmed to your entry into the world. I can't stress enough; it isn't sadness.

I've stuck around (pretty obviously), and as a result I've found places where I do sort of fit. I made those things. It's not easy to stick me into any one category as I won't really align myself with many nomenclatures, and I don't seem to obviously "be" anything in particular. It makes you look like a maverick to some people. Not many, but enough.

The reason I never killed myself? Because I somehow have an ability to comfort. And if I did kill myself, people that were comforted by my presence would be upset. I would not be alive, and therefore I'd be incapable of easing their sorrow. Sorrow that I'd have created.

See, as many would call suicide a selfish act, I believe that my reluctance to kill myself is much, much more selfish. I am too self-absorbed to not be around to make the people that I care about feel better. That can be through music, being nice, sharing my own stories, or having a snappy response at the wrong moments.

Suicide is easy. I don't like the easy answers so much anymore. My birth disrupted the natural order of things. I have to use my life to leave happier faces. I must do something good with it. Music is one way, but sometimes just letting people know I'm there is good enough. I don't mean that in a big-headed way, either. Some of you reading this have probably seen me send you an email when you mentioned having a rough time. I probably gave you my number and told you that you weren't alone. If I didn't, it's because I maybe didn't know you were hurting, or I was already trying to reach out to other people.

(I've had to try to curb this behavior, too. I've found that many times, people are just complaining to complain, but I take them being upset really seriously, and it's embarrassing to some that I'm behaving like an unlicensed suicide hotline, but they're merely writing "FML" because someone spoiled *Game Of Thrones*).

I'm still alive because if you're reading this? You gave me a reason to live. And if you're reading this and would be sad if I died? That's the reason it'd likely never be by my own hand – assuming I didn't end up in Guantanamo Bay or something, because, y'know.

8-11-17

Just a couple of things today. Remember Kim? We tried to bring her into my band to play flute? Her boyfriend, Patrick, is the drummer in a killer jazz-funk band that I can't ever remember how to spell the name of — you probably pronounce it "muse," though. His group is opening for Donald Fagen of Steely Dan tonight, and he got me a spot on the guest list. I all but begged for him to do so because it costs around $75 to get in. While I'm a stupidly big fan of Donald, I just can't afford that ticket right now. I'm excited to see Mr. Fagen be crotchety, as well as to possibly get in some tunes from his overlooked solo records. Plus, I get to see Patrick's band play, and I like their EP a lot. I'm in the perfect mindset for a night of dad rock.

When I went to the dentist, though? It was all going okay. They wedged me in as an emergency visit. While they took X-rays of my mouth, there was some nice music playing in the background. Mellow indie folk. Some Ben Gibbard, Rufus Wainwright, and right as they left the room after shooting me up with Novocaine? "Drunk Classic Rock Fans."

Yes. My song. In a dentist's office.

With a numb and slurring mouth, I was trying to tell the assistant that we were listening to my song, and maybe at first she took it as "my jam," so she turned it up — f-bombs and all. Eventually it must have dawned on her: she said my name and realized that somehow she didn't recognize me while playing the Marc With a C Pandora station. I guess I look pretty different after dropping a bunch of weight. Before the drilling started, her phone also played "Slick & Unused" of all things, and I had to ask her to switch it off so I didn't laugh with the drill in my mouth. She put on the Spice Girls channel instead. Seriously.

Folks have been publicly bemoaning the loss of Nerdy.FM online all week, especially right when we'd made the announcement. People were acting like a family member died. I would have been flattered if I couldn't see via our backend that while people were "mourning," there were only ever around three listeners tuned in at a time concurrently.

Been in kind of a funky mood for the last two days. Noticed a toilet leaking, which made my mind jump to "oh no, the septic tank is clogged" to "a pipe under the house must have burst" to "our house will be condemned" within five minutes. It was fixed by a plumber today in under 10 minutes. Can't wait to go and bliss out to some yacht rock tonight because I clearly am carrying around too much stress.

8-18-17

It feels like we live in a completely different world than the one in which I wrote that last blog. The day after I wrote it, I was violently ill. Emphasis on "violently." My body definitely decided to do/not do a whole bunch of things independent of what my brain wanted to happen.

I was debating calling for an ambulance while Charlottesville, VA held a street war between Nazis and people who oppose Nazis. The fallout has left countries divided. Nearly everyone in America has an opinion that someone else can find fault with. Last night, Tina Fey made a joke about stress-eating, and today it's what all the ruckus seems to be about. Our attention spans got pretty short, especially considering that there's around nine other "Aren't white people the best"-type of rallies scheduled around the nation this weekend.

Opposing hatred and bigotry in all forms has been the walk of the week. People arguing about whether violence is okay if it might stop another round of genocide, etc. Feels like a silly time to be shoving my music down people's throats. At the same time, though? That's how I make money. Haven't sold a single thing all week. I don't really know how to operate right now. All I can do right now is to publicly oppose hate, but sooner or later, I'll have to get back to work.

Got booked for my annual round of *Rocky Horror* opening slots with The Rich Weirdoes, so at least there's one bit of expected normalcy on the horizon!

The band and I got back into rehearsals this week. Slowly trying to learn a few songs from *Obscurity*, which sounds like the name of the "official cologne of Marc With a C" the more I say it, while shaking off the rust of a vacation. I'm feeling pretty passive at rehearsal lately, happy to let the other guys dictate what we'll play and how we'll play it. It's becoming my default setting. I have too many songs, and I've got no idea how to integrate even more new tunes into rotation while not neglecting old standbys that audience members might hope to hear. It's becoming easier to say, "I dunno, what're you into, Emmit?"

Though I'm writing words here, I don't want to write songs at the moment. I already have too many. And I don't want to blow out my voice while trying to get them right. I'm letting limitations win in hopes of preserving what I've still got left to give.

9-3-17

I probably shouldn't check social media as soon as I wake up. I think I'm going to try to break that habit for at least a little while. I woke up today to a fan notifying me through Facebook that Walter Becker, co-founder of Steely Dan, had passed away.

You wouldn't know it on a cursory listen, but Steely Dan made a huge impact on me and what I'd go on to make as Marc With a C. They were among the few bands that decided "Touring is for the birds, so we're going to stay home and write the best songs possible." The template for what I do wouldn't exist without them, though they invented standards of quality no one else could ever hope to reach. True perfection.

People recently knew Walter Becker as the guy that noodled away endlessly over songs during the reunion tours. Walter was seemingly also the guy that brought the true snark to the Dan, lighting fires under Donald Fagen.

People have made jokes about the band for years, but they missed the point entirely. Every punk that joked about getting a job to "fuck shit up from the inside"? Steely Dan did that for you. Made the most smooth-as-butter songs about heroin, underage dating, sports doping, gambling addictions, and the inventors of LSD. You hear those songs in Walgreens and make fun of the dad rock, sure. Some of us heard a way to communicate rough topics without being alienating.

Thank you for everything, Walter. Thank you in advance to Donald Fagen who has vowed to keep their music alive for as long as he is able.

9-6-17

I write this from the waiting room of yet another courthouse. My throat is very sore. I initially thought that I'd pushed myself too hard during rehearsals, but Nicole is feeling the same raspiness, hoarseness, and malaise. We're both hitting the apple cider vinegar quite hard.

On one hand, I need to keep practicing because I'm having a hard time remembering the lyrics to many of the newer songs that I'd like to play at this weekend's show. On another hand, one of the strongest hurricanes in the history of the Atlantic basin seems to be hurdling toward us, a large portion of Southern Florida is under mandatory evacuation, and it's too soon to say for sure if air travel will run as usual, meaning that the headliner, Schaffer The

Darklord, may either not be able to come, or possibly not be able to go home, all depending on what the hurricane does. And when.

Most of Florida is justifiably in a panic. I believe the show should be postponed, but the promoter has to make that call. It's his money on the line. As an entertainer, I should be happy to do a short set to get people's minds off of the potential disasters. As a human being, I'd rather stay at home and prepare for the worst.

Saw some folks talking about the show on Facebook. Someone was surprised to see that I was still out performing. One person confirmed my continued existence but added "unfortunately." One person in the comments, which I really shouldn't have been reading in the first place, mentioned that I'd had the "original nerdcore beef." Besides me and Klopfenpop having a silly problem concerning a song about cereal? I really can't think of any arguments that stuck. There are musicians I'm not fond of as people, as I'm sure there are plenty of people that don't like me, but I don't really know of anything circulating out there in the public sphere. Weird. I'd like to think I'm one of the least dramatic musicians around (relatively speaking, of course), but people are going to think whatever they're going to think, no matter how fictitious and removed from reality.

I've been told that it's a positive thing that people are talking about me at all. I can't think of a rebuttal to that. I can only offer the following to those who do not like me: unless I've truly wronged you, I don't care if you like what I make. I can merely hope that you do.


9-12-17

Amidst some bickering, it finally took the airports closing down to get last weekend's show canceled. On the night the gig was supposed to take place, I did a livestream on Facebook to try to play some songs to keep our minds off of the impending hurricane doom.

On Sunday the tenth, the rains began in Orlando during the early afternoon. A window immediately started to leak in Nicole's office. We listened to the radio for tornado warnings, and as the wind started to howl, we'd occasionally take cover in our hallway.

It was an hour after dark that the power went out. Hurricane Irma was downgraded to category two, but that's still no joke. No power meant that there were no sounds to mask the beating that our neighborhood would take.

I found myself genuinely frightened for my life. Nature could just fuck us all up any time it pleased, and this particular hurricane decided to dip east only long enough for the eye wall to pass right over my house.

Since that night, I've had a mixture of panic attacks and debilitating depression. No power at all – and there are rumors about Duke Energy lying about their readiness that are too ugly for me to process or repeat. The lack of power equals no air conditioning.

It's Florida. It's 95 degrees. A company lied about their ability to restore normalcy. It's hard to go look for more supplies like batteries, food, (All of ours is spoiled.) or just a nice place to cool off because the traffic lights are down. A ball of anxiety like me can't take that kind of confusion right now. Some of the richest neighborhoods do have electricity, and so do all of the tourist attractions. The places where the lower-income folks might store or procure food? Nothing.

In contrast, there are two other power companies in Orlando. Each of them has worked on restoring at least a third of the power per day. Ours? Still sending out automated tweets about being in the "assessment" phase.

It's not healthy to be here right now. If you struggle with mental or emotional disorders, there's not many safe ways to get anywhere else. The bunnies are showing signs of heatstroke, so we're boarding them into pet hotels.

The sun is out. Beyond a few uprooted trees and the aforementioned leaky window, our general area seems to be fine. Yet for no good reason, the power stays off. Duke Energy hardly even has any trucks in the field working. I have to stop writing now because I'm a little too upset to process much more, let alone even imagine the thousands that aren't lucky enough to have spoiled food, panic attacks, and a lack of power as their prime concerns.

9-20-17

I can't pinpoint exactly when I knew something was fishy. Potentially the way Duke Energy had radio ads a-blazing before the hurricane touched down boasting of the crews that were on standby. The disconnect between their PR lady that was doing the news-radio rounds and how many trucks were actually entering the state. I do know that I'd figured out their game when we learned that Duke had stationed their ~9000 workers in Georgia, waiting to enter our state, and then sent a bunch of them back to North Carolina, their home base, where their PR is in the toilet after scamming funds for a fake nuclear plant. Because they wanted to be ahead of the tropical storm.

That's right. They sent a bunch of the trucks back to work on a weaker storm. It wasn't until late Tuesday-ish that video appeared of trucks actually entering Central Florida. Any work being done before then was that of crews likely already in the state. When the new workers came to Florida, though? They were under union rules. They weren't allowing help from the Florida "storm standby" crews, experts, and specialists who are incredibly familiar with the grids and how to get them back up and running quickly/safely. There are receipts for that if one digs far enough.

I'm mad that they drastically underprepared for restoring Florida and my community. That the corporation sent out false restore dates and lies just to keep an angry and rightfully confused public at bay. That they dumped outage reports from their systems multiple times to cook the numbers that they were releasing to the press, one moment saying, "You don't have to make reports anymore; we know you're out," and later saying, "Uh, please re-report your outage, kthxbye." That they intentionally released robotic and minimal statements so that there would be a consistent party line of verbiage – the more they'd have released, the more people could have twisted their words.

Nope, Duke fucked up, knew they fucked up, and then stayed relatively silent to cover their asses. They have no emergency infrastructure that places emphasis on the disabled. As a result? Many elderly and differently abled people had to be jetted off to hospitals. When neighborhoods stayed pitch black? Prowlers knew precisely where to go. My neighborhood was one of them. Duke straight up messed with my community and didn't have to care because, what, are we going to drop our service? It's Florida. Air conditioning isn't a luxury, it's pretty much mandated by law. This heat will kill you. Duke didn't care about that.

The linemen were working unrealistic hours and deadlines under union rules that didn't really apply to the state of emergency situation. Their Twitter PR person reminded us that they couldn't be up in buckets at night unless it was "an emergency," despite the fact that we were under a state of emergency. Those linemen clearly did the best that they could, and Duke knew it was in over its head as it continued to ship more people in from as far away as Canada very late last week. The call center folks? Unless you were escalated to a supervisor? They could see your account and the same infographics that we could from our phones. That's pretty much it, and it didn't change until the weekend. This was confirmed by multiple Duke sources internally as I fought for my neighborhood while battling my own depression and anxiety. Duke did not want you to know how poorly they'd planned.

It'd take a short novella to tell you about the maneuvers I had to pull just to get a truck into my neighborhood to even look at the damage. It became my full-time job, really. Also wrote and recorded an EP's worth of throwaway songs about being mad at a power company with a battery-powered Zoom recorder. Gave it away on my Patreon. A song that I filmed on my camera's phone about hating Duke garnered a few thousand views in a single day.

One can argue that we all should have been more prepared, surely. It's a hurricane. We expect to lose some power. But this wasn't Houston. It wasn't Harvey. Orlando was not underwater. By the time it reached us, it turns out that it was only a Category 1 hurricane. Much of the frustration came from watching the company complain that conditions weren't safe for them to "assess" the situation, despite the weather being bright, warm, and sunny just hours after the storm had passed. And Irma did do some damage, that can't be denied, but just as we should practice hurricane safety and preparation, Duke also should have done the same. They did not. They sent out inflated bills while collecting government money from the emergency situation. They ran out of parts left and right.

Duke. Was. Not. Prepared. It literally had the one job.

It is my belief that a different company that is more familiar with our seasons and how to combat them should be allowed in – some friendly competition at the very least. Petitions and making our voices heard are a good start. Duke has clearly demonstrated that it can't handle the area it bought. Honest communication about the gravity of the situation would have eased the public and allowed for the affected to make proper arrangements, but it intentionally chose not to do that. Remember how people initially evacuated and whatnot? They did so because they had the most up-to-date info to base their decision around. Duke gave you silence. Your power could have been on in the next hour, or during one of their continuously missed deadlines.

This was a complete and total disaster. Some communities were more adversely touched by Duke than the storm itself. I shudder at the thought that we may ever have to ask them for assistance again.

Meanwhile, with some power restored, the band has gotten back into the swing of rehearsals. I'm having a really hard time remembering lyrics lately, sometimes resorting to using cheat sheets for songs that I've sung upward of a thousand times.

There's been a few months of depression now for me. Some days it's a bit easier to manage. Today is one of them, thankfully. I still feel covered in a glaze of "why bother" and "why can't I be bothered." I must be an absolutely impossible person to deal with as of late.

The bunnies got to come home, though! They were so excited and darting all over the place. Watching their sprints is my happy place.

10-20-17

Feeling pretty low right about now. On one hand, I fear that recording a diary of my experiences as a DIY artist will ultimately be incredibly whiny. On the other, the great experiences are becoming fewer and fewer with longer spaces between them. I spend a good portion of my time working hard to merely power through physical/emotional pain or general disappointment.

A few months ago, I worked at a breakneck pace to have the *Shock Treatment* covers hit vinyl as soon as possible. After the plant assured me that the LPs would be shipped to me on October 13, 2017, I made plans to sell them after my yearly *Rocky Horror*-opening slots.

Yesterday, the rep from the plant laid the news on me: they might not ship for another four weeks. This means that I can still eventually fill pre-orders in an almost-timely fashion, but there is literally no better gig to sell these LPs at than a showing of *Rocky Horror Picture Show* on Halloween. The money I had anticipated making was to pay for the compact discs of *Obscurity*, as well as a portion of the first video from said album. And now? No telling when they'll arrive. The good news is that I usually err on the side of "underpromise/ overdeliver," so I (hopefully) won't miss the release date of late November. The bad news is that all of those practically guaranteed on-site sales are just simply gone.

I have spent the days since the last entry trying to come up with how to raise money in the interest of a worst-case scenario, but I am coming up short. I am just feeling defeated overall. There is little I can do here. Putting the pressing plant on public blast will do me precisely no good. If I piss them off, they can do any number of things to stretch the problem out.

I suffer from bipolarity. I fight anxiety with medication. Today, those afflictions are winning. I wanted to tell you about the first nerd music concert I've ever gone to that I was not working at in some capacity. I hope that I would be able to find some excitement about talking a bit about the first meeting with a press agent for the *Obscurity* roll-out.

Instead? Today, I am losing the internal battle. My inbox continues to pile up with things that I need to respond to, but I can only bring myself to focus on the way that I am being screwed by an overseas company.

Fine. The illnesses can win today. I will lie down for the rest of the day and watch (hopefully) comforting movies. Tomorrow? Watch out.

10-22-17

As a vinyl enthusiast, I window shop for records online even when I can't afford them. Sometimes this yields disastrous results. I will find an offer that I believe that I can't pass up, and I'll spend money that I truly do not have to acquire yet another piece of plastic stored in cardboard.

I have spent the last few days being so angry at the music industry that I have done said window shopping without any urges to spend, spend, spend. Let's use a really rare EP by the group Twa Toots for an example. It's called *Please Don't Play A Rainy Night In Georgia*. It's okay if you haven't heard of it. I'm not being willfully obscure by mentioning it, either. It's one of those weird "holy grail" items that just hardly even exists but has been on my "holy grail" radar for many years.

Twa Toots barely made a blip when they were current in the early '80s. As such, there was no need to press oodles of this cute little EP. The folks that are holding onto their copies are probably doing so for one of the following three reasons:

- The band was so obscure that the owner has no idea that anyone else might want this vinyl.

- The band was so obscure that the owner has sentimental attachments to the vinyl, likely knowing a member of the group.

- The band was so obscure that the owner believes that it will be "worth something someday."

It is "worth something." The market metrics available on Discogs (currently the foremost website for buying used vinyl online) shows that people on average will spend between $55-$200 to get a copy of this seven-song release. But it is only worth that when someone actually spends the money. When it's listed for a price online, and it sits unsold? It ain't worth dick: it's just plastic and cardboard. Value is in the eye of the beholder.

Could just be the mood of the week, but I am having a hard time finding the value at the moment. I know it is valuable, but I am starting to feel more and more guilty about putting price tags on passion, heartbreak, and the life's work of people that were potentially hurt by the music industry.

It's not as if creative types are usually all that stable in the first place.

11-2-17

I sit before you a sore and tired man. The yearly Rich Weirdoes shows went pretty well. I didn't change my setlist once in the three nights. By Halloween, I'd really found a groove. I performed "All I Want For Christmas" at each show to represent the most recent EP while knowing that there were better song choices, but I decided to use it as a vehicle to stop in the middle of to make a statement about consent. Very, very loudly.

Merch sales were sparse. Half because people are less and less involved with physical media, and half because, well, I cannot count the number of audience members that would come up afterward, thank me for what I do, tell me how they were singing along with every word, how I take up half of the space on their iPod, etc. A lot of playing to "the converted," if you smell what I'm stepping in. I felt like I matter to some people, and I cannot put a price on that.

The *Shock Treatment* LPs may arrive tomorrow. When I would mention the film during my opening slots at Universal, fan recognition was pretty low, so I may not have lost the amount of sales I'd previously thought, but this puts me in an interesting position:

- I'm playing at a festival this weekend. I cannot possibly start shipping out orders yet.

- I cannot possibly sell the LPs at the festival, or it would appear preferential.

- Some folks that have pre-ordered the LP will attend the festival. While I could hand the album to them, it may appear that I'm trying to screw them on shipping costs. And some folks might see it, want it, and that leads me back to the previous point.

- On Monday, I'm filming some sort of YouTube thing about "digging through used records." I'm not in control of it, and details are scant, so that's a day I cannot spend packing and mailing records.

- I have to stay up all night on Monday as Nicole is leaving town for work at about five in the morning the next day, and I'm to take her to the airport. This means I will sleep Tuesday away and will not be able to take the hundreds of LPs to the post office.

The end result? I will have to keep it secret that I've got the LPs at all for about a week just to treat those who believed in/loved the project enough to pre-order the vinyl fairly. But there's a bit of smoke and mirrors to it.

The worst kicker? Between the copies of *Obscurity* that I can't yet sell and the boxes of *Shock Treatment* that will coat each bit of floor space? I wanted to let StarF crash here while he was in from out of town, but I simply don't have room to do it.

A really interesting thing happened at the Halloween shows, though. On the second night, a guy made his way to the front of the post-show merch line to demand an album with "Blowjob Queen" on it. Somehow, I miraculously had one in my suitcase. On Halloween night, he walked up to me again while I watched the Rocky "virgin games," handed me one hundred dollars in cash and walked right out of the building. Wordlessly. Didn't even respond when I asked what the money was for. Did he just want to support what I do but didn't want records? I'm still mystified. But thankful. It is buying food and helping to pay for a future music video.

Last night, Cap and I drove to Ft. Lauderdale to see Roger Daltrey do a random solo show in a club. He played a bunch of unexpected tunes that The Who have mostly never done onstage. He embraced his current vocal abilities. This club was affixed to a casino, and he did a lot of the more power ballad-y stuff, seeming to embrace the shlock that one would mentally associate with a casino resort gig.

I still think that Marc With a C comes with an expiration date, but it was inspiring to watch a man find his personal identity away from his "brand name" while not trying to pretend that he wasn't older and with less hearing, hair, and vocal range. It can be done. Something to keep in mind.

But we're not all Roger Daltrey. He looks better in his 70s than I do at the end of my 30s.


11-9-17

My last few days have been nothing but boxing up copies of the *Shock Treatment* vinyl to mail them out. It's pretty repetitive and time-consuming, but it was a nice way to kill some of the inherent loneliness I feel when Nicole leaves town for work. Also a nice excuse to try out some of the new records I found on the "dig" that I mentioned before. Found a smaller post office tucked away in a place called Gotha. A real small-town vibe to this place. Just two clerks, and it looks like hardly anyone knows this place exists. It was beneficial to not have to stand in a long line each day, but those poor postal workers were clearly unhappy with the amount of boxes I was bringing in, especially the large amounts of international orders, which are hideously time-consuming and tedious to mail. But thanks to them, all current orders are out for delivery, and I'm free to work on recording for podcasts.

Played at a two-day festival thrown by Orlando Nerd Fest called Fantoku. Overall pretty fun but pretty lightly attended, especially considering I was headlining with acts like The Returners, Dual Core, and Professor Shyguy, who are all usually quite bankable for a full house in Orlando's nerd music community. Our set was merely okay by my count. Emmit was really ill, so I held back on the tempos just a bit for his sake, and even though we'd done a soundcheck, something happened halfway through where I simply couldn't hear myself sing anymore. This resulted in the most off-key rendition of "Fighting For Love" I'm capable of. Well, truth be told, I could certainly sing it worse if I tried, but I was attempting to hit notes but flat-out failing. Usually I'm at least in the vicinity of the proper pitch. The real star of the event was Lauren Leibowitz, lead vocalist and flautist for The Returners. She's so talented and pure in her interactions. I adore her. She always has audiences right in the palm of her hand.

The trio was supposed to be rehearsing this week, but Jim has some personal things going down, and we couldn't make it work. Hopefully we can get back to it soon. The holiday show is a month away, and it takes an unreal amount of preparation.

Rather excited and surprised at the demand for the vinyl of *Shock Treatment*. Who knew that those recordings that sprung from depression and experimentation would be in demand in 2017?

12-3-17

Juliana's become quite a big fan of MegaRan. Worked our way into his sold-out gig at The Geek Easy last night. Seeing the place hoppin' that way made me really nervous about the upcoming holiday show that we've been prepping so hard for. Right now, if Facebook event invites are to be believed, we'd have around 150 attendees. That's cool, but I'm also seeing people dropping off as the date gets closer. Maybe they have to work, they have a different engagement planned, or any number of reasons. The idea of playing to a nearly empty room wouldn't do wonders for anyone's ego. I've been fighting back a cold this weekend, and I get incredibly emo when I don't feel well, so the pre-emptive nervousness just isn't something I can shake yet. You never lose the "what if no one shows up," no matter how long you do this.

I haven't talked much about the publicity firm I'm hiring for *Obscurity*. They're called [NAME REDACTED]. I feel a bit rotten that I'm finally starting to talk about it here under these feelings, but I just didn't get around to it until now.

I contacted them and told him my game-plan to release *Obscurity* in … October, I think? Last week, on a day off – my first in months, which I'd actually made a public declaration about in the hopes that no one would contact me – I finally got a slew of information from him. Unfortunately, some of the huge to-do list he sent me raised more questions about the "how," and since I responded? No answers. Nothing besides him feeling squeamish about having such a short window to work in. He needs a bio and a press release. I hired Katharine for the job, and she had plenty of questions about what she needed to make. I lobbed the questions to him since they felt time-sensitive: no answer. Meanwhile, he's posting things on Facebook about how frustrated he is with the music industry.

I'd promised the folks that back my Patreon that I'd be using some of their money to hire a PR firm to push the album. My gut feeling is to fire him. If I can't get in touch with him to field questions about how to do what he's asked now? What do I do when I am really depending on him to set up coverage and interviews? If I fire him, I'll have lied to fans and taken their money. I haven't fired him right now purely based on ethics. I'm going to call him in the middle of next week and voice my concerns to him. He's stressed the trouble of the timing to me, but he also waited a month and a half to send me a kit to know how to get started with him. This feels like a disaster in the making.

On a different note, I played the whole of *Obscurity* to Juliana last night. She loved it, which made me feel pretty fantastic. She talked about how different it was for me, and her stand-out songs were "One Of These Are Gonna Be Your Day" and "Why" – not what I expected. She has a good ear for hits, and I may change the planned third single based on her suggestion. It was going to be "Perfect For Me," but "One Of These" might be the better pick. I didn't think about it as a single because it'd already been out in a lo-fi form on the *Songs For Aubree* EP. I couldn't see it as a good single because I'm just too close to it, and usually the ones that I like best tend to fare the worst. And here I was thinking that we'd do "The New Normal" or something.

These would be easier decisions to make if the back and forth with the company that has to push this stuff was a little more, well, back and forth.

12-7-17

I'm glad I gave it a day before I wrote this entry. I really wasn't okay yesterday.

I ended up firing [NAME REDACTED]. When I called him to ask if my gut feeling that he just wasn't into it was correct? He mostly went on a tangent about how weird "the industry" is. How no one responds to emails that you can see that they've opened, etc. He went on about this for a fair 15 minutes before I interjected to tell him that he was doing those very things to me.

Since firing him, it's dawned on me just how impossible it's going to be to replace him. He didn't give me enough time to get a new PR person in place and keep the intended release dates and scheduled shows. I either find someone last minute to do as much of the job as they can (which is unlikely), or I do it myself.

In a few hours, I have a meeting with someone that I'm trying to pitch the plan to. His name is Curtis, and he is/has been a writer for *Wired* and *Forbes*. He's seen enough bad pitches to probably know how to do a good one, though being on the pitching end might be new to him. I've also sent out an email to one very talented PR lady from Riot Act, but I don't expect her to respond.

What few seem to understand is that I'm not expecting a Grammy nod here. I just want a few more people to hear about this album than usual. There's no expectations of anyone to do some superhuman sword-in-the-stone maneuvering. Just do some pitches. Get a few extra reviews. Maybe an extra interview in a new blog. For some reason, everyone is terrified to take this job, and that's rubbing off on me: if they don't want to do it, what business do I have doing it myself?

If these meetings go south, it'll be on me to admit to Patreon backers that I'm not spending their money where I promised that I would and to start coming up with my own game plan for PR. I can kiss medicated sleep goodbye for a few months. We've gone from go-go-go to make the album to go-go-go to fill people's inbox with press pitches to go-go-go to pack records and hit up the post office, plus I'll need to rehearse, play shows, and be nice to people when I go to the supermarket.

Yesterday? I had a mini-breakdown, but I was too stressed out to actually cry. Firing people does not come naturally to me. And sure, it might've been firing someone who didn't want the job in the first place, but that's still telling someone they did a bad thing, and I really don't like spreading that negativity. I blew a rehearsal with Jim and Emmit; I couldn't concentrate on remembering the lyrics and chords because I was trying to figure out who would replace the PR guy. By the next day, I felt like I couldn't do anything right. Whiny Facebook posts were made, and that's not a good look for me. I was fraying publicly, and I really shouldn't have done that.

And then, there's Katharine. Dear, sweet Katharine did such a great job writing the press releases and bios that I begged her to do the PR job. She exclaimed that it was pretty far outside of her skill set, and I just ignored her and groveled for her to do this because I believe she would be amazing at it, and in the meantime? I completely ignored how uncomfortable it might feel for her to turn down a job, especially having to turn down a friend that was clearly on the edge of losing it. I need to write her an apology. She's just so good at everything that I can't imagine her failing at doing a project with anything less than stellar results. But I may have infringed on her comfort zones. That guilt was also part of yesterday's mini-breakdown.

I have been doing this for far too long. Some days I want to chuck it all and just work in a roller rink. I'm going to go write an apology to Katharine now.

12-14-17

As of maybe an hour ago? A bunch of Net Neutrality protections were rolled back. People on my Facebook feed are flipping out. I don't know how to feel. Everyone says it's bad, but when I started digging into the issue, I instead started reading positive things about the Telecommunications Act Of 1996 – and I didn't think there were any – so it always confuses me to the point where comprehension wasn't a possibility for me. One of those deals I just can't wrap my head around, but I'd be better if I could.

Hired Curtis to do the PR for *Obscurity*. He won't get the type of reach that I had banked on, but he'll do **some** work, and that's the most I can ask for at this point. I've slowly just digested the fact that this album will not be hitting as many ears as I hoped. It's a self-fulfilling prophecy; I wrote the line "Obscurity is success." Now I'll have to see if I meant it.

I am still stressed to the gills. Had a talk with Nicole last night about the possibility of trying to schedule a weekly day off. It hasn't failed that each night in December, I find myself still working at 5 a.m. and wishing that there were more hours in the day. My tensions are boiling over, and I have very little to show for it. There are good things happening today: tonight I'll see a private screening of *The Last Jedi* with Juliana, but before and after, I still have to mix/release part of last week's holiday show for Patreon supporters, pack the records I'm to send out tomorrow, and another big thing that I've completely forgotten.

The plans for the annual holiday show are usually generally static: play for a really long time, and make audience requests the backbone somehow. This year, the plan was to do a set in the audience with only acoustic instruments – to hush the people that tend to talk over the band – and then a long second set comprised of only what the Trio enjoys playing. That first set went over very well. Much better than I'd hoped for, actually. It became even more intimate than I thought it'd be. While we'd initially hoped to go unmiked, Fishtoaster (The Geek Easy's house sound person) invented a sound plan with lavaliere microphones. We'd be pumped through the PA ever-so-slightly, but to the untrained ears and eyes, it'd appear that we had gone completely acoustic. To make this a reality? We actually spent more money than we made to rent those damned microphones. But everyone seemed to have a good time, and that's really all that I ask. I was physically useless the next day. This show clocked in at about eight hours of work with three-and-a-half hours of singing,

Tuesday was spent with Emmit taking my picture in a variety of locales. We did a shoot in a record store, one outside of our rehearsal space, and one at Parliament House. Usually the latter has huge strands of lights at Christmas that aren't just predictably green and red, but this year they went a bit more low-budget with plain ol' Christmas trees. That shoot didn't go the way I'd hoped, but the first two locations yielded some really great shots, so I'm good with it.

We also did a video shoot for "Terribly Popular." It was intended to be two live takes of us miming to the song with a practice take for safety. Instead? We did so many takes under Emmit's direction that we didn't really have time to rehearse afterward. This was a bit of a bee in my bonnet, but in truth, doing a quality-over-quantity type of shoot may be better for the future. Just the raw clips that I saw that night have me very excited for a cool video. While I traditionally hate appearing in music videos, Emmit makes it fun.

I'd love to write more, but I just don't have time. Too much to do before I go and see the movie. Busy enough that I almost forgot that I'm seeing the new Star Wars movie tonight, and that it's nothing to be stressed over. I'll be surrounded by friends. I'm going to soak up some entertainment. It'll be a nice break for a few hours.

12-24-17

I'm writing this on Christmas Eve, and with any luck, it'll be the last entry for the year. Not because I don't like to write, but because I'm hoping that tomorrow will be a break, and that the rest of the week can be straight work.

Nerdy FM has manifested itself as a monthly podcast. This has given us a slightly different format than we used to have: the old format used to just be song after song, occasionally broken up by station IDs and ads. This time around, I'm the voice, the host, the personality. And while my heart isn't always in it, I do believe that it's sort of a duty. The nerdy music community has been so good to me that I feel like I ought to give back.

This month, I did an interview with Hex. The objective was that since Nerdapalooza's first events were in 2007, it'd be fun to do a 10-year anniversary retrospective wherein we'd look at how it got started. Unfortunately, I was halfway through that entry when Hex pretty much discounted that whole first year and, in turn, basically wrote off the work of everyone that made the 2007 events happen while deciding that they were no longer canon. I tried to stay an impartial host, but this wasn't the episode I'd signed up to do. Instead, he mostly talked about 2008. People noticed. There's been a lot of backlash – mostly pointed at Hex, as he's already a polarizing personality – but a few people were actually mad at me, calling me an "enabler." I didn't know that the show would go in that direction. I didn't think to interview anyone else, as the average Nerdy FM listener would likely peg Hex as the founder of Nerdapalooza. And sure, maybe he founded the name, but some other shows took place under that name before he did what he's known for.

The coming week will see me trying to set things right, doing another episode where I'm talking to Rob Tobias (the organizer for the 2007 show) and a few members of Magitek who performed at that gig. Even if that first Nerdapalooza was smaller in stature, it's disheartening to know that all of that initial scene-building had been dismissed in a quick swoop. Hopefully the next episode sets it right. I don't like when people don't get credit for hard work. Hex's wife has noticed some of the internet fervor and has called to check on me a few times. I adore her.

I was able to put the ticked-off nerds out of my head for a little while to do December's livestream for Patreon backers. This time around I performed all of _Linda Lovelace For President_. Had a really good time doing it as well. If there was a hang-up, it's that "Debt Is Only What You Make Of It" just wasn't built to be played live, and it felt thin and clumsy, but it gave me an excuse to break out a favored arrangement of "Satellite" and the always-hard-to-fit-into-a-usual-show "San Diego Doorways." Few people watched it live, most settling for replays, and that's a bit tough, performing live for a tape-delayed audience. One person who watched live requested "Long Time Listener," which was all too fitting. I love that song and was happy to oblige. Also tacked some drapes to the office ceiling so it looks like I've got stage curtains for livestreams now.

Feels a bit early to talk about this, but there's a chance I'll be hired by Consequence Of Sound for a podcast they'll be leasing from me called *Discography*. Sort of like *The Real Congregation*, but I'd pick a "legacy artist" and go through their whole catalog with fan-tinted glasses. This morphed from the big Frank Zappa project I'd made into this, a totally different format so the work wouldn't go to waste. And it seems as if they liked the initial samples enough to want more. I'm thankful that Cap is spearheading this proto-network because the CEO of Consequence had some pretty grand ideas for the podcast that were the antithesis of everything I pitched, as well as what was offered in my pitch demo. The show he was suggesting to me would need a full crew, months of lead time, and a lot less of me focusing on my own music. Which I'd be happy to do for the right price, but I don't think they could afford the stars they wanted to shoot for. Cap got us back on solid ground, and hopefully I'll be able to move forward with it really soon. I've always wanted to be that music geek that people call on to write liner notes for reissues and whatnot, and this is just one step closer to making myself employable by having spent my life obsessing over music.

Of course, if *Discography* takes place, I won't have time to do the Nerdy FM podcast. That doesn't really hurt my feelings given the current circumstances.

It's 40 minutes until Christmas Day. I'm going to drink some tea and watch the *Star Wars Holiday Special*.


1-4-18

I can't explain the anxiety that's been inside of me all day, but it's there. Gnawing at my hiatal hernia from the inside. Feeling as if something horrible is going to happen, and it's got me checking my social media feeds compulsively. Potentially related to making people unhappy with that Nerdy FM podcast, possibly due to being so "pregnant with album," and possibly because the president is teasing nuclear war on Twitter.

Today was my first interview about *Obscurity*. I've become so accustomed to not answering questions directly that it must make me seem like an incredibly evasive interviewee. My default mode is having this album that I'm increasingly proud of under my belt but not sharing it with the rest of the world. While I know that my job is to make the art and then let the world do what it's going to do with it, I'm already having a hard time "letting go" of this one.

Been getting a number of compliments lately on looking healthier and younger than I have in years. Emmit sent me my smorgasboard of 2018 press photos, and I can't get over just how old I look in them. On some days, I feel that I don't look like I'm about to turn 40. In Emmit's unflinching lens, I absolutely look my age. It doesn't actively bother me because mortality doesn't freak me out. I earned every wrinkle and pockmark on my face. It was just a bit disarming – not how I thought I looked. He's a really honest photographer, which has everything to do with why I wanted him to do the pictures, but besides my weight being in a relatively good place, I'm not sure where the compliments are coming from.

Maybe I'm just entering the "you look good for your age" phase of adulthood.

Did the follow-up Nerdy FM episode to further tell the Nerdapalooza origin story. Didn't seem to get much traction, but at least I can rest easier knowing that I tried to get the correct information out into the world. Also trying to get a bunch of things done in the next few days so I can take a few days off before the push for the new album starts. There simply won't be any days off for quite some time after January 15. I'll need to be rested and as centered as possible.

Too anxious to write much more today. Brain feels like a leaky dam.

1-18-18

Haven't written here for the last few weeks. Just been too busy. We announced the pre-order for *Obscurity* a few days ago, and it's gone just about as well as my last few album launches. A Bandcamp chart-topper, but the real work lies ahead: getting it into new ears. PR guy hasn't been able to get a single nibble, but I've set up numerous interviews on my own, a few of which came out yesterday. Haven't heard anything negative about the album yet, but it isn't officially out yet.

Years ago, around the time of the *Popular Music* demo process, [NAME REDACTED] approached me about wanting to do a theater show, a sort of one-person play based around my songs. I got the impression that they merely wanted to rearrange the stories and songs I'd already been using onstage for years, basically making their own sort of "greatest hits" show. There are worse fates that could befall a DIY musician, but at the time, I wasn't in the mood to stand still creatively. Claire and The Potatoes was an exciting thing that sort of popped out of nowhere at the time, and the theater talks eventually ended. I don't remember how or by who, but I do recall feeling that not a single new idea of mine was being entertained, so I might've distanced myself?

Either way, over the years, I'd been working on putting my own ideas for a one-person show together. The very words "one-person show" seem scarily self-indulgent to even read, I thought I'd bunch together every idea I'd had for the show and just do it one day, if only to be able to say "here's an audience that liked it, it was a good idea," etc. To tell myself, the ideas you had were not rejected due to quality issues or even just so I could show it off to prove that most times, I'm a fairly good judge of what the stage act Marc With a C should do. So I wrote it. It started as "beats to hit." It progressed to "themes to hit." It became a script dictated by songs. And over time, it was mostly the songs from *Obscurity* that found their places as beats in the script, the ones that brought those initial points home best.

I was able to workshop *The Obscurity Show* last weekend for a relatively unsuspecting audience at The Geek Easy. It was a weirdly triumphant show. I didn't quite end up with a standing ovation, but the cheering in the room sometimes didn't leave room for continued speech. Most folks just told me that they cried – some from a long bit on toxic family members, some from a bit on impostor syndrome that becomes a bit victorious. [NAME REDACTED] happened to be there for the second half and raved about it, so I've sent them a copy of the recording of the show to see if they'd like to help me get it into theaters. I really believe in this show, and with some tweaking, it could be the show I was meant to be doing all along.

See, I think it'd be more fun to tour to places where I knew ahead of time that people would be receptive to listening. The theater circuit seems kind of neat to play, and more exciting than trying to be heard in a bunch of rock clubs. I'm realizing that I like telling stories just as much as I like singing songs. Theater is a good place for it. We'll see what shakes out. It's not **the** show I'll be doing all year, but rather a specific show that I'd like to take to theater festivals, if I'm able. That's really where [NAME REDACTED] might come in – I haven't got the first clue about how to source those venues, let alone how to hire a lighting person? But I've been feeling good this week about the future after the show was received well and more initial positives responses to the album came my way.

Doesn't do as much validating as one'd think, though. It'd be easier if I just defined myself by the success I'm having at any given time. But besides Nicole? Family isn't in the best place. I like that I'll have a lot of work to keep me occupied for a while. Keeps me distracted from micromanaging things I have less control over than I initially thought.

Yesterday was my birthday. Nicole made sure that I had a nice and low-key day. We watched a movie, ate some poutine, and generally kept a low profile. She bought me some shirts, flowers, and snacky treats that I like (popcorn and éclairs). She always works really hard to make me feel appreciated on my birthday, and while mine doesn't often mean too much to me, this year of turning 40? I feel like I'm a better person than I've ever been. My creativity is having a more positive influence than ever before. Hell, what's left to strive for, really?

Finding a better poutine source in America, that's for sure.

2-6-18

*Obscurity* is as "out" as it'll ever be. Since I last wrote here, it's been nothing but interviews, rehearsals, and general work. Last week was when it really intensified:

THURSDAY: Went to record an appearance on the wildly popular *Tom & Dan* radio show. 1 p.m. taping for a radio show that goes on at 7 p.m. Yet you have to look okay on camera, as they broadcast the tapings to the Twitch streamers. You can see a live feed of people saying "GAY" after you answer questions and whatnot. The guys wanted to ask questions about my daughter, which was a bit gauche, but I got to play "Terribly Popular" for a decently sized listening audience.

Then the work-stress made me stomach-sick.

FRIDAY: Band went to do an interview/radio performance/video shoot on WPRK with Captain Chris for WPRK. We played "Please Don't Let My Art Die," "Low Rent Truman Show," "Terribly Popular," and "One Of These Are Gonna Be Your Day" while multiple cameras captured us playing them in the CD library. It was around 30 degrees outside, but the air conditioner was broken in the literal bomb shelter-basement of WPRK, so it had to be over 100 degrees in there while we played. Did well, had fun, puked in the bushes during load-out, not just from the heat, but the continued work-stress. No one caught me, though.

SATURDAY: *Obscurity* release party at The Geek Easy. Said venue has brand new owners, so there were (minor) extra headaches involved. From the parking lot, the venue looked closed and under construction. Once you entered the doors, they'd lit the place up like the colors of the album cover. We had AJ doing an ambient set as Peephead for an opener. We played to a respectable amount of people, but our original agreement was that we were to play for about 75 minutes and then clear the stage for The Geek Easy's dance night. Due to the regime change, we now had a whole night to fill with very little notice. During the band's set, I forgot words and chords to the new material left and right, but during the extra all-request set? Oh wow. I was nervous and shaky and barely holding together. The saving grace was the very-polite-and-quiet audience that got louder (in a good way) as the night went on. The band played well, while I was relatively stationary for a Marc With a C rock show. Tried some windmills, but couldn't land any of them. Everybody danced to a finale of "I Hate This Song" and seemed to have a really good time. As soon as the hourlong encore was over, I went to throw up behind the club.

SUNDAY: Threw up on and off all day during what was supposed to be a day off, but I actually spent it mixing audio of Saturday's show.

MONDAY: Threw up in between business meetings and interviews for future podcasts.

Is it nerves? Is it a flu bug? Have I filled my quota of "making music for the world," and now my body is rejecting it? The latter seems more likely than you think.

I keep getting told which songs are making people cry good tears on the album. Fans are telling me the profound ways that the songs are resonating with their lives. I'm reacting with a "thank you" and a "that means so much to me," but I feel like I've done what I set out to do. I made the best things I can ever make. Every attempt at future work is overkill. The reception of the album is everything I hoped for. (It's currently something like #2637 on Amazon's music charts, making the name a self-fulfilling prophecy, yet it's touching the right people, just as intended.) I don't feel like further work is necessary now. My body is rejecting it.

Or I have the flu and haven't been able to stop to notice. It could be either one, really.

I used to work with a burlesque/art troupe named AntiBabe often in my first decade. Jodi was the brains behind the operation. Xoe is her 18-year-old kid, who was at the *Obscurity* release party, front row, raving about how much fun they had. Transcending generations with pop songs is really cool.

I still have a long way to go to make it to 20 years. Here's to hoping I can physically hold together for that. I'm trying. There's nothing else I'm supposed to be doing with my time on earth.

I'm happy.

2-13-18

I really like the Yes album called *Union*. You're "not supposed to" like it. The party line is that it's a cut-up cash-in.

Here's the story on it: Yes was a '70s prog-rock band. Mostly known for mammoth epic-length songs, impeccable musicianship, and that singer with the super-high voice. They had a revolving-door lineup; members came and went inexplicably. In the '80s, they had a huge hit with "Owner Of a Lonely Heart," and they'd had sort of an MTV-ready makeover. That's how I heard about them, and I like that cheeseball '80s material still for sheer dumb fun, but the '70s stuff is the real honey hole.

Anyways, in 1989 or so, the band was fractured. Half of the group started performing as Anderson, Bruford, Wakeman & Howe, which sounds more like a law firm than a rock band. These cats had the upper hand because they wanted to do the big-huge-long tunes, plus they had the instantly recognizable vocalist. There was still a Yes, though: Chris Squire was the bassist that was arguably "the sound" of the band both musically and harmonically, and to my understanding? He had the rights to the name, plus the guitarist who wrote "Owner" in tow. Could've gotten ugly.

Some industry folks decided that if the warring factions just stuck all of their musical works-in-progress together on an album under the name Yes? No one would ever know the difference, and they'd all have a nice payday. They were certainly right about the latter.

When I got the cassette in 1991, I didn't know anything about the infighting, that all eight members were never on the same track, and that those with their ears to the ground knew that this wasn't really Yes. To me, it was just a Yes album. Had some longer songs − but not TOO long − so it was kind of a nod to the past, as were some of the guitar tones. The shorter songs sounded like an updated version of the fun-cheese found on the *90125* and *Big Generator* albums.

Got to see the band on that tour. They only played two songs from *Union* onstage that night, but I didn't know it was maybe because of fan backlash. I just figured that they were trying to play "the hits," and most of those hits were eight minutes or longer, so how would they even have time, right?

Played the tape like crazy. Was so into it at the time that when I'd get depressed and think about hurting myself, I'd also think "but I'll never know what the next album sounds like if I'm dead," and that's literally why I didn't off myself during a massive and early depressive swing I had around the age of 13.

It isn't my favorite Yes album. Not even in the top 10, probably. And though I like Yes quite a bit, they might not even make it into my "top 20 favorite bands ever" list. But, just now? Was playing the record for the first time in a long while. I'm enjoying it as I write this, actually. Thought about all the people that would laugh at me for being really into it because, again, I'm "not supposed to" like it.

This silly and dated money-grab record has melodies that I like, and I suppose that it technically saved my life once. I don't give a shit that someone might laugh at my enjoyment of the platter. Or rather, I keep telling myself that because I do feel a bit guilty. Not because I think it's bad by any stretch but because of all of the truly wonderful music in the world that I'm not listening to instead of this fuzzy warble. Like I'm doing a disservice to "real art." Sometimes it's actively hard to just like what you like without apology.

*Union*'s follow up album, *Talk*? Didn't like it much at first, but hey, if just the mere thought of missing out on the next major statement by Yes kept a chubby and acne-covered kid from harming himself, it's probably worth another spin one day.

2-19-18

Forty is a weirder age than I thought it'd be. I watch myself age, never having had any fear of it, and now I'm grappling with not being thrilled about the way my body matures – again. I simultaneously feel like I've passed my expiration date while having a nagging feeling that I've left more work for myself than I could finish in one lifetime. I've had my iTunes on shuffle this weekend in the office, and I feel like I haven't heard whatever song is playing in years. I can hear how dated they are, how it must sound incredibly foreign to kids, and just how much guitars overtook pretty much everything. Yet, I continue to make music with guitars. Wish I'd have paid more attention to the piano lessons I had for a few months in my early teens.

This is the tail-end of four straight days of either interviews or shows. The most memorable of the shows took place on the second floor of our local library: there's a neat audio/visual studio that anyone in the community (with a library card) can use known as The Melrose Center. Music studios, virtual reality studios, you name it. They had me do a little 30-minute session in their studio. It was nice, as I played to around 10 people, but I could look them all in the eye. I know I didn't fully connect with them, but I was under a "no swearing" rule that severely limited which songs I was able to draw from. I enjoyed it. Struck up a conversation with the engineer about our favorite digital audio workstations.

All the reviews for *Obscurity* have (so far) been very positive. After only a few weeks, sales have slowed to a trickle. This is pretty common until I get back into the promo swing of playing to new faces.

Darren from Kid Dakota and I have struck up a Facebook friendship. He keeps trying to ask for contacts in northern Florida, and I'm realizing just how few contacts I have anymore. Haven't been able to help him in the least. Still a little starstruck that he's hitting me up for advice, though.

**3-4-18**

Exhausted and sitting at an empty merch table in Minnesota. Came up to sing some of my more humorous material at MarsCon again. Had a really fun set despite jet lag. I'd asked The Great Luke Ski if I could go five minutes longer than my originally agreed-upon set length, ensuring I wouldn't have to cut "Life's So Hard." Luke agreed, but the stage manager wasn't clear on the situation. She started flashing a red light in my face repeatedly during my penultimate song as if to say GET OFF THE STAGE NOW. This made for the most rushed renditions of "You're My Princess" and "Life's So Hard" I've likely ever done.

It seems that 75% of the audience was made up of folks that saw me here last year and came back with friends, which is one of the best feelings you can have when you fly across the country for these standalone-type shows.

Last night I went out with StarF to see the Mall Of America. Found some poutine in one of their 80 or so food courts. That place is almost unnecessarily big and definitely overwhelming, and we fittingly parked on the "Florida" level of the parking garage. Afterward, Carrie Dahlby had me go out with her to see her dad play pedal steel in a roots-rock band. She was iffy on going out alone and thought that I seemed relatively respectful and non-threatening. There are worse reasons to be asked to accompany a lady downtown. Had fun, though. We both geeked out about Steely Dan and The Monkees.

Today, I'm oddly singing precisely one song onstage before I hop on a plane home. StarF is accompanying me onstage but in a silent role. Hard to explain. We've hardly thought it out, honestly.

Softening my no-touring stance over this weekend. Every audience I've seen came to listen, which is getting increasingly rare in Florida. I'm interested in coming back. Last night I nearly slipped on the icy ground twice, so I'd be interested to see what the place is like when the sun is out. I love snow but hate walking in it.

Through no fault of my own, a deadline was blown for the delivery date of the video for "One Of These Are Gonna Be Your Day" for a really high-profile website premiere. I'm handling it oddly well – or I think I am, at least. Pretty mad about it inside, but as the ball has been dropped by someone different at nearly every stage of the *Obscurity* promo cycle, I'm a bit numb to it now.

3-17-18

I think I'm depressed.

I know. It seems like the kind of thing that you'd either know was happening or not, right? If it's happening, it's pretty mild. But that's the only reason I can think of that I'm so disinterested in things that I used to love. I pick up my guitar to see what sounds might come out of me, plunk around for five minutes, and then I just set it back down. I don't feel excited for upcoming shows. I haven't even sang a song in full since the show in Minnesota. Not by myself. Not in a car. Nothing. Just no interest in it.

Initially, I wanted to attribute the phenomenon to being overworked. Obviously, being overworked is relative, but finishing up the first season of *Discography* is pretty all-consuming if I want it to be any good. And when I finish something for that show, I feel accomplished, but not, say, "into it."

I've been quite enjoying laying on the couch at night and watching television. That's not been the highlight of my days since I was under 10 years old. I usually kick off with a sitcom: *Love*, *Crazy Ex-Girlfriend*, or on super adventurous days? The rebooted *Battlestar Galactica*. I love that show. Bigger fan of *Caprica*, actually. I feel that the avatar/afterlife subplot is the most important story that science fiction may have ever told in my lifetime. Then I watch a music show until I fall asleep on the couch. Documentaries. Old episodes of *Behind The Music* on YouTube.

I've struggled with bipolarity since long before I was diagnosed with it. Sometimes the depressive side wins. It's rarely something that completely wrecks my life, though. I can usually force myself out of bed and talk myself into self-care mostly because I get paranoid about smelling bad, and I don't want to make Nicole deal with it if I do. But the two places I'm noticing it? I can't force myself to make music, and I can't even force myself to engage with people. I wouldn't mind disappearing, really.

I know this is just today. This week. This month. It'll pass. That's why I've taken no drastic measures. But it needs to pass faster. Lack of interest for a prolonged period of time worries me. They are relatively few in numbers, but there are some folks that'd like to hear me sing and play guitar. I'm having trouble forcing myself to even rehearse just to keep my voice and dexterity in shape for the next time I'll be doing that in front of 'em.

I can't shake the "I've done what I set out to do. Why do more?" ennui and malaise.

I really hope it's just depression. Otherwise, I'm gonna be phoning it in for a good long while.

4-3-18

The malaise has continued, but I'm trying to work despite it, not letting on. Brave face and all that. Did a few shows – two at Universal Studio with The Rich Weirdoes were so sparsely attended that I was literally able to hand out free copies of Obscurity to all attendees. Did two livestream shows, and I felt nothing for any of the music I performed. This is really bizarre. I don't recall ever having "checked out" of my own music on this level before. I'm not sick of listening to it, though. The other day, I listened to *Exactly Where I Am*, and I found that I still really liked it. It didn't feel as foreign as it does to actually sing the songs so there's a good chance that this'll pass.

Right?

I keep booking shows in hopes that one day soon I'll just wake up and the haze of numbness about my silly little songs will have been lifted. Meanwhile, a few little things have changed.

- I've found myself very overworked with all of the Marc With a C admin work mixed in with the addition of *Discography*. Stretched so thin that the only day I could have off turned out to be Easter. I found myself so wiped out that I was unable to attend Easter dinner with Nicole's side of the family. I missed out on watching my niece and nephew do an egg hunt and the like. So I've instituted a schedule – Monday through Friday, I work from

12 p.m. to 8 p.m. After that, I have to shut off and make room for leisure time. There's the "all work and no play" element, sure, but I also need to make sure I don't find myself too exhausted to see loved ones. Of course, this schedule doesn't account for doing shows as well. I probably cannot realistically stick to it, but life might get easier if I can do this.

- I've been approved for a medical marijuana card. I'm such a teetotaler with the stuff that it merely takes one draw from the vape, and I've hit on a panic attack. Meanwhile, if I take a very, very, very small puff, the anxiety that I take other medication for goes away (mostly), and I stop craving my other prescriptions. Doesn't really help with my throat pain, but it makes sleeping easier, and if I take the aforementioned puff right before bed, I wake up with a slight enough carryover that my anxiety doesn't go quite as apeshit through the day. It should be noted that I'm only using it right before bed. I don't enjoy "the high" (or even being high, in truth), but I can't argue that it makes listening to records even more fun than usual. Also, my tolerance for shitty television changes drastically on the stuff.

In a cowardly way, someone made their displeasure known that I changed a common/oft-retold joke in my shows that was once solely about drugs to instead be (non-jokingly) about stressing the need for acquiring enthusiastic consent before sexual contact. I used to do a "Hey, who's got vicodin" joke in the same place, every show. Lately, it's been replaced with framing audience participation as practicing enthusiastic consent which you're free to revoke at any time. Someone made a Facebook sock account (which they swiftly deleted or blocked me from, not sure) to make it clear that they liked me better when I "was funny" and not "an SJW." They were referencing one of the Universal Studios shows.

I addressed this on social media since I had no other recourse to respond to the person. Mostly just reminding people that it's my show, I'll say what I like, and I'm not wrong. Folks that appeared to be fans started arguments about the word "enthusiastic" and tried to do it in what looked like crummy lawyer-speak. Their spelling was atrocious, so any finer points they were trying to make weren't clear. Spelling "interpreted" as "interrupted" and the like.

It's 2018, and I'm having to explain consent instead of playing songs at my shows. Based on the guys trying to get into the semantics of the term, it's something that I clearly need to do.

On a positive note, I used last month's Patreon money to acquire a new cassette four-track so that I'd be able to transfer tapes of pre-2009 shows to digital. I'm pretty excited to see what I uncover!

4-16-18

Growing pains have abounded with this whole "keeping to a schedule" thing, but I'm committed to trying. The key has been to avoid computers when I need to take a day off. Yesterday was Sunday, a designated day off, but I'd also been sent the multi-tracks for my appearance on *Live From Dope City*, and since we're hoping to slice that version of "Please Don't Let My Art Die" out of the footage and make it a standalone music video, I was certainly tempted. That's my downfall: I sit in front of the equipment, telling myself "this'll only take a minute or two," and then I wrap up ... in the middle of the night. Yesterday, I did well. Just sat on the couch and shot the shit with Nicole for what felt like the first time in ages.

This month, I've seen concerts by Japanese Breakfast, Snail Mail, Mitski, and Run The Jewels – all are artists I adore, and all of them put on good shows. My malaise felt like it sat between me and the stage, blocking my view, sometimes sitting on my lap as a barricade hell-bent on being an emotional shield. Now, to be fair, the audience was really rude to Snail Mail. The audience talked over one of her very, very quiet songs, and it appeared to me that she walked off the stage without warning. I felt anger at that moment. But that's about it for even feeling moved by music. The numbness continues unabated.

*Discography* has been pretty successful so far for an upstart podcast. We only have first-week numbers, but it's certainly blown any podcast venture I've ever taken on out of the water. I believe that's due to the promotional machine of Consequence Of Sound and ... well? Frank Zappa. His fans are ravenous, and I'd know because I'm one of 'em. The listeners that have reached out to me have been really nice. There's even been a few that simply don't agree with my take on his output, and they're still just happy the podcast is happening at all. I like that type of response: "I don't agree, but I get it, and I'm glad you said it."

I pitched an idea to Emmit and Jim: they could be equal partners when it comes to the Marc With a C Trio. Emmit seemed into it, but I could tell that Jim was hemming and hawing a little bit. In his case, he's spread so thin that I imagine that it must have sounded like just something else to put on his overflowing plate. We did a set at the Orlando Overdrive set this past weekend, playing almost exclusively newer material. I thought it was a pretty good set, but Emmit seemed to take the few musical mistakes he made pretty hard. This was surprising to me, because I certainly played far more bad notes than he did. We're in a good place musically, but I'm not totally sure what the future holds for us besides just playing together here and there whenever we can.

Really feeling my age on stage. After 35 minutes, I felt like I usually do at the end of a marathon show. You could practically wring my Steamed Hams shirt into a glass and fill it with liquid after the show.

4-28-18

I am absolutely, assuredly, and without a doubt fully in a low swing, but I don't know how to tell you about it. I'll just ramble and hope I can get it across. My computer went on the fritz, rendering all attempts at further work on *Discography* futile. As well as all surrounding work. Everything I do has a digital step now, and I'm at a standstill due to what seems to be a mixture of planned obsolescence and bad luck. I fought so hard to keep my work away from being purely digital for so long, and right now I remember why.

I get antsy and think, oh, well, I guess I'll go and transfer some old 4-track tapes to – GODDAMMIT, I NEED THE COMPUTER FOR THAT AS WELL, DONT I? and then feel even lower. I use a lot of very specific proprietary stuff to get certain microphone tones, so I can't just go to, say, Cap's house and edit the last episode of the first season of *Discography* at their place because it wouldn't sound uniform, and I'd lose the consistency and quality I've been striving to achieve with this show. And now that I'm used to writing on a keyboard with a word processor-type of program for the show, I'm finding it very difficult to continue to absorb the Janet Jackson records for the second season and write anything worth a fuck about them. Tried writing here on the cell phone (where I'm typing now, sans desktop computer) but it just isn't the same, and I know that my voice gets a little lost in the script somehow when just using my thumbs to type.

A family member died unexpectedly yesterday. He was a man that I quite liked but didn't know very well. We weren't close, and we mostly only ever talked about our latest e-cig rigs and a few of the bands we both liked. The family on Nicole's side is pulling together very tightly, but I'm trying to keep my distance to an extent. I think that I'll say the wrong things. Drugs were a factor in his death, I've seen this rodeo before, and frankly, I have a modicum of first-hand understanding of what transpired. In comparison? Those that were closest to him weren't as savvy about these matters. It's best that I stay away, keep my mouth shut and not interfere with the grieving. They are all struggling to understand, but few want to hear answers in times of this nature. Just last night, I found Nicole furious with me without allowing me to complete my sentences. We yelled, I decided to sleep on the couch and let her be mad. I can't fix death, but I can certainly shut the fuck up.

There are times where being right won't get you anywhere. I'm in one of those periods. I can't answer questions incorrectly if I'm not near those with skyrocketing tensions. I'll stay alone as much as I possibly can, but this time, I can't escape through immersing myself in work. I'm just alone here with my thoughts and few outlets.

I'm writing this on a Saturday, and I may not have the computer back until Tuesday. It feels like an eternity to be unable to work and create.

On top of that, I know that I'm becoming increasingly hideously depressed. It's been going on for months now. I don't know how to get out of it. I don't know how to tell people without seeming whiny. I'd tried to cancel my May gigs but wasn't allowed to do so. Promoters don't give a fuck how I feel inside. The closest I've been able to get to clearing my calendar was getting the band to agree to only rehearse once every two weeks. Beyond that, I still need to finish *Discography*, play shows, do promo, and all of the stuff I have to stay on top of to keep Patreon backers entertained.

I'm not having a good time. Physically, I simply do not feel right, but I'm not ready to talk about that yet. I currently find little joy in the work I surround myself in, but I'm finding out this weekend that even when the ability to work properly is stripped away, I'm not actually feeling any better.

There doesn't seem to be an obvious answer: I'm depressed whether I'm working or not. Today, besides writing this diary/journal thing, I've laid on the couch and watched silly music documentaries, the type that are made by fly-by-night companies who don't have the rights to use the music of whoever they are talking about, so you end up with two hours of talking heads you've never heard of talking about Stevie Nicks or something. It's a lot like having friends with a bunch of musical knowledge drop by to talk about famous songs, but they also understand that you're not feeling your best, so they don't expect you to join in. Weirdly comforting.

Anyways, back to the numbness. I'm hoping that a good thing happens soon. Everything feels either hopeless or – on good days – merely doldrumesque.

5-11-2018

Yesterday, I posted a thing on social media, and people dogpiled on me pretty quickly. It was done on my personal Facebook page. After an initial few seconds of confusion and anger, it dawned on me: I get upset because I think/hope people take words seriously. Sometimes they do. Sometimes they don't. I'm horrible at reading tones and intent when it's directed at me via computer. I'm fine for business matters because we're all usually working toward a common goal of creating something good, but actual sharing of my personal feelings or "hot takes"? Weirdly, it took me until yesterday to realize that's where a good portion of my inner bad feelings are transpiring.

I wrote a song called "Ethics In Gaming," and it reminds me that I've often come up with my own answers and forget to ever actually apply them to my own situations. Take any social or political issue you'd see people arguing about on Facebook, for example. There might be some small and puny exceptions, but mostly, these conversations are just an attempt to "win." They don't really want to change a way of thinking because then they've got nothing to talk about. The other party likely feels the same way. Or there's one thing that one party doesn't know that'll change **everything**, and the commenter MUST be the one to show them the light.

We're at a place where everyone is showing up ready to fight, yet we forget that we don't need to do that with our friends, so we complicate things by constantly one-upping and trying to show "how things oughta be" in our particular mental space. These fights are pointless, and they make me scared to talk with friends or others on screens and rectangles unless it's about business matters. Or maybe pop culture once in a while.

My answer? Step out of it. I still need Facebook for professional reasons, but trying to talk to my friends and acquaintances through it upsets me. I hadn't narrowed it down until yesterday. I thought it was just "social media" in general, but this is the part that disrupts my own inner peace – and I'm bringing it on myself. As I'm not built for that kind of discourse, my knee-jerk reaction to the knee-jerk "let's argue" reaction of everyone else is to curl up in a ball and be sad that I've upset my friend. Meanwhile, they've probably forgotten that they even typed anything.

Thankfully it was a pretty stupid topic that made me realize what should have been all-too-obvious to me in the first place: I pointed out that the world is globally kinkshaming DJ Khaled (because they are), while everyone hides under pretending to be mad that he said misogynistic things at the same time (which he did). The whole world is breathing down this guy's neck to start giving his wife cunnilingus though he doesn't want to. His reasoning sounded pretty chauvinistic, sure, but ... yeah. I don't think I need to explain further. Shaming is still shaming.

*Discography* has done shockingly well over the last few weeks. Seeing lots of impossible-to-please people leaving reviews about what I should change, but in some of their cases, they just don't like my voice. Not much I can do about that, so it doesn't really get under my skin. Turning in the last episode of the season made me breathe a huge sigh of relief. I battled the computer problems to finish the season, but, unfortunately, it left some audio errors and glitches that cannot be removed due to computer malfunctions, and mostly those affected interviews with Alex Winter and Weird Al.

Yes, I got to interview Weird Al about Frank Zappa. He's such a pro. I asked him the same set of questions I'd asked the other guests. It had taken the full 45 minutes to get their answers each time. With Al? Since he knows how to speak in sound bites, we were done in a flat 15, and he hadn't glossed over anything. I could learn a lot from that style of speech.

I'm leaving to go and open for MC Chris in about an hour. I'm weirdly looking forward to performing tonight. It feels like the healthiest outlet I can use at the moment. No nerves. Little anxiety. Just ready to roll, get some energy outta my chest, hopefully entertain some people, and maybe even make some new fans while I'm there. Since I haven't been enjoying my performances lately, this is a nice internal change.

And I'm working on a special 10-inch record for hardcore fans, but it's in some pretty early stages of development, and I'm not sure what to say about it yet. I think it will make more sense when I can instead talk about someone's reactions upon receipt of the item. I could get used to releasing music to people on a subscription-basis, I must admit.

6-2-18

This has been the biggest gap between journal entries so far, and that's been because I've been procrastinating. I knew this one would be difficult to write, so I waited until I kind of knew where things were headed. It's painful, and I wasn't sure if this was going to be a blow-by-blow account or just boiled down to a "Today I Learned" sort of deal.

Due to a cavalcade of miscommunications, it appears that Katharine and I will no longer be professional partners. It's difficult to even type that, but it was more difficult to live it. If I spelled everything out, neither party would likely come out looking too rosy. If I don't give some context, I've pretty much given everyone license to let their imaginations run wild. The latter is almost preferable, but it'd make me a lazy writer.

I wasn't sure until today if our friendship would survive at all. It looks like we'll go forward as friends while putting the kibosh on anything professional that might wreck our besties-without-borders arrangement. And until today,

I've been a wreck about the situation. Must've been ugly to watch. I had to get legal advice, and then I cried my way through a rehearsal, and that was just the first few hours of the problem. Most things I've had to do since then have been half-hearted "what's the point of doing anything at all if you lose friends?"

This type of argument is precisely what people like to read about in these types of books, right? Spilling tea, sharing the drama, revealing secrets from behind the scenes, etc. I'm afraid I'll have to disappoint you; it's just for the best that Katharine and I don't work together going forward, and you'll have to trust that it's the only proper way to continue. I respect that you want to know more, so I'll tell you something a bit "meaty," maybe?

The issues that arose were even changing the shape of the book you're involved with right now. I wasn't sure if I was going to have to rewrite this book altogether because of a sea change that interrupted what I'd set out to make. Based on a misunderstanding, I had to come clean about a secret that I don't really like to share because I don't believe it's anyone's business at all: if you're assuming that the personal "identity" of Marc Sirdoreus: Human Being/Private Citizen is 100% masculine, you'd be incorrect. There's more femininity internally than you might have first thought. That said, I don't feel the need to break it down into specifics. It only really jolts me when someone mentions that I'm doing something "typically male" because then I think, wait, is it? I figured out how to be a guy, finally? or something like that.

I'm just Marc. My body is recognizably male, but internally, I couldn't even begin to break down where I am on any spectrum for you without authoring a second book. I'm just Marc, male pronouns are fine, yet in my thought processes I don't necessarily match any of the ways that I'm able to "present." Truthfully, if I were pressed to give myself a named identity, the only one that feels right is "monogamous," but I've been told that it doesn't count/isn't an identity, so who the fuck knows? I guess I use the words "guy" and "man" for myself because I'm used to it, but it isn't altogether accurate. I'm fine with living somewhere in limbo mentally and fluidly, though, it doesn't tax me much until situations like these come about.

Moving on.

I'd really wanted for the band to do a low-pressure gig in which we could just be a bar band that no one had any expectations from. We booked one, and then the venue changed from the hole-in-the-wall we'd first booked to Will's Pub (which is a bit more high-pressure) and had to come up with a hook to get people in the door. We'd decided to go the "Bizarro World" route – the Trio would go on stage as a democratic band that was seemingly run by Jim and Emmit. We'd poise Emmit as the main songwriter, Jim as the frontman, and I'd just be the guy that played guitar and sang. I didn't really even talk onstage. We got to do this gig for about 12 people. Emmit's other band, House Of I, opened up, and I think they gave us a real run for our money. Super good. Meanwhile, in the early stages of planning, we expected our setlist to be really alienating, but it didn't turn out that way. When it comes to the tunes we like to play best, we all actually seem to be on the same page. I mostly thought it'd be a neat way to do a show without "Nerdy Girls," "Love My Little Squiddy," and "Life's So Hard," but enough relatively well-known songs found their way into our program ("Stuck With Me," "Drunk Classic Rock Fans," and "Dickpuncher") that our intent may have been lost on some. We did a good show, and as it's probably the last gasp for The Trio for a while, I'm happy with it, though I can hear in the recordings that the physical issues I'm hesitant to get into are starting to really appear in my voice more than ever. I mean, I can hear it. Maybe everyone is too kind to say anything about it directly to me?

I'm starting to feel like there might (emphasis on "might") be a little bit left in me to say. I also feel that those things might only be said for the benefit of others. I'm not doing much creating "for myself" at the moment, and that's where I feel I'd need to get back to before I actually try to make any new statements. *Obscurity* is a fine final word for now.

6-13-18

After years of having a nasal voice, I'm used to pretty much anything that I put into words being misconstrued by those who are unfamiliar with me as "whiny." That claim was lobbed at "Every Single Friend" (a song quite obviously not sung from my perspective), "Where's My Giant Robot," (I don't even have the words.) and the title track to *Exactly Where I Am*. But despite pushing forward because that's just the most attractive solution? I feel like a light has gone out within myself. The place where the excitement to create would usually ooze with contagious jubilation, but right now said internal place is merely getting by on my ability to fake it. I pick up my guitar to play for fun, but the strings and finger placement feel foreign. I try to sing at the same time, but there's no register that feels right. It isn't just the throat pain or other physical problems; I just feel incredibly out of place when I try to make musical sounds. No one seems to notice when I'm onstage – or at least no one has admitted that I appear to be faking it. Or maybe they haven't said it to my face?

Ditto for actually writing down words for potential song usage. I feel like Marc With a C might have ended at *Obscurity*. I had suspicions, even secretly planned an endgame, but I figured it'd go like it normally does: I finish a record, feel as if it's the best thing I've ever done, and then I tell those closest to me that I'm "done" while I'm still scribbling ideas, and then I'm finished with another album before I'm even ready to do anything with it.

Not this time. Very few scribbles. Though, *Obscurity* does feel like it's arguably my strongest record, but I haven't done anything new of substance in one whole year now.

Allow me to emphasize: I wrote so many songs between 2003 and 2006 that I'm still occasionally stripping the unused material for parts. Meanwhile, 365 days in one of the most fascinating times in American history, and I haven't felt the need to write many songs at all. I can think of a few verses that I jotted down, but each time I tried to marry the words to chords? Guitar felt alien, I'd look at the words and realize that I didn't mean anything I wrote, I'd decide that it wasn't "happening," and then I'd move on to working on *Discography* or something.

I have captured little doodles of sound for Natural History Museum. I've also recorded a few covers to try to kickstart myself. The facts remain that I'm not having a good time with playing, singing, or writing music. I thought it might be a phase.

Is one year a phase? Or does one year mark a "new normal?"

Or maybe it's that usual post-album cycle, but it's taking a bit longer to reset myself because the album was "bigger?"

I'm scared. And that probably sounds silly to you. But if you've had one constant invisible muse in your life that was one of the few reasons you'd get out of bed, and it inexplicably leaves you? You might find yourself scared as well.

I mean, who the hell am I if I'm not the minutia-obsessed songwriter I've known myself to be? I suppose I could just take stock of the other things that are good in my life and focus on those in the interest of self-definition. Thing is, I can't decide if this is comfortable or not. Am I good with this?

This whole songwriting issue predates the current depression. They could both just be parts of my psyche post-turning 40! And why fight it? If it's who I'm supposed to be, I see little reason to engage in fisticuffs with fate.

Domenico Marini passed away a few days ago. I'm still reeling and nauseated from the news. I knew that he had cancer, but something in me thought, Dome is super tough, he'll shake that illness right off. I really believed that, too. But he took a turn for the worse a little while before this writing, yet he didn't tell me. A quiet and sometimes shy man, he still had his prideful moments, and maybe he didn't want to admit that the illness had won? I can only guess. And marvel at how much I relate.

We all need role models. We need to know that someone believes in us. And we need those folks that can be both, rain or shine. Dome was always that person to me. He told me that I was family; the son he never had. I didn't wince when he said that. I believed him. I still do. He was a sweet and genuine man that always bent over backward to ensure I felt special and loved. Starting as a fan, clawing his way over my own protective wall, and ending up as a person that I'd trust my life to? That simply doesn't happen, and if it does, it's once in a lifetime.

When I learned that Domenico passed away, it gave me a moment to wonder why I wasn't running to a guitar and a notebook to work out what he meant to me in a melodic way. That's when I realized how serious this case was for me. I'm not sure that the depression, the feuds, and the lack of musical drive are actually connected at all because when something as relatively earth-shaking like the death of one of my very best friends can't pierce the malaise, I have to imagine myself as a temporarily lost cause.

Make no mistake: Dome's passing did make me sadder, and it made me think about just how different my life could have been if he hadn't flown from Italy to Florida to see a show of mine and decided that he needed to back me as an angel investor to get my music out on vinyl. Really, I could spend the whole rest of this book talking about the effect Dome had on me. And while I do feel even more down than before, there's surprise in the lack of the internal jolt at such news.

And then I feel worse for not feeling even worse than I already do? It's a fuckin' weird cycle.

Hopefully, I'm coping by throwing myself into work while I still have any drive at all. The work is usually either *Discography*-related or something revolving around the 20th anniversary objects, like the "best of" compilation and this book.

If it's *Discography* work, I'll bog myself down in minute things; I had Chris LeBrane on as a guest for a few segments in our upcoming season of *Discography*. There's a buzzing sound in his microphone around the 200 hz range, and I've spent hours trying to remove without resorting to tricks and plug-ins. Anyone in their right mind would use a quick fix-it plug-in and get on with things. Me? I'm clearly trying to avoid thinking.

Regarding the "best of," I've been playing with countless variations on the tracklist. Most of those tracks have been decided on by audience votes and the opinions of trusted longtime hardcore fans. As I'd tally the results of the polls I'd find weird shit like the title track of *Exactly Where I Am* placing not just high enough in the polls to practically guarantee its inclusion but placing much higher than "Free Bird" and "You're My Princess" – both of which now shan't be making the cut. Literally no one has ever spoken to me about that song, nor does it go over well live, so the shock of finding out that it's quite loved almost feels like a practical joke at my expense.

See? That's the shit my head comes up with: didn't expect a song to place so high in poll results? It's clearly because my fans got together to fuck with me. How ludicrous is that? Living in my head can really suck sometimes.

I'm typing this all on my phone while I'm waiting to do a solo show opening for Champagne Jerry. Another gig where I had to show up three hours before show time, wait a half hour to soundcheck for less than a minute, and then kill two and a half hours – all for a slot that I accidentally ended up with. And the promoter isn't even sure he can pay me. Initially, I was trying to get on the bill with TV Girl, and instead I got slapped on the more comedic bill. Didn't even know it was supposed to be a "funny" gig until last night. As a result, I had to toss my initial set list in favor of a whole bunch of songs that I've not rehearsed.

Writing this has eaten up a lot of time. Still have 75 minutes to kill. Maybe I'll call my friend Shannon. She tried to reach me on Monday, but I was knee-deep in trying to get the buzz out of Chris LeBrane's recorded vocals, so I didn't hear the phone.

And sure, if I call Shannon, I run the risk of wearing my voice down a bit, but I'm past caring at this point. If my voice doesn't work, maybe it's time to stop hiding that?

6-29-18

Last weekend, I did a show at a really, really cool venue called [NAME REDACTED]. Afterward, I tried to get paid and found myself in the center of a really strange match of he-said/she-said. It's my belief that threatening to go public with the exact problem and names of people involved are the only reason I eventually got paid because the club shut down with no warning a few days later, rendering my gig the last one that'd ever actually take place there.

But let's not move on so quickly; at times on that night, I was surrounded by three people who would sort of "bow up" at me each time I made a move. My crime? Being the opening act that insisted on getting paid when I was told I'd be paid by the guy who said it was his job to pay me. One person would ask who I made the arrangement with. Another would ask why I couldn't produce a written agreement. Another still would marvel that I was considered "worth" my rate by some (and that party really, really seemed to dislike me).

If I'd have left with a check like they initially wanted? I doubt it'd have been cashable, because again, they shut down days later and removed all their social media.

It's true that I did threaten to be very public with names and the multiple businesses that were encircling me, but beyond that, my evening consisted of showing up on time, soundchecking when told, playing one minute shorter than my stage time called for, and then waiting around and trying to sell merch. One minute I'm singing "Happy To Be Alive" to a moderately attended club half-full of people in Marc With a C shirts, The next, I'm trying to justify why I deserve money at all.

That's not all that happened, but it's the gist of an all-too-common occurrence. People just don't want to give musicians money, but they sure like the income provided by our listeners. Too many nights are spent being the opening act, watching your audience leave, seeing the headliner play to a now-quite-spacious room, and then noticing the money that my audience gave the venue is being handed to the act that didn't bring as many warm bodies to the gig.

This isn't a persecution complex. Ask any other culty musician at/around my level and they'll tell you the same story. The only way to change it is to convince the entire world that all artists deserve compensation. Let me know how that works out for you, please.

Beyond music, this has been a painful month. It wasn't just the loss of Domenico, but there was also a huge problem in my household that's so hurtful that words won't do it justice. It was a no-win situation, and I just wanted to survive, I know that Nicole and I are still shaken, and I also can tell that it's becoming obvious to people that something has been going on with me: so many people are reaching out to me that I've had to ask that listeners and fans stop contacting me through Facebook because I just can't keep up with their nice and heartfelt letters. Even the once-teen lady that inspired "Life's So Hard" wrote me a letter after seeing a recent show and being able to read sadness all over my face.

Unfortunately, I'm the one who has to make positive changes in my life, so while it's nice to know that people have my back, writing back to everyone takes me away from trying to actually enact the needed changes. Or even figuring out what those are!

Today, I'm listening to Yes records while I finish up work for Patreon backers. This is a cool type of workday because I'm doing things that actively need to get finished, but I can listen to music that isn't mine while I do it. Rarer than you'd think. At the end of my workday, I'll be able to show something for it. Those are the days that fulfill me most as of late.

7-15-18

I think I'm beginning to see light again. A bit of forward momentum. I've spent a bunch of my mental and emotional energy in recent months asking myself, why go on? I always come back to only one answer, which is "because that's the best option."

I needed the question, though! As someone who has (mostly) set fairly attainable goals for themselves, after the release of *Obscurity*, there's been an intense period of soul-searching, asking myself overall what I should do with myself now that I've (more or less) done what I set out to do in the first place.

Make records? Check.

Make up some songs that mean something to me and maybe other people, too? Check.

Make some kind of legacy for myself, even a teensy one? Check.

Make a record with one of the inspirations that made me love music in the first place? Check.

After achieving those things, the rest is a weird and surprising gravy for me. But it puts me in an odd place, as there's income which makes me "a professional," and sometimes there's profit and reinvestment of funds which makes Marc With a C "a business." But what now?

That's pretty much been the bulk of this year. The backbone of this odd internal drift. Importantly, not what next?, as my heart was searching for immediacy.

Hosting things without actually playing any music actually feels oddly comfortable. Last night, I hosted a gig at The Geek Easy thrown by Ongaku Overdrive called NEXGEN. The idea was that they'd show off the future of nerdcore hip-hop with acts like Wreck The System, EyeQ, None Like Joshua, Lex The Lexicon Artist, and SPF. I'd be the liaison between audience and performer, talking up raffles and whatnot. I did sing a little as EyeQ had me do the chorus to "Gettin' Lucky," which I did while wrapped around his (very, very long) right leg. It was fun. I didn't exhaust myself. I didn't get into a bad mood at the slightest sign of trouble. I got to actually watch the other artists on the bill. Just a really good night all around. Do I feel like a Ryan Seacrest-type in my heart? No, not really. But I'm used to speaking to audiences, projecting my voice comes naturally to me, and people seem to think I'm okay at it. There could be more of this in the future, mayhaps.

Though it's the next day, and my voice is still shattered. And I only sang for maybe a combined 60 seconds. That's a factor.

The most recent gig where I played my songs was a few towns over in a place called Sanford. Played a show in a brewery with Lando The Roadie (he played guitar and sang in a completely separate set, we didn't revive "the roadie show"). At first the venue reminded me of Sleeping Moon – the place where *The Real Live Sound Of Marc With a C* was recorded. As the crowd trickled in, it became clear to me that this should have been an atmosphere gig. And I could've chucked my setlist to provide that, but the left side of the room was fully made up of Marc With a C fans that drove for an hour to hear me play. I nicknamed them "left beef" for the night after a popular meme. I had to do my show while the left side of the room listened and the right side talked, getting drunk and a little rowdy. Also, there was literally nothing in the venue even resembling sound equipment. I had to pack an entire PA into my Scion, unload it at the venue, set it up alone, etc. I was visibly exhausted by the time my set was supposed to begin and didn't have the energy to fight with the talkative portion of the crowd. It was fine, I guess, but I was tired, bored, and generally not at my best. Plus I'm getting restless with playing the same songs so often. Not the *Obscurity* tunes, but nearly every show has "Unicorns Get More Bacon," "Life's So Hard," and "Dickpuncher" and I think I need to swap them out for a bit to keep myself engaged. Everything needs a break sometimes.

That was the first show where a fan had ever asked me to sign a coaster, though.

I'm listening to the last record by Sammus while sipping ice water on a gloomy and humid Sunday. Mere days from now, season two of *Discography* goes live – the season about Janet Jackson – her fan base is still one of the most loyal and passionate clubs of fans I've ever seen. A little scared of their potential reactions. I don't have the kindest words for some of Janet's later records, and I don't imagine that will excite the fans that have stuck by her side all these years. And then there was watching the Zappa fans turn away in droves when we announced who I'd be covering next because, well, I guess you can't get further away from Frank Zappa musically than the sounds made by the Jackson family, can you? I think this is just the way of the walk now. I'll always be nervous about fandoms, no matter which artist I explore on the show.

7-31-18

Okay, let's talk about the burgeoning illness that sidelines me (on and off) for the last little while. It was nefarious. I didn't even know it was happening until seeing a rash on my leg. My doctor looked at it, I told him what I thought the issue was, and they sort of tossed some "hail Mary" antibiotics at me without any real diagnosis. Those antibiotics were not to be trifled with, as I'd come to learn.

The last 10 days have been a blur. It's like the pills put me into some type of pissy trance while also wrecking me even worse physically. If you can name the side effect, it happened. I had to do a live online performance for Patreon backers in the thick of the antibiotic mess. I'd not been keeping food (or liquid) down, but I still had to play. I considered canceling up until five minutes before my start time. I remembered that even big movements look diminished on camera sometimes, so I'd just be upfront with viewers: I'd play all the songs I'd planned to play, but if I needed to leave "the stage" to throw up, that was the end of the show. I think that was a fair compromise. Made it to the 13th song, said my goodbyes, ducked around the corner to puke, and then promptly canceled every bit of professional work I had for ... well, all the work in general. Interviews, rehearsals, you name it. Because I don't know if I can do it.

That's unlike me, but I had to. I don't mind looking sickly, but I was finding it hard to be entertaining (let alone to follow conversations started by others) so I realized that even if I did "show up to work," I might be a waste of time to watch or listen to. That sealed the deal. First time I said no to a big swath of work and didn't feel guilty for it, maybe?

In a potentially ironic twist, I'm listening to Alice Cooper's *DaDa* while I write this; an album Alice claims he doesn't remember making. Of course, Alice was on cocaine, and I was on Doxycycline and Keflex, so maybe those aren't as comparable as I thought, but I'm good with that. That's my rock and/or roll lifestyle: do what the doctor says. That's kind of its own form of rebellion for musicians, maybe?

The first time I ventured out of bed was to see The Smashing Pumpkins with

Cap and Juliana. Musically, it was fine, but the stage show was perplexing. But that's part of dealing with the Pumpkins. You might get what you want on a pure technicality, but it's going to come with so many head-scratching moments that you don't always notice all the good stuff. The big draw for this tour was the return of James Iha, who was barely lit/visible from our seats. Also from my seat, it looked like most of his solos and tweedly-meedly bits had been handed over to a different guitarist altogether. Really, beyond his lead vocal turn on "Blew Away," if you didn't already know James was back, you might not have believed me afterward when I told you that James Iha was onstage for 95% of the show. Of course, there's more to it – it's Billy Corgan, so one can't run out of hairs to split – but hey, loud rock and roll show, and I wasn't sequestered in bed, so it was a better night than I'd have had otherwise. And it was a good lesson that nostalgia only works in your head most times.

Of course, the next day, all the folks that went were all over social media talking about how great it was, so I'm obviously in the minority. Why share a bunch of negative stuff and wreck people's good time? And I have something to think about for a few days after a concert I've paid to see, so it was a better time than I may have made it sound.

I'm elated to find that Janet Jackson's fan base are very sweet and welcoming on the whole. They've been really cool to me, even when I'd get an occasional factoid wrong, and it actually makes me dig the records even more because they quite obviously inspire kindness in her fans, and I'm hard pressed to think of similar fandoms in 2018. Of course, the only time I really hear about a fandom is when they're pulling some toxic shit – don't even get me started on the Star Wars contingent that straight up harass the actors – so I'm mostly trained to believe that they're ready to pounce at all times. Halfway through the season of *Discography* airing, and there's only been one person pulling a bunch of "well, ACTUALLY" so far, and that is a pretty good batting average.

8-22-18

When I woke up and turned my phone off of airplane mode, I was greeted with a cavalcade of congratulations, as I'd just placed second as Best Singer/ Songwriter in that yearly *Orlando Weekly* popularity contest. Coolest part is that my friend EyeQ swept his category, and I know that being voted Orlando's best hip hop artist means an awful lot to him. I'm oddly happier for him than I am for myself.

Crossroads. That's the current position for pretty much, well, everything I do.

I'm not driven to make new music right now, but I'm annoyed at myself for being mildly okay with that situation. I've been considering recording a new version of a song called "Tired Old Dicksucker Revue," which is a track I've always kicked myself for leaving off of *This World Is Scary As Fuck*. But every time I sit down at the drum kit to begin cutting the basic tracks, I get a flash of "you've already put enough music into the world, so go do something else now." I obey.

As far as "family" goes and all that the word entails? There's either been a disruption in relations or completely severed ties on my part. There's few exceptions to this phenomenon, and when I have to think really hard about family members that wouldn't fall under either category? I realize that it's ridiculous that I'm thinking that hard about it. If it's not a blood relative, we're probably a-okay. If we share any DNA, I can't really say where things stand one way or the other unless I've walked away out of mental self-preservation. I feel like pretty much everyone gets wrecked by their family at some point, and I also (probably mistakenly) feel that being aware of that fact means that I should be allowed to just not deal with it.

I've been alive for far too long to have to put up with people who can't accept me as I am. It'd be one thing if I was out to hurt anyone, but mostly I bolt when keeping the peace fails. Or I'm fearing for my life.

Let's talk about the health thing: I haven't felt right for months, and since I didn't know what it was, I didn't want to track my assumptions. Basically, one of my bones was literally infected in some freak decision that my body made to revolt against me. I didn't know that's what was happening until it appeared on my skin. Round after round of antibiotics seemed to kick the first infection out, but I'm noticing the beginning stages of those same symptoms appearing on top of other bones. It may not be fixed at all, which means I'd better not make many plans, otherwise everything'll come with a 50% chance of being canceled, depending on how I feel on that day. It's not "fixed," and I'm not sure that it isn't spreading. I'm not going to tell you more than this. Sorry.

This weekend, I'm returning to Universal Studios to open for The Rich Weirdoes again – breaking my live hiatus – because, get this: Universal bought the AMC theater that's been their home. And though they're quite a consistent draw as a *Rocky Horror* shadowcast, no one has approached them about continuing to perform at the theater post-buyout. So, basically if something doesn't change very quickly, these shows will be their last performances at the theme park. Of course, this makes emotions run quite high. I'm planning to show up and do three songs that have historically seemed to mean a lot to that audience and cast: "Drunk Classic Rock Fans," "Nerdy Girls," and "Life's So Hard." "Nerdy Girls" is especially poignant as, if memory serves, it's one of the songs I would've played during my first appearance with them. Though I'm likely the one holdover from that period almost 15 years ago, so it may only be poignant to me and a few longtime fans.

I'm starting to gear up to get back to playing songs onstage for at least a little while. After this year ends, I think I'd like to kind of celebrate the brevity of my catalog a bit more in the shows rather than putting so much focus on newer material.

Of course, that may only be a pipe dream. All the records in the *Obscurity* Trilogy are being reissued on cassette by Needlejuice Records, a label that's released stuff by King Gizzard and Lemon Demon. And of course, eventual stagings of *The Obscurity Show* would absolutely depend on those newer tunes. For all I know, I might need to plunk away at those newer songs for a bit longer in regular shows though, depending on the reception they receive. The cassette release is the first object we're making without Katharine doing the layout since 2014, and that doesn't feel quite right to me yet, but I know that this is how things have to be. Excited for the tapes, though. It'll be the first time there's a canvas that plays the albums and EPs straight through as intended, and I hope people like it that way.

I've seen longtime businesses close. I've watched people drift away. I see myself drifting. Change is the only constant right now. Much like mortality, I try not to fear it because it's simply going to come up anyways. As it stands, I'm currently doing better talking about other artists with *Discography* than I am at pushing the music I've poured my blood, sweat, tears, and other genetic material into.

I don't know if I'm okay with this. I also know that it doesn't make a lick of difference if I'm okay with this or not. It's my story. I'm writing it, but it has to happen first.

9-2-18

I don't know where to begin.

I don't intend to take such increasingly long breaks between entries now, but in fairness, research for season three of *Discography* has proven to be quite the time-suck. I thought it'd be easy, doing a season on The Who. I know just enough to shit that out, right?

Nope. Not even close to my own standards. I'm taking everything I know to be true and doing my best to independently confirm each kernel of truth and rumor. One of the hardest parts to get right has been talking about *Quadrophenia*. It's a beautiful and complex piece that's like a musical Mount Everest, and much like *The Wall*? It's one of those records where if you've got the ears to hear it, you don't really ever walk out of the mindset. It's a very personal record to many people, and depending on how you slice it, it's either the most meticulous work of Pete Townshend's life or a series of accidents that all somehow coalesced perfectly.

Three days straight were just spent researching the *Quadrophenia* period because it's so wonderfully dense, right? I thought I'd gotten it right the other day, and I plopped onto the couch to watch an official documentary. In my head, I was thinking it'll be so great to watch a visual confirmation of everything I just wrote for the script, and by the time it was over, I was frantically writing again after realizing all that I'd gotten wrong.

Well, not necessarily "wrong," but there's a narrative that's so commonly accepted that you kind of don't want to fight against some strongly held beliefs, so why muck about with it, right? Somewhere up the middle of the spectrum of truth seems to be where musical journalism lies. I've never had any official training for this kind of thing. More exhausting than method acting.

Or I'm just exhausted in general. While not having much to show for it. Or prove it, rather.

I feel that I should tread very carefully here: there has been a rash of things popping up from my earlier life, my pre-Marc With a C life, and watching them drift into my everyday "try to look forward, most times" goals messes with my brain, because it involves some measure of looking back, which I'm not great at.

Okay, this is where you should be yelling at me: MARC, WHAT DO YOU MEAN YOU DON'T LOOK BACK. THAT'S ALL YOU HAVE FUCKING DONE IN THIS BOOK.

You're right. But I'm personally doing this TO move on. I don't want to spin these yarns as an older person. I don't want to always be looking back in some sort of "high school glory days" manner, hoping to impress eventual grandkids and shit. It's just not attractive to me. I'd rather get it out now while it's still relatively fresh - and that way, if you're ever curious about my first 20 years? You've got a reference book, and I'm free to go on to have new adventures. That's the main reason for this period of my "looking back." (Though I don't discount the chance that I may see all of this very, very different 20 further years from now. In which case, I hope you'll enjoy that book as well.)

But many folks are already beginning to set their rear view mirrors to around 20-ish years ago, seeing where they fit in now, what went wrong, what the future can be, and measuring the distance between where they are versus who they thought that they might be, maybe? Or maybe the present in 2018 is bleak enough that we all can't even imagine a future of any sort? Either way, it's been a bit of an epidemic in my life lately, and one that's actually quite distracting for me.

I should give you an example, but the one that's most pressing for me would involve telling you things that are not my endings to share, if that's clear enough. It's consumed me greatly. Turning my brain into a spin-cycle of circular thinking. Had to call people that knew me way, way back to make sure I hadn't gone completely insane.

I might actually be completely insane, too. There wasn't really a consensus. I'm potentially a little too screwed up to see anything squarely at the moment.

Looks like a bunch of word salad, right? Trust me on this: to tell you what's going on would probably necessitate a whole other book, but a lot of it is already in my lyrics if you know what you're looking for. The only hint that I can give you is that it's not familial.

Meanwhile, the (potentially final) shows with The Rich Weirdoes at Universal Studios took place and were every bit as emotional as one might assume, but not always for predictable reasons. Friday night, word spread that a drunk lady was threatening to shoot people. I heard about it while I was backstage after my opening set, and only learned about it when some folks that had survived the Pulse shootings were having panic attacks after whatever verbiage the lady allegedly used. I didn't hear the voice actually say those things, so I can't confirm that, but the panic that spread through the theater was very, very real.

I don't want to relive it. It wasn't a good position to be in. It was also timely.

Saturday's show was beyond sold-out. the building was made up of about 95% people that have a deep, deep emotional bond with this cast, community, and the soundtracks that I sometimes provide. Juliana seemed taken aback by some of the beautifully pure "here's how your music fit into my life" stories we were told at the merch table again (in the best possible way). While we loaded the gear up and said goodbye to the building, watching a corporation further kill local culture yet again, and she just offered up, "Your fans are really sweet."

But on the last note of my last song? I was doing my end-of-show windmills, and I missed one after slicing my thumb open, which sent the final swing of my arm directly into the body of my guitar, right against the metal stud that the strap locks on to. I haven't been able to play properly since, and I'm trying very hard to not freak out about it.

The next day, someone shot up a game store three hours away from me. My connections to the nerdy industries meant that I was frantically checking on people, while hundreds of names of potential victims flooded my mind.

My mind is just fucked right now. I can carry on conversations. I can do daily tasks. I can wipe myself. I'm thankful for all that I've got. But upstairs, right now? I'm burnt toast, at best.

9-20-18

I've got a bunch of Guided By Voices albums on shuffle, and I'm excited for this. The songs are usually pretty short, and as I've literally been listening to nothing but The Who for weeks on end now, I was quite excited to listen to as many songs as I could by literally anyone else. This'll either be the best season of *Discography* yet, or it'll straight up kill me. The jury is still out. Today alone, I reviewed three albums and spanned the "connective tissue" between them from 1982 to 1985. I never thought I'd be craving a break from Pete Townshend, yet here we are.

I think I'm going to wrap up this section of the book fairly soon. There's too much going on that I can't tell you about and that's simply not fair to you. I don't have any remove or hindsight. Unsure what's fair game to talk about and what isn't.

Many things are in flux, and I can hardly even imagine what my life might look like a month from now. My initial plan was to just write until the end of 2018, then we'd go through the motions of putting this book "together," and it'd be all wrapped up for release right at the 20th anniversary of that fateful night at the Precious gig. Now I just feel like I'm wasting your money and time because I can't tell you anything.

In the interest of not leaving you hanging: some folks from my past have shown up after a long absence, and while I'm happy when they are in my life, I know all too well the heartbreak that will set in when they inevitably leave for reasons I'll never understand or have explained to me. Family problems had gotten bad enough that I found myself sitting in an abandoned parking lot trying to figure out where the hell I'd go next, assuming that I'd have the energy left over to make a move. I'm currently watching life kick the living shit out of my daughter without having any real way to help. I questioned why I'm alive at all.

The drama just doesn't stop. Did a radio interview on WPRK at 7 the other morning. By 3 p.m., the whole campus the station broadcasts from was on lockdown because of an active shooting. I can't even promise myself that I'll live through doing my jobs at this point. Not an easy thing for a person with my thought patterns to deal with or even face. And it's not damage to my person that scares me about shootings – though I don't imagine I'd enjoy having a bullet in me – but rather the pain it would inflict on others.

Somewhat related to the above: a few days ago, I finally announced to a large number of people that I've had an honest-to-goodness stalker for quite some time now. I've referred to them in this book, but it likely wasn't always obvious, and for reasons too painful to share, I'm unable to let this part of my life be known in a very specific way. I have to leave something for myself, even if what I keep for myself hurts. I mostly made the announcement because they seem to be starting to watch my fans, and I was tired of blindsiding said fans with surprise emails that their new follower was actually trying to keep tabs on me through them. Instead, I decided it'd be better to put something vague "out there" so I could point to it whenever I need to. These moves were made after trying to put this all out of my head for the better part of two years, yet seeing this person unable to actually leave my life.

From where I sit, it feels like they've got an all-consuming desire to "win." The trouble is that I'm not playing. I simply have a wall up regarding them, and they just aren't a person in my life any longer, nor will they ever be again, if I can help it (and I'm trying to help it). They just seem to want to provoke a response. When people have an endgame, I can at least fight back against manipulation. When they're just fucking with me, I've got nothing as a defense. It just hurts, and I think that they get off on that, if emotional sadism is a thing.

I'll say that they've brought up that I'm a public figure, which would allow them to get away with much more than if I were just some regular person working in a garage or something. Joke's on them because I'm at least not MUCH of a public figure outside of a few ZIP codes.

It makes me want to quit. Just for safety and peace of mind.

Public figure or no, my friend Heather said something that got through to me during the constant circular thinking and the depression which surrounded. And it was so simple: "Marc, you are a limited resource."

That might not read like much to you, but when she said that, it was like she scrubbed my brain clean for a few minutes. I'm under no delusions that I'm immortal or indestructible. I know I'm far more fragile than I might appear to be. But if I see a situation that I can make better? I'm going to run into that burning building and not even be concerned about my own safety until I've passed out from smoke inhalation. Always been this way, and it just grows as I age. Her reminder that I can't go on this way (with protecting everyone first but putting my own needs and self-care last all the time) was worded so precisely that my own vocabulary fails me to share that sense of relief with you. At this point, Heather has been my longest running friend without interruption, and she gets through to me like no one else can. Her birthday is like two days away. I sent her the new Mitski record because that thing has pretty much saved me on especially bad days in the last few weeks. It may be just a record, but it's a bigger gesture. She'll know.

Despite the tension, the drama, the pain, the illnesses? Glimpses of the muse returned. Finally did that second recording of "Tired Ol' Dicksucker Revue," but I didn't feel that it improved on the original much. Also made a cover of Mitski's "Townie" to go on a new EP released to benefit Aubree and her fight against cystic fibrosis. I have other ideas percolating. Even made a few demos.

I'll even go as far as to say that I've come up with the aim for another Marc With a C record. Not so much a concept or a theme, but the general "what I'd like to make." This step is crucial because then I write a little bit of music, and then the songs start to tell me what they want to do. It's merely my job to listen. I'm good with this.

There's at least a hint of a direction, and that's been evading me since *Obscurity* got so mangled due to that PR firm fuck-up. I saw the interest in the work slipping away, and it's not something I was mentally prepped for. It's been easier to live with, weirdly, because a bunch of other drama distracted me. If I only focused on *Obscurity* not really making much of an impact (that I can see, at least), I'd be leading a pretty charmed life. Instead, all of the drama makes me happy that anyone listened to the new album at all, and it becomes a happier thing. A clear bit of proof that music can't be all that I do, no matter how much I think that's my calling.

And this is only what's happening in my house, yard, inbox, and head. I'm not even touching on the completely ludicrous political environment that I'm surrounded by. There's too much right here in front of me to care about the size of the 45th president's dick.

That's seriously what everyone was on about today.

I am going to get through this. So are you. I will be stronger, happier, and better able to care for those who would like to accept care from me. So will you.

We're going to make it.

Light at the end of a tunnel.

Some other platitudes.

Either way, it can't rain all the time. But if it somehow does? I've found my internal umbrella again, and it might be a little rusty and ragged, but damn it, I'm not letting the dreary shit stop me anymore.

## 10-25-18

Two days ago, I woke up to an email from Tim Labonte alerting me to the fact that the video for "One Of These Are Gonna Be Your Day" is somehow on the official ballot for the 61st annual Grammy awards. This had nothing to do with me, I was the last to know, and the shock still hasn't worn off. The video was fraught with deadline problems, but Tim and Madison Durand made the perfect video for a song that I absolutely love. And now? It's everywhere. Fox News affiliates, Orlando's papers, blogs, etc. You name it, and all of the sudden, this video, single, radio airplay in states I've never been to, and the *Obscurity* album itself ended up with a second lease on life.

To make this clear: I'm quite honored but am a little in shock. I know there's no chance of us making it to the top 5 actual nominees for Best Music Video, and awards don't really mean a ton to me in the first place, but the idea that more people can hear the song? That's what matters to me. It's a song of hope and how endings aren't always something to be feared. I think this is the perfect time for such a song to be heard. And frankly? If I have to be remembered for one single song, this is the one I'd have picked.

But if we're being serious? I almost didn't make it here. Allow me to try to explain.

I've (clearly) been in a not-so-great place for a while. Besides my usual battles with anxiety, depression, and bipolarity, I've also been incredibly overworked to get the new season of *Discography* done, and there have been uproars and even displacement for/from my loved ones.

I found myself so in need of a day off in early October that I literally went to a town in a state I've never been to (if we're not counting airport layovers).

No one could reach me besides those closest to me, and even if you could, you couldn't find me. It shouldn't have gone this way, but there were multiple breaking points, and each one brought me closer to things I couldn't undo.

I'll focus on one seemingly unimportant thing: around a week and a half ago, I'd gone to see David Byrne at a seemingly nice Orlando venue that I'll not name in hopes that I won't be sued. It was a miserable experience at that venue: their sightlines were so bad that there was literally no way to see the show from our section once people stood up. Let alone the stage. I tried to tell an usher, and after keeping me in the hallway while they scrambled to come up with something (though one usher confided in me, "This place wasn't really built for rock concerts; happens every time people stand in that section," making me believe that this was a known problem). They got a different vantage point for us by the final song. With another completely obstructed view.

It took the venue four days to even bother to refuse a refund, but they (for some reason) offered me free tickets to see another show there, but, um, how would I actually see it? Smarmy and rude, they were. Not a fan.

But a bit about why this show was so important to me. The album *Stop Making Sense* was the soundtrack to early traumatic experiences. Also the soundtrack to some good times. But on one specific occasion —

I was forcibly removed from my home (for good reason) at around 12 years old. I didn't (completely) realize at that time that what happened at home wasn't normal or healthy and that a kid DEFINITELY shouldn't have been involved, but I mentioned something about my situation to one teacher, and by the end of that day, I was being shipped out of state.

The situation was bad enough at home that I decided to have a prepacked bag "just in case," which should illustrate just how untenable my living situation was. No one had ever suggested such a thing to me that I can recall. If I'd not done that, I'd have likely left with nothing. I made it out with the suitcase that I now sell CDs from at my shows and a Walkman with a tape inside.

On that plane, circa 1990 or so, upon realizing just how beat up the Walkman was, it also dawned on me that I didn't have headphones. That was when I finally cried. A sweet lady on the airplane gave me her headphones, I plugged them in and – nothing. But if I bent the cord JUST right? I could get one earphone to kind of work. "Once In a Lifetime" filled one half of my head, and I sobbed tears of joy.

Those nine songs that David Byrne had done with Talking Heads on that tape were the soundtrack to losing everything, a terrifying prospect for a traumatized child with anxiety, low self-esteem, and a newfound PTSD (which went undiagnosed for years).

When I could hear the strains of "Once In a Lifetime" through the concert hall door in 2018? I felt ripped off. Taken advantage of. Like no one cared. Small stuff, yes, but it internally rewound my heart and the rest of my insides to the memories of losing everything years ago. Turned out to be a massive trigger. I lost it. I really, really lost it. People could see it but didn't seem to care. Those who would hear me out also didn't care.

Ultimately, I realized I needed some closure but wasn't sure how to get it – especially as David would only be doing a few more shows in the USA. To even see the show? I'd have to rearrange EVERYTHING, and I'd have to fly to San Antonio to see the one non-sold-out gig left. (After that, he'd be going to Europe, and it's not like this guy tours constantly, nor is he getting younger, so ...)

It wasn't cheap. It wasn't easy. But if you'd seen me since the Orlando venue debacle versus today, being home, having seen the show properly in San Antonio? You'd get why this HAD to go this way. And you could see the closure all over my face.

Three songs into that show in Texas, around "I Zimbra"? I just started uncontrollably sobbing. But it was the best cry ever, and it lasted for 90 minutes. A happy cry. A restorative cry. A cry of closure after years of not even realizing that closure could be found this way.

Music really CAN heal. After that experience, and the closure I was lucky enough to acquire? I felt strong enough to fight for another day. Since then, I've seen two surprise shows by The Breeders, Emmit got a Squiddy tattoo, and now the Grammys know about a song that might make someone else feel better one day.

It's worth fighting your demons to stay alive.


11-20-18

Here I am forgetting to even write journal entries. I don't want to leave anything out, but I can't possibly remember everything that went down since my last writing.

Basically, all that Grammy stuff? I don't know how it'll pan out, what'll come of it and how seriously I should take it. Insert – "it's an honor to even be-" statement here – but it's propelled a bunch of other stuff into motion. A couple of appearances on (get this) Fox News. The first one was the most interesting to talk about:

At 11 on a Monday morning, I was to meet a cameraman and a news anchor at The Geek Easy to film some B-roll and an interview so the network affiliate can run a feel-good "local boy makes good" story. Cool. I know how to do that. The anchor never showed up, though. Instead, I was interviewed by a poor camera dude named Nick that had no idea why he was in a closed-down empty nightclub first thing in the morning.

After he kind of got wind of what his story was supposed to be, and after maybe 10 minutes of asking me questions while the video played in the background – thanks to Jay from The Geek Easy being the best one-night-stand-roadie imaginable – he asked if we could get some B-roll of me actually playing the song in question "live." Perfectly cromulent thing to ask because I'd brought my guitar, and we were in front of a stage and PA, so that didn't seem egregious.

An important thing to note: for reasons beyond my control, I'd been awake for somewhere between 36 and 48 hours at this point. I figured that at worst I'd play the song twice, you know? I downed a bunch of energy drinks – very out of character for me – so I could look halfway conscious during the interview. I'm pretty good on my feet, so I wasn't concerned about the brain fog that energy drinks sometimes instill in me. Besides, I've got a lot of experience performing and interacting while deprived of sleep, so this should have been a piece of cake, right?

I lost count of how many times the cameraman had me perform the song at around the 10th rendition. The energy drinks wore off halfway through the first verse of the first performance. Each subsequent run-through suffered for some reason or another. More or less, I did a private hourlong show for a camera guy and a freelance roadie consisting of only one song over and over. That was the first bit of "Marc needs to be there" press coverage for this strange little "One Of These Are Gonna Be Your Day" thing. The weirdness continued, but by the time I was doing interviews with people I already knew at *The US Show*, I started getting pretty comfortable talking about it all.

Played one gig with The Rich Weirdoes at a really beautiful venue called Plaza Live, and the song was getting enough traction to where I needed to start wedging it into even the Rocky Horror pre-shows, which are traditionally reserved for more "edgy" fare. But somehow, even in that environment, this intensely earnest song went over, the audience was quiet and respectful, erupting into loud cheers at the end of the tune. It's bizarro world stuff. A thousand people singing your song back to you when you thought the song was a flop just a week prior will confuse you.

Since then, I've watched Spotify and YouTube numbers creep up. It's not "huge" or anything, but the song is entering "minor hit" territory. Spotify is sticking it on official playlists, and I'm pretty sure it's on some "viral chart" by now, but I wouldn't know how to look that up.

I'm good with all of this, by the way.

Last weekend, I played a benefit show called Snipfest, which was trying to raise money for trans youth to get their top surgeries. I was certainly the oldest person on the bill by a country mile. Many of the band members would come up to me through the night, thanking me for playing for free and telling me how much they used to love me when they were in high school.

I am "I loved you in high school" years old. I'm good with this, as well.

Did a photoshoot with this cat named Mike Dunn who seems to have thrown every single bit of his human energy into putting on the most intense three-day, DIY folk music festival that Orlando has ever seen. It's called Folk Yeah, and I'm closing the second day. I'm happy that I can play predominantly punk shows like Snipfest and make sense but also make sense on a folk bill. I can do comedy festivals. I can play nerdy music shows with folks who make chiptunes, heavy metal versions of video game music, and nerdcore hip hop. I'm strangely malleable, yet I don't really waver from "the muse."

I'm good with that, too. Really good with it. It's all just music, anyways.

In the "poetic justice" department, the venue that treated me so horribly during the David Byrne show dropped the ball on putting Hamilton tickets on sale, and the entirety of Orlando can see just how inept they actually are. That was pretty nice, but I should probably try hard to not find delight in watching people fail.

Been struggling with writing stuff that I like. I can write and even consider something to be finished, but the finished music isn't exciting me at all. I'm finding a lot of joy in revisiting older material lately. Had to do a livestream gig for Patreon backers where I'd perform the entirety of *Normal Bias*, but I didn't have much time to rehearse the album in the week leading up to the show, so I played the LP a lot. I found myself really excited that this album even exists. I couldn't get over how little I'd even want to go back and change it assuming such a thing ever needed to be done. To an extent, I do sort of wish that "Please Don't Go" had found its way to the final track order, but I also doubt I'd have liked any future recordings of the song more than the initial demo, so it's a moot point. *Obscurity* feels like the best record I've ever made, but

*Normal Bias* trails it by fractions of points. It's exactly what I wanted to make, and the lack of compromises went a long way. Something I'll be keeping in mind as I try to figure out what is going on with this inability to finish a song that I feel is worth releasing.

It's not limited to that album, either. The band has been working on relearning the title track to my first album, *Human Slushy*, in rehearsal. I've been looking forward to each attempt. Like, I'm really, really digging it. It's not the best tune or anything, nor do I even relate to it, but it's fun to play and sing, and I'm happy that it gets to be a Marc With a C thing. As I look back on my history, as anniversaries approach, all of these records are starting to really and truly make sense to the guy that made them for – in some cases – the very first time.

12-3-18

Y'know, I'd actually hoped that this would be my final word for this book, but the last week or so was pretty strange, and I'm in such a state of limbo that there's no real burn out or fade away type of ending. I only have one more show scheduled for the year, and I suspect that after the dust settles from that annual Holiday show, I'll be able to boil this all down to something.

I'm sick. Like, really sick. Not "gonna die" sick, but "can't do much of anything" sick. It hit me last week so suddenly that I actually had the "gonna die" thing run through my mind. Still here, though.

Last week, I'd played at that Folk Yeah festival. Turns out that I was closing the smallest stage, and very few people seemed to know that said stage existed. And by stage, I mean a patio hidden behind a bar with one speaker stick and a microphone. I already had a pretty weird setlist lined up (since I couldn't plan for atmosphere and had no idea how the interactive stuff would work there), but as I was the last act, I could play for as long as I felt like it, but I didn't feel right.

I'd woken up to a bit of personal news that kicked me in the face and couldn't shake it all day. I also felt physically drained, but I thought I was maybe just taking some complicated news quite poorly. I felt like I'd played for two hours to around four people, but not only did I barely clock in at 33 minutes on "stage," I inadvertently skipped songs on my written setlist. Talked with a Canadian fan about music for a few hours, and my spirits lifted a bit. The next day, I didn't feel wonderful, but I thought it was just remnants of being at a music festival: few places to wash your hands, everyone is sweaty, germs everywhere, etc. By the following Tuesday?

Ugh, I don't want to describe it. It even makes me squeamish. Nicole hadn't seen me in that kind of state pretty much ever, and it took days to be able to walk from the bedroom to the bathroom without some fluid trying to escape my body without vertigo also trying to knock me down.

Five days in, and I'd canceled every rehearsal, interview, appearance, etc. Again. Even some type of NPR interview which really killed me to bail on, but I couldn't even drive myself to the hospital, so there wasn't much I could've done. Hell, I was too weak to complete sentences for the first two days. Now I'm walkin' and talkin', but I wouldn't describe it as comfortable. I know I need rest, but this is already a big week on top of needing to make up the time where I was out of commission. Really hoping the holiday show goes well considering I lost a week of promo and prep. I'm really thankful that Emmit and Jim were so understanding.

By now, I'm hoping that you've picked up that my intent with this book was to answer most of what one could ever ask about the recording act named Marc With a C. One day, if I tell you what my process for making this book up was, I think that'll be clearer. At the same time, I tried to leave things and actions that belong to Marc Sirdoreus: The Human Being, mostly out of this. There's little about that guy that would interest you, and frankly, it's better this way. I get to keep things for myself, and you don't get useless information. Really, at best? This book should only ever enhance existing Marc With a C records.

12-9-18

It's very late at night, the day after the annual holiday marathon show. It's the first one where I've genuinely thought to myself that I'm getting too old for this. I mean physically, not in some ageist way. I've recently been falling asleep to the pro-shot shows from The Who's 2006 tour, an infamous string of dates where Roger Daltrey battled his own throat every single night. Sometimes unsuccessfully. You could feel that the audience was rooting for him, too.

But I don't want to become that. I'd rather you had a good time because I gave you something of quality, not because I'm trying really hard but ultimately unable to deliver what you've paid for. It's just how I'm wired.

I mention all of this because, well, remember how I was sick? It came raging back at the show. I played my first song at 8:30. We were offstage by 12:30 a.m.-ish. But by 12:47, I was throwing up outside instead of signing records that people were buying at the merch stand. Halfway through the third set, every part of my body had started to cramp exactly as it had when the sickness really blindsided me. We dropped two songs in the encore, but by one fans count, we still did 46 songs. I felt horrible, as it turns out I have an intense flu. Plus, I could see that people were waiting to talk to me and take pictures, but I needed to be at home in bed. I rushed out of there, and thankfully, Nicole was running merch, so she was able to load that stuff out while I took the drive home, eventually collapsing into a cramped vomit-ball.

I'd only eaten a banana and a protein bar. I'd only consumed water. But what I'd not done was take care of Marc Sirdoreus: The Human Being. He wasn't ready to do his job again, and especially not for four hours straight.

I should have canceled for my health. But all the folks that would say things like "I didn't know you were sick!" "You sounded great!" "[insert song here] really meant a lot to me, thank you for playing it," etc.? They wouldn't have seen the show. And frankly, there wasn't much reason to think I wasn't out of the proverbial woods. Nicole and I talked this morning about how anyone that would have seen me the day of the show in the afternoon, yet had later seen me cancel the show due to illness? They'd have no doubt thought I was lying. Faking. A hypochondriac. Any number of things, but definitely not ill. I know that, and there was just no other way for this to go. Besides, I'd made it through my rescheduled NPR interview and performance, so I kind of already was working again!

Usually I spend the day after most gigs checking out recordings of the previous night to see what went wrong/right, and what needs improvement. Today, I didn't do that. I laid on the couch listening to the newly minted vinyl issue of Paul McCartney's *Red Rose Speedway*. That album is from around 1973, I think? I always liked it, but everyone always treats it like some lesser work of his, and I can't fathom why. It has everything anyone likes about him in one place (besides the other three Beatles, I guess). But? Dig this – initially, it was a double album. That double album was rejected for some reason and shelved. This month, they've finally put it out as originally intended under the moniker *Red Rose Speedway Reconstructed*. Of course, it has a very different vibe than the single-disc version that I grew up with, but it's the rare case where it's absolutely improved in every way. To my ears, at least. And it's chill enough that you can listen to it while being sick to your stomach and not feel like you're listening to nails on a chalkboard or something.

But back to the show! We all flubbed a bunch of things through the evening, but the three of us at those points would just give the player that screwed up a knowing smirk, as if to say, "I heard that, but don't worry, I'm gonna fuck up wayyyy worse in a minute." I think it's kind of cute.

Oh, and I'd guess that according to the date, I've been Marc With a C for 19 years this month. Cool!

12-19-18

This past Sunday, I did my usual monthly on-camera livestream concert for Patreon backers. For the last few months, I've been performing one of my own albums in full. This time? I made it available to everyone that supports me on that site – and frankly, those supporters are why this book even exists at all – and though I did do my best to make it especially clear that this one would be different? When I began to play the *Linda Lovelace For President* in full album on Sunday, I started with "It's All Gonna Be Alright" in front of my makeshift stage curtains like usual. And after the line "please direct your attention to the stage," I launched into "All My Drug Use Is Accidental," and ...

Chris Zabriskie popped out from behind the curtain, sat to my left playing an updated version of his old makeshift drum set made of tin cans, cardboard boxes and the like (usually referred to as the "wuckarnnn"). And you know, after having a few days to process it all?

I think that was the best time I've had playing music since I was in Canada.

I wanted to wait a few days before I made that kind of declarative statement. There have been good shows. In fact, on some days, I'd consider the barely announced 2018 run-through of the one-person *Obscurity Show* might be in my top five favorite shows I've ever done, but few have felt so natural. Like the music was just leaking out of me (if you don't count having to use a lyrical cheat sheet for "Debt Is Only What You Make Of It" because that song has always been a nemesis for me to perform for some reason).

Thought about all the variables, but ultimately, though Chris and I decided to do this maybe a month prior? We didn't rehearse at all until two hours before the show. We knew the songs, and however they came across would be honest: exactly what it sounds like when two dudes play songs together with minimal rehearsal after nearly five years apart musically. But? It worked. It completely worked. It was all happy vibes, and there's nothing at all that I'd change. Refreshing.

There were a few people asking if this meant we'd be doing more together in the future. The answer is: I have no idea, but there's been no discussion of a future for us musically. We're better to each other when we don't work together, I feel. Besides, I love playing with Jim and Emmit and see no need to have competing lineups. But ultimately, I think it was so much fun because we made it super low-pressure. Little was riding on this. Basically, if we just appeared together and tried? That would have been good enough. Instead, two pals naturally fell right back into what we used to do. It's nice knowing that we could if we wanted to. But that's not what the muse is telling either of us to do.

I'm sure it's glaringly apparent that I have a strange relationship with the *Linda Lovelace For President* album. To me, the record plays through like a million half-finished compromises. However, the people that it touched are heavily passionate about their emotional connection to the thing, so technically, it's just right! But it's odd, this position. To be the creator and not have any real understanding of what made this work so well for those folks. I can never do anything like it again because I don't know what I did "right" because the whole album feels ... yeah. You get it. A circular fascination with a record I don't always like to hear, but I like all of the songs contained on it.

Of course, there's also the fact that Chris wrote three songs on the album. Singing the harmonies to "Born Vintage" with Chris again after so many years was just ... it was right. It felt good. It makes me want to keep making things to find more situations that feel just as right.

There are a lot of uncertain factors heading into next year. Factors that blindsided me right as I got even more ill this year. But that 50 minutes that Chris and I spent playing and singing together made me feel like "hey, music is gonna help me get through this," and I haven't felt that way in a good long while.

Thanks, music. (If you're reading this.)

1-28-19

Well, that's been a massive gap between entries, huh? I don't even remember the last thing I talked about, and a lot has happened since. Today, though? I thought I'd tell you about my cats.

I am not actually a cat owner, mind you. In fact, I'm deathly allergic to them. The only pet that currently lives in my house is our dwarf hotot rabbit named Alice Cooper. When Alice's twin sister, Tammy Faye Bakker, passed away, we noticed Alice was spending a lot of time staring out of the sliding glass door. We sort of have the dining room blocked off as a big room that Alice can run around in, you see. I thought at first that she might be wistfully missing her sister. And for a while, I even thought that maybe when she saw her own reflection, she thought she could see her sister on the other side of the glass. (Really, these bunnies were practically identical.)

Nope. Turned out she was lonely and getting as close to the feral cats that hang out in my backyard as she could.

I thought it'd be a good idea to start feeding them so they'd stick around for Alice's sake. First, I dumped out some tuna for the kitty we saw most often, one I'd named Bleedin' Gums Murphy. Gave him a can of tuna. He has a bad leg and had an injured eye, so it felt like the least I could do.

Word spread to the other feral cats in the neighborhood, I think. The very next day, Bleedin' Gums arrived with two other kitties in tow. We named them Snowball and Snowball II. I started buying a lot more tuna.

But then the Snowballs started bringing baby kittens around that were also hungry. After a quick call to Cap Blackard, cat owner extraordinaire, they told me I should be going toward dry food since I couldn't afford THIS much tuna every day.

There was one particularly bad night almost a month ago. One of those no-sleep/the-whole-world-hates-you/your-life-and-career-are-over-forever nights that just would not let up, even when the sun rose. I left the bedroom I'd been stewing in and found the Snowballs waiting outside of that window. And then they moved back to the sliding glass door when I walked to the dining room. They were ... following me? Checking on me, maybe? I went outside and dumped some food out. They just stared at me. They weren't hungry.

Look, I know this sounds insane, but I have a witness to these events, and I swear that this actually happened.

Those two cats in particular now just sort of live under the window to whichever room in the house I happen to be in. When I go outside, they keep a few paces from me as if to say, "Hey, we know we'll make you sick, so we aren't getting any closer than this," and it's super bizarre. I wouldn't believe this was true if someone tried to describe it to me either, in all honesty.

But somehow? There it is. Some very real connection that these two cats seem to have with me. They just want to be close to me, but not too close. It's like they just want me to know that they care. I've never seen anything like this. The cats don't even do the same to Nicole, even though she makes sure they are fed when I'm away. Just me. It's a really weird and beautiful situation, one that made me cry legitimately happy tears at a time where there was no happiness to be found.

*Discography*'s season on The Who is live, and people seem to be digging it. It got pretty buried under the band doing a bunch of press to announce another tour, one that very few of us could have predicted, least of all me.

I'm currently putting together info on our next two seasons: on The Breeders and Black Sabbath. The Black Sabbath stories are especially fun to research, truth be told. Some of their early '80s excesses inspired the script of *This Is Spinal Tap*, so there's no way you can't have a pretty good time when you immerse yourself in that world.

Oh, and ... *The Obscurity Show*. Nothing with this show has gone to plan, due to illness and pretty much any factor one can dream up. I know it's worthy to push through and make the show happen, but it's been like playing Paperboy on difficult the whole time.

Yeah, I said that in a silly way, but it's best that I do that rather than go into the gory details. Really, about 20 things happened consecutively to turn a dream into ... well, nearly nothing but a dream that never came true.

But now?

We have dates. We have a venue, the Downtown Arts Collective. But at a very high cost: though many of the ideals and general points of the show will not change too much, the folks I'll be working with will be different. It's going to look a lot different than originally envisioned, but it's been becoming "minimalist DIY theater," which is what the script was demanding as it was being tightened on sleepless nights, and that's something that suits what I do much better than where it could've headed.

Unfortunately, I think I lost a beloved friend in the process. A few things I'll admit: I was trying to juggle personal problems, a massive bout of depression, a case of vertigo so intense that it demanded medical care, and a familial change I was completely unprepared for that I'm not going to mention just yet. My head was just unable to handle it all, and when it all came together at me, all at once, I just straight up had a breakdown.

The phone wouldn't stop ringing. The inbox wouldn't stop dinging. I couldn't collect my thoughts or even have a moment to decide how to proceed at all. Eventually I found myself hanging up on people each time they gave me a new reason to cry. Not my finest hour, but bipolarity sometimes makes decisions for me, and I hate that I can't always be completely in control of what might push me into a low swing. I tried to write letters of apology, but it feels like I'm apologizing for having a disability, which also feels not quite right.

Nicole saved the day with *The Obscurity Show*. There's so much more that could be said about that, but none that is fit to print. Just know that this gap in writing? The book nearly ended without being finished or released, and? So did Marc With a C as a going concern. Having the chance to complete what I've begun is why I'm still here at all.

And the cats, if we're being totally honest here.

There is now hope were there was previously none to be found. Maybe the future will be good?

## 2-6-19

I'm writing this on the back-half of one of the most eventful 24 hours I've ever seen on a personal level. I'd delve into it here, but it's not my story to tell. I'm a bit shaken, but hey, I've gotta keep up these diary entries, right?

If you've made it this far? Yeah, I definitely fought a hideous depression through 2018, had breakdowns in both October and December, and I think I've been pretty clear about that. I mention it because I'm anticipating a specific word from folks around that section of the book: "whiny."

If that's the word that came to mind for you? Please remember that I fight genuine diagnosed mental illnesses on a daily basis. Sometimes I lose the fight – even for a whole year, as it turns out.

I mention this because I lose friends over this kind of thing often. I've learned to not "blame" my actions on the illnesses because they aren't an excuse; they are a hurdle. I don't always jump high enough. I could list 'em all to everyone I meet on a business card upon first meeting people, I suppose, but what'd be the point? That feels more like an excuse. But here's why I was tempted to maybe do that very thing as the introduction to this book:

I don't tour for long stretches, and even one-off shows around the country are rare, and that's for a very, very good reason: I have too many of these illnesses to be stuck away from home all by myself in a potentially bad situation. Whether it's the leg issues, the throat troubles, or the struggles "upstairs?" It's pretty simple, really; I don't want to make my already-sometimes-dodgy quality of life any worse by throwing travel stress into the mix.

Let me stress that again. It's not that I don't want to see your town. It's not that I don't want to sing my songs in front of you. It's truly, genuinely, an "I might not make it home" thing, if I were to be gone for more than about two weeks.

And even two weeks is pushing it. Keep in mind that if you want to leave the state of Florida from my house? It'd still take you at least four hours to make it to Georgia, and that's just to cross a state line. This is one big, big state. If I happened to live in, say, Ohio, with a bunch of other states adjacent? I could probably "tour." My disabilities, fears, and general location all lead up to: "Meh, I'll just stay home and make records, I guess."

But that's not what I'm doing this year! I want to fight all of that and try it out, one more time, before my body really lets the aging process go nuts. Maybe a few one-offs, maybe a week of shows up the coast, but I need to at least attempt it, for my own head. To never think about "What if you LIKE life on the road" on my deathbed.

I mean, assuming I get a deathbed. You never know how or when you're gonna go. And assuming that the upcoming familial changes allow for any manner of touring at all?

I plan to work on *The Obscurity Show* until I can't work on it anymore. It's becoming something that I'm feeling very strongly about, just as I did when I finished *Bubblegum Romance, Normal Bias, Popular Music, Exactly Where I Am, Obscurity* itself. I felt closure and a sense of "this is exactly what you're meant to be doing." I just had to let the muse change the shape and scope of the show. That's not always the easiest thing to notice about yourself, that you're fighting the muse. Instead, I think it'd be more fun to give the muse free reign in 2019.

As in: does it inspire me? Good. Let's go.

It's been too complicated for far too long. Now's the time to just run right at the elusive inspiration and see what it really wants with me. I've paid my dues. Now it's time for the muse to point me in the right direction. It usually does.

One thing I do need to work on is being better about saying "no." It's a powerful and simple word, but I've never been able to shake that whole "I'm lucky anyone wants to listen to me at all" thing. It's meant that up until now, you pretty much could have booked me to play at the opening of a bag of chips. I'm gonna stop playing shows that I don't want to play, as best as I can.

Today, I released "Perfect For Me" as the fifth single from *Obscurity* with a video that Mike Dunn shot, and while I haven't "officially" announced *The Obscurity Show*, there was some accompanying verbiage that made mention that it's a single from an upcoming theatrical presentation.

Just this past weekend, Vikka Leoni did a photoshoot with me, styled kind of as the stage set for *The Obscurity Show* might be, which is heavy on harsh white and washed-out surfaces. They did some really cool practical effects – busted out a prism on an overcast day, had their partner hold up my guitar just out of frame, and used the crystalline object to reflect the guitar back onto me and into their lens. It was pretty neat to watch, and the results were even cooler. Once upon a time, Vikka and I had a misunderstanding, and I didn't think we'd be friends anymore, but I think we both fought our individual anxieties to do our best to keep the friendship intact.

That's why people like me are driven to fight our inner demons rather than to let them take over. Good things happen when you overcome. And even if there isn't a literal pot of gold at the end of your figurative "overcome rainbow," the sense of accomplishment for jumping high enough to clear the hurdle is more than enough.

## 2-14-19

Last Saturday, a local record shop named Foundation got a vinyl copy of the not-so-easy-to-find mono mix of Jefferson Airplane's *Surrealistic Pillow* LP, the famous record with "Somebody To Love" and "White Rabbit." I really love the group and have since I was a kid, and it was only in the last decade or so that I'd heard about how punchy the original mono mixes of their first three albums were in comparison to their stereo counterparts. This was the last of the three I'd need to complete that l'il collection. Called the shop, had 'em put the album on hold for me, and set off on the road, excited to come home with my long-lusted-after LP.

I was about three miles from home and approaching an intersection. At said intersection, I had a green light, but I'd noticed a police officer with their lights on at the perpendicular cross-street. He was clearly trying to get traffic to stop so he could rush off to a call. So I yielded to the right, slowing down, I reached over to turn on my hazard lights just in ca—

WHAM.

I think I was in pure shock when someone slammed into me from behind. Ever get into the mess of a car accident simply for following the law? If not, please allow me to assure you that it sucks. It also sucked when the police officer explained that the driver who'd hit me did so on a suspended license after receiving a number of tickets in a very short amount of time. Their car got it pretty bad, but ...

It *really* sucked when the insurance inspector told me that there's a good chance that my relatively new-ish car would have to be totaled. That'll teach me to do the right thing, eh?

The suckiest part are the injuries. Basically, something went all screwy in my back, and according to the fine folks at the emergency room, that pain is just going to radiate all through my body for a while. It's in my thighs, my feet, obviously in my back itself, and, yup, I had to cancel a show that we (thankfully) hadn't been able to announce to the public yet.

Nicole has been a great help in this period, of course. Can't put the guitar on yet, too much weight. I basically just have to take the rest of this month as easy as I can physically, and then maybe I can get back to work if I allow myself time to heal – not something I'm great at. Luckily, *Discography* can be written while I'm horizontal.

The car will probably be fine. I'll be fine. Still shaken, but it seems like everyone has a good car accident story, and I was probably due for mine. Story of my life: punished for doing the right thing.

I did leave the house to get the Jefferson Airplane record in a rental car yesterday, though. Priorities, you know?


3-3-19

Was able to wear a guitar comfortably about a week ago, so I got riiiiiight back to work. I mean, I hardly even stopped, but I definitely didn't play the guitar much at all due to pain. It was almost a month without playing guitar and— oof. I'm not doing that again. You can forget a lot REALLY quickly. The instrument felt foreign at first, but now it at least feels a bit like something I did once upon a time again.

Two days ago, *The Obscurity Show* was announced. A lot of "OH MY GOD" and "I MUST GO TO THIS" responses were seen, but it didn't seem to spread much. I'm going to really have to come up with something interesting to get this event in front of new eyes. I even screwed up the early press releases: the images I was sending to news outlets were too large and kept getting lost in spam folders. Either way, there's at least enough interest to kind of get a little momentum going, and that's as good of a promotional starting point as any, right?

Today I did another session at Orlando's Melrose Center to record some tracks in front of a live studio audience for the upcoming compilation: namely, I initially wanted to use the versions of "Music Geek," "Amy, It's Kevin," "Music Can Heal," and "Happy To Be Alive" from *The Real Live Sound Of Marc With a C,* as they are (to my ears) superior to their studio counterparts, and the songs have had massive lyrical changes in the intervening years. But there was a problem with the vocal tracks from that show, and unfortunately, almost any further attempts to master it a different way would only exacerbate it and make the issues more obvious. Some friends and hardcore fans crammed into the live room of the studio, and I went for it with a short little seven-song session. Right now, I'll likely use five of them. Had to restart "Music Can Heal" because somehow the lyrics went completely off my radar mid-song. I thought it was embarrassing, but it actually worked out fairly well – the room was pretty understanding. I mean, sometimes you blow a take in the studio. It happens.

Actually, the more I think about it, it's weird that I only screwed up the one thing.

I found out a few days prior that Melrose wanted to film it, which I was initially not happy about, but that was because I was told at the worst possible time. I mean, this might be hard to believe, but I'd just come from trying to meet with an insurance agent to settle some stuff for my accident, but they'd given me an address that was a cow pasture. A legit cow pasture. Literally led me to the middle of fucking nowhere. No cell reception. No insurance adjustor. Nothin' but cows.

I'd refused to get out of the car because this seemed a lot like the kickoff to a horror film. Finally got it resolved. The agent isn't a serial killer, but they are very bad at their job. Can't even get the address to their own office right?

When I was finally reaching civilization again and was half-scared out of my wits and half-fuming from this treatment, THAT is when the phone rang, and I was told that the session was to be filmed. I bit the hapless caller's head off but apologized mightily. I didn't really have a problem with it. I knew they were potentially trying to start a TV show out of some sessions filmed at the Melrose Center, but I also know that I swear enough that little of my footage would ever be usable.

The session went nicely. Actually, too nicely. Everyone was so respectful and docile that I had to do some creative editing to make it all fit together properly.

But beyond that (and being sick to death of studying Black Sabbath for *Discography*), I'm in the best spirits I've been in since ... I don't know. Years. I know what I'm doing. I know what I'm making. I know why I'm making it. I know what I hope to achieve: completing the vision.

Oh sure, that seems silly, right? "Really, Marc? You're excited to finish what you've started?"

Yes. Because you have no idea how many times I was faking it while I was falling apart inside. Now that I'm back to being happy to play, excited to write, and have secretly been doing some work behind the scenes to figure out what Marc With a C and Marc Sirdoreus even **have** in common anymore? I know where I'm going and what needs to be done. Creating hasn't felt so positive since maybe the first draft of *The Obscurity Show* script.

This is a massive internal change, and I refuse to squander it.

3-9-19

Just woke up, sipping on coffee. Played in Tampa last night for the first time in ages. Bit of a funny story about it – well, maybe?

A few months ago, I start getting emails from a band named Cartridge Carnage, a VGM band, and they really, really want to play a show with me. I make it clear that I love playing, but I am quite busy, so it's hard to book me at the moment, but if they should have a good gig lined up, give me a ring, right?

They book that gig at a place called Lowry Parcade. I asked upfront (because I have to): is it a "listening" room or an "atmosphere" room? If it's the former, I can do my usual solo Marc With a C storytellin' show. If it's the latter, I'm not uninterested, but I do have to play a very different show than some attendees might have expected. I just needed to know upfront so I'd know what to rehearse! I was assured that it's a "listening" room.

I arrive, and immediately I'm overwhelmed by the noisy atmosphere. It's a rad place, we have a bunch of bars like this in Orlando: kind of like a sports bar, but for geeks. Pinball and arcade games line the walls, craft beer is served at the bar, and it's a generally feel-good/good-time place! Trouble is it's very noisy, and no matter what, I'm gonna end up mostly being atmosphere. Which happens to be what I didn't rehearse.

Showtime nears. A number of fans show up: they'll want to see the Marc With a C storytellin'/interactive show. My sound options are a small mixer and two small speakers provided by the venue. I can't turn it up too loudly or my acoustic guitar will feedback with a low hum that'll drive everyone crazy. I'd just have to hope for the best at a lower-than-I-would-like volume.

At the center of the room, in my direct line of sight? Probably 40 people who came for me? But they are flanked on the left and right sides of the room by multitudes of people who really didn't come for this, and they're quite loud. This began a 55-minute set where I tried to tune the wings of the building out and focus on the folks up the middle of the venue, who I dubbed "center beef" for the evening, and just do the show I'd prepared. Sometimes it was tough – gentler songs like "Music Geek" and "One Of These Are Gonna Be Your Day" would get lost in the noise and excitement and flashing lights. Reviewing the tape of the show, I can hear me trying to win everyone over, smatterings of applause, but the smatterings got louder after each song. By the time I got to the closing "Motherfuckers Be Bullshittin"/"Life's So Hard"/"Happy To Be Alive" trifecta, participation had succeeded (at least with center beef), and it sounds like I drew more and more people in. I had to work for it, but I think I got 80% of the place on the same page with me, which is not always the case when you do very specialized shows like mine.

But the confusion lingered in my mind: why would they tell me it's a listening room when it's just clearly the exact opposite of that? And then Cartridge Carnage started.

The earth practically shook under our feet. They weren't even going through the PA – they were oppressively and unapologetically loud. You had no choice but to listen. Every time they'd played there? Everyone listened. They had told me the truth! They have a lot of young and nervous energy but some serious raw talent as well. I did get a kick out of them playing video game soundtracks while people played completely different games around the perimeter – must've led to some real cognitive dissonance for some!

It was a nice distraction from documentaries that the world is currently obsessed with that don't present any facts. I really don't want to experience the death of truth in my lifetime, but I don't know how to stop our overnight willingness to just accept disinformation. Eventually, I just had to do my best to not look at social media anymore. I can't let the current darkness impede my newly regained drive. I feel like I'm almost ready to take the training wheels off again, which has been a long, long, long time coming.

3-26-19

Last week, I canceled all plans for public performances until summer. Every interview. Everything. I'm finally ready to start talking about this.

Juliana is pregnant. Yes, I'm currently staring down the barrel of becoming a grandfather. But that's not the important thing so much as – she's due in May, yet when she'd gone to the "find out the assigned gender" ultrasound appointment, she was met with some pretty scary news about the baby's development. She still hasn't been told the gender of her child, but they also made it clear that there's reason to be afraid. There may even be an emergency C-section.

And yes, that could get as bad as someone having to say, "Okay, which one are we going to save." Once that part was made clear to me, **it wasn't even a question about putting everything on hold**. Juliana needs her father more than anyone needs me to sing songs. While I'd hope no one would be disappointed in me, this is a situation where anyone who gives me any amount of guff for not showing up to sing, say, "Liana"? They're free to go fuck themselves a few thousand times over.

I'm sure you've gathered by now that canceling work of any kind isn't exactly my default setting. And canceling something like *The Obscurity Show* feels especially unnatural to me. Not to complain; obviously, I'd rather Juliana was in good health and that the shows could all take place. And I initially booked it all hoping that'd be the case. It took two days of twisting my own arm, but the decision was eventually made by Juliana herself. I asked her if I could cancel everything to be here for her, for whatever she might need, and if that would help her feel less scared. She said yes. That's all there was to it.

Though this is obviously the sole way that this can go, you don't unlearn your strong work ethic overnight. So even though I know that it's good and proper that until the baby is born, I'll now never be in a position where I can't drop everything to do whatever Juliana needs – including *Discography*, Patreon duties, and even working on this book, but the spaces when nothing is going on? My brain still kicks my body into that whole "WHY ARE YOU NOT WORKING, THIS IS YOUR WHOLE FUCKING LIFE, IF YOU DO NOT DO THIS STUFF NO ONE ELSE CAN DO IT FOR YOU" anxiety. I keep trying to internally yell back to say, "Fuck you, I'm here for my daughter," but the anxieties don't listen.

I know I'm doing the right things, and thankfully, though I can't explain this all publicly at this moment – mostly because I don't think Juliana really wants anyone knowing that there might be a problem – most seem to have understood that if I'm canceling the summation of the entire *Obscurity* project, I clearly have good reason to do it.

Downtown Arts Collective seems keen on restaging *The Obscurity Show*, looking at this as a postponement rather than an outright cancellation. Until I know an "it's okay to get back to work" date, I can't entertain potential show dates. And beyond that? *The Obscurity Show* is literally built on a through-line of "hope," and hope is the only thing keeping me going right now.

I can't work on it, anyways. Here I'd be trying to memorize all the speech and stories but trying to ignore that hope might not actually get us through. If something happens to Juliana or the baby? I don't know when I'd feel okay about working on a show ultimately about the potential healing power of music. Because I'd have just experienced something where "hope" didn't fucking help in the least. There's no way to go forward with this show at the moment. I can't do it and believe in it while this is the situation. There's no music that I know of that currently makes me feel like they might be okay. This one is too big for music to fix.

I especially needed to postpone further research on this upcoming season of *Discography*. Since it's all about Black Sabbath, well, there's a lot of lyrics about death. And the cover of the *Born Again* album? I can't be immersed in such bleak and death-related material right now and expect to retain any sort of sanity. I was just a few albums away from having finished the script for the season, but it was *Dehumanizer* from around 1992 when I just couldn't focus on this stuff anymore.

*Dehumanizer* is pretty rad, though.

Been hideously upset, and there aren't words to describe what this is doing to my insides. I keep trying to focus on just "doing right," and that's the only thing that seems to help at all. I clench and tense up every time the phone makes a noise, scared that this is the one where I'll find out that my family shrank again.

As I'm sure you can imagine, this even changed the ending of this book. My last plan was, in the most recent *Obscurity Show* script, I spend the entirety of the hour prior to the start of the performance backstage. But, what makes that odd, you ask? The backstage is clearly and visibly on stage. The lit-up makeup mirrors and everything. It'd look to the audience like I was doing all of my pre-show rituals in plain sight, eventually dawning on them that I've taken the rare step of utilizing "the fourth wall," while usually deconstructing said wall in some form is the hallmark of most Marc With a C activity, really. And on opening night, it'd have looked to the waiting audience that I was writing some notes to myself, but really, I'd have been writing the final journal entry for the book.

We won't be doing it that way now. I can't even say with 100% certainty that *The Obscurity Show* will even take place. Again.

But I will trade it happily if it means that my daughter feels some comfort in me stripping away all that I am and have worked toward just to be there for her without question or hesitation. Especially if she makes it through. I'll trade absolutely anything for that. I'm even getting to the "try to bargain with the deities you hardly even believe in" phase of fear. So if you see me release a whole bunch of worship/praise music at some point, now you'll know why.

Juliana did try to tell me that there could be a positive in all of this: that I'd finally get a bit of "a break." Leave it to her to find the silver lining, right? And I certainly do need a bit of distance between my brain and these worries, but, oof, I didn't want it to show up like this.

I'd say this is at least a contender for Worst Reason For A Vacation Ever.

4-26-19

On the 13th of this month, I became a grandfather to a beautiful baby boy named Ian Marcus.

Oh, sure. There's all the prerequisite "you're too young to be a grandparent" stuff, and I do suppose it's pretty early for me to be one, no matter how you slice it. Especially since Juliana wasn't due to deliver until the end of May.

It was late on a Friday night when Juliana called to tell me that she wasn't sure if her water had broken. I guess it's probably not a sensation that one would be used to, and I was busy tending to a few household crises already, but I can hardly remember them now.

Ian was born on the Saturday morning, and the abdominal defect that had first given us cause to worry, his gastroschisis, had not subsided, meaning that he came into the world with a hole near his waist with most of his intestines literally hanging out. He was rushed into emergency surgery.

There had been a few "which person should/could/would they save" worries at numerous times during Juliana's traumatic pregnancy. I'm not able to even hint at around 90% of it all, but suffice to say that the story could easily fill a book all by itself, especially the legalities.

But the nerves? Oh, those I can tell you all about. I was literally chasing Juliana's ambulance through downtown Orlando on a Friday night, and that's next to impossible due to the amount of drunk pedestrians falling about in a maddening crowd, speaking of playing Paperboy on difficult. And I was freaking out as the ambulance took Juliana to the wrong hospital. This was a super high-risk pregnancy, and she'd literally only met her pediatric surgeon the previous morning, but here she was, being rushed to the wrong place who had no expectations for what'd be coming through the door on that fateful night.

I don't want to say too much more because I'm not sure what's right or wrong to say in these situations. I think I'd be okay if I told you that my heart did happy things when Juliana first looked into Ian's eyes, and I saw her light up exactly as I did when I first saw her eyes. I currently feel good with saying that his continued healing and growth is nothing short of a hard-to-explain miracle. And I cannot even begin to tell you how relieved I am that Juliana's health is just fine.

There's a whole other component, though. He was premature. So was I. I wish I had access to the first pictures ever taken of me because this kid is basically my body double, especially in his facial structure. Specifically with a line that runs down the right side of my face. It almost looks like a scar from one side and looks like heavy eye-bags from the opposite side. It's surreal to look down at a tiny version of myself and feed your own face. It's uncanny. Maybe that's why I feel such a strong connection to him?

It's not like I only love him because he looks like me, of course. That's just a temporary thing, too, since Juliana looked identical to her mommy upon birth, but as of late, people have been confusing her as my sister.

But no, there's just something really magical about Ian.

I don't have a ton of family left, and certainly not much of one full of people I'm close to. Juliana is in a similar boat. By extension, the same applies to Ian, but he especially has a dearth of obvious male role models. And it's true that I'm not mentally 100% masculine, but this may be the first time it comes in handy that I can so easily "present" as a man because I think I have a new purpose: be Ian's example.

I can't "lead" because he's not my child. But I can cry in front of him. I can show respect properly in front of him. I can be the person that enthusiastically supports anything he wants to try. I can show him why it's important to know his own strength because that's how you (mostly) avoid inflicting pain on others. I can take the high road in front of him at every possible turn. And though he's hours away from being two weeks old, I've already begun. He'll never not know me this way. It's never too early to set an example. And of course, he doesn't have to follow the example I hope to set, but if he chooses not to, it won't be for lack of resources.

It's not lost on me that he turns two weeks old tomorrow, and that just happens to be the day that *The Obscurity Show* was supposed to begin its run of performances. As I type this at Ian's hospital bedside, I'm not as upset as I thought I'd be. Actually, I'm not upset about it at all. I'd rather be here with him.

I'm happy to reschedule the show when Ian is home and safe. And all the other stuff, too. Even excited to get back to writing new music. I've got a direction in mind for a possible new album now, and I've been jotting down ideas at this hospital, though the ideas predate this situation.

I see a whole new phase opening up. One where I'm able to make music solely because I'm inspired to do so, rather than making music because it's "what I do." One where I'm just as known for being a fairly well-read music geek as I am for the songs I've made up. One where when I shut the door at the end of a day? I can go from being Marc With a C: Public Figure to Marc Sirdoreus: Private Citizen.

I spent the first 20 years of my life becoming Marc With a C. I spent the next 20 years being Marc With a C while Marc Sirdoreus clawed to get out. I think I can spend the next 20 years being Marc With a C at work but being Marc Sirdoreus on a more consistent basis. I owe it to myself to just be me a little more often.

I don't know what that phase will look like. I don't know what it'll sound like. Not even sure what I'll wear. I'm proud of what I've made, and this oncoming phase will certainly be informed and influenced by what has come before, and I'm excited to try out a new way to balance it all. A phase with more "passing the torch" to my loved ones. A phase with only music that I'm too passionate about to ever consider keeping under wraps. A phase with the occasional day off. A phase where I can have friends rather than just "people I know because I make up songs."

Or maybe the next phase will be drastically different from what I'm hoping for here right in front of you. The muse does what it wants to do, after all. But I'm not scared.

Because? I've got a fairly decent moral compass by now. And?

Maybe it'll be good.

# Part III: Fan Reviews

One last thing! I'd asked some long-time listeners to share anything they wanted to about any albums of mine they chose. You've seen me prattle on about my records, but I thought it might be nice to include some writings from those who grew up with the music. These are the words and opinions of a teensy cross-section of people who have let Marc With a C music impact their lives, and I'm grateful for every single set of ears that has ever given what I do a chance. Thanks, everyone.

-Marc With a C, July 2019

*HUMAN SLUSHY*, ACCORDING TO DAVID KINSEL:

A brilliant man once wrote "Time is an illusion, lunchtime doubly so."* As a newer convert to the world of Marc With a C, courtesy of *Unicorns Get More Bacon*, exploring his first release *Human Slushy* was an interesting time travel experience. Going back 14 years in the career of Marc With a C, but having a subjective experience of *Human Slushy* as a "new" album, made for some fascinating contrasts.

At its heart, *Human Slushy* feels like a concept album. If you take the singer as the central character, there is a definite story of growth and change in the structure of the songs on the album. Listening to this knowing where Marc Sirdoreus is at currently, how his songwriting has grown, adds dimension to the album.

*Human Slushy* is an apt title. The subject of the songs is definitely a sticky mess, barely constrained within the cup of his life. Listening to the songs, it feels like the guy will fall apart at any given moment. Musically, there are the sweet melodies and vocals that exemplify Marc's work, with a very icy core. Marc can wield words like a sword when he wants to, cutting to the quick with very nasty efficiency.

Nowhere is this more prevalent than in what I have come to think of as the Stalker Suite. "Groupie Sex," "Left for Her," "Victoria's Girls," and "Laura, I Need Medicine" are harsh. This is a totally different guy from the writer of "Anything But Plain" The music is catchy, but the subjects can make you cringe at times. Particularly "Left For Her." I found myself laughing nervously as the song progressed. We've all had very dark thoughts about ex-lovers, but to hear those thoughts voiced with such venom is unsettling. (Seriously, Marc. What the hell, man?) "Laura, I Need Medicine" is funny but with a dark core. Where does fantasy become obsession? And what do our obsessions say about us? For the character in the song, he's definitely looking to escape reality, first through a fantasy love with an unobtainable actress, then through self-medication. This is seriously a person on the edge.

Keeping with the concept album idea, those songs do seem to serve a purpose in the narrative. Our hero (?) does move from the self-absorbed guy in "Groupie Sex" to a more self-reflective person over the course of the album. "Not There At All" helps us transition in our story. It has a line that feels like the honest center of the story, "All I ever wanted was someone who'd inspire love songs, so I could mean them for once." Our hero is moving forward in his journey, trying to become less of an egotistical jerk.

"A Very Special Episode" is one of the prettiest songs on the album, with a creative conceit of comparing a relationship to television shows. "Melena" gives us a slight return to our stalker from "Laura, I Need Medicine." This time he's more self-deprecating, less in his fantasy world. "Why Don't Girls Like Me" and the title cut "Human Slushy" find us almost 180 degrees away from the Stalker Suite. This is someone who is unsure of how to connect, searching for something real.

Finally, we get to "Well Fucked Sailor." Great song. This feels like a confessional, exposing the writer for what he is: a complex, flawed human. It addresses things in the past that may have shaped his behaviors without using them as an excuse. If our hero has gotten to this point, and really means what he says, there is hope. Hope that we can see our own flaws and do something to improve.

The album closes with a cover of the *Charles in Charge* theme song. Quick and fun, and an interesting choice when we have spent the album with someone very out-of-control. Marc shows a love for popular culture and treats this cover well.

If you are a newbie to Marc With a C, like I am, this is an interesting choice. Understanding the past helps to inform the present. If you've been a fan for a while, give this a revisit. A flawed but vital work. There are treasures here if you dig.

## *HEY RAPE GIRL,* ACCORDING TO A.J. IN EVOLUTION:

From the very opening song, I was transported to an all too familiar place. As if the past was being sung before me. A story unfolding of a human soul and their desires, their passion, their obsessions. An individual who I felt I knew all too well. A lost love who had their vices that were not quenched by one source alone as they constantly needed to find that next level of temporary contentment, at any cost. But underneath it all, *HRG* is a story of all souls, of all our discontentment, addictions, and thirst. The lengths one will go to in order to satisfy those inner desires/wants/needs. It started as a memory and ended as a self-realization. Of all of Marc's works, this one haunts me, as it should ... longing for more.

## *HEY RAPE GIRL,* ACCORDING TO CALI KEENE:

*HRG*, or *Hey Rape Girl*, is a 6-song EP "based on a character that seeks out fantasy rape."

First and foremost, it's imperative to remember that sometimes music is simply meant to be a journey — letting yourself experience something new and unknown. I recommend approaching this record with an open mind.

Now, this is by far my favorite Marc album. It's rare to see a musician explore a topic of such controversy, and rarer still, to see an entire album dedicated to it. *HRG* deals with some pretty dark subject matter, and the music itself is just as blackened. Recorded on a 4-track, it is the definition of lo-fi. A few repeated themes are those of self-induced pain, disenchantment with the real world, humiliation from men, and sexual fulfillment from all three. I'd like to briefly discuss all six tracks, starting with the very first:

"MWS"

The pacing of this song is so pleasant and melodious. It just barely touches the surface of having an interest in non-typical sexual relationships. This introduction is short but well-suited. Watch out for the last few lyrics of this one, as they end up being repeated in the last song, really bringing this album full circle.

"Chasing The Bug"

A quick Google search tells me that "chasing the bug" is a term for seeking sexual interaction with someone that is HIV-positive. Further research proved that these "bug chasers" often seek to contract the disease as a form of self-harm, sometimes even suicide.

I'll be damned if that isn't the most fucked up thing I read all week. The song itself maintains true to the set tone and is the gift that keeps on giving. I mean, if your idea of a gift is a no-holds-barred peek into a twisted mentality. Take these lyrics for example: "The congregation holds my head under the water / Until the bubbles stop rising up / And I won't be saved until the liquid fills my lungs / I'm dirty like I'm chasing the bug."

This song is about a desire to be abused. It's a very open view into someone that almost obsessively puts themselves in a position to get hurt. Really hurt. As in stripped and defiled in every way, hurt. They get off on being used and thrown out, both emotionally and physically. To quote an exact line from this song, "It makes you want to throw up, but that's the allure." All of this, accompanied by fuzzy guitars and a slow, dizzying melody, sends me into a vehement despondency.

"HRG" is the title track of this album and is arguably the liveliest of which. Starting out harmonious and upbeat, as the ending nears it becomes ever more fast-paced and unnerving. It builds and builds into layers of intensity, creating this disconcerting stupor.

This could be a reflection of the character's eagerness to dive into dangerous situations and the results thereof (i.e., "I don't mind the whip but I prefer your bare fist / To lay me out with no dignity intact"). Or it could be a representation of the flying emotions during these extremities. One word to describe this song? Antsy.

"She Loves The B-Sides" showcases a woman's fervent love for her favorite band. This is probably the most relatable song on the album, at any rate the most vanilla. Its repetition is calming, and I find it to be a refreshing break in between the heavier songs.

"Every Inch Of You" features masochism, a staggering avoidance of self-betterment, and whimsically diluted life views. ("Life's just something I do to pass the time / The only thing that's real and free is when I cannot breathe.")

These lyrics sucker punch me every time simply because I relate to them. This entire song could have been a chapter from my own life.

Lastly, "Long Distance Dedication" is presumably about a complex relationship with a prostitute. This song is slow, pointed and distorted, and it features an eerie backing vocal intoning the presumed prostitute. LDD embodies the feeling of being overcast, that implicit detachment, and even delusion.

Everything about this album makes waves. From the concept, to the lyrics, to the pacing and instrumentals. *HRG*'s hypnotic sounds of perpetual turmoil will make you feel like you're being pulled apart. The messages of suffocating dysphoria will force you to face the most well-hidden bits of yourself. If you have an inclination to the grotesque and an affiliation with the taboo, you are going to fucking love this album.

A WRITING INSPIRED BY *BUBBLEGUM ROMANCE*, ACCORDING TO ASHLEY THOMPSON:

It was 4:30 a.m. when he told me he loves me.

No one else was there to see.

The privacy of all of this scared me.

I washed the dishes. I cleaned the countertops. I swept the floors.

The idea of him loving me honestly scares me more than the idea that he doesn't.

I folded up every linen on the coffee table.

I woke him up. I asked him to help me fall asleep. Knowing that he wouldn't be able to stay awake long enough to make me sleep.

I am so scared that he loves me. I am .... so scared.

How could he love me when he doesn't know the me that thinks, "Let's do drugs because I have something strenuous coming up? How could he love me when he doesn't know that for two years, I believed the only path to salvation was 'Get married in the church.'"

Maybe I am scared that I am not worthy of love. Maybe I am scared that in this rash decision of a relationship, nothing will work out.

The only thing I am sure of right now is that I am scared. I want it to be well documented that I am scared.

But I am also in love. I am in love. I am in love. I am in love.

I love the way he looks at me without fear.

I am in love with the way he falls asleep, even though he snores as bad as I do.

I am in love with his idea of going out, only to stay in for the night.

I am in love with the way he holds my hand.

I am in love, and I AM scared of letting the whole world see.

Not because the world doesn't deserve to see love.

The world deserves a love like this.

I know I love him because he holds me in the way I never thought was possible.

I know he loves me because he said it out loud.

I know I love him because he makes it easy for me to love him; he opens himself up.

I know he loves me because he tells me in a hundred million different ways.

He tells me when he holds me close.

He tells me when he asks what's wrong.

He tells me when he asks if I have eaten.

He tells me when he asks the other people I am close to.

He tells me he loves me every day.

I am scared he is telling the truth.

The fear I feel right now is inconsequential. I know I love him. I know he loves me.

*BUBBLEGUM ROMANCE,* ACCORDING TO CHARLES BOWMAN:

I have been a fan of Marc With a C since the first time I saw him perform live at a pre-Nerdapalooza show back in 2008 or 2009. I had heard some of the more popular songs of his at the time being played in A Comic Shop but had never actually been listening until that ungodly warm night in parking lot. I bought as much merch as I could find at his table and even got to say some kind words as he was packing up. On the way home the first album on top of the stack was *Bubblegum Romance.*

There are songs on here ranging from the love songs of "Prettiest Girl in the Whole World" and "Freezing in Florida" to the constant crowd favorite of "Nerdy Girls." But in between these you will find nuggets of audio gold like "Just a Few Words." You can even listen to him profess his love of listening to music on 12 inches of wax on "RetroLowFi" with just the right amount of tongue-in-cheek humor. You even get a little more of the humor on "Honda Civic Paint Rocket."

Overall, *Bubblegum Romance* is a pretty simple listen with some insanely catchy melodies and more than a few earworms that will stick with you for a good while. If you are just looking for a mix of ballads and upbeat toe-tappers, this is the perfect album for you. But if you are willing to sit with the record for a while and really listen to the lyrics you get, in my opinion a pretty good glimpse into the mind of Marc With a C circa 2004.

*THIS WORLD IS SCARY AS FUCK,* ACCORDING TO MATT ODOM:

*This World is Scary as Fuck* is not the first Marc With a C album I heard, and it's not my most favorite of his albums, but it does have what I consider one of the most quintessential Marc With a C songs: "Music Geek." I think this song really encapsulates a lot of Marc's music and gives a good insight into his past and why he's into music in the first place. Although I'm not even sure if it's about him. Some of Marc's songs are from his perspective, and some are from a different character. It's hard to tell, but I think this one is about Marc.

The album starts off with a pretty good bang and has a good mix of slower and fast songs. The only song I really ever skip is "God Save the Queen from Navy Seals"; it's a little slow, and I'm not too fond of the organ. Toward the end of the album is where the album gets its title, from "Stuck With Me." He sings about how scary the world is, which I think is something everyone can relate to. It's my other favorite from this album.

The final song "Amy, It's Kevin" is a really nice guitar song. It's a very pleasant song to listen to, except that the lyrics are very nasty. He really seems to have a problem with this woman and that she slept with the door guy. It gets a little funny the way he stops singing and starts just talking during the song.

I've never really thought about the album as a whole, but it seems to be mostly about how life sucks and people make it suck more. I think a lot of Marc's songs and albums are about this, but this is mostly from his older albums. I think we were all a little more cynical and angry when we were younger; I know I was. I don't think this reflects poorly on Marc as a person because he's a pretty swell guy.

*LIFE'S SO HARD*, ACCORDING TO DAVID BOWIE (We know. Not that one. Yes, it's his real name.):

So it's sometime in 2006 or maybe early 2007. Our family has settled into the rhythm of living in Central Florida after moving there a couple years prior, and we've discovered WPRK and its eclectic (to put it mildly!) musical range. Among the artists in regular rotation on the station is Marc With a C, and everybody in our family likes his music. But you know who really likes his music? I mean, really, really likes his music? My oldest child, then 7 years old.

And it's cute, watching her bounce around to the music, even (maybe especially) when the music she was bouncing to was music that some people wouldn't expect a 7-year-old to ever even begin to enjoy. But the cutest thing of all, the one that I'll remember forever as one of the great musical moments of my lifetime? Listening to her voice coming from the next room as she sang along with the radio, altering the lyrics to "Life's So Hard" ever so slightly so that they fit her life a little better: "I'm so sad/I'm se-e-ven/Life's so hard/Life's so hard."

Epilogue: She still loves the song. I still love it, too. In fact, the moment she turned 15, that song became her ringtone on my phone. It's a regular singalong when we're on family road trips. Really, not a lot more you can ask from a song, you know?

*LIFE'S SO HARD*, ACCORDING TO JONATHAN PAMPLIN:

It's late after a long day. A friend invites you over to hang out on their back porch. You listen to music, maybe have a drink or two, and spend most of the evening talking and laughing. Even though you're tired, you're having a good time. Later that night, you leave feeling worn out – doubly so when you dwell on the day you know you'll have tomorrow – yet with a smile on your face. That's what it feels like listening to *Life's So Hard*.

*Life's So Hard*, unsurprisingly, is an album about the ways in which life is hard. Billed as "A somewhat satirical album about 'those damn kids,'" it explores many of the broad social forces that make early adulthood thorny, whether it's the disappointment in our parents in "What The Hell Were You On?," the disappointment of our parents in "Military Brat," the conflicted feelings toward self-centeredness and self-care in "The Problem is Me," or the difficulty of learning how to control budding superpowers in "Diane Works For Ozzy."

Crucially, it also explores the ways we make life easier on ourselves, from the unequivocal joy of spending time with true friends to the rejuvenating power of music. It's an album about finding the joy in small things and silliness, and about the power (good and bad) of relationships. All of which resonates with me. [1]

"Life's So Hard" (the track) is one of the first Marc With a C songs I ever heard, and the one that most firmly wormed its way into my head during the two years between when I first saw him, opening for *The Rocky Horror Picture Show* and when I eventually met him after his performance at the first Orlando Nerd Fest. Yet when I listened to its eponymous album for the first time, it wasn't the crowd favorite, title track, and personal gateway song that hit me most. That distinction goes to "Counting Down," a short yet oh-so-sweet song anticipating a visit with a close friend. It's so genuinely, unironically affectionate that I can't help but smile listening to it. In an age when genuine expressions of love between friends are often smeared as saccharine or exaggerated to cloying levels for comic effect, it warmed my heart encountering something so earnest in its sentimentality. That earnest capacity for feeling, if we can push past the jadedness that too often comes with age, is responsible for much of what makes life great.

Conversely, fakeness, in various forms, is responsible for much of what makes life hard, whether it be the toxic effect of people who call you "friend" while dragging you down ("Every Single Friend") or the deluded angst and anger that comes from only seeing the world through the lens of your expectations ("Military Brat," "Life's So Hard"). Phoniness, either through deception or self-deception, damages relationships. Expectations cause problems or cause us to see problems when we shouldn't. Happiness, then, comes in part from being real and realistic with how you navigate the world.

Following this ethos, there's a strong current through the album about taking delight in the small things. Playing records, dancing, hanging out with friends: given how limited our time is — and given how much of it is taken up by life's headaches, let-downs, and a-holes — it's important to hang on to the little stuff that makes us happy.

Ironically, given its name, *Life's So Hard* is a positive album, and it achieves this by avoiding irony. Whether it's the unfiltered seriousness of youth rebellion in songs like "What The Hell Were You On?" and "Life's So Hard," or the imploration to enjoy yourself in songs like "We're All Gonna Die" and "Counting Down," there's a refreshing honesty to the characters and messages on the album, even if they're not always endorsed [2]. With that honesty comes clarity: if you're willing to take it for what it is and appreciate the small victories, too, life's a little easier to bear.

And it's easier still with some good music to go along with it.

[1] Except the bit about having superpowers. I suppose I dodged that bullet, though I also suppose I could dodge bullets even easier if I had superpowers. [shrug]

[2] Hence the album being *"somewhat* satirical:" there's some criticism in its messages, and some characters who roundly deserve it, but the edge of condemnation is sheathed in gentle mockery, as these aren't perspectives to cut down, but people whose perspectives deserve them a bump on the head. Ok, maybe a harder hit for some of them.

*SHOCK TREATMENT INTERPRETATIONS*, ACCORDING TO MICHAEL DOMANGUE:

I don't believe in gateway drugs.

I do believe in gateway songs.

The work that introduces you to an artist is like a first kiss. You don't know what the hell is happening, but you know it's good and it's right, and you want to experience it again and again. I know where I was the first time I saw a Tarantino movie, and I really know the first weird corner of the internet I was in when I discovered Marc With a C.

I've been a *Rocky Horror* fan since my sister showed it to me at the ripe old age of 7. A little less than a decade later, I finally discovered its sequel/ equal *Shock Treatment*. For those of you who have seen the former but not the latter, I would describe *Shock Treatment* as lacking in all sense of plot or narrative structure, but with a far superior soundtrack showing Richard O'Brien evolving as a songwriter.

I wore out that VHS tape listening to those songs and started going on *Shock Treatment* fan sites to find out word about a DVD release. That's when I found it, the Marc With a C covers. They were still being made when I found them, not quite the whole collection you see now, but it was like peering through the looking glass and seeing that somewhere on this blue planet was someone who loved this weird little movie as much as I did.

I treasure these covers, as they became my gateway to an artist whose work continues to inspire and comfort me. But I still don't know who the bird belongs to.

NORMAL BIAS, ACCORDING TO CALI KEENE:

*Normal Bias* is the album you listen to on the drive home from a full weekend with your friends, windows rolled down, and the slowly setting sun warm on your face.

Childlike simplicity with uninhibited emotion, you'd be inclined to sing along and clap to these tunes around a bonfire with the family. And then you realize you might be singing about domestic abuse and parental absence. Even then, this album is so catchy, who really cares?

That's one of the special things about this album: it has songs that make you cry while also making you dance. I can think of none other that exemplify this more than "Already Dead." Upon listening, I'm reminded of the people I know and love that struggle with addictions. That may not be what the song is about, but it brings poignant visuals to mind. With that being said, I can't help but fight a smile and bob my head along to it. How is that possible? How does he do it?!

Another incredible trait of Marc's, which is evident in all his work, is how self-aware he is. He integrates that awareness into every song, the more famous of which on this album would surely be "Drunk Classic Rock Fans" (which talks about an old rocker that can't see the reality of his life) and "Dear Son" (which is the honesty those of us with disappointing fathers have been waiting for).

Fret not: this album isn't all callous reflection to the sound of rainbows. It's just mostly so. The ending track on *Normal Bias* is also one of the most positive songs in the Marc catalog. It's called "Happy To Be Alive" – need I explain further? No? I will anyway.

With Marc crooning about accepting himself and his life as it is, and taking a moment to appreciate the very two, you begin to do the same. Nothing feels better than freedom from your own cynicism and a pleasant ditty in your ears. *Normal Bias* is integral in helping accomplish that, making it quite the indispensable addition to any proper collection.

*NORMAL BIAS*, ACCORDING TO DOMENICO MARINI:

Polvere. Polvere sottile, quella che si deposita sui mobili di una stanza chiusa per molto tempo. Una lieve corrente d'aria piano piano la solleva lasciando intravedere qualche contorno più definito. Piccole rivelazioni. Piccole cose quotidiane, tristezze, gioie, paure, rabbie. Volti, oggetti perfettamente riconoscibili. La polvere li ha preservati dall'usura e li svela quasi con crudele orgoglio. Arrendersi alla sua impalpabile dolcezza.

(Editor's note: Domenico's review is preserved in the original, unedited Italian.)

*LINDA LOVELACE FOR PRESIDENT*, ACCORDING TO CHRISTINE VEASEY:

My first exposure to Marc With a C was a birthday party my cousin threw for their self. They rented the upstairs of a bar/restaurant (in Philadelphia), hired Marc to play a private show, and didn't give a damn what anyone thought of the whole thing. I learned a lot that night. I also walked away with a few new friends, including Marc. Marc's show was intimate and honest, like his lyrics. Letting go of your checkered past and striving for better is a theme that never gets old. What can get old are people's misconceptions about you based on rumor. To me, this is an album about getting to know people for who they are and accepting them and yourself without adding the baggage of other's opinions. In Marc's own words: "There's nothing worse than carrying on when there's nothing left to carry at all."

*LINDA LOVELACE FOR PRESIDENT*, ACCORDING TO TRISTESSA PLUME:

I had forgotten that the first track on my dear friend Marc With a C's 2008 album *Linda Lovelace for President* was the incredibly comforting. "It's All Gonna Be Alright."

But the second I put it on, especially at night, I am transported to a humid and lonely night on the Florida Turnpike in July of that year. It was a pivotal night and a pivotal time for me.

How I got on the road that night is a story that Marc was a part of. At strange intervals throughout the non-chronological story, various tracks from *Linda Lovelace* start playing in my brain.

In essence, the story starts in November of 2007 at Stardust Coffee & Video in Orlando. I was there, wearing a pink T-shirt and a jean jacket, while my boyfriend stood behind me, very likely wearing a Guided by Voices shirt. Marc and friends were filming that particular show for a future release. (Coincidentally, the video would be released with *Linda Lovelace for President*, and me wearing that outfit, holding my hands up in the air, talking about the show being greater than the sum of its parts, was part of its trailer.)

After that particular weekend of visiting Orlando was over, my boyfriend and I drove down the Turnpike back to our apartment in suburban South Florida, where I had moved to be with him. I'd found a job and reconnected with at least one old friend, so things seemed to be going alright thus far. "All My Drug Use Is Accidental," which another close friend titled, sort of served as a longstanding soundtrack to my day-in day-out life at that point, the start of my career.

In reality, the story starts long before that. The boyfriend and I met Marc together in 2004 at a show at Austin's Coffeehouse. He sang about nerdy girls and rhymed John Stamos with Tori Amos, and the boyfriend and I looked at each other, mouths agape, and were hooked from there. The boyfriend featured him in the paper that we both wrote for at the time. We were audience fixtures at all of Marc's shows for years, the fun, dance-y couple always there. Shortly after we met him, Marc met my friend Nicole, and they began to date soon thereafter. Things were happy for everyone in Orlando.

Boyfriend graduated and moved, kept driving up to see me and Marc shows, and two years later, I graduated and moved South for him. After I moved, I visited Orlando as often as possible, as it was really my home, which the boyfriend expressed concern over. We had made the dual trip for Marc's much ballyhooed show in November of 2007.

Just over a month after that show, on a Friday afternoon, the boyfriend ended things, six weeks short of four years, and left me alone in the apartment. I was planning on driving to see friends in Orlando that night, of course, who were in from out of the country. I did drive, back up and down that dark and lonely three-point-five hour stretch of Turnpike, on the phone and with the windows down most of the way. It was not a pretty night, suffice to say.

I decided that weekend to stay down in South Florida, as my job and moreover my new students needed me more than I needed to be with my own family. I stuck to my guns, which made my mother somewhat upset, but I made it work. I was emotionally worn down, but "I'm Not Coming Home" helped me through that particular feeling.

Beyond my own biological family, I had a massive network of friends in Orlando who took care of me, several of whom I referred to as the Cult of Marc: friends who played with him, friends who I met at his shows, and, of course, Marc and Nicole themselves. I guess what made the breakup harder was that it was like losing a family member.

At the end of that year, I spent my own holiday break in Orlando as a self-care measure. I visited Marc at [a record store] one rainy afternoon, and he gave me one of the most restorative hugs of my life, promising to help rebuild my music collection after the boyfriend took all of his things (including the Darren Hanlon Christmas 7-inch we got together in Athens, Georgia earlier that year – that one stung). I had also made the decision that the former boyfriend didn't get to steal my love of any of the bands he had introduced me to (There were a lot.) or music that we'd discovered together (like Marc). Boyfriend was not the sole proprietor or distributor of The Magnetic Fields or The Mountain Goats. Hell, I bought my own copy of *Tallahassee* that day, and it helped me tremendously through that time. Marc also talked about lack of faith in most of the relationships he knew based on the sheer number of breakups he'd witnessed that year. He and Nicole got married that following February.

I spent the New Year's Eve transition from 2007 to 2008 with much of the Cult of Marc crew. Even without boyfriend as a family member, they helped to make my transition from abandonment to hopefulness a little easier. When I hear "Born Vintage," even though it hadn't been released at that time, I think of that New Year's, and sitting on a friend's living room floor in Altamonte, shouting "WE'RE EARLY!" at 11:45pm EST off of the balcony, and Chris Zabriskie saying to Marc, "Remember that New Year's that I shaved your head?" with clippers in hand.

In 2008, I found new friends, new purpose in my new locale, and even a new relationship with a gentleman who, of course, I brought to Orlando to meet my family, biological and extended, and to see Marc play. We returned to Stardust, and that March seemed to be when I heard "San Diego Doorways" for the first time. Something about Marc singing that song, aching to connect with the past, looking for someone who wasn't there got under my skin that particular night. It is still my favorite Marc With a C song to this day.

As much as I felt like I was moving forward, especially that night in March 2008, back in town with family, I met a girl who had met ex-boyfriend and heard the entire rundown on me and just had to talk to me to get my side of everything. The gentleman tried to extract me from the conversation, but I was tugged too hard, and had grabbed on myself, borne ceaselessly into the past.

The year wore on. The new relationship wore on – tough, just as all rebound relationships are. We argued through a weekend in Key West, through nights on the town in Miami and parking mishaps, through termite mating rituals and more unintended shaved heads, through orchestra concerts. As much as that gentleman gave to me at the time, he wasn't the thing that would keep me grounded. My job tested me tremendously, but I soldiered on. I comforted myself cynically, knowing that every other person who'd moved to be with a significant other had experienced a breakup as well. Surely countless others have suffered tremendously more than I was at that time, but the loneliness and awful homesickness that pervaded my heart during some of those long nights started to spread.

The summer took me away from my job as purpose, gave me some adventures (but left me broke), and gave me a fully solo move to look forward to. After an enjoyable camping road trip in early July of 2008, I came home to my mother's house, bills pilling up, without plans for the immediate future, full of problems I couldn't reasonably solve, in a bad spot in my relationship, and with a car that was not exactly functional.

One fateful night, I decided that I had to get home, and I rented a car. A green Ford Focus, different color but the same model the ex-boyfriend used to have. I left too late in the evening, a rookie mistake I made often that first year of living away, so the trek down the Turnpike through the isolated center of Florida was especially dark. My mother had always asked me to call to ensure I wasn't in a ditch at Yeehaw Junction, which became a longstanding joke of ours.

On that particular drive, I started to feel untethered. The stress of getting my life together, mundane as it may seem, had started to untie me, or rather unravel me. I had been a tightly wound ball of keeping my shit together since the breakup, since the move south, really, and whatever mission or purpose I sought in the near future kept me moving. It was the same way I dealt with the death of my father – just keep pushing forward.

But I wasn't in college anymore. I didn't have a clear mission. I sort of did hope someone would call me on a mission. I knew I was driving home to sleep in my own bed and see the gentleman I was dating at the time after several weeks away, but the rest of the details became hazy. Without a prime directive, it became hard to see any future clearly.

So unlike my Turnpike trek the night of the infamous breakup, I didn't call my extended family of friends on the phone – instead, I slipped *Linda Lovelace for President* into the rented Focus's CD player. I had not listened to it in its entirety yet.

And my friends all seemed to appear. They were in the car with me, transparent, but their phantom presence was enough. Nicole was dancing and clapping as Marc asked for clapping on one of the tracks. My tall blond friend was there, shouting out the line "I don't want to get in your pants / just inside your tape machine." Chris was there, drumming on the back of the front seat. The friend who first coyly uttered "All my drug use is accidental" was there in the front seat, lurching forward as she laughed, blonde ringlets shaking every which way. And Marc was singing. He was singing about my financial issues on "Debt Is Only What You Make of It," and I got nervous, but as the first track said, it was all going to be all right.

And I found myself tethered again. It took a lot of repeats of a lot of tracks. I can't count how many times I played "Satellite" or the title track toward the most isolated part of my journey, from Vero Beach to Stuart. I indeed felt like the coldest satellite, removed from everything and seemingly everyone I'd known and loved. But I was being drawn back into my galaxy through these songs.

I don't remember walking up from my parking lot to my otherwise empty apartment that night. I don't even remember if I turned in my rental car that night or the next morning, and I have a very hazy recall of the next week, or even the rest of the summer until my move to a tiny one-bedroom near work. But through that period of questions, through that period of quiet unravelling after too much tightness, *Linda Lovelace for President* kept my wheels on the highway. I've always driven with my St. Christopher medal on my visor, even as a lapsed Catholic, and I don't remember if I brought him into the rented Focus. St. Christopher has seen me through major accidents and flat tires on same Turnpike, but that night in July of 2008, Linda Lovelace running for president, as interpreted through Marc, served the purpose of keeping me safe. I guess that it kept me from jumping the gun.

Although the remainder of the details of that summer are fuzzy, aside from merely pushing through it, the internal emotional cacophony quieted down after that night. A long drive may seem like a poor apex to a story, but the music carried me through. I'll never be able to thank the long crescendos and decrescendos on "Linda Lovelace for President" enough.

The epilogue is a lot brighter. The gentleman and my local best friend accompanied me to get a new car after summer's end. I worked with my best friend to get Barack Obama elected that year. Gentleman and I broke up, but I was burrowed well into my surroundings. I got through that unscathed. We're still friends to this day, and he lives in Hawaii and has a wonderful girlfriend.

The next summer, I met a dude who eventually took many pilgrimages to Orlando with me and accompanied me to many of Marc's shows, where he and Marc joked about Wang computer monitors. He wowed Nicole with his knowledge of weird Spin Doctors lyrics. And the whole crew danced until dawn at our wedding in November of 2011. We hope to bring our baby daughter to her first Marc With a C show within the next year.

My story is, in essence, a happy one with a couple of ugly delays. But on the road, literally and figuratively, the album *Linda Lovelace for President* kept me driving forward, even through the darkest of nights.


*LINDA LOVELACE FOR PRESIDENT,* ACCORDING TO STARF:

The year was 2009, the location Orlando, Florida. At 19 years old, I had only been out of high school for a single year, which meant that I was a full-fledged adult who truly understood the world and had all of the answers. As you may expect of someone with all of the answers, I found myself constantly in awe of the world, embarrassing myself and learning all of the time.

2009 would prove to be a truly transformative year in my life, and it's all thanks to one event: Nerdapalooza. In what was not the first official happening of the event, but certainly the first larger-scale one, I would find myself exposed to heaps of brand-new music and friends. I had been listening to a handful of nerdcore artists for about three years up to that point and had only recently been interacting with them via online message boards for a year. Making the trek to Florida alone all the way from Minnesota was somewhat daunting, but I knew that what lay in store was nothing but a grand time. I was correct.

I don't remember which day of the festival it was, but I do remember wandering the convention center around midday with nothing pressing to do. That entire event was enchanted for me and would lead me down some interesting paths. I found myself sauntering into the main room, unsure of who was playing. From the stage a man with incredible charisma was entertaining the crowd with no backup – just him and a guitar.

Oh sure, I'll check this guy out, I thought.

The first song that played after I had entered the mid-progress concert was "All My Drug Use Is Accidental." I was immediately hooked by the catchiness, the quirkiness, and the animated performance of it all. I stuck around for the rest of the set, and I only became more enamored with the music. I didn't know it at the time, but I was witnessing the performance of someone who I would come to greatly admire, and unbeknownst to me would one day be honored to call my friend.

After the set, I made a direct line to the merch table. I had no idea who this guy was or what his deal was, but I knew I needed to purchase *something* of his. There certainly must have been more albums available, but in my memory the only one that mattered was *Linda Lovelace For President*. I think it was because it was the most recent one available on the table. So I snatched it up with glee, stoked to listen to it once I had returned home.

This story may feel less about the actual album than it is a personal experience, but it is an extremely important album in my life. I have fond memories of listening to it on repeat for countless nights to come after that. I remember it keeping me company on one particularly "rough" night when I confessed feelings for a girl and got rejected (truly the worst fate that could befall any of us, I was certain of it at the time). After that, I drove through the night listening to *Linda Lovelace For President* on repeat in a car that didn't belong to me. I parked somewhere secluded, laid on hood with the windows open, and simply took in the tunes with the night. I learned a little something more.

People say that going to college is one of the most important formative experiences in a person's life. I didn't go to college out of high school; instead I had music festivals and awkward experiences. I grew up in a music scene, and as such this album will always take me back to a magical place of naivety and wonder. A time in my life when I was still learning how to be myself.

It's one of those albums that will remain constantly embedded in my head, no matter what happens. It reminds me of a time when everything felt way more intense, a scary and exciting time.

And hey, the tunes are pretty bitchin', too!


*LOSING SALT,* ACCORDING TO TIM LABONTE:

In February 2014, I found myself sitting with Marc Sirdoreus at a restaurant in

Orlando, which I arrived late to. (I didn't how Orlandoan peak traffic worked.) We had only talked in email before. He was just doing a Massachusetts fan a favor while visiting Disney, but soon enough we were sharing nachos and avoiding an awkward waiter. We talked about ourselves, family, life, other stories … We then began to talk about Marc With a C, and soon Marc said, "Man, I don't get why *Losing Salt* is your favorite album."

Well, then it was. It's still Top 3. Who can explain why anything is their favorite anything? It hits them some way. This is how *Losing Salt* hit me.

When I found Marc the previous summer, I was in a funk, left Facebook, joined twitter, and was reading an article about They Might Be Giants that Marc was interviewed for. Something about his story led me to look up his music. His latest album was titled something I found bizarre to name. I listened and bought *Motherfuckers Be Bullshittin'* during its first track (I had gotten the vinyl bug a couple years prior.) and proceeded to download the rest of his catalog. I would play them here and there, but one I kept returning to.

There's something so raw and honest about *Losing Salt*. The opening track "I Will Repossess Your Heart" still remains my favorite songs of his, and which I still throw on mix CDs. There's this awesome subtle build, and the melody never leaves my head. And hey, an eccentric love song I'll take any day.

I'm a sucker for drum machines. And in the next couple tracks, what really gets me, is the drum machine. However, the way Marc recorded it, he seemed to make it his own. Maybe he just put a mic to it;ce maybe it's the brand he used? (I notice Casio in the album's keywords.) I don't know, but it's not recorded as a typical "plug in and play with." But "Chicken Pox and Star Wars Guys" definitely hits that kid in you when you'd be home sick from school – and for me – I had the Star Wars 1995 *Faces* reissue on VHS, which we hadn't returned to my neighbor for years. It's an awesome memory to return to every time I hear the song, covered on the couch re-watching the trilogy over and over again.

But the nice transition from the drum machine to drums is seamless in "A Woman's Duty." And still, the melodies and layering continue strong. The content is tongue-in-cheek – but it's just enough to get right into "You've Got the Curse." Another quirky love song, good arrangement and harmony – the album is still holding strong. "He Left You For A Punk Rock Girl" – man, what a fun song. I was in the punk scene for a little bit, and the drama. THE DRAMA. Marc nails it. He also nails the backing vocals and response.

As many fans know, Marc does this awesome job of taking something macabre but making it pleasant to experience. The rest of the album (the second half, really) goes down this path. My favorite track on *Losing Salt* is "You Do Not

Exist." I know it's a favorite for many, but for me was this out of left-field, piano-led track. And as the lyrics set in (which is the last thing to happen for me with songs – I'm an instrument-and-melody guy), memories return from my workaholic ex, which brought out the worse in me. But it's a good sort of wallow.

"This Stuff Is Gonna Kill Me" is a nice little answer to the previous song. When I listen to "You Do Not Exist," I have to make sure this has to play after. Not that it's the same song – I just feel it's the second part. Not sure if that's what Marc intended, but it works for me.

Lately I find Marc doing more "epic" songs, which I've always just called longer or bigger songs. (Yes, I agree the word has lost its meaning, but that came after my time.) "Magazines" remains my favorite epic of his – I love every layer of it – especially the guitar during the instrumentals. There's a feel to it I don't find in the later big songs of Marc With a C – but an artist changes at every album, so it's no use to compare, but enjoy the art as it is. I just can't really make out what the recording is that takes up the majority of the song – some cable access religious service? I don't care, it works.

What an awesome little closer. "If These Walls Could Talk" is a great reflection of your life at a point. Getting older, I've made so many friends, and as we get to know each other I hear what they've been through – and I think back on my life and how cookie-cutter and dull it is. I'm not depressed – I'm a very happy person – but boring. Or I just don't know how to tell stories, which usually end with me finding $5.

I know Marc finds *Losing Salt* a weird collection of songs, which I also learned when talking about the album he was very sick when putting it together and recording (which made me respect the album even more). Maybe because of that it left a certain taste in his mouth as the artist? But the album works for me. For my nostalgia and music-loving ears, this is his album that speaks to me the most. Thank you for making it.

*POP! POP! POP!*, ACCORDING TO CHAD WALKER:

When Marc put a call out for people to write about their experiences with his albums, my mind immediately went to *Popular Music*. Upon scanning the list of available albums, however, I realized that it had been taken. And, quite honestly, as I thought about it, I'm not sure I have more to say about that one that I haven't already said, either in writing or on my podcast. That's when I noticed that *Pop! Pop! Pop!* was still available. I seem to recall having heard that it's one of Marc's favorites but not exactly a fan favorite (though that may be a faulty memory). In fact, I originally purchased the album without having listened to it, though I knew a couple of the songs on it. Despite this, the first time or two that I listened to the album, it just sort of washed over me and passed on. Nothing quite stuck with me. Possibly I wasn't in the right mood or conditions for it, but regardless of the reason, I basically shelved it, playing it far less than any of Marc's other albums.

Upon choosing this album for Marc's project, however, I knew I needed to give it a proper listen. (Several, actually. And on vinyl, of course.) When I did this, I realized a couple of reasons why it hadn't grabbed me before. The first time I listened, I had been immersed in *Popular Music* and *Motherfuckers Be Bullshittin'*, both heavily concept-/theme-based albums. *Pop! Pop! Pop!* is not that at all. It's a collection of great pop songs (as the title implies). I just didn't quite have the context for the album when I first heard it, but now, having explored more of Marc's back catalog, I have a better idea of what to expect.

I suppose this would be a good time to mention a few of the songs that particularly stand out for me as an illustration of the type of album it is. Of course I'd be remiss if I didn't mention "Ammonia," one of the tracks that almost certainly lead people to expect Marc's music to just be funny all the time (something Marc has told me happens all the time). It is certainly a funny track about how important ammonia is in our lives, though it's not really representative of all of his music. "Fighting for Love," a track I knew before purchasing the album, has one of my favorite lines from any of Marc's songs, the titular chorus: "Fighting for love is like fucking for virginity." It's just such a great simile, especially in the context of a song about a failing relationship. I'm also particularly partial to "The Audience Is Listening." I love it when Marc tells stories during his live shows, and this track integrates that perfectly given that the song is actually about listening to the artist on stage (an idea he also uses on the title track for *Unicorns Get More Bacon*, though in a slightly different way).

I've also noticed something about the tracking of Marc's albums that I doubt I would have recognized if I only listened to the digital versions. Side one of many of the albums, including this one, tends to have one or two more songs than side two. And side two, then, tends to have the longer tracks. The penultimate track of the album also has a tendency to be the longest, though it might also be the last one. I don't know if that's any kind of spectacular insight or anything, but I find it interesting. Regardless, it's quite clear that the tracking on Marc's albums is something he spends quite a bit of time with (and in fact, he had the help of Chris Zabriskie on this particular album).

It's so weird how expectations can transform the enjoyment of the exact same music. A different setting, a different context, and I had a whole new experience. I'm not going to say it's my absolute favorite of Marc's albums, (That's still going to be *Popular Music*.) but I can definitely say that I have a much better understanding and appreciation of it than I did going into this. I'm really glad I got the chance to hear this album again, almost as if for the first time.

*MOTHERFUCKERS BE BULLSHITTIN'*, ACCORDING TO MATT ODOM:

*Motherfuckers Be Bullshittin'* was one of the first things I heard from Marc With a C. I remember seeing him at Nerdapalooza and a friend of mine really liked the title of the album. I just remember Marc's sweet pajama pants.

"Love My Little Squiddy" is one of my favorite songs. I have great memories of listening to this song while giving my son a bath. We even played with a squirting squid (or maybe octopus) toy. I know it sounds weird, but it's a fun song. It always gets me in a good mood. According to my play count on Google Music, this is my number two-played Marc With a C song. Curiously, the top is "You're My Princess" (also from this album). That song may be a little problematic, but it's enjoyable. I didn't let my son listen to that one. I decided to check the bottom song (that isn't 0) just for the hell of it, and it's "Long Distance Dedication" from *Unicorns Get More Bacon*. I'm not sure why this is important.

I don't own a physical copy of this album. Over half of my (very small) vinyl collection is Marc's, but for some reason I haven't bought this one. I love it though. I tend to use different music for different moods, and lots of songs can evoke a feeling in me. Or remind me of an event that happened in my life. This album, as mentioned earlier, always reminds me of the fun times at Nerdapalooza and drinking way too much NOS. All of the standing around for hours, sweating in the Florida heat, and listening to all of the great nerdy music for days; all of it was great times. Marc was a part of that. And part of my memories. This album, and a lot of his albums, is part of my memories. And they always will be.

*MOTHERFUCKERS BE BULLSHITTIN'*, ACCORDING TO "KJKW":

*Motherfuckers* came to me in a weird point in my life, both personally and as a music fan. I had actually heard Marc With a C first perform at Nerdapalooza 2011, when this album was still very much fresh, but neither he nor the album really resonated until around two years later. I had gone through a serious breakup and had lost a number of people close to me, and I was looking to bury myself in whatever hobbies or activities I could, and Marc just happened to be playing a show that was only a few miles out from where I lived. (Note: I live on the west coast of the state, so it probably wouldn't have been an impulse decision I would've followed through on if it were back in Orlando.)

While I won't focus too much on the show itself, lest I eclipse what the album is to me, I'll just be brief about it; it was a show in a small cafe in Tampa, and Marc was opening for Steve Poltz, who I know held some personal significance to Marc, but I'll be damned if I remember what that was at the time. (My apologies, dude.) But it was my first small personal show, and it just oozed this charm like I hadn't ever really noticed with him before. I ended up impressed enough to pick up *MFBB* that night on vinyl, purchasing an album on vinyl being a first for me that night, and I really found myself relating to it.

It's no big secret that *MFBB* is a concept album, following the character of Brian as he ends up separating from Jenny and all the different forms of escapism he goes through and other self-destructive tendencies, whether it be religion, music, and plenty of different actions he goes through: stalking, threats, and other general creepiness while ultimately culminating in an uneventful "life moves on" conclusion. Maybe it was just a case of this album turning into a "right time, right place" for me, but it provided a proper insight to a lot of shit I was going through at the time, and dare I say kept me off some of the more self-destructive paths I could've taken dealing with a similar situation.

If I had to pick a favorite track, it'd be "Try to Just Stop." While in the context of the album, it might have been a very passive-aggressive excuse to back out of a difficult time, (I think?) it spoke to me on a very literal level. Before listening to it, I had burned myself out on a dying relationship that I just couldn't let go of to save my life, and I ended up taking it more as an anthem to live for yourself once in a while. It could go either way meaning-wise, I suppose. Music transcends and shit like that. All I know is if Marc did requests, you'd bet he'd be playing it those nights for at least a six-month period, if not longer.

While mentioning what stuck out to me, I do have to mention the odd thing out for me being that the actual title track of the album absolutely doesn't speak to me whatsoever. Don't get me wrong, it's a catchy little song about how privacy in the age of the internet is inherently bullshit, and I love hearing it whenever it may pop up at a show, but at least for me, it seemed to be the only song that didn't fit into the theme the album was trying to set up. It didn't feel like it really furthered any of the story that the album was trying to put on the table. That being said, it has made me acutely aware of any Stanley Steemer vans in my vicinity.

Personal biases aside, *Motherfuckers Be Bullshittin'* is maybe not the best Marc With a C album, but it's certainly one of the more unique records in his catalogue and certainly stands well on its own. This album holds a very special place in my heart. I probably wouldn't even be a fan if it weren't a thing. It's totally worth a listen.

*MOTHERFUCKERS BE BULLSHITTIN'*, ACCORDING TO JO LOUDEN:

If you only remember one thing about Marc With a C, please remember no matter where you go, no matter what you do, *Motherfuckers Be Bullshittin'*. This album holds a very specific and important place in my heart, as it managed to be the main thing that helped me through a really rough patch in my life during 2015. My relationship with this record has always been one I've struggled to articulate, and even if I find it very musically impressive, there are a few tracks that make it may be a bit difficult to recommend to everyone (as some concept albums often have). But none of that detracts from how I feel about it.

I hyper-fixated on this record for months, much like the speaker in this record does with flossing. I got into Marc's work what feels like forever ago, but really it's been maybe five years – it just so happens to be those were the five years where I really grew into who I am now after becoming some approximation of an adult. And my relationship with Marc's music, and especially this album, has provided an odd representation of my own growth over that time.

Going back to some of these tracks at a considerably more emotionally mature place is telling particularly as well as how differently they make me feel now, but most of all my favorite track on the record is even more powerful to me now than ever. That is, without a doubt, "The Kindergarten Steely Dan." This song has a really powerful message buried under some tongue-in-cheek lines, which might be an apt blanket statement for several tracks Marc has written. But that style of songwriting means a lot to me, and lines like "And I don't really care what songs we play / as long as everything's gonna be okay" really speak to what the song is really about and are very heartwarming and honest.

This record starts with some songs that come from a cynical speaker in a bad spot, and it ends with songs about how important a strong unity can be, and it champions togetherness above anything else. That feels like not only an arc I personally relate to but one that seems to paint an image of what things could and should be like for a lot of folks still being cynical in the world. "We could all do better than we're doing right now, we're just doing all the right things wrong."

In 2015, I talked to Marc at a show about how much I enjoyed a song he put out in 2006 and how I felt it described a considerably different experience when I heard it nearly 10 years later. He said it was a testament to how some things don't change, and I think about that a lot, more so since he went to reprise that track on the closer to his 2018 album, *Obscurity*. Some things never change, and some things should and do, and that's a big part of why Marc's music, and especially *Motherfuckers Be Bullshittin'*, means so much to me.

*POPULAR MUSIC,* ACCORDING TO NICOLE M. CAREY:

"Your New Voicemail Message (For Bethany Taylor Myers)"

Hilarious introduction song/skit! I love it

"Popular Music"

I absolutely love this song! In Marc With a C-style, the music is relatively simple though this song has everything it needs. There aren't many instruments, but each one fills its part and there are enough rhythm changes to make it even more interesting. One of my favorite parts is toward the end when he brings in the line "This has all been nothing more than a soundcheck." I absolutely cracked up when I first heard it. That line is also a great lead-in to the next song.

"The Proper Amount of Snare"

I've always wondered about this song. It sounds almost as if it was actually written in the recording studio. That is not to say that it is poorly made, it is just a reflection on the subject matter, which is also great.

"DJ Danny Treanor"

I have lots of questions about this song. It seems to be about a local DJ that thinks he is really cool because he plays songs at a small radio station. Though I guess he really isn't that cool in light of the details about him, but he gets to tell his listener what the hits are. I guess in this case the DJ decides what music is popular.

"Obedience"

This song has a very catchy beat, really easy to sing along with even on the first time hearing it. I love how the fun, danceable beat kinda clashes with the angsty lyrics. I remember hearing this at a concert and singing along with the chorus, and it wasn't until later that I actually heard the lyrics. Interesting to think about how I could so easily follow along and later realized it was about criticizing people who just follow along.

"Brand New Thing"

This song is just fun, and it plays well after the last one. The music is very similar to the previous song, but slightly more complex. I love the key changes; they make it really fun to sing along to. The one question I have is: did he actually tell us about the brand new thing?

"Free Bird"

This is one of my favorite songs! There is always that one guy in the audience that has to yell "Freebird!" whenever the artist on stage asks for requests. This song is the perfect answer to that. The first time I heard this at a concert I about died laughing. It is a wonderful play on that stereotype with very creative rhymes.

"Daddy, Make the Sun Come Out"

Kinda funny that I am listening to this, and it is currently raining. I love the sweet lyrics about a kid talking to their father who is also their protector. When we are young, our parents are the most powerful people in the world, so of course the child would think their father could control the sun. I still wonder whose perspective this is from. Is Marc the kid, or is it his kid?

"Slick and Unused"

This song seems to be about getting older and leaving the nice safe days of being young. It makes some statements about leaving home and getting famous and I suppose "selling out." Being young is so simple, and it goes by so fast.

"DIY"

This song is hilariously dark and very short. Upon first hearing it, I was not sure what to think, but it is an interesting point that some things (such as trying to cut off your own hands) can be hard to do on your own.

"Whack Jite"

Not sure what to say about this one. It is a little hard to hear the lyrics, so I'm not sure exactly what it is about. I guess it is about a white guy playing music in a church, though the subject of the song doesn't really make any good points. Maybe that is the point.

"Dickpuncher III: The Dickening"

This is another absolute favorite of mine – absolutely hilarious! I always love when I hear this one in concert, the tone is so epic yet the subject is ridiculous. I also have to say that the assortment of euphemisms is impressive.

"The True Story of Triforce Mike"

I also remember hearing this one on Nerdy.FM a while ago. I never actually met the guy, though I had heard of him. I've always wondered if this was actually true, hard to say. This song is simultaneously fun, awkward and comical.

"The End of Popular Music"

Nice outro, very good note to end the album on.

Overall:

I love this album; it has a great mix of chill hangout music, sweet thought-provoking songs, and hilarious lyrics that seem to come out of nowhere. Some songs make you dance and some make you think, some actually do both. One of my favorite songs is the title track. I think that was the first Marc With a C song that I ever heard on Nerdy.FM, I remember hearing it in my car on the way to work. Overall, this is a great blend of fun music and thought-provoking lyrics that make for a great journey.

*POPULAR MUSIC,* ACCORDING TO CHAD WALKER:

When Marc first put out his call for personal stories about his albums for his book, I wanted to snag this one, but I missed it. Then he put out a second call, so I was able to jump on it at that point. It's probably still my favorite Marc With a C album, although *Obscurity* gives it a run for its money (which is, of course, appropriate since the two albums represent the beginning and ending of a sort of meta story about music-making and the nature of celebrity/popularity, among other things).

It wasn't the first Marc With a C album I heard. I'm not quite sure which one that was, actually. I became aware of Marc at Nerdapalooza 2010, but I think it was a bit later, with *Motherfuckers Be Bullshittin'* that I really started to become a fan. Regardless, it was *Popular Music* that made me into a die-hard fan. (Perhaps you could even say obsessive – I've seen Marc perform live more times than any other artist, even if you don't include live online performances.)

What is it about this album that inspires such passion? As a fan of postmodern literature (if not necessarily of postmodern philosophy – but that's a story for another place), I recognized immediately that this is what Marc was going for on this album. There's irony ("DIY"), black humor ("Dickpuncher III: The Dickening"), intertextuality, (There are so many examples here, but I'll mention a relatively obscure one: the last lines of the album, "It's the end of popular musics. I'm just saying" is a reference to the "Segue" titled "Baby Grace (A Horrid Cassette)" from David Bowie's *Outside*) poioumena, (OK, I'll admit that I looked up that word; I was going to say "metacommentary" but *poioumena* is such a better word. Examples are "Popular Music" and "Proper Amount of Snare."), pastiche ("Whack Jite"), and probably more that I'm missing.

When I wrote up a review for this album over on Fandomania.com, one of the things I said was, "In fact, it seems that each time I listen to the album I discover something else that makes it into a postmodernist masterpiece." That still holds true today, especially in light of subsequent releases like *Obscurity*. Now when I listen, I think of it as the beginning of a much longer story that basically turns the typical trajectory of a musician around. For Marc, it starts with *Popular Music* but ends in *Obscurity* (which was the goal all along, of course).

This was also the album that finally prompted me to purchase a record player. (I now own three, one of which is in my classroom.) I had, of course, known that Marc wanted his music to be heard that way; I even backed the Kickstarter to bring *Normal Bias* to vinyl (although I went for the CD version at the time. I've since rectified that and bought the vinyl, of course). I just didn't necessarily want to invest in something that would end up taking up so much space. (I'm enough of a pack rat and collector of stuff as it is!) But I just couldn't resist the lure of that tri-colored disc. And as it turns out, it actually added to the meta nature of the album, with the disc representing a pie chart of the album's creation (equal parts "Music, Media, and You" as the key explains) plus the Squiddy from *Motherfuckers*, which is itself holding an album. And, of course, it led to me buying all of Marc's catalog on vinyl (as well as plenty of other music – yeah, once you start collecting vinyl, it's kinda hard to stop).

So basically, in short, I tend to think of this album as the true beginning of my journey into the mind and music of Marc With a C. I hope that journey will continue for many years to come.

*HAVE AN OKAY TIME WITH CLAIRE AND THE POTATOES*, ACCORDING TO LAUREN FURZE:

I was a little late to the Claire and the Potatoes party. I'd seen Marc advertising this new side project, but as often the case with me and side projects, I'd bookmarked it with the intention to check it out and taken my sweet time in doing so.

Orlando Nerd Festival 2014 rolls around, and I spend the whole weekend watching the livestream. It was a great weekend, but one memory sticks out in my mind. I tune in to watch the Claire and the Potatoes set so that I can support Marc and finally hear this new band of his. I kick myself now for not checking them out immediately!

I was completely blown away. It was what I'd come to expect from a Marc With a C record but on a whole new level. Here was a group of musicians that gelled so well with one another. A group of people who reached out through the screen to me and made me feel something extraordinary. Awe. Happiness. Belonging. Jim was a force to be reckoned with on the drum kit. Guy was working all sorts of magic on the bass. Marc was channeling his inner rock star more than ever. And then there was Leslie. This amazing frontwoman, with an incredible voice, fun, and charismatic. I found myself thinking, where has this band been my whole life? I had a more than okay time watching them do their thing and had purchased the CD from their website before the set was over.

Any time I listen to *Have An Okay Time*, I'm still struck with that sense of awe. It's so beautifully made. The heart and the soul pour out of it, and I can only imagine that these four people had the greatest time of their life working together on it.

When I'm having a bad day, and need a pick-me-up, I know that record is their waiting for me like a warm hug or a good cup of tea.

*HAVE AN OKAY TIME WITH CLAIRE AND THE POTATOES*, ACCORDING TO AMANDA ALEXANDER:

My first experience with Claire and the Potatoes was a small concert at The Geek Easy. I liked the groove of what I heard, and when I started dating a friend, he shared the album *Have an Okay Time with Claire and the Potatoes* with me, and I quickly fell in love with it. It gave me an upbeat way to deal with the pain and anger I felt when that relationship ended. Then it became a quick and easy way to brighten up my day, and it still is no matter what kind of day I'm having.

I know I can listen to any of the songs off that album, and, even on my worst of days, I'll be able to smile, even if it's just for a short while. When I hear their music, it's like I'm being enveloped in a warm group hug, and it's as if the entire "band" is telling me that everything is going to be okay.

Everyone has one album by one band that they hold close to their hearts for whatever reason. For me, *Have an Okay Time with Claire and the Potatoes* is that album, and it's by the best fictitious band that I've ever had the pleasure of listening to.

*EXACTLY WHERE I AM*, ACCORDING TO NICHOLAS COTTRELL:

It's 9 p.m. on March 19, 2016, and I know exactly where I am. I've just left a gas station in Gainesville, Florida and am blazing up Interstate 75 on my way to what I can now only think of as my father's house in Georgia. "Bootwater Suite: Americana" is playing through a shaky aux cord, adding a dimension to the relentless authenticity of Marc's words. I, like he, "sometimes ... feel useless, like I never had much to give." And also like him, "When it comes to writing about it, I just give up on it." Sometimes, anyway.

It's 4 a.m. on March 20, 2016, and I know exactly where I am. I'm in the house that is now my father's and my father's alone; as I was getting out of my beater car in his driveway, "I'm Gonna Miss You" was the last track I heard. For Marc, it's a love song and a song of loss; a surgical excision of emotion. For reasons entirely unrelated to the narrator of his song, I too have someone I'm going to miss. Like the bridge of the song says, "It's late but I don't wanna go to bed, it's cold and your side is still tucked in." Mom always kept it exceptionally cold in the house; a 68-degree oasis from the Georgia heat. Her "side" of the bed is definitely still tucked in.

It's 1 p.m. on March 21, 2016, and I know exactly where I am. I'm in a conference room at McMullen funeral home, having been tasked by my father with writing, in most people's minds, the last and most important thing about my mother anyone will ever write. I reflect on their marriage, spanning decades, and her life, stretching a bit longer, and "Bootwater Suite: Staying Dormant" is in my head as I sit with a pen and paper. "What do they have in common? Not much at all; but I put them together so they won't be forgot." They were seemingly a mismatched pair – he, the long-distance runner with the high-pressure corporate job who long ago learned not to sweat the small stuff; she, the consummate worrywart and fussbudget. I put them together not solely so they won't be forgot but because that is where they belong.

It's 11 a.m. on March 23, 2016, and I know exactly where I am. I am sitting in the church where I first called myself a Christian; it is coincidentally the same place that shattered that faith. As I look around at the multitudes of faces streaming in to pay their last respects, I find myself thinking of a song by a man I'm pleased to call my friend, Marc Sirdoreus. In what I consider to be the standout single of his album *Exactly Where I Am*, which this writing is ostensibly a review of, he laments a condition I've suffered from all my life: "I can't remember your name, but I see you all over the place / you're friends with my acquaintances and I know I've seen your face." I smile in spite of the setting, in spite of the occasion, and I stand up to tell the assembled group of strangers that I loved my mother, I miss her now that she's gone, and that we should all take care to express our love to everyone we love, however we love them, as frequently and loudly as possible. Exactly where I was when these songs resonated in me is not the same place Marc was when he wrote them. I hope for all of you that you find yourself exactly somewhere else when they hit home for you. But Marc is a singularly talented songwriter, and no matter where you find yourself, at least one song on this album will be exactly where you are.

*UNICORNS GET MORE BACON*, ACCORDING TO DAVID KINSEL:

Sometimes, you discover an artist when you need them most. *Unicorns Get More Bacon* by Marc With a C was released in early 2016, the latest release from a veteran indie pop singer/songwriter. Thanks to a post about the album by Kyle Stevens of Kirby Krackle, I found this album, and the artist behind it, at the moment in my life that I needed to.

This wonderful compendium of quirky pop songs hit at a time of personal chaos and change. A widowed guy, still processing the grief of that loss, embarking on a new relationship and the changes that accompany those feelings. A swirling mix of sadness, confusion, excitement, insecurity and awe. The former friend, now romantic partner, and I discovered Marc's music at the same moment. It hit a resonant chord in both of us; music full of strong melodies, pop culture references, and snarky lyrics. Since we were separated by four hours of driving time, I was able to spend some quality time with the record. Traveling down back roads in the dark, discovering the songs one by one.

The social commentary of "Celebutantes" was an early favorite. "Anything But Plain" hit close to home. The song expressed a lot of my feelings about my new partner Kristyn, my late wife Sandy, and my respect for them both. "I Hate This Song" and "The Ballad Of Dick Steel" both provided much-needed laughter during a complicated time. The honesty of "Unicorns Get More Bacon" was inspiring, Marc directly asking the listener to stay with him on this journey.

The more I listened to this album, the more I got out of it. "Where's My Giant Robot" expressed the quiet frustration that I think plenty of people feel around their mundane daily lives: where's the excitement, where's the brave new world that we all hoped we would have when we adults. "Falling Sometimes Down" was an emotional bombshell after the mostly upbeat songs that comprise the rest of the album. Complex feelings around fears of failure and disappointing my loved ones echoed in the notes of that song.

The song with the most impact on my life was "Long Distance Dedication." A long-distance relationship with one partner who is obviously at a low point in his life, a reflection of the complex emotions that I was dealing with. "Does she slow down when it's too much for her weary feet" always makes me think of just how hard Kristyn works. "But if life permitted I'd give you what's left of the best years of my life" overwhelmed me, voicing my efforts to deal with my pain but move forward. And "Love like you've never been burned", well. ...

An artist can never predict how their creations will impact people. They hope the work is enjoyed, but sometimes the connection is so much more. On October 1, 2016 ( "October is just too far away"), at The Milestone Club in Charlotte, NC, "Long Distance Dedication" played over the speakers as Kristyn and I danced for the first time as husband and wife. Not something that Marc would have expected when he added the song to the album. Life just happens that way sometimes.

*UNICORNS GET MORE BACON,* ACCORDING TO ROB TOBIAS:

There are a select handful of albums that I've listened to in my life so many damn times that I don't even need to listen to them again to enjoy them. Their recordings have been uploaded into the ultimate in portable meat-based mp3 players, the long-term memory.

*Unicorns Get More Bacon* is one of those albums. I blame my children.

Hey, I'm not shitting on the *Frozen* or *Moana* soundtracks, they're obviously good soundtracks, but if I'm going to have to listen to the same album over and over on trips to the water park and the library, I want it to be something I already kind of enjoyed. And, well, they didn't really like a lot of the rap I usually listen to, so I figured, with a title like *Unicorns Get More Bacon*, this should be an easy sell.

Prior to this album becoming a soundtrack to our family drives, I'd been more of a Marc With A Single kind of guy. I'd stick his individual tracks into mixes to promote Nerdapalooza or maybe play a track on my now long-defunct radio station on Radio KOL. I knew he was a conceptual guy, so it didn't really surprise me that the album was cohesive, but that amount of cohesiveness while exploring so many sounds really impressed me a lot. Marc's ability to tell a story on multiple levels permeates this album —a surface level, a subtext, an underlying theme. His use of harmony is perfectly chosen but not so overproduced as to sound sterile. I didn't really even like lo-fi all that much before Marc, but with a guy like him pumping out the tracks? Yeah, man. I get it. Musically, it's a really great album. More importantly, it's also a really human album.

*Unicorns* has important messages to share that frankly, kids don't hear often enough. "We're all going to fail in public" is a permission to try, even if you don't succeed. "Everything everybody does these days is a game" reinforces that. "If somebody tells you that you're a dick, you might be a dick" — a call to self-criticism. The plaintive question, "where's my giant robot?" is a warning that the future isn't all sunshine and roses. Ultimately this album carries that thread of a slightly immature take on the subject of learning maturity itself, a dichotomy that I think everyone of all ages can relate to.

And then there's the profanity. Sorry, let me correct that. And then there's the *fucking* profanity.

Look, man, it's funny to hear a kid sing along to the chorus of "I Hate This Song." "The chords are fucking stupid, it's predictable as shit"? Comedy gold. If you can't appreciate the sound — or at least the irony — of a kid singing "my songs are like my kids — some are great and others are just assholes," you have no soul in your body.

So if you're a parent, I highly recommend you do what I did. Take a deep breath and play *Unicorns Get More Bacon* for your small children. It'll teach them something about life. It'll teach them something about music. And it'll teach them the comedic value of simply chanting "Dick! Dick! Dick!" for hours on end.

Sure beats Kidz Bop.

*HALF SERIOUS HALF KIDDING*, ACCORDING TO LANDO THE ROADIE:

If you've come this far in Marc With a C's discography, the words "prolific" and "motherfucker" should come to mind, both separately and together. Dude's released more songs than ___. He's like John Darnielle in that regard. (And only that regard, guys. Let's not get carried away. We're all living in the shadow of Robert Pollard, anyway.) When he and I first met, he was just about to release his 10-year compilation. Think about it, how many non-touring artists can claim to have done the same? Not many. There aren't many like him, and I'll spare us all the Hunter S. Thompson quote.

Now that we've covered the "prolific," let's address the "motherfucker" in the room. My name's Lando. You might know me as "Lando the Roadie." What, you thought I was going to talk about Marc? This whole thing's about him, and we'll get to him, but context is important.

I was Marc's roadie a few years back, right around the time of the release of *Motherfuckers Be Bullshittin'*. I guess that technically makes THREE motherfuckers, huh? Well, being close to the source allowed me to see a little bit of the creative process and how a Marc With a C full-length album would come to exist in this world. There were several methods in play, but no matter what off-the-cuff jokes or Ambien-fueled hazes resulted in the embryonic stages of songs, there was always a great deal of care that went into each release, no matter how lo-fi. Now, this is important, because *Motherfuckers* marked a shift in the paradigm. It was arguably the first album that didn't explicitly sound like it was recorded in his living room.

Why am I talking so much about *MBB*? Isn't this about *Half Serious, Half Kidding*? Yes, yes, it is, but like I said, context is important. In March of 2016, Marc released *Unicorns Get More Bacon*, another important milestone. Lots of work went into that album, too. There was press and a buildup and everything. It was rad as hell. Growth, perspective, a third thing. Then, in June of 2017, Marc laid this EP on us.

EPs are an interesting bit of Marc's career. There are more full-length releases than there are EPs, with compilations to boot. Of the ones he's released, *Half Serious, Half Kidding* is my favorite. Despite being released almost a year later than the full-length that precedes it, it picks up right where *Unicorns* left off. Those who've been around the guy know that he's the kind of motherfucker who doesn't just walk the line between dour and sardonic, he built himself a house there with a yard that has a pergola, some shrubberies, and a little place for bunnies. It's really very lovely. You know in Star Wars when a Jedi Master is just sort of fed the fuck up, so he becomes one with the Force in a sort of sci-fi/fantasy disappearing act? Well, in this analogy, Marc is the Jedi, and the Force is that silver hammer between dour and sardonic.

Marc's not a comedian. He doesn't make "comedy albums." He's a funny guy, but that's about where it ends. Same goes for "nerd music," but that's a horse of a different color altogether, though, this EP does include a song written by StarF, an underrated nerdcore genius if one ever existed.

This record came out, and I felt fucking SEEN. I've never pirated any of his music, (I either bought hard copies at shows, or downloaded them directly from his website.) but I'll be the first to admit that from 2007 to 2013, I didn't "get" Clutch. Marc's never been one to mince words, and satire's been a tried and true medium for those who really just want to get the fuckin' point across sometimes. This record's full of it. This has all the ingredients of a Marc With a C record, complete with a track that just barely makes it past 1:30 in length. It's got all the bubblegum harmonies that Marc loves. Listen to "First Time Collar" or "All I Want for Christmas." It's not saccharine; it's pure organic free-range sugar. It's also hilarious in a way that's incredibly cutting. It's half serious, and it's half kidding, so was I the subject of "Clutch"? Well, I was, and I wasn't. We've all been that person in "This Meeting Is Bullshit."

This is the Marc With a C EP for the first-time listener, and the longtime fan. It's a bottle episode that also maintains continuity. In this way, aren't we all Marc With a C? Well, we are, and we aren't.

MY LIFE AS A MARC WITH A C FAN, BY SHAMMUS ODDISH:

There I was, standing in the humid summer heat of Florida, surrounded by about 250 other people. We were all in the parking lot of A Comic Shop, a local provider of comics, graphic novels, and good times. The shop was attached to a small plaza of about six other stores and featured a gas station on the corner and a Chinese restaurant on the other end. I had arrived a little late to this party due to work, but the evening was setting in, the sun had set, but the heat was still very present.

It was the Fourth of July weekend 2008, and all of these people were in Orlando for the second Nerdapalooza to be held in Florida. The name of the event explains why the crowds were there, but I had joined in due to it being a reunion for myself and several others from the inaugural event a year earlier as well as a first time meeting some people from the music scene online that

I had been a part of for a few years by that time.

I remember being drawn outside of the shop's struggling A/C into the crowds by a girl I had just met recently because she said I absolutely had to hear the next performer. I was only really familiar with the nerdcore hip hop acts that were in town for the weekend, but I made the decision to see what this next "group" was about.

I don't recall how the full set went, but I do remember the girl saying to me to call out the name of a song for an encore. So in the heat of the parking lot I shouted out to the artist a song that I had never heard it before. I shouted at the top of my lungs, "Life's So Hard." What happened next made me a fan for life.

Marc With a C is a special kind of artist. He is a one-man band who strums on his guitar like a rocker from the '60s but normally carries a very lo-fi style. His sound fills up whatever venue he is performing in, and his songs are those kind of catchy ear bugs that will stick in your head for days after hearing them. I had never heard a single song by Marc ever, but in that one instance when he started, the first few notes of "Life's So Hard" caught my attention immediately. The song itself is not a very complicated affair. The lyrics are all about a generation of teens who were growing up with the immergence of social media and how they had to take to the internet to complain whenever anything in their life goes wrong. Being in my mid-20s, I was a little off from the demographic the song would seem to be about, but there was a resonance. The guitar melody, Marc's voice as he laments about not going to the Warped Tour, and the crowd reaction built into a memory I will not soon forget even as I type these words more than 10 years later.

There is a simple callback section Marc does at the end of "Life's So Hard" where he allows the audience to suddenly become his backup and take the chorus themselves. I do not know how many people knew of Marc 30 minutes before this, but he had all of us following along with his instructions. "Sing it quiet," Marc would shout out to the audience. We sang the song quieter, almost comically. "Sing it louder!" Marc would tell us. We sang this song at the top of our lungs. It was one of those moments that you know you are tangled in something special.

I have a ton of other amazing memories of Marc performing. The following day to that pre-party at the comic shop, Marc took the main stage at Taste, the venue that Nerdapalooza was at that year, everyone crowded into the space set for the 250 attendees to witness his set. The instant Marc put his guitar behind his head to finish off the final few licks for "Nerdy Girls," he had created quite a few more fans. I remember there was bra thrown on stage after that performance.

Since that time, I have tried to make it to every Marc With a C performance I can be at. In recent years, Marc has elevated himself and created an amazing, eclectic discography that ranges all over the place. He has songs about a fictional movie that involves dick punching. He has songs that talk about the most important part of performing, that the audience is listening.

There are two songs though that have resonated with me so hard in recent years though. One is from his most recent work at the time of me typing this up, and that is "Please Don't Let My Art Die." I was at the pre-release show for the album *Obscurity*, and sitting in the crowd for part one of the show, Marc went into the song to close out before an intermission. It was a very powerful moment as he started to unstrap his guitar and kept on with the lyrics, "Please don't let my art die." It was as heartfelt and sincere as anything I had heard him do before. It was both a chilling realization that nothing really lasts forever but also a signal of hope that as long as we remember and keep playing the songs in our heads and hearts, memories will never fade.

The other song is more of a personal favorite that never fails to bring some tears to my eyes whenever i hear it. "Music Can Heal" has become a cathartic experience for me every time I hear it performed live. I lost a dear friend of mine back in 2013, and for some reason I can see her face while that song is playing, almost as if she had heard this song it might have saved her life. This loops back into "Please Don't Let My Art Die" because as long as I keep holding onto those memories of that friend, she will never really die. "Music Can Heal" allows me to remember all the amazing times we had.

At any rate, I have had some spectacular times at Marc's shows. I have made many memories watching him perform and am looking forward to what comes next for Marc With a C.

*OBSCURITY*, ACCORDING TO CHRISTINE VEASEY:

A friend of mine once said something to the effect that she imagines cameras are watching her all the time to keep her on the path of being a good and decent person. I was taken aback, as I had just had a nervous breakdown centered around thinking I was on a prank reality show. Then, Spotify suggested "Low-Rent Truman Show" on my Release Radar. These coincidences helped me feel much less crazy and more like a person who was just readjusting to finding their place in the world after trauma.

The album is cautionary, contemplative, and hopeful all at the same time. You can easily go astray if you're always looking for validation. Finding your place in the world is much different when you don't try to force yourself and others into an unrealistic vision of success. It's a much-needed album of reflection in these fast-paced digital times where everyone seems to be seeking validating feedback constantly in varying ways. There's a lovely build up throughout from simple acoustic guitar to full, lush orchestration, which adds to the wonderful lost-and-found, soulful feeling.

*OBSCURITY*, ACCORDING TO RANDY PENCE:

In an age where information comes and goes at the speed of electricity, it's easy for thing to slip by unnoticed. Art can easily be one of these things. We have music, photography, graphics, videos and a whole slew of media presented to us every day. It's hard to know what will go viral, be seen by millions of people, and ultimately be remembered for only a few short days. But what can we do to make sure that art is held on to and preserved in our modern culture. How do we make an impact with an artistic creation that transcends generations and is remembered by the general populace well past our ultimate demise? Or do we delve into a realm of obscurity where the work is remembered by only a select few, but they are the ones that preserve it forever?

Perhaps one way to answer this question is to look into the Marc With a C album, *Obscurity*. The album, which was created as a labor of love by its artist and addresses this topic in the way only a Marc With a C album can, is what can ultimately be described as the album he always wanted to make. The album is the result of careful planning and a long trip to Canada to have the album produced and mastered.

Thinking about the story of how the album was made and seeing Marc talk about the process of creating the album stuck with me as I listened to the album. The track that kept sticking out to me in particular was the track "Please Don't Let My Art Die." This was the track that really made me stop and think.

It starts out on a bleak note but gets straight to the punches: "I'd say I don't want a funeral but nobody'd listen / Funerals are like birthday parties and they ain't always 'bout the victim / What matters is how it feels when all the attendees leave / Like when I was at a funeral and I heard my songs sung back to me."

Death many times is where art can truly shine. That can come in many forms, such as through the end of a band, an artist retiring from their medium or taking on other interests, or even the passing of the artist themselves. Many artists don't achieve the recognition they deserve until after they stop making the art or it is given posthumously. Many artists try to think of and comprehend what impact their works will have when it is all said and done. That many times is the ultimate goal of an artist, to have their work remembered and know that it brought joy into someone's life. The chorus of the song can sum up this thought process.

"Please don't let my art die / It's about the only thing I did right with my life / I tried so hard to be obscure to make the right people smile Please don't let my art die."

In ways, that is how the best art works. Sometimes, only a select few will get the art and truly appreciate it. But they will be the ones to preserve it and make sure it is enjoyed by future generations. Movies experience this all the time. Many films perform atrociously at the box office and are considered flops due to not bringing in enough return to even recoup the cost of the film's budget. This rings true for Tommy Wiseau, the director of *The Room*. The movie performed particularly dismally, but word-of-mouth from some critics that the movie was so bad it had to be seen to believed sparked a new life into the movie, and it now a cult classic with the reputation of being the manifesto of bad movie-making. The true test of art is its longevity – who will remember it, and how will it be remembered. A work can be easy to explain while we are still here to explain it or shape its meaning as we exhibit it. We can go along for the ride and play off a bad reaction to art as well a good reaction, which can only add to how we remember art and allow it to exist.

This is something I have worked on and thought of myself. In creating Geek World Order and running it for the past eight years, I am always trying to craft the site's voice and make it distinct and memorable. This album and this song specifically strike a chord with me and have helped my shape a way of thinking as I look to shape the site for future growth and to keep myself revitalized in wanting to continue its operation. The whole journey from starting out as a geek with a camera wanting to document conventions has turned into a journey of exploration into what my true passions in life are. The people I have met and the experiences I have had all add a new nuance to the mix and continue to shape the product I put out and continue to drive me in putting out something that people will remember.

That want and desire to make something memorable, whether it be the photography I focus on or new avenues I seek to explore, I keep asking what will the ultimate impact of doing this be. What am I leaving behind as a legacy? Is what I'm doing even art? Will someone consider it art? I know my photography may be considered art, but will the whole of what I'm doing be considered art? Ultimately, will what I bring to the table be remembered fondly and put a smile on people's faces when they talk about it? As I continue on this journey of life, I keep aspiring to create the best thing I can create and ultimately find myself saying please don't let my art die.